Issues and Options for U.S.-Japan Trade Policies

SIE *Studies in International Economics* includes works dealing with the theory, empirical analysis, and evaluation of international policies and institutions, in the area of international macroeconomics and finance, international trade theory and policy, as well as international legal and political economy.

Keith E. Maskus, Peter M. Hooper, Edward E. Leamer, and J. David Richardson, Editors
Quiet Pioneering: Robert M. Stern and His International Economic Legacy

Bjarne S. Jensen and Kar-yiu Wong, Editors
Dynamics, Economic Growth, and International Trade

Jagdish Bhagwati and Mathias Hirsch, Editors
The Uruguay Round and Beyond: Essays in Honor of Arthur Dunkel

Kala Marathe Krishna and Ling Hui Tan
Rags and Riches: Implementing Apparel Quotas under the Multi-Fibre Arrangement

Alan V. Deardorff and Robert M. Stern *Measurement of Nontariff Barriers*

Thomas Cottier and Petros C. Mavroidis, Editors
The World Trade Forum, Volume I: State Trading in the Twenty-First Century

Rajesh Chadha, Sanjib Pohit, Alan V. Deardorff, and Robert M. Stern
The Impact of Trade and Domestic Policy Reforms in India: A CGE Modeling Approach

Alan V. Deardorff and Robert M. Stern, Editors
Constituent Interests and U.S. Trade Policies

Gary R. Saxonhouse and T. N. Srinivasan, Editors
Development, Duality, and the International Economic Regime: Essays in Honor of Gustav Ranis

Charles P. Kindleberger *Essays in History: Financial, Economic, Personal*

Keith Acheson and Christopher Maule
Much Ado about Culture: North American Trade Disputes

Alan V. Deardorff and Robert M. Stern *Social Dimensions of U.S. Trade Policies*

Thomas Cottier and Petros C. Mavroidis, Editors
Regulatory Barriers and the Principle of Non-Discrimination in World Trade Law

Bernard Hoekman and Jamel Zarrouk *Catching Up with the Competition: Trade Opportunities and Challenges for Arab Countries*

Jun Fu *Institutions and Investments: Foreign Direct Investment in China during an Era of Reforms*

Robert M. Stern, Editor *Services in the International Economy*

Keith E. Maskus and John S. Wilson, Editors
Quantifying the Impact of Technical Barriers to Trade: Can It Be Done?

Robert M. Stern, Editor *Issues and Options for U.S.-Japan Trade Policies*

Issues and Options for U.S.-Japan Trade Policies

Robert M. Stern, Editor

Ann Arbor

THE UNIVERSITY OF MICHIGAN PRESS

Published in the United States of America by
The University of Michigan Press
Manufactured in the United States of America
♾ Printed on acid-free paper

2005 2004 2003 2002 4 3 2 1

A CIP catalog record for this book is available from the British Library.

Library of Congress Cataloging-in-Publication Data applied for
ISBN 0-472-11279-1

Contents

Preface

This volume contains the papers and comments that were prepared in connection with a conference, "Issues and Options for the Multilateral, Regional, and Bilateral Trade Policies of the United States and Japan," which was held at the University of Michigan, Ann Arbor, on October 5-6, 2000. It represents the first year of a two-year program of research on "Analytical and Negotiating Issues in U.S.-Japan International Economic Relations," which has been funded with a grant from the Japan Foundation, Center for Global Partnership (CGP). Partial funding for local arrangements for the conference was provided by the University of Michigan's Center for Japanese Studies and by the Mitsui Life Financial Research Center of the School of Business Administration.

The two-year program of research is being directed jointly by myself and Professor Mitsuhiro Fukao of Keio University, Tokyo. We wish to thank the funding organizations for their support as well as our respective institutions for providing facilities for the conduct of program meetings. I wish also to thank Violet Elder and Sonja Page of the Gerald R. Ford School of Public Policy for their assistance in administering the CGP grant and organizing the conference arrangements. Finally, I would like to give special thanks to Judith Jackson, for her outstanding and unflagging assistance in the typing and editing of the conference papers and comments and the preparation of camera-ready copy.

Robert M. Stern
Ann Arbor, Michigan
August 6, 2001

CHAPTER 1

Introduction and Overview

Robert M. Stern

I. Introduction

This book contains the papers and selected comments that were prepared in connection with the conference, "Issues and Options for the Multilateral, Regional, and Bilateral Trade Policies of the United States and Japan," which was held at the University of Michigan, Ann Arbor, October 5-6, 2000. It represents the first-year of a two-year program of research on "Analytical and Negotiating Issues in U.S.-Japan International Economic Relations."

The book is designed for a broad audience consisting of academic economists and lawyers, policy makers and staff, and students interested in U.S.-Japan international economic relations. This design is reflected in the choice and organization of the topics and the expertise brought to bear upon the topics. In constructing the program of research under the terms of the grant from the Japan Foundation, Center for Global Partnership, an effort was made to identify economic and legal scholars in the United States and Japan who had the knowledge and ability to address many of the central issues faced by the United States and Japan in the global trading system and in their regional and bilateral relations. The topics and bi-national authorship of the papers contained in the book were chosen consciously, and individual authors were given leeway to choose their particular focus within the overall selection of topics. The individual chapters thus represent a spectrum of approaches, including theoretical analysis, quantitative measurement, and evaluations of policies and institutions from both an economic and legal perspective.

The design of the program of research reflects recognition of the fact that the United States and Japan are now inextricably linked both to each other and to the rest of the world. These linkages arise through trade, foreign direct investment (FDI), and financial flows, as well as through the exchange rates, international prices, and government policies that influence all of these. The overall purpose of the program of research is intended accordingly to develop a better understanding of these links, and how they may be turned to the advantage of all involved by improvements in the international policy environment. The two major parts of the research program deal, first, with the potential for such improvements as part of formal government-to-government negotiations, and, second, more broadly with changes in policies and institutions that the two nations can implement individually to improve their economic relations with each other and with the world. The negotiating issues, which are the subject of the present volume, arise in the multilateral, regional, and bilateral contexts. The broader policy considerations, which require an understanding of international economic relations themselves and their implications for policy, are being addressed in the second year of the research program and will be included in a subsequent volume.

The multilateral issues of importance are centered on the multilateral trade negotiations that have begun in 2000 and will be continuing under the auspices of the World Trade Organization (WTO). The United States and Japan have played leading roles in the previous multilateral trade negotiations conducted under the auspices of the General Agreement on Tariffs and Trade (GATT), the most recent one being the Uruguay-Round negotiations that were concluded in 1993-94. The WTO, which came into existence in January 1995, subsumed the GATT. A WTO Ministerial Meeting was held in early December 1999 in Seattle for the purpose of establishing the agenda for a new negotiating round to begin in 2000 and to continue thereafter.

It was mandated in the Uruguay Round that negotiations covering agriculture, services, and several other "old" issues would commence in 2000. In addition to this "built-in" agenda, it was anticipated that "new" issues such as trade and investment, competition policy, the environment, and trade and labor standards were to be discussed in formulating the agenda for a broader WTO trade round. Agreement on the agenda could not be reached, however, at the Seattle Ministerial Meeting. The meeting ended in an impasse for a variety of reasons, chiefly because the main participants had adopted inflexible positions on agricultural liberalization, the use of antidumping policies, and the insistence by the United States especially that issues of international trade and labor standards be placed on the WTO negotiating agenda and that sanctions be directed particularly at developing countries that did not adhere to these standards.

In the wake of the failed Seattle meeting, there have been efforts made to get a new negotiating round underway. Negotiations had to commence in any event, since, as noted, the built-in agenda items from the Uruguay Round had already been scheduled starting in 2000. It is acknowledged that a number of the "new" issues may be addressed as well, either in the WTO or in some other forums. At the time of writing (August 2001), it is anticipated that an agreement will be reached at the WTO Ministerial meeting in Qatar in November 2001 on the agenda details for a new trade round. Given the interests that the United States and Japan have in achieving a successful outcome of a new round, it is obviously important that their negotiating options be carefully designed and backed up by sound and authoritative economic analysis.

In addition to the multilateral negotiations, the United States and Japan are engaged in a variety of ongoing regional negotiations, including the forum for Asia-Pacific Economic Cooperation (APEC) and the formation of new free trade agreements (FTAs) and expansion of existing FTAs. In this regard, there is an ongoing debate in both policy and academic circles about the desirability of pursuing regional arrangements such as APEC and other preferential trading arrangements. The question is whether these various arrangements make it easier or more difficult to pursue the benefits of freer trade according to the Most-Favored-Nation (MFN) principle of non-discrimination, which is a pillar of the GATT/WTO multilateral system. That is, regional and preferential arrangements may be faulted on the grounds of possibly being detrimental to global economic welfare to the extent that they discriminate against non-member nations. Presumably, the policy of "open regionalism" associated with APEC is designed to avoid such discrimination, but it remains to be seen how and whether or not this can be achieved. The North American Free Trade Area (NAFTA), which was created in 1994, is another important regional arrangement of concern. The question with NAFTA is whether it has resulted in the diversion of trade and FDI especially to Mexico, to the detriment of Japan and other trading nations in Asia and elsewhere. Finally, in what may be an historic change in its trade policies, Japan has become engaged in negotiations and discussions to form FTAs with a number of its trading partners, including Singapore, Mexico, Korea, and Chile. Regional issues thus constitute an important set of topics in their own right that are addressed in both years of the program of research.

Then, there are several ongoing and prospective bilateral U.S.-Japan trade and FDI issues that command attention. For many years, the United States has been critical of Japanese domestic and external policies and regulations on the grounds that they limit access of American exports to and FDI in the Japanese economy. The United States has accordingly sought to bring pressure on Japan to institute policy changes that will promote greater market access. In addressing bilateral issues, the U.S. trade authorities are responding to complaints by U.S. firms about specific Japanese policies that are perceived by these firms to be harmful to their interests. It is not surprising therefore that there have been several instances in which the complaints have become highly politicized in the United States, recent examples being automobiles and parts, film, steel, and a variety of food and other agricultural products. For its part, Japan has been highly critical of U.S. trade actions designed to limit imports from Japan, in particular U.S. antidumping and other unilateral measures that are believed to be motivated in large part by U.S. protectionist interests.

What is now important to note is that there has been a significant change in the context in which these bilateral disputes may be addressed. That is, as part of the creation of the WTO, the process of dispute settlement was recast and reinforced in ways that have speeded up resolution of disputes and the binding of dispute settlements. The issue then is under what circumstances the United States and Japan will decide to use the WTO dispute settlement mechanism to address bilateral complaints rather than pursue these complaints through political channels.

With the foregoing by way of background, the next section contains summaries of the individual conference papers and selected comments. The final section will consider the main themes and conclusions reached and the implications for the design and conduct of trade and FDI policies in the United States and Japan.

II. Chapter Summaries

For the benefit of the reader, summaries of the individual chapters are presented below.[1] These summaries should assist in sorting through the chapters and, depending on the reader's interests, selecting those to be read in greater depth.

Part One: WTO Multilateral Negotiating Issues

The chapters in Part One deal with a variety of issues that are pertinent to both the United States and Japan in the context of a new round of multilateral negotiations under WTO auspices. The issues include an assessment of the welfare and employment effects that may be experienced from multilateral and regional negotiations, the reform of Japan's agricultural policies, services liberalization, dispute settlement, antidumping, intellectual property rights, investment, and competition policy

In Chapter 2, **CGE Modeling and Analysis of Multilateral and Regional Negotiating Options**, Drusilla Brown, Alan Deardorff, and Robert Stern use the Michigan Model of World Production and Trade to simulate the economic effects on the United States, Japan, and other major trading countries/regions of: the Uruguay Round of multilateral trade negotiations completed in 1993-94; a prospective new round of WTO multilateral trade negotiations; and a variety of regional/bilateral free trade agreements (FTAs) involving the United States and Japan. They estimate that the Uruguay Round negotiations increased global economic welfare by $75.1 billion annually, with gains of $12.9 billion for the United States and $15.6 billion for Japan. An assumed reduction of all post-Uruguay Round tariffs on agricultural and industrial products and of all services barriers by 33 percent in a new WTO trade round is estimated to increase world welfare by $613.0 billion, with gains of $177.3 billion for the United States and $123.7 billion for Japan. If there were global free trade with all post-Uruguay Round trade barriers completely removed, then world welfare would increase by $1.9 trillion, with gains of $537.2 billion (5.9 percent of GNP) for the United States and $374.8 billion (5.8 percent of GNP) for Japan.

Elimination of APEC-member country bilateral post-Uruguay Round tariffs on agricultural and industrial products and services barriers is estimated to increase world welfare by $764.4 billion, with gains of $294.7 billion for the United States and $283.1 billion for Japan and losses of $7.0 billion for the European Union/EFTA and $1.0 billion for South Asia. Separate bilateral

FTAs involving Japan with Singapore, Mexico, South Korea, and Chile and an ASEAN Plus-3 FTA involving Japan, China/Hong Kong, and South Korea would have positive, though generally small, welfare effects, but potentially disruptive sectoral employment shifts in some member countries. Depending on the agreement, there may be detrimental welfare effects on some nonmembers. The welfare gains from multilateral trade liberalization are therefore considerably greater than the gains from preferential trading arrangements and more uniformly positive for all countries.

In his comment, Keith Maskus notes that Brown, Deardorff, and Stern (BDS) provide timely analysis of the potential economic effects of various trade liberalization possibilities in the Asia-Pacific region, and that their model advances the literature in two important directions. It incorporates product heterogeneity in the monopolistically competitive sectors, accounting for entry and exit decisions and cost reductions from scale economies. It also includes measures of barriers to trade in services. The tariff equivalents of these restrictions are quite large in the model and their removal dominates welfare impacts. While the welfare computations are noteworthy and point squarely to the potential gains from expanding market access in services, Maskus questions the underlying estimates of the services distortions. He notes in particular that it is unlikely that fixed entry costs for multinational enterprises are captured by the lowest national margin, for there may be large differences in such costs. He suspects also that the choice of substitution elasticities is critical for assessing the distribution of scale effects and trade-diversion impacts. He further suggests that it would be interesting to know the extent to which the large impacts of service liberalization are associated with maintaining the same substitution parameters in services and manufacturing. Finally, an unexplored point that BDS might consider is that regional free trade areas (FTAs) may alter critical parameters within a region relative to those outside the region. If the elasticity of substitution between imports and domestic goods, in particular among FTA partners, were to rise as a result of better information about the quality characteristics of imported goods, a further gain would emerge through reducing imperfectly competitive markups.

In his comment, Keith Head notes that the CGE analysis conducted by Brown, Deardorff, and Stern (BDS) should be valuable to policy makers for a number of reasons. First, the BDS model allows for gains or losses associated with changes in terms of trade or changes in scale and variety in addition to the familiar gains from exploiting comparative advantage. He notes that the BDS model employs a version the New Trade Theory that differs from some better-known variants in the theoretical literature. Second, the quantification of the gains from trade can help policy makers decide between allocating scarce political resources to trade liberalization as opposed to other policy initiatives. Third, comparisons between multilateral and bilateral agreements show that there seem to be strong economic reasons to prefer the former even though the latter may be more politically appealing. While useful in their current form, Head concludes that CGE models would benefit from incorporating three items that are omitted from the BDS model: additional factors such as land and skilled labor; search-related unemployment; and "natural" trade barriers such as distance and language effects.

In Chapter 3, **Reforming Japan's Agricultural Policies,** Yoshihisa Godo seeks to clarify the political dynamics underlying Japan's rice policies. For this purpose, he estimates the PSE (Producer Support Estimate), CSE (Consumer Support Estimate) and DWL (Dead Weight Loss), and conducts a simple simulation analysis regarding major rice policies. His major findings are: (1) the magnitude of the government's intervention in the rice market is significant—namely, the PSE, CSE and DWL divided by the total value of rice production (or rice consumption) are nearly 0.8, -1.0 and 0.3 respectively as of 1997; and (2) most of the PSE, CSE and DWL are attributable to non-budgetary policies such as import prohibitions and the cartel effect of the acreage control program, which have escaped public attention whereas budgetary policies such as subsidies for the domestic rice marketing, which have repeatedly attracted public attention account for minor portions of the PSE, CSE and DWL.

These findings imply that Japanese consumers are generally tolerant about the rice-protection policy unless it involves a large budgetary cost. Using this consumer tolerance, farmers have succeeded in obtaining government income support mainly by non-budgetary policies. This situation should thus be regarded as a kind of "logrolling" that is detrimental to the overall efficiency and equity in the Japanese economy.

Godo also notes that the "clean tariffication," which the WTO authorities have advocated, may undermine the rice-income-support effect of the non-budgetary policies. In this respect, the new round of WTO negotiations that will include agriculture can be seen as a prime opportunity to reform Japan's agricultural policy.

In his comment, Will Martin asks for clarification of the uses that were made of the land withdrawn from rice production and that a clearer distinction should be drawn between self-sufficiency and food security in the context of Japan's agricultural protection. Martin also shows how Japan's protection has changed over a longer time span to reach their now unprecedentely high levels. In the Uruguay Round negotiations, Martin notes that Japan could have set its minimum-access levels for rice at 5 percent rather than 8 percent. Nonetheless, Japan made significant concessions in the Uruguay Round in reducing protection on wheat, sugar, and dairy products. Martin expresses concern about Godo's ad hoc demand and supply curves since it is then difficult for Godo to calculate welfare changes, including assessment of the effects of land-withdrawal policies.

Sadao Nagaoka notes that Japan was able to achieve "dirty" tariffication for rice because the price comparison used reflected a premium for Japanese consumption of high-quality rice. He also suggests that Godo may possibly exaggerate the political difficulties of liberalizing rice imports. Nagaoka further notes that Godo has perhaps underestimated the cost of rice protection because of the assumption of a low domestic supply elasticity. The welfare losses of the acreage-control program may have been overstated because Godo did not allow for land withdrawn to be used for alternative and more profitable crops. The welfare impact of the minimum-access commitments of the Uruguay Round may also be questioned because Godo did not take the sizable depreciation of the yen into account in 1994-97. Nagaoka reinforces Godo's conclusion about the need for clean tariffication and an income-support program to assist Japanese farmers.

In Chapter 4, **Tariffication in Services,** Alan Deardorff argues that the prospects for achieving significant liberalization of the international provision of services will be greatly improved if something like his proposal for tariffication of services is followed. By amending the General Agreement on Trade in Services (GATS) to permit countries to tax foreign providers of services in a manner that is roughly analogous to tariffs on imported goods, countries will be encouraged to bring most categories of services under GATS discipline.

Of course, that discipline will be much weakened by doing this, since the tariffs may be set so high that little if any trade will occur. However, once this is done, it will become possible for countries to negotiate reductions in these services tariffs in exactly the same way that they have done for goods over the last fifty years. Considering the amount of time it has taken to achieve significant liberalization of trade in goods, we should not expect to achieve it in services any time soon. However, by starting the process with tariffication, we place services upon the same well-traveled road that has been followed before, and we can be more confident that the future negotiating process will take us where we want to go, even if we cannot know how soon we will get there.

In his comment, T. N. Srinivasan notes that spreading the cost of adjustment over time is the only argument for gradually liberalizing tariffs, and that tariffication may not be the only or the most desirable way of spreading adjustment costs. He questions Deardorff's view that countries may never agree to full national treatment in services, and he notes that there could be a quota analogue to achieving liberalization without having tariffs initially. Further, Srinivasan states that Deardorff exaggerates the "lumpiness" of services and the problems of balancing concessions, and fails to take into account the gains from unilateral liberalization. Finally, he questions whether it would be feasible to implement tariffs on a nondiscriminatory basis because of difficulties in identifying foreign suppliers.

Kyoji Fukao notes that there exist foreign services affiliates in Japan in sectors already subject to discriminatory regulations, so that the introduction of tariffication would be highly disruptive to these affiliates. He also suggests that the GATS schedules do not provide sufficient detailed information on which tariffs could be devised. Further, there would be problems with tariffication arising from bilateral investment treaties that guarantee national treatment for existing foreign affiliates but not for future entrants. Finally, Fukao notes that different types of taxes on services will have different welfare implications, and that it is not clear how tariffication would be applied to other modes of services supply such as consumption abroad and the presence of natural persons.

In Chapter 5, **Japan, WTO Dispute Settlement, and the Millennium Round**, William Davey notes that the new WTO dispute settlement system was a major accomplishment of the Uruguay Round. Compared to the prior GATT system, it is more legalistic, with more stress on compliance with agreed rules. Davey's chapter contains a brief overview of Japan's involvement with GATT/WTO dispute settlement and then catalogs some of the more important issues that should be raised in any near-term WTO negotiations on dispute settlement procedures.

Japan should view its participation in the dispute settlement system positively. It has generally received satisfactory outcomes in the cases where it was a complaining party. Its threatened action against the United States in their 1995 auto dispute seemed to be a useful tool in leading to a settlement with the United States that Japan could accept. In the highest profile case against Japan—*Film*—Japan prevailed in a claim against the United States.

At the end of the Uruguay Round, it was decided to have a full review of the dispute settlement procedures before the end of 1998. The review has ended, but to date, no changes have resulted from it. In addition to clarifying the procedures to be followed when there is a dispute over implementation of WTO recommendations, WTO Members should consider: (1) ways to improve remedies in cases of noncompliance; (2) the establishment of a permanent panel body; (3) increased transparency and access to the system; and (4) greater support and training to enable developing countries to use the dispute settlement system more effectively.

In Chapter 6, **Antidumping as Safeguard Policy,** J. Michael Finger, Francis Ng, and Sonam Wangchuk note in the realization that trade liberalization would require periodic adjustments because of problems in particular industries, GATT's framers provided that tariff reductions that led to such problems could be renegotiated. In an emergency, a country could raise its tariff first and negotiate compensation with the principal exporting countries later. GATT lists many provisions that allow import restrictions, provisions that, over time, have proven quite fungible. Renegotiations were replaced by negotiated quantitative restraints (VERs), which were replaced by antidumping. The problem (troublesome imports) was always the same, but the instruments changed.

Antidumping is by far the most popular instrument today. Its increased use by developing countries is particularly alarming. Since the WTO Agreements went into effect in 1995, more than 50 developing countries have informed the WTO of their antidumping regulations, and 28 have notified the initiation of antidumping cases. Developing countries since the Uruguay Round (in 1995-99) have initiated 559 cases, developed countries 463 cases. Even transition economies have entered in, 4 cases by Poland, 2 by the Czech Republic, and 1 by Slovenia. Per dollar of imports Brazil has initiated five times as many cases as the United States, India seven times as many, South

Africa and Argentina twenty times as many. Transition economy and developing country exports are the usual victims—as much for antidumping actions by developing countries as for actions by developed countries.

Finger et al. argue that the use of antidumping makes neither economic nor political sense. It does not help a government isolate those import restrictions for which the benefits to the domestic economy would exceed the costs, and it undercuts rather than reinforces the politics of opening the economy to international trade. The key characteristic of a sensible safeguard procedure is that it treats domestic interests that would be harmed by an import restriction equally with those domestic interests that would benefit. The "morality" of the foreign interest is irrelevant—the issue is the plus and minus on the domestic economy. The important considerations are: (1) identify the costs and losers as well as the benefits and winners; and (2) give potential losers and potential winners equal voice in determining if an import-restricting action will be taken.

In Chapter 7, **Intellectual Property Issues for the United States and Japan: Disputes and Common Interests,** Keith Maskus notes that there has been marked convergence of intellectual-property standards between Japan and the United States since 1994. In large part, this reflects the introduction of stronger legislative and judicial standards in Japan covering patent scope, examination procedures, and copyrights. However, the United States has also clarified its patent regime and moved partially toward early disclosure of patent applications.

Despite this convergence, there remain substantive differences in the national systems of protection. Among other issues, Japan expresses concern about the ability of the U.S. "first-to-invent" patent system to foster submarine patents and raise uncertainty for foreign inventors. Japan also protests the weak U.S. provisions for third-party invalidation procedures. The United States remains concerned about slow patent litigation, weak discovery procedures, and patent flooding in Japan. It also argues that Japan has weak protection for well-known trademarks and urges reform in its trade-secrets regime. Despite these differences, both countries have mature systems and remaining disputes are more in the realm of small irritants than significant conflicts.

On an international scale, Japan and the United States share a broad commonality of interests in shaping the global system of intellectual property rights (IPRs) over the next decade. Both are significant suppliers of intellectual property, with Japan taking a leading role in transferring technologies to the industrializing nations of East Asia. Creative firms in both countries should earn higher returns on the international exploitation of new technologies and products as standards are strengthened. Econometric computations demonstrate that, in the short term, inventors in the United States would earn considerably greater net rents on their portfolios of international patents, while the same would be true for Japanese inventors as regards their patent stocks in developing Asia.

Despite this long-term joint interest, it is likely that the United States would place greater emphasis than Japan on implementation of strong IPRs in developing countries through the TRIPS Agreement of the WTO. In part this could reflect strategic views on the part of American firms in relation to Japanese competitors, which must deal more closely with extensive Asian production networks. It could also reflect recent history, in that Japan's patent system in place after World War II promoted diffusion and small innovation, with a positive impact on productivity growth.

In the wake of TRIPS and stronger home standards, Japan may need to exercise vigilance in monitoring and disciplining anti-competitive business arrangements arising from the combination of intellectual property protection and private market restraints. Because such issues will reach increasingly across borders in the future, there is scope for multilateral consideration of the basic framework of an international competition agreement.

In Chapter 8, **Prospects for Investment Negotiations in the WTO**, Fukunari Kimura reviews the multilateral effort of establishing policy discipline for investment-related policies and discusses the prospects for WTO-based negotiations. He argues that FDI-related policies currently conducted by a number of countries are often distortive, and the establishment of multilateral-investment-policy rules is essential to enhancing economic efficiency and reducing politico-economic costs in the globalization era. He also attempts to draw some lessons from the failure of the negotiation of the Multilateral Agreement on Investment (MAI) and the implementation of the Trade-Related Investment Measures (TRIMs) Agreement. He further extends his discussion to issues of the treatment of developing countries, possible conflict with "pure domestic" policies, and the relationship with bilateral/regional investment rules.

In Chapter 9, **Trade and Competition at the WTO: Competition Policy for Market-Access Development,** Jiro Tamura focuses on the challenge of gaining market access in the new global economy. He notes that it is now time to take stock of the progress that has been made in implementing market access, regulating restrictive business practices, and enforcing and maintaining free and fair competition. Antimonopoly issues affecting market access in Japan such as cartels, boycotts, and trade associations have been effective to a certain degree but there is room for alternative approaches. Tamura argues the necessity of market access being treated as a trade issue, first through the examination of competition law in Japan, and, second, by looking at some of the problems and questions left behind from the U.S.-Japan Fuji-Kodak Film Case. He proposes a multilateral approach to the issues. The idea of having a multilateral organization to monitor anticompetitive activities and a committee at the WTO can play a key role by having a forum for members to report situations of competition issues to further develop international competition and trade. In addition, Tamura discusses how a WTO Competition Committee that can contribute to the regulation of restrictive business practices together with other bilateral approaches offers the most flexible and effective means available to deal with trade problems among industrialized and developing countries.

Part Two: Trade and Environment; Regionalism

The chapters in Part Two deal with trade and environment and analysis of regional negotiating initiatives of interest to the United States, Japan, and other major trading countries. The chapter on trade and environment describes so-called eco-labelling programs and provides a theoretical analysis of their effects. One chapter on regionalism is a theoretical analysis of the choice between a preferential trading arrangement and open regionalism as envisaged in the Asia-Pacific Economic Cooperation (APEC) forum. The other chapter uses simulation methods to analyze different trade arrangements to determine if APEC is a building or stumbling block towards liberalization.

In Chapter 10, **Eco-Labelling, Environment, and International Trade,** Kenzo Abe, Keisaku Higashida, and Jota Ishikawa note that many countries have recently introduced eco-labelling programs. These programs are expected to change consumer behavior to buy more environmentally friendly products and in this way to improve the quality of the environment. Abe et al. review recent discussions of eco-labelling programs, in particular in terms of their effectiveness and trade effects. They construct a theoretical model incorporating domestic and foreign eco-labelling programs in an international oligopoly.

They first describe both expected and unexpected effects of eco-labelling programs on consumer behavior and the environment and then discuss concerns about possible unfavorable trade effects of these programs in the context of a life cycle assessment in individual countries. They also discuss the effects of eco-labelling programs on investment in environmentally sound technology.

The significant features of the effects of eco-labelling on the domestic economy are analyzed using a simple international oligopoly model. They first show that the effects of eco-labelling depend on whether pollution is emitted during production or consumption. They then show that the introduction of eco-labelling or the recognition of a foreign eco-label could increase local emissions. Finally, even if foreign firms cannot obtain the domestic eco-label, this does not necessarily mean that the foreign firms lose from it. Moreover, domestic firms may not benefit from such eco-labelling.

In his comment, Stephen Salant notes that Abe et al. are not able to conduct a welfare analysis because they do not specify a social damage function for emissions and the preferences underlying the consumer demand curves for labelled and unlabelled products. This latter issue suggests the presence of a second externality that relates to consumer preferences about the technology used to produce a good. In this event, a Pigouvian tax could be placed on emissions, and eco-labelling might then be a way to deal with the technology that consumers would prefer to be used in producing the clean good that they will buy.

John Whalley suggests that the term "eco-retailing" might be more appropriate than eco-labelling since it reflects more of what concerns consumers about the ways in which products are packaged. While environmental concerns reflect externalities, Whalley points out that eco-retailing restrictions are an inefficient policy because they may worsen the externalities. It would be preferable to use a tax instead. Since developing countries may have the most to lose from product identification schemes, they will need to be offered some offsetting concession if called upon to negotiate trade and environment issues in the WTO. Finally, Whalley notes that Abe et al. do not consider that mandatory labelling may be welfare improving if consumers are uninformed or if information gathering is costly.

In Chapter 11, **Preferential Trade Arrangements vs. Open Regionalism: A Theoretical Analysis of APEC,** Taiji Furusawa notes that the Asia Pacific Economic Cooperation (APEC) forum adopts open regionalism as its fundamental principle. Among several possible definitions of open regionalism, he focuses on the aspect of offering unconditional most-favored-nation treatment (MFN), which is the most prominent feature of APEC. That is, open regionalism refers to a principle of regional arrangements such that any internal agreement is extended to nonmember countries. Because of this inherent feature of openness, regional economic integration is complementary to global trade liberalization if it adopts the principle of open regionalism. Furusawa examines the choice between a Preferential Trade Arrangement (PTA) and open regionalism when countries form a trading bloc. Whether a PTA is preferred or open regionalism is adopted cannot be determined *a priori*. In a simple three-country model, he shows that when countries engage in economic integration, they always choose not to adopt open regionalism. Indeed, if the status-quo tariff rates are large enough, it is possible for PTA member countries to select the best tariff profile that maximizes their social welfare in the absence of any constraint on the feasible tariff profiles. This result, however, is not universally true. Furusawa discusses a possible extension of the model, so that politically motivated governments of member countries adopt open regionalism when they are economically integrated.

In his comment, Gordon Hanson notes that there is a tradeoff between a preferential trade agreement (PTA) and open regionalism insofar as a PTA eliminates all trade barriers among a small number of countries whereas open regionalism reduces, but does not eliminate, barriers among several countries. It is especially noteworthy that the welfare benefit of a PTA could dominate open regionalism in cases in which member countries have relatively small tariffs so that there would be little trade diversion. The opposite would be true when the PTA members have relatively high tariffs. In asking why APEC members might then opt for open regionalism rather than a PTA, Hanson suggests that with APEC and open regionalism, there might be lower variance in tariff rates, a large dependence on trade with non-APEC countries, and geopolitical concerns in avoiding conflicts with politically powerful countries.

Chong Xiang suggests that Furusawa might extend his analysis of open regionalism to take into account that some countries, like the United States, Canada, and Mexico, are members both of APEC and the North American Free Trade Agreement (NAFTA). Xiang also suggests that, contrary to Furusawa's results, open regionalism might be preferred to a preferential trading arrangement (PTA) if trade diversion is strong enough. Finally, in case a member country of a PTA may be harmed, this country would have an incentive to create non-tariff barriers against other members to offset the harm involved in its membership.

In Chapter 12, **Is APEC a Building Block or Stumbling Block towards Trade Liberalization?,** Masahiro Endoh examines the conditions under which APEC may become "a building block" or "a stumbling block" toward trade liberalization by using a political-economy framework combined with computer simulation. The market structure is assumed to be imperfect competition, with oligopolistic firms producing goods that are perfect substitutes for each other. Twenty countries with asymmetric market size are taken into consideration to compare the effects of five methods of trade liberalization on each country's welfare, world welfare, and the world trading system.

Three main criteria of being "a building block" that promote trade liberalization are evident in the simulation results. First and foremost, the inclusion of many large countries in APEC is crucial. Second, "open regionalism" has significant and positive effects on world-trade liberalization and each country's welfare if it goes along with WTO-based liberalization. Third, when trade liberalization is by a preferential trading area (PTA), it is important to deter non-APEC countries from "free-riding" on APEC efforts towards trade liberalization. In actuality, the form of "open regionalism" still remains at the proposal stage, and it is not clear whether any of the present economies or groups in APEC would follow it. However, the analysis shows that this policy has the potential ability to become "a building block" in the world trading system.

In his comment, Jeffrey Bergstrand notes that, in contrast to other models of preferential arrangements, Endoh has a more comprehensive representation of consumer behavior and the government's objective function. Endoh also analyzed the welfare implications of APEC's open regionalism both with and without FTAs. While Endoh concludes that unilateral liberalization by APEC is welfare decreasing, Bergstrand suggests that this result could be changed if account were taken of such matters as product variety and dynamic aspects of competitiveness and economic growth.

Arvind Panagariya takes issue with Endoh's government-objective function in which it is assumed that only the welfare of wage earners matters, and not profit earners as well. Endoh's negative conclusion about unilateral liberalization is also called into question insofar as no account is taken of changes in the terms of trade, the role of exports, and the forward-looking behavior of the economic agents. With regard to the definition of open regionalism, Panagariya notes that open entry does not mean speedy entry so that some countries may experience discrimination during the sometimes lengthy entry process.

Further, entry may require some onerous and costly side payments that may be detrimental to welfare.

Part Three: U.S.-Japan Bilateral Trade and FDI Issues

The chapters in Part Three focus especially on issues of U.S.-Japan bilateral trade and foreign direct investment. These chapters seek to identify the main issues of bilateral concern and frictions, the factors determining the dispute-settlement actions and outcomes of cases brought by the USTR in the WTO dispute-settlement mechanism, the trade impacts of U.S. unilateral measures directed at Japan, and international legal issues arising from some high-profile trade disputes.

In Chapter 13, **U.S.-Japan Trade Policy and FDI Issues,** Robert Stern presents background information on the patterns of trade and the foreign direct investment positions of the United States and Japan. He then reviews the multilateral dimensions of each nation's trade policies, focusing especially on the dispute settlement actions that they have instituted against each other since the creation of the WTO in 1995. He discusses at considerable length U.S.-Japan bilateral trade relations and policies from the perspective of each nation and has a brief discussion of regional trade relations and policies.

Stern notes that U.S.-Japan trade relations have become relatively quiescent compared to earlier years. This may reflect the increasingly important role and use of the WTO dispute settlement mechanism as well as the rapid rate of U.S. economic growth in the 1990s that may have moderated domestic protectionist pressures. It is also the case that Japan has made genuine progress in promoting domestic deregulation in several key sectors and eased access to its domestic market. Finally, Japan's recent decisions to negotiate free trade agreements represent an important departure from its longstanding support of multilateralism.

In her comment, Yoko Sazanami reinforces Stern's points about the importance of the WTO dispute settlement mechanism and Japanese deregulation as important reasons for the current quiescence in U.S.-Japan trade and FDI relations. She suggests that the restructuring taking place may help to foster Japan's economic recovery from its protracted recession. Further, Japan's recent policy shift towards negotiating free trade agreements has strong business support and may at the same time provide an incentive for additional deregulatory measures that could improve domestic economic performance.

John Ries also remarks that the trade relations between the United States and Japan in recent years reflects progress in Japan's deregulatory program that has eased market access for imports and FDI, the continued rapid growth of the U.S. economy that has muted protectionist pressures, and a shift in the ideology of Japan's policy making towards greater emphasis on the role of unfettered markets. Ries expresses some concern about future repercussions stemming from possible reductions of Japan's trade surpluses and problems that may arise if environmental issues become of greater importance in generating trade disputes.

In Chapter 14, **Dispute Settlement at the WTO and the Dole Commission: USTR Resources and Success,** Gary Saxonhouse notes that at the time the Uruguay Round Agreements were passed by Congress in 1993, particular concern was expressed about their implications for U.S. national sovereignty. Concern was sufficiently great that the Clinton Administration committed its support to the creation of a commission that would review each adverse decision against the United States by the WTO. The commission was designed such that the outcome of its review process might trigger a serious Congressional consideration of U.S. withdrawal from the WTO. While the so-called Dole Commission was never created, the Congressional controversy surrounding the ratification of the Uruguay Round Agreement has led to particular concern with USTR performance at the WTO. Curiously, enhanced Congressional concern has not gone hand in hand with more resources for USTR. Over the 1990s, USTR has rarely asked for, but it did receive additional resources for its work at the very end of the Clinton Administration in 2000.

In his analysis, Saxonhouse shows that if the USTR is concerned not only with the number of cases it wins but also with its rate of success, then having more resources may have an ambiguous impact on USTR's rate of success. Depending on how relatively promising are the additional cases that may yet be brought by USTR to the WTO and how usefully additional resources may be applied to existing cases, it is possible that more resources can lower USTR's success rate. This is true, though for different reasons, when explicit allowance is made for the response by Japan or some other party to the dispute to a USTR commitment of additional resources.

More resources cannot explain the increased use that the USTR has made since the WTO was established, because, until 2000, USTR has received no additional resources. Rather, the DSM is being used more because its newly acquired speed and automaticity may make the WTO more predictable than before, notwithstanding the inevitable vagueness of a new trade treaty.

In his comment, Jude Hays suggests that Saxonhouse does not assess the domestic political risks that may arise if there is dissatisfaction with the WTO dispute-resolution procedures. While perhaps not altogether important currently, political opposition to the WTO could conceivably be of future importance. Hays also questions the functional form in Saxonhouse's second strategic model involving the USTR and MITI insofar as it may not be generally the case that the USTR's success rate in winning WTO uses will be reduced if USTR receives more resources. Hays asks finally whether or not it is really the case, as Saxonhouse concludes, that the dispute-settlement mechanism will be used more because the texts of the Uruguay Round are unambiguous.

In his comment, David Weinstein commends Saxonhouse's focus on the actual implementation of trade policies and, in particular, on how WTO disputes are handled by the USTR, given the size of its budget to be used in pursuing dispute actions. Weinstein poses some questions concerning the origin and weights for the variables in the utility function attributed to the USTR in its agency role, the optimal funding levels for the USTR, and the costs of legal fees in preparing cases and private-sector lobbying.

In Chapter 15, **Do U.S.-Japan Bilateral Trade Agreements Affect International Trade?**, Theresa Greaney notes that the 27 industry-agreement cases reviewed in her study provide evidence for both skeptics and advocates of US-Japan bilateral trade agreements. The skeptics, however, can embrace the bulk of the cases for which the trade data from 1980-95 do not support a conclusion of significant positive impacts of the trade agreements on Japan's imports of targeted manufactured products. At the bilateral level, most cases showed a decline in Japan's real import growth of targeted products from the United States after an agreement was signed. Of the cases where import growth from the United States increased in the post-agreement period, only one case displayed instability in the trade growth path at the time of a bilateral trade agreement. In this particular case, involving the automobile agreement in 1987, the trade data suggest trade diversion benefiting U.S.-based producers at the expense of European producers. The semiconductor agreement in 1991 is a less-definitive second case where the trade data can be used to support a claim of positive impacts on U.S.-based producers from a bilateral trade agreement. In this case, the agreement may have served to soften the negative impact of Japan's economic downturn in 1991. At the multilateral level, only two cases were found where the trade evidence and details of the agreements support a claim that non-U.S.-based producers benefited from the increased market access sought by a U.S.-Japan trade agreement. These cases involved bilateral agreements covering telecommunications equipment and semiconductors signed in 1986.

In his comment, Shujiro Urata notes that there may be a mismatch between the objective of trade arrangements and Greaney's method of evaluation. That is, the objective of the trade arrangements may not be to increase the volume of imports of particular goods but may involve other types of concessions or market-share arrangements. He also suggests that it would have been preferable to estimate a structural model of import-demand and export-supply functions to take a broader range of explanatory variables into account. He also recommends more in-depth industry studies. Finally, he suggests that Greaney's country/region coverage might be expanded to include East Asia, which may be affected by the various market-opening initiatives.

In Chapter 16, **Multilateralism, Unilateralism, and Bilateralism in U.S.-Japan Trade Relations: A WTO Law Perspective**, Robert Howse notes that, although Japan and the United States have frequently resorted to dispute settlement under multilateral (GATT/WTO) rules to settle their trade disputes, unilateral trade-policy instruments such as the U.S. Section 301 legislation, as well as bilateral-market-access agreements (auto parts, for example) have played an important role in the management by the United States of its trading relations with Japan. Howse examines recent WTO jurisprudence that has clarified the legality, or legal preconditions, for certain kinds of unilateral and bilateral trade policy instruments. The cases are *Turtles*, *Section 301* and *1916 Anti-Dumping Act* cases, and *Canadian Autos*. The *Turtles* case concerns an embargo of shrimp imports imposed by the United States, where shrimp are fished in a manner that causes high levels of mortality of endangered species of sea turtles; the Appellate Body ruling in this case has important implications for trade and environment disputes between Japan and the United States, including the recent whaling dispute. In the *Section 301* and the *1916 Anti-Dumping Act* cases, the extent of the obligation to ensure through legislation that domestic authorities do not resort to unilateral trade remedies in a manner inconsistent with WTO law was considered. The *Canadian Autos* case applies WTO disciplines to a long-standing bilateral, managed-trade arrangement between Canada and the United States, with important implications for the WTO-consistency of any future such arrangements between the United States and Japan.

III. Conclusions and Implications for Policy

It should be evident from the foregoing chapter summaries that a wide range of issues of concern to the trade relations and policies of the United States and Japan have been covered. Some of the most noteworthy conclusions are as follows.

1. WTO Multilateral Negotiating Issues

- Substantial welfare gains for all the major trading countries can be attained with a new round of WTO multilateral negotiations. These gains are much larger than the gains from regional/bilateral preferential trading arrangements.
- Japan's new initiatives to negotiate bilateral free trade agreements will have comparatively small welfare and employment effects in Japan but potentially disruptive employment effects in some partner countries.
- Japan's intervention in its domestic rice market results in significant deadweight losses, due especially to non-budgetary policies such as trade restrictions and acreage controls. There remain significant domestic obstacles to the political reform of Japan's rice policies. But the ongoing WTO agricultural negotiations may provide an opportunity for such reform.
- Services liberalization in the ongoing WTO negotiations will be beneficial to the interests of the United States, Japan, and other major trading countries. One way to anchor the basis for services negotiations may be to seek to "tarrify" existing services barriers.
- Japan has generally experienced satisfactory outcomes in the cases that it has brought to the WTO dispute-settlement mechanism (DSM). There remain nonetheless a series of measures that need to be considered to improve the functioning of the DSM.

- Antidumping (AD) is currently the most popular method for addressing allegedly "unfair" trading practices in setting prices, and it has become increasingly used by developing countries. However, AD actions are subject to abuse and should be replaced by safeguard measures that take into account the domestic costs and benefits of import restrictions.
- There has been increasing convergence of intellectual property (IP) standards between the United States and Japan, and existing disputes are minor. Both nations have a strong interest in an effective IP regime, given that they are both major suppliers of IP.
- Because policies relating to foreign direct investment (FDI) are distortionary in many countries, there is a case for developing multilateral rules in the WTO to enhance economic efficiency.
- There is a case to be made for addressing questions of market access by having the WTO monitor anticompetitive activities in member countries.

2. Trade and Environment

- Eco-labelling may be a way to induce consumers to buy more environmentally friendly products. It is not clear, however, that eco-labelling in itself may be welfare improving. There also may be a need for the tax treatment of environmental externalities.

3. Regionalism

- Whether a preferential trading arrangement is more desirable than an APEC-type arrangement with open regionalism depends on the height of existing tariffs, trade with non-member countries, and political factors.
- APEC efforts in conjunction with WTO-based trade liberalization may reinforce the global movement to freer trade.

4. U.S.-Japan Bilateral Trade and FDI Issues

- U.S.-Japan bilateral trade relations have become more quiescent compared to earlier years due to the increasingly important role and use of the WTO dispute-settlement mechanism (DSM), rapid U.S. economic growth in the 1990s, and the genuine progress that Japan has made in deregulation and easing access to its domestic markets. From Japan's perspective, the U.S. resort to antidumping actions taken against imports from Japan, especially iron and steel products, is a continuing source of bilateral friction. The increased availability of resources to the USTR to apply in cases brought before the WTO DSM may have an ambiguous effect on USTR's success in winning cases.
- There is not much evidence in support of the effectiveness of U.S.-Japan bilateral trade agreements in increasing Japan's imports of targeted products from the United States.

- Attention must be given to WTO dispute settlements insofar as they have a direct bearing on policy instruments used bilaterally in U.S.-Japan relations as well as unilateral policy actions that may be taken.

The foregoing conclusions are not meant to be exhaustive in terms of what the individual chapters contain and the depth of their analysis. Hopefully, then, depending on their specialization, readers will be encouraged to consult in detail those chapters that may be of greatest interest. It should also be mentioned that there are many issues in U.S.-Japan international economic relations that have not been addressed in this volume. These include especially issues of policies and institutions that are more domestic in nature but which nonetheless have a bearing on the relations of the two countries with each other and with the rest of the world. Such issues comprise the agenda for the second year of the program of research that is entitled "Analytical Issues in the Trade, Foreign Direct Investment, and Macro/Financial Relations of the United States and Japan." A companion volume to this present one is in progress and will contain the papers from the second-year conference that was held at Keio University in Tokyo on May 18-19, 2001.

Note

[1] Chapters 5-9 and 16 were presented at the conference in a panel format and therefore do not include separate comments. Comments by James Levinsohn on Chapter 15 were incorporated in the author's revisions and are not included. It should also be mentioned that there was a conference keynote address on "Japan's Perspective on a New Trade Round" by Shinichi Kitijima, Minister for Economic Affairs, Embassy of Japan, Washington, D.C. Minister Kitijima did not prepare a written text for this address. He touched on many of the issues dealt with especially in Chapters 5, 6, 13, and 15 in the context of a new trade round.

Part One: WTO Multilateral Negotiating Issues

CHAPTER 2

CGE Modeling and Analysis of Multilateral and Regional Negotiating Options

Drusilla K. Brown, Alan V. Deardorff, and Robert M. Stern

I. Introduction

The United States and Japan are two of the key players in the global trading system even though they have at times been at odds regarding each other's trade and domestic policies. What we wish to explore in this paper are the options that the two nations have in prospective trade negotiations at the multilateral and regional levels. For this purpose, we use the Michigan Model of World Production and Trade to provide some quantitative assessments of the economic effects of different options. The Michigan Model is a multi-country, multi-sector computational general equilibrium (CGE) model that we have used now for more than 25 years to analyze changes in multilateral and regional trade policies.

In Section II we first analyze the multilateral trade liberalization provisions of the Uruguay Round Agreements. For this purpose, we use a 20-country/18-sector version of our CGE model. Then, in Section III, we consider the potential economic effects of the liberalization of trade in agricultural products and services, which are currently in the early negotiation stages of a new WTO trade round as part of the built-in agenda mandated in the Uruguay Round. We also consider the liberalization of trade in industrial products, which is yet to be decided pending agreement among the WTO members on the agenda for a new trade round. In Section IV, we analyze regional negotiating options of interest to the United States and Japan. These options include the removal of trade barriers between members of the Asia Pacific Economic Cooperation (APEC) forum and possible bilateral free trade agreements between Japan and Singapore, Japan and Mexico, Japan and Korea, and Japan and Chile. We also consider a possible ASEAN Plus-3 free trade agreement involving the ASEAN member countries together with Japan, China/Hong Kong, and South Korea. Conclusions and implications for policy are discussed in Section V.

II. Computational Analysis of Multilateral Trade Liberalization in the Uruguay Round

In this section we analyze the trade liberalization provisions in the Uruguay Round. As mentioned, we will use CGE model-based simulation analysis to assess the potential economic effects arising from the implementation of the liberalization provisions. The computational experiments consist of simulating the economic effects of reductions of tariffs and nontariff barriers on the countries/regions included in the model.

Overview of the Michigan CGE Model

The distinguishing feature of the Michigan Model is that it incorporates some aspects of the New Trade Theory, including increasing returns to scale, monopolistic competition, and product heterogeneity. Some details follow. A more complete description of the formal structure and equations of the model can be found on line at www.Fordschool.umich.edu/rsie/model/.

Sectors and Market Structure

The version of the model to be used here consists of 20 countries/regions (plus rest-of-world) and 18 production sectors. The country/region and sectoral coverage are indicated in the tables below.[1] Agriculture is modeled as perfectly competitive and all other sectors as monopolistically competitive with free entry and exit of firms.

Expenditure

Consumers and producers are assumed to use a two-stage procedure to allocate expenditure across differentiated products. In the first stage, expenditure is allocated across goods without regard to the country of origin or producing firm. At this stage, the utility function is Cobb-Douglas, and the production function requires intermediate inputs in fixed proportions. In the second stage, expenditure on monopolistically competitive goods is allocated across the competing varieties supplied by each firm from all countries. In the case of sectors that are perfectly competitive, since individual firm supply is indeterminate, expenditure is allocated over each country's industry as a whole, with imperfect substitution between products of different countries. The aggregation function in the second stage is a Constant Elasticity of Substitution (CES) function.

Production

The production function is separated into two stages. In the first stage, intermediate inputs and a primary composite of capital and labor are used in fixed proportion to output.[2] In the second stage, capital and labor are combined through a CES function to form the primary composite. In the monopolistically competitive sectors, additional fixed inputs of capital and labor are required. It is assumed that fixed capital and fixed labor are used in the same proportion as variable capital and variable labor so that production functions are homothetic.

Supply Prices

To determine equilibrium prices, perfectly competitive firms operate such that price is equal to marginal cost, while monopolistically competitive firms maximize profits by setting price as an optimal mark-up over marginal cost. The numbers of firms in sectors under monopolistic competition are determined by the condition that there are zero profits.

Capital and Labor Markets

Capital and labor are assumed to be perfectly mobile across sectors within each country. Returns to capital and labor are determined so as to equate factor demand to an exogenous supply of each factor. The aggregate supplies of capital and labor in each country are assumed to remain fixed so as to abstract from macroeconomic considerations (e.g., the determination of investment), since our microeconomic focus is on the intersectoral allocation of resources.

World Market and Trade Balance

The world market determines equilibrium prices such that all markets clear. Total demand for each firm or sector's product must equal total supply of that product. It is also assumed that trade remains balanced for each country/region, that is, the initial trade imbalance remains constant as trade barriers are changed. This assumption reflects the reality of mostly flexible exchange rates among the countries involved. Moreover, this is a way of abstracting from the macroeconomic forces and policies that are the main determinants of trade imbalances.

Trade Policies and Rent/Revenues

We have incorporated into the model the import tariff rates and export taxes/subsidies as policy inputs that are applicable to the bilateral trade of the various countries/regions with respect to one another. These have been computed using the "GTAP–4 Database" provided in McDougall et al. (1998). The export barriers have been estimated as export-tax equivalents. We assume that revenues from both import tariffs and export taxes, as well as rents from NTBs on exports, are redistributed to consumers in the tariff- or tax-levying country and are spent like any other income. When tariffs are reduced, this means that income available to purchase imports falls along with their prices, and there is no bias towards expanding or contracting overall demand.

Model Closure and Implementation

We assume in the model that aggregate expenditure varies endogenously to hold aggregate employment constant. This closure is analogous to the

Johansen closure rule (Deardorff and Stern, 1990). The Johansen closure rule consists of keeping the requirement of full employment while dropping the consumption function. This means that consumption can be thought of as adjusting endogenously to ensure full employment. However, in the present model, we do not distinguish consumption from other sources of final demand. That is, we assume instead that total expenditure adjusts to maintain full employment.

The model is solved using GEMPACK (Harrison and Pearson, 1996). When policy changes are introduced into the model, the method of solution yields percentage changes in sectoral employment and certain other variables of interest. Multiplying the percentage changes by the levels projected for the year 2005, which is when the Uruguay Round provisions will have been fully implemented, yields the absolute changes, positive or negative, which might result from the various liberalization scenarios.

Data

Needless to say, the data needs of this model are immense. Apart from numerous share parameters, the model requires various types of elasticity measures. Like other CGE models, most of our data come from published sources.

As mentioned above, the main data source is "The GTAP-4 Database" of the Purdue University Center for Global Trade Analysis Project (McDougall et al., 1998). The reference year for this database is 1995. From this source, we have extracted the following data, aggregated to our sectors and regions:

1. Bilateral trade flows among 20 countries/regions, decomposed into 18 sectors. Trade with the rest-of-world (ROW) is included to close the model.
2. Input-output tables for the 20 countries/regions, excluding ROW
3. Components of final demand along with sectoral contributions for the 20 countries/regions, excluding ROW
4. Gross value of output and value added at the sectoral level for the 20 countries/regions, excluding ROW
5. Bilateral import tariffs by sector among the 20 countries/regions
6. Elasticity of substitution between capital and labor by sector
7. Bilateral export-tariff equivalents among the 20 countries/regions, decomposed into 18 sectors

The monopolistically competitive market structure in the non-agricultural sectors of the model imposes an additional data requirement of the number of firms at the sectoral level. These data have been drawn from the United Nations, *International Yearbook of Industrial Statistics, 1998*.[3]

We also need estimates of sectoral employment for the countries/regions of the model. These data have been drawn from: UNIDO, 1995, *International Yearbook of Industrial Statistics*, and the World Bank, 1997, *World Development Report*. The employment data have been aggregated according to our sectoral/regional aggregation to obtain sectoral estimates of workers employed in manufactures. The *World Development Report* was used to obtain data for the other sectors.[4]

We have projected the GTAP-4 1995 database to the year 2005 by extrapolating the labor availability in different countries/regions by an average weighted population growth rate of 1.2 per cent per annum. This figure was computed from the growth-rate forecasts for the period 1997-2010 provided for various countries in Table 2.3 of the World Bank's 1999 *World Development Indicators*. All other major variables have been projected, using an average weighted growth rate of GDP of 2.5 per cent per annum, for all of the countries/regions of our model during the period 1990-1997, as per Table 11 of the 1989/99 *World Development Report*.[5]

Computational Scenarios

The projected database provides us with an approximate picture of what the world could be expected to look like in 2005 if the Uruguay Round (UR) negotiations had not occurred. The UR reductions in trade barriers were implemented beginning in 1995 and will be completed by 2005. Accordingly, we have analyzed the impact of the UR-induced changes that are expected to occur over the course of the 10-year implementation period as a consequence of the negotiated reductions in tariffs and non-tariff barriers. The scaled-up database for 2005 is then readjusted to mimic the world as it might look in the post-UR implementation. In Section III following, we use these re-adjusted data as the starting point to carry out some liberalization scenarios for a forthcoming WTO negotiating round, involving possible reductions in tariffs on agricultural products and manufactures and reductions of barriers to trade in services.

In this section, we report on the following four scenarios:

UR-1 *The Agreement on Textiles and Clothing (ATC) is analyzed by simulating the effects of phase-out of the Multi-Fiber Arrangement (MFA) under the Uruguay-Round (UR) agreement. This is done by assuming complete elimination of the MFA export-tax equivalents on textiles and wearing apparel for the developing countries/regions subject to the MFA and other quotas imposed on their exports to the industrialized countries.*

UR-2 *Agricultural liberalization is modeled according to the percentage reductions in import tariffs and export subsidies for the industrialized and developing countries as agreed upon in the Uruguay Round. Agricultural import tariffs were reduced by 20 percent for the industrialized countries and by 13 percent for the developing countries. Agricultural export subsidies were reduced by 36 percent for the industrialized countries and by 24 percent for the developing countries.*

UR-3 *All the countries/regions in the model are assumed to reduce their bilateral import tariffs as per the UR Agreement on mining and manufactured products.*[6]

UR-4 *This combines UR-1, UR-2, and UR-3.*

Computational Results

Table 1 provides aggregate, or economy-wide, results from the scenarios listed above for the countries/regions that have been modeled. Disaggregated sectoral results for the UR-4 scenario for the United States and for Japan are reported in tables 2-3.

To help the reader interpret the results, it is useful first to review the features of the model that serve to identify the various economic effects that are being captured in the different scenarios. Although the model includes the aforementioned features of the New Trade Theory, it remains the case that markets respond to trade liberalization in much the same way that they would with perfect competition. That is, when tariffs or other trade barriers are reduced in a sector, domestic buyers (both final and intermediate) substitute toward imports and the domestic competing industry contracts production while foreign exporters expand. With multilateral liberalization reducing tariffs and other trade barriers simultaneously in most sectors and countries, each country's industries share in both of these effects, expanding or contracting depending primarily on whether their protection is reduced more or less than in other sectors and countries. At the same time, countries with larger average tariff reductions than their trading partners tend to experience a real depreciation of their currencies in order to maintain a constant trade balance, so that all countries therefore experience mixtures of both expanding and contracting sectors.

Worldwide, these changes cause increased international demand for all sectors, with world prices rising most for those sectors where trade barriers fall the most. This in turn causes changes in countries' terms of trade that can be positive or negative. Those countries that are net exporters of goods with the greatest degree of liberalization will experience increases in their terms of trade, as the world prices of their exports rise relative to their imports. The reverse occurs for net exporters in industries where liberalization is slight—perhaps because it already happened in previous trade rounds.

The effects on the welfare of countries arise from a mixture of these terms-of-trade effects, together with the standard efficiency gains from trade and also from additional benefits due to elements of the New Trade Theory. Thus, we expect on average that the world will gain from multilateral liberalization, as resources are reallocated to those sectors in each country where there is a comparative advantage. In the absence of terms-of-trade effects, these efficiency gains should raise national welfare measured by the equivalent variation for every country, although some factor owners within a country may lose, as will be noted below. However, it is possible for a particular country whose net imports are concentrated in sectors with the greatest liberalization to lose overall, if the worsening of its terms of trade swamps these efficiency gains.

On the other hand, although the New Trade Theory is perhaps best known for introducing new reasons why countries may lose from trade, in fact its greatest contribution is to expand the list of reasons for gains from trade. It is these that are the dominant contribution of the New Trade Theory in our model. That is, trade liberalization permits all countries to expand their export sectors at the same time that all sectors compete more closely with a larger number of competing varieties from abroad. As a result, countries as a whole gain from lower costs due to increasing returns to scale, lower monopoly distortions due to greater competition, and reduced costs and/or increased utility due to greater product variety. All of these effects make it more likely that countries will gain from liberalization in ways that are shared across the entire population.

In perfectly competitive trade models such as the Heckscher-Ohlin Model, one expects countries as a whole to gain from trade, but the owners of one factor—the "scarce factor"—to lose through the mechanism first explored by Stolper and Samuelson (1941). The additional sources of gain from trade due to increasing returns to scale, competition, and product variety, however, are shared across factors, and we routinely find in our CGE modeling that both labor and capital gain from liberalization. That is often the case here.

A final point to note about our model is the modeling and role of nontariff barriers, such as those applying to textiles and apparel. These are quantitative restrictions, captured in the model by endogenous tariff equivalents that rise and fall with changing supplies and demands for trade. The tariff equivalents generate quota rents that accrue to whatever group is granted the rights to trade under the restriction, which in the case of the MFA are the countries that export textiles and wearing apparel. Liberalization of these nontariff barriers reduces or eliminates these quota rents, and this can be costly to those who possessed them disproportionately beforehand. Therefore, it is not the case that exporting countries necessarily benefit from relaxation of these trade barriers, since their loss of quota rents can more than outweigh their gains from increased exports. Indeed, the exports of particular countries can actually decline, along with their national welfare, if increased exports from other countries displace them in world markets.

In the real world, all of these effects occur over time, some of them more quickly than others. Our model is however static, based upon a single set of equilibrium conditions rather than relationships that vary over time. Our results therefore refer to a time horizon that is somewhat uncertain, depending on the assumptions that have been made about which variables do and do not adjust to changing market conditions, and on the short- or long-run nature of these adjustments. Because our elasticities of supply and demand reflect relatively long-run adjustments and because we assume that markets for both labor and capital clear within countries, our results are appropriate for a relatively long time horizon of several years—perhaps two or three at a minimum.

Table 1. Summary Results of the Uruguay Round
Change in Imports, Exports, Terms of Trade, Welfare and the Real Return to Capital and Labor
Percent Change and Millions of U.S. Dollars

Country	Imports (Millions)	Exports (Millions)	Terms of Trade (Percent)	Welfare (Percent)	Welfare (Millions)	Real Wage (Percent)	Return to Capital (Percent)
UR-1: Elimination of the Multi-Fiber Arrangement							
Industrialized Countries							
Japan	268.1	465.1	-0.031	-0.009	-589.5	0.004	0.016
United States	5,320.9	3,528.5	0.137	0.083	7,556.2	0.056	0.076
Canada	690.2	601.0	0.068	0.149	1,084.9	0.047	0.103
Australia	90.7	74.6	0.017	0.002	7.2	0.006	0.021
New Zealand	14.4	12.5	0.011	0.004	2.6	0.006	0.011
EU and EFTA	2,123.7	1,880.5	0.047	0.030	3,296.3	0.023	0.039
Developing Countries							
Asia							
Hong Kong	2,208.0	2,405.3	-0.208	-0.099	-127.7	1.027	-0.103
China	2,393.9	3,304.0	-0.354	-0.020	-183.7	0.067	-0.028
Korea	436.7	436.0	-0.001	-0.006	-35.7	0.037	-0.019
Singapore	-333.8	-378.4	0.030	-0.106	-78.5	0.021	0.031
Taiwan	285.3	286.6	0.002	-0.093	-324.6	-0.010	-0.098
Indonesia	157.9	217.0	-0.087	-0.071	-180.8	0.030	-0.038
Malaysia	-39.3	-3.1	-0.034	-0.163	-195.1	0.150	-0.035
Philippines	199.1	276.4	-0.240	-0.020	-17.5	0.228	-0.012
Thailand	189.0	298.7	-0.133	-0.058	-118.6	0.188	-0.008
Rest of Asia	2,055.1	2,703.4	-0.813	0.307	1,757.1	0.123	0.204
Other							
Chile	15.4	15.5	0.000	0.038	30.3	0.005	0.012
Mexico	-42.5	12.8	-0.026	-0.059	-208.5	-0.012	-0.011
CCS	-161.9	-136.4	-0.030	-0.041	-681.2	-0.001	-0.007
RME	159.7	171.1	-0.007	0.034	289.8	-0.012	0.084
Total	16,030.6	16,171.1			11,282.9		

Table 1 (continued)

Country	Imports (Millions)	Exports (Millions)	Terms of Trade (Percent)	Welfare (Percent)	Welfare (Millions)	Real Wage (Percent)	Return to Capital (Percent)
UR-2: Agricultural Trade Liberalization—Import Tariffs and Export Subsidies							
Industrialized Countries							
Japan	1,925.1	2,558.5	-0.119	0.039	2,521.1	0.060	0.080
United States	2,377.7	1,850.7	0.078	-0.024	-2,219.0	-0.029	-0.032
Canada	100.5	-56.6	0.041	0.003	25.3	-0.023	-0.027
Australia	270.3	163.4	0.150	-0.022	-96.1	-0.061	-0.081
New Zealand	20.0	3.3	0.068	-0.018	-13.0	-0.050	-0.061
EU and EFTA	1,307.0	1,289.7	-0.022	0.011	1,256.3	0.013	0.016
Developing Countries							
Asia							
Hong Kong	48.7	68.1	0.018	-0.014	-18.5	0.024	0.022
China	342.4	233.5	0.022	0.070	633.6	0.018	0.006
Korea	447.7	609.4	-0.086	0.067	380.1	0.099	0.104
Singapore	132.5	148.3	-0.006	0.046	34.5	0.113	0.110
Taiwan	446.4	516.9	-0.061	0.286	1,004.3	0.148	0.317
Indonesia	74.9	52.7	0.024	0.020	49.5	0.014	-0.006
Malaysia	200.3	222.9	-0.030	0.118	141.6	0.096	0.116
Philippines	85.5	104.5	-0.022	0.063	55.5	0.035	0.052
Thailand	154.3	127.7	0.049	-0.016	-32.3	0.185	-0.076
Rest of Asia	201.8	218.7	-0.007	0.168	963.4	0.010	0.019
Other							
Chile							
Mexico	1.6	-5.9	0.031	-0.035	-28.2	-0.021	-0.062
CCS	19.1	-45.3	0.029	0.015	52.6	0.012	-0.024
RME	536.2	376.9	0.123	-0.024	-403.3	-0.041	-0.070
Total	294.9	288.0	0.006	0.031	269.3	0.011	0.006

Table 1 (continued)

Country	Imports (Millions)	Exports (Millions)	Terms of Trade (Percent)	Welfare (Percent)	Welfare (Millions)	Real Wage (Percent)	Return to Capital (Percent)
UR-3: Mining and Manufactures Trade Liberalization							
Industrialized Countries							
Japan	7,549.2	7,527.0	0.004	0.274	17,763.3	0.066	0.092
United States	11,296.0	12,329.8	-0.125	0.133	12,029.2	0.086	0.074
Canada	1,213.1	1,446.1	-0.074	0.084	615.8	0.132	0.100
Australia	2,246.9	2,136.5	0.142	0.357	1,566.2	0.345	0.348
New Zealand	635.5	393.6	1.112	1.006	738.3	0.438	0.340
EU and EFTA	14,885.8	13,646.7	0.119	0.291	31,919.5	0.080	0.086
Developing Countries							
Asia							
Hong Kong	617.4	372.3	0.239	0.294	379.2	0.243	0.260
China	3,191.9	1,789.8	0.518	0.454	4,116.1	0.205	0.207
Korea	2,277.2	2,176.7	0.055	0.627	3,568.3	0.212	0.219
Singapore	2,414.4	2,430.4	-0.017	1.207	897.4	1.528	1.745
Taiwan	1,297.7	774.1	0.323	0.531	1,863.6	0.260	0.258
Indonesia	884.2	870.3	0.026	0.314	795.1	0.303	0.216
Malaysia	2,179.1	2,746.0	-0.518	0.956	1,142.9	1.272	1.454
Philippines	2,197.4	2,771.9	-1.749	1.598	1,410.3	1.422	1.530
Thailand	1,436.9	1,105.4	0.378	0.899	1,853.1	0.839	0.176
Rest of Asia	7,658.8	10,719.6	-3.848	0.119	679.1	0.681	0.761
Other							
Chile	165.6	78.8	0.380	0.311	249.9	0.147	0.127
Mexico	168.2	256.7	-0.056	0.104	365.9	0.044	0.042
CCS	4,257.2	3,615.3	0.381	0.206	3,444.5	0.080	0.032
RME	2,620.3	2,036.1	0.263	0.572	4,940.4	0.188	0.340
Total	69,192.9	69,223.1			90,338.0		

Table 1 (continued)

Country	Imports (Millions)	Exports (Millions)	Terms of Trade (Percent)	Welfare (Percent)	Welfare (Millions)	Real Wage (Percent)	Return to Capital (Percent)
UR-4: Uruguay Round Combined Liberalization							
Industrialized Countries							
Japan	8,400.3	9,437.4	-0.213	0.240	15,600.5	0.112	0.166
United States	17,743.8	16,852.3	0.075	0.142	12,853.0	0.095	0.103
Canada	1,742.2	1,701.4	0.026	0.182	1,328.6	0.145	0.168
Australia	2,414.3	2,098.7	0.433	0.277	1,214.6	0.293	0.307
New Zealand	599.8	276.1	1.475	1.256	922.2	0.642	0.592
EU and EFTA	14,176.1	10,731.0	0.307	0.344	37,744.8	0.137	0.174
Developing Countries							
Asia							
Hong Kong	2,559.2	2,700.0	-0.027	-0.031	-39.4	1.185	0.085
China	5,296.4	4,654.6	0.148	0.330	2,994.2	0.267	0.136
Korea	2,749.1	2,910.2	-0.078	0.434	2,469.5	0.277	0.231
Singapore	1,971.4	2,024.0	-0.027	0.892	663.2	1.452	1.660
Taiwan	1,752.6	1,281.4	0.243	0.505	1,770.9	0.338	0.350
Indonesia	632.2	742.1	-0.211	-0.713	-1,804.0	0.265	0.018
Malaysia	2,068.9	2,690.0	-0.599	0.576	688.6	1.458	1.452
Philippines	2,131.8	2,891.0	-2.122	0.496	437.4	1.558	1.422
Thailand	1,022.9	494.2	0.662	0.982	2,023.9	0.078	0.412
Rest of Asia	9,631.9	13,443.9	-4.740	0.243	1,391.4	0.787	0.883
Other							
Chile	150.5	53.9	0.420	0.108	86.8	0.113	0.029
Mexico	-255.0	-127.2	-0.152	-0.334	-1,178.1	0.028	-0.064
CCS	3,639.0	3,179.9	0.355	-0.152	-2,531.7	-0.026	-0.120
RME	113.8	338.0	-0.082	-0.181	-1,564.6	0.094	0.039
Total	78,541.2	78,372.9			75,071.6		

On the other hand, our model does not allow for the very long-run adjustments that could occur through capital accumulation, population growth, and technological change. Our results should therefore be thought of as being superimposed upon longer-run growth paths of the economies involved. To the extent that these growth paths themselves may be influenced by trade liberalization, therefore, our model does not capture that.

Aggregate Results

As already mentioned, table 1 reports various economy-wide changes for each of the countries/regions of the model. These include changes in exports and imports in millions of dollars, changes in terms of trade, real wage rate and real return to capital in percentages, and changes in economic welfare measured by equivalent variation, both in millions of dollars and as percent of country GDP. The terms of trade is the world price of a country's exports relative to its imports. The equivalent variation is the amount of money that, if given to the country's consumers at initial prices, would be equivalent in terms of their level of welfare to the effects of the assumed liberalization. In general, as discussed above, a worsening (fall) in a country's terms of trade has an adverse effect on its consumers' welfare. But this can be outweighed by the other gains from trade due to increased economic efficiency and the other benefits modeled by the New Trade theory.

UR-1: Elimination of the MFA Quota Constraints—The results for the Uruguay Round elimination of the MFA quota and other bilateral constraints on developing country exports of textiles and apparel, shown in Scenario UR-1 of table 1, indicate an increase in global welfare of $11.3 billion. In interpreting the results, it should be noted that, with increased exports of these goods to world markets, their prices will fall and the terms of trade of the MFA exporting countries and possibly their economic welfare should deteriorate. This can be seen in column (3) in table 1, with the exception of Singapore and Taiwan that had minimal quota premiums to be removed. It is interesting that the Rest of Asia, which includes mainly India and Sri Lanka, shows a welfare gain indicating that their exports are stimulated and efficiency is enhanced. The developed countries gain from MFA elimination, except for Japan, which did not maintain MFA quotas and thus is faced with higher world prices for its imports when the quotas are removed.

Changes in returns to labor and capital are mostly small.

UR-2: Agricultural Liberalization—This scenario includes the reductions in both tariffs on agricultural imports and in export subsidies that were negotiated as part of the Uruguay Round Agreement. The results shown for Scenario UR-2 in table 1 indicate that world welfare falls by $26.2 billion. The decline in welfare in Japan is $1.6 billion and in the United States, $6.7 billion. In the underlying results, which are not presented here but are available on request, the reductions in agricultural import tariffs are welfare enhancing in most countries as consumer prices fall and resources are reallocated. Thus, for example, Japan's welfare rises by $2.5 billion. It is noteworthy though that U.S. welfare declines by $2.2 billion, which in this case reflects the negative scale economies experienced in the nonagricultural sectors as resources are shifted to permit the expansion of agricultural output. In the case of export subsidies, their effect is to reduce the consumer price below the producer price, whereas the import tariff raises the consumer price above the producer price. Since tariff rates are generally larger than export-subsidy rates, the nature of the distortion is that consumer prices are too high relative to producer prices. Thus, in order to take a step towards efficiency, the consumer price needs to come down relative to the producer price. That is, the percent change in the ad valorem equivalent separating these two prices has to be negative. In the simulations that we have done, it turns out that the agricultural export subsidies were reduced at almost twice the rate as the agricultural import tariffs. Consequently, the ad valorem equivalent separating consumer and producer prices actually increased, taking us away from the optimum. In this event, Japan experiences a welfare decline of $4.1 billion when agricultural export subsidies are reduced, and U.S. welfare declines by $4.5 billion. It turns out, then, that when the reductions in agricultural import tariffs are combined with reductions in export subsidies, the overall effect as shown in Scenario UR-2 is welfare reducing for most countries, the European Union (EU)/EFTA being an exception.

UR-3: Liberalization of Industrial Products—Scenario UR-3 covers the reductions in import tariffs on mining and manufactured products that were negotiated in the Uruguay Round. Global economic welfare increases by $90.3 billion and the gains are positive for all countries/regions. The largest welfare increases noted are for EU/EFTA ($31.9 billion), Japan ($17.8 billion), and the United States ($12.0 billion). The effects on returns to labor and capital are uniformly positive.

UR-4: Combined Liberalization Effects (UR-1 + UR-2 + UR-3)—The combined effects of the Uruguay Round liberalization are indicated in Scenario UR-4 of table 1. As noted, this table is the linear combination of UR-1, UR-2, and UR-3. Japan's welfare gain is $15.6 billion and the U.S. gain is $12.9 billion. The other industrialized countries/regions gain, as do the Asian developing countries, except for Hong Kong and Indonesia. Mexico, other Western Hemisphere developing countries (CCS), and the Rest of Middle East (RME) show welfare declines.

Sectoral Results

A major contribution that this sort of CGE modeling can make is to identify those sectors that will expand and those that will contract as a result of various patterns of trade liberalization, as well as the sizes of these changes. Given our assumption that expenditure adjusts within each country to maintain a constant level of total employment, it is necessarily the case that each country experiences a mixture of expansions and contractions at the industry level. This must be true of employment, and it is likely to be true as well for industry output. To report these sectoral results in any detail is tedious, since there are 18 sectors in each country/region. We therefore report the sectoral results only for Japan and the United States in tables 2-3, both for the Combined Liberalization of the Uruguay Round Scenario UR-4. The sectoral results for the other countries/regions are available from the authors on request.

For Japan, in table 2, there are declines in output in agriculture, food, beverages, & tobacco, textiles, and wearing apparel, and increases in all other sectors. The changes in employment mirror these changes in output. Thus, the declines in the numbers of workers are: agriculture, -39,859; food, beverages, & tobacco, -8,262; textiles, -1,672; and wearing apparel, -11,162. There are employment increases in the remaining manufacturing sectors and also in services. For the United States, in table 3, there are notable increases in employment in agriculture (60,893) and other manufactures (25,707) and decreases in textiles (-26,604), wearing apparel (-69,387), and government services (-11,689). The results for the EU/EFTA, which are not reproduced here but are available on request, show reductions in output and employment especially for agriculture, food, beverages, & tobacco, textiles, wearing apparel, leather and footwear, and other manufactures, and increases for the other manufacturing and services sectors. There is evidence of positive scale effects for most of the sectors.

III. Computational Analysis of the Prospective WTO Round of Multilateral Trade Negotiations

As already mentioned, the built-in agenda of the Uruguay Round mandated that multilateral negotiations under WTO auspices would commence for agriculture and services in 2000. It had been expected that the agenda for a broader WTO negotiating round would be approved at the WTO Ministerial Meeting held in Seattle in December 1999. However, because of the lack of consensus in Seattle among the WTO members, decisions on the details of the negotiating agenda for a new round were put off until some future date. Although at the time of writing (January 2001) nothing definite yet has been decided, it may nonetheless be instructive to use the Michigan Model to assess the magnitudes of the economic effects that may result from a new round. Accordingly, we have run what we refer to as the Millennium Round liberalization scenarios. These scenarios assume 33 percent reductions in post-Uruguay Round tariffs and services barriers, as follows:

MR-1 *Agricultural liberalization is modeled as a 33 percent reduction in post-Uruguay Round agricultural import tariffs.*[7]

MR-2 *Liberalization of industrial products is modeled as a 33 percent reduction in post-Uruguay Round tariffs on mining and manufactured products.*

Table 2. Uruguay Round Liberalization
Percent Change in Exports, Imports, Output, Scale and Employment
Japan

Product	Exports (Percent)	Imports (Percent)	Output (Percent)	Scale (Percent)	Employment (Percent)	Employment # Workers
Agriculture	-11.78	11.44	-0.97	0.00	-0.96	-39,859.1
Mining	1.49	-0.30	1.11	0.21	1.00	679.1
Food, Beverages & Tobacco	1.83	5.72	-0.16	0.22	-0.25	-8,261.8
Textiles	2.57	2.44	-0.20	0.09	-0.22	-1,671.7
Wearing Apparel	-2.89	4.70	-0.78	0.08	-0.80	-11,162.5
Leather Products & Footwear	1.27	0.08	0.21	0.14	0.10	109.7
Wood & Wood Products	2.04	0.52	0.12	0.13	0.02	432.6
Chemicals	1.69	1.28	0.14	0.08	0.13	2,030.0
Non-metallic Min. Products	1.95	0.55	0.17	0.08	0.13	1,752.3
Metal Products	2.43	-0.15	0.36	0.11	0.29	7,312.9
Transportation Equipment	0.80	4.78	0.11	0.12	0.08	448.1
Machinery & Equipment	1.77	0.95	0.52	0.14	0.43	9,982.5
Other Manufactures	2.31	0.73	0.52	0.13	0.42	2,157.0
Elec., Gas & Water	0.56	-0.13	0.13	0.12	0.09	3,071.1
Construction	1.26	-0.03	0.07	0.07	0.06	5,025.3
Trade & Transport	0.60	-0.66	0.13	0.10	0.07	12,327.9
Other Private Services	0.93	-0.30	0.12	0.10	0.08	14,788.9
Government Services	0.70	-0.02	0.03	0.03	0.02	837.9
Average	1.52	1.57	0.11		0.00	0.0

Table 3. Uruguay Round Liberalization
Percent Change in Exports, Imports, Output, Scale and Employment
United States

Product	Exports	Imports	Output	Scale	Employment	
	(Percent)	(Percent)	(Percent)	(Percent)	(Percent)	# Workers
Agriculture	9.28	0.55	1.51	0.00	1.51	60,893.1
Mining	1.52	-0.88	0.43	0.11	0.32	2,229.4
Food, Beverages & Tobacco	6.38	9.35	0.14	0.12	0.03	799.1
Textiles	-0.14	8.80	-2.16	-0.02	-2.15	-26,604.5
Wearing Apparel	1.18	19.69	-5.67	0.40	-5.99	-69,387.3
Leather Products & Footwear	0.94	0.02	0.05	0.07	0.00	-4.5
Wood & Wood Products	1.25	0.42	0.07	0.07	0.03	1,169.7
Chemicals	1.33	2.03	-0.05	0.07	-0.11	-3,109.4
Non-metallic Min. Products	1.10	3.44	-0.20	0.06	-0.23	-1,804.7
Metal Products	1.50	0.91	0.13	0.11	0.03	906.8
Transportation Equipment	1.87	-0.27	0.41	0.14	0.28	5,508.8
Machinery & Equipment	1.12	1.46	0.03	0.12	-0.04	-1,300.5
Other Manufactures	5.20	-0.42	1.49	0.08	1.43	25,707.2
Elec., Gas & Water	0.05	-0.01	-0.02	-0.01	-0.01	-295.6
Construction	0.84	-0.21	-0.01	0.00	-0.01	-1,241.4
Trade & Transport	0.68	-1.67	0.06	0.04	0.03	9,973.6
Other Private Services	0.78	-0.55	0.08	0.07	0.02	8,249.0
Government Services	0.50	-0.30	-0.07	-0.03	-0.04	-11,688.8
Average	1.83	1.63	0.03		0.00	0.0

MR-3 *Services liberalization is modeled as a 33 percent reduction in estimated post-Uruguay Round services barriers.*

MR-4 *This combines **MR-1, MR-2, and MR-3**.*

In addition to the foregoing scenarios, we thought it would be of interest to run a scenario of global free trade, as follows:

MR-5 *Global free trade is modeled as complete removal of all post-Uruguay Round tariffs on agricultural products and industrial products as well as services barriers.*

Data

As noted in Section II, our basic data source is the GTAP-4 Database, supplemented with employment data, and projected to 2005, which is when the Uruguay Round will have been fully implemented. The projected database has in turn been readjusted to include the results of the Uruguay Round implementation as analyzed above.

While services issues were addressed in the Uruguay Round, the main accomplishment was the creation of the General Agreement on Trade in Services (GATS), which is an umbrella agreement setting out the rules governing the four modes of providing services transactions. These modes are: (1) cross-border services (e.g., telecommunications); (2) services provided in the country of consumption (e.g., tourism); (3) services requiring a domestic presence in the form of foreign direct investment (FDI); and (4) movement of natural persons. In an earlier study, Brown and Stern (2000) developed a new version of the Michigan Model for the purpose of analyzing the behavior of multinational firms, which are major providers of services, both intra-firm as well as in the production and sales of foreign affiliates located in host countries.[8] To approximate existing services barriers, Brown and Stern used estimates of barriers to FDI provided by Hoekman (2000), based on the gross operating margins of services firms listed on national stock exchanges for the period, 1994-96. These gross operating margins, which were calculated as the differences between total revenues and total operating costs, are indicated in percentage form in table 4 for construction, trade & transport, other private services, and government services. Some of the differences between total revenues and costs are presumably attributable to fixed cost. Given that the gross operating margins vary across countries, a portion of the margins can also be attributed to barriers to FDI. For this purpose, we have selected as a benchmark for each sector the country with the smallest gross operating margin, on the assumption that operations in this country can be considered to be freely open to foreign firms. The excess in any other country above the lowest benchmark is then taken to be due to barriers to establishment by foreign firms. That is, the barrier is modeled as the cost increase attributable to an increase in fixed cost borne by multinational corporations attempting to establish an enterprise lo-

Table 4. Average Gross Operating Margins of Services Firms Listed on National Stock Exchanges, 1994-96 (Percent)

	Construction	Trade & Transportation	Other Private Services	Government Services	Average
Japan	14	23	27	43	27
United States	20	35	46	40	40
Canada	14	21	42	15	33
Mexico	26	35	47		39
Chile	69	32			41
Australia	15	8*	15*		13
New Zealand	15	21	27		21
Hong Kong	14	16	23		19
China	42	36	72	75	49
Korea	15	24	41		24
Singapore	11*	13	21	26	18
Taiwan	21	28	50		35
Indonesia	23	32	58		44
Malaysia	19	17	22	26	18
Philippines	41	42	50		45
Thailand	38	42	49	41	45
EU/EFTA	20	24	34	38	29
Rest of Asia	23	23	34		27
Rest of W. Hemis.	29	40	49	32	38
Rest of Middle East	40	35	48		39
Rest of World	12	19	32	19	22
Average	22	27	35	36	

*Taken as benchmark country.

Source: Adapted from Hoekman (2000).

cally in a host country. We further assume for purposes of our analysis here that we can interpret this cost increase as an ad valorem equivalent tariff on international services transactions generally.[9] Our simulation MR-3 assumes then that these services barriers are to be reduced by 33 percent in a new trade round.

Aggregate Results[10]

The aggregate results of the individual Millennium Round scenarios are presented in tables 5-6, and the sectoral results of the combined scenarios (**MR-4**) for Japan and the United States are presented in tables 7 and 8.

MR-1: Agricultural Liberalization—The assumed 33 percent reduction in post-Uruguay Round agricultural-import tariffs is shown in table 5 to increase global welfare by $10.8 billion. Japan experiences a welfare increase of $4.3 billion, while the United States records a welfare decline of $4.1 billion. As was the case in our analysis of agricultural liberalization in the Uruguay Round, the expansion of U.S. agriculture has the effect of drawing resources away from the monopolistically competitive, non-agricultural sectors, thereby producing negative scale effects in these sectors. Similar negative welfare effects are also noted for Australia and New Zealand, both of which are net exporters of agricultural products.

MR-2: Liberalization of Industrial Products—The assumed 33 percent reduction of post-Uruguay Round manufacturing tariffs results in an increase in global welfare of $210.7 billion, which is considerably greater than the $90.3 billion welfare gain from the Uruguay Round liberalization of manufacturing tariffs. As was the case for the Uruguay Round, liberalization of manufactures in a new trade round is seen to increase welfare in all of the countries/regions listed and to have positive effects as well on real wages and the return to capital. The largest welfare gain is for EU/EFTA ($63.3 billion), while Japan's gain is $57.8 billion and the U.S. gain is $31.3 billion. While the welfare gains for the developing countries/regions are much smaller in absolute terms, the percentage gains range from 0.5 percent for China to 3.5 percent for the Philippines. There are also sizable percentage increases in the real factor returns in the Asian developing economies.

MR-3: Services Liberalization—As noted above, the Uruguay Round negotiations on services resulted in creation of the GATS, but no significant liberalization of services barriers occurred. Following the conclusion of the Uruguay Round, there have been successful multilateral negotiations to liberalize telecommunications and financial services. While it would be desirable to assess the economic effects of these sectoral agreements, we cannot do so here because of lack of data. What we have done then is to use the estimates of services barriers based on the calculations of gross operating margins for services firms in the countries/regions in our model, as already

Table 5. Summary Results of the Millennium Round Change in Imports, Exports, Terms of Trade, Welfare and the Real Return to Capital and Labor

Country	Imports (Millions)	Exports (Millions)	Terms of Trade (Percent)	Welfare (Percent)	Welfare (Millions)	Real Wage (Percent)	Return to Capital (Percent)
MR-1: 33 Percent Reduction in Agricultural Tariffs							
Industrialized Countries							
Japan	3,405.0	4,449.4	-0.193	0.066	4,301.9	0.102	0.136
United States	4,651.0	3,502.0	0.157	-0.045	-4,062.8	-0.057	-0.064
Canada	170.9	-107.2	0.073	0.009	66.8	-0.043	-0.049
Australia	508.4	298.7	0.282	-0.043	-188.8	-0.118	-0.162
New Zealand	28.3	1.7	0.108	-0.041	-29.8	-0.093	-0.113
EU and EFTA	2,076.7	1,942.0	-0.026	0.020	2,193.6	0.019	0.024
Developing Countries							
Asia							
Hong Kong	139.0	153.4	0.038	0.016	20.0	0.060	0.052
China	748.9	593.6	0.028	0.176	1,598.9	0.037	0.038
Korea	1,106.5	1,511.0	-0.214	0.164	933.9	0.247	0.258
Singapore	299.8	338.7	-0.019	0.124	92.2	0.267	0.258
Taiwan	1,098.1	1,331.4	-0.170	0.714	2,502.3	0.370	0.804
Indonesia	154.0	118.1	0.038	0.055	140.1	0.029	-0.003
Malaysia	484.9	561.8	-0.085	0.275	328.3	0.226	0.276
Philippines	206.6	253.8	-0.080	0.197	173.8	0.073	0.166
Thailand	321.5	300.8	0.053	0.031	64.4	0.276	-0.075
Rest of Asia	446.5	474.5	-0.018	0.398	2,280.1	0.025	0.058
Other							
Chile	6.8	-5.9	0.053	-0.053	-42.3	-0.034	-0.107
Mexico	23.5	-82.5	0.044	0.032	111.1	0.017	-0.039
CCS	812.5	590.6	0.175	-0.029	-485.5	-0.060	-0.102
RME	539.7	562.0	-0.005	0.091	789.3	0.017	0.040
Total	17,228.7	16,787.9			10,787.2		

Table 5 (continued)

Country	Imports (Millions)	Exports (Millions)	Terms of Trade (Percent)	Welfare (Percent)	Welfare (Millions)	Real Wage (Percent)	Return to Capital (Percent)
MR-2: 33 Percent Reduction in Manufacturing Tariffs							
Industrialized Countries							
Japan	26,163.0	22,288.2	0.655	0.890	57,818.6	0.261	0.369
United States	28,638.2	27,341.3	0.083	0.345	31,289.1	0.245	0.268
Canada	2,997.1	3,288.8	-0.081	0.382	2,787.2	0.290	0.302
Australia	4,244.9	4,135.9	0.127	0.558	2,450.2	0.638	0.658
New Zealand	1,408.4	1,001.0	1.838	1.883	1,382.8	1.060	0.819
EU and EFTA	36,312.4	34,161.2	0.235	0.578	63,333.0	0.208	0.228
Developing Countries							
Asia							
Hong Kong	3,747.5	2,497.8	1.130	1.559	2,007.9	1.348	1.028
China	21,400.1	24,846.5	-1.256	0.539	4,882.4	1.094	1.081
Korea	9,551.2	9,597.4	-0.031	1.404	7,990.4	0.990	0.711
Singapore	5,202.8	4,618.9	0.362	2.854	2,122.3	3.432	3.629
Taiwan	8,423.5	7,458.8	0.582	1.584	5,554.2	1.067	0.561
Indonesia	154.0	118.1	0.038	0.055	140.1	0.029	-0.003
Malaysia	4,792.1	5,443.1	-0.580	1.988	2,376.6	2.994	2.888
Philippines	4,191.7	5,122.1	-2.615	3.525	3,110.8	2.906	2.799
Thailand	4,509.4	4,946.9	-0.529	1.468	3,025.1	2.139	1.147
Rest of Asia	12,262.9	15,109.9	-3.002	0.904	5,173.9	1.093	1.108
Other							
Chile	978.8	1,009.5	-0.131	1.286	1,032.5	0.910	0.932
Mexico	921.1	1,170.6	-0.191	0.323	1,139.1	0.170	0.173
CCS	10,459.6	11,436.3	-0.627	0.307	5,121.3	0.216	0.106
RME	8,982.6	10,219.9	-0.566	0.922	7,962.2	0.417	1.007
Total	195,341.1	195,812.0			210,699.6		

Table 5 (continued)

Country	Imports (Millions)	Exports (Millions)	Terms of Trade (Percent)	Welfare (Percent)	Welfare (Millions)	Real Wage (Percent)	Return to Capital (Percent)
MR-3: 33 Percent Reduction in Services Barriers							
Industrialized Countries							
Japan	14,330.2	16,743.0	-0.328	0.948	61,570.1	0.199	0.232
United States	33,320.6	35,501.0	-0.306	1.653	150,047.9	0.434	0.464
Canada	5,832.0	6,646.3	-0.248	1.461	10,649.6	0.695	0.787
Australia	1,252.7	784.4	0.534	0.648	2,845.6	0.498	0.402
New Zealand	419.0	411.5	0.048	1.201	882.1	0.856	0.857
EU and EFTA	30,839.3	25,607.1	0.499	0.943	103,416.1	0.201	0.207
Developing Countries							
Asia							
Hong Kong	3,672.5	2,647.3	0.871	1.784	2,297.0	1.900	2.170
China	3,821.5	4,528.4	-0.190	0.786	7,118.3	0.205	0.206
Korea	3,725.0	3,534.4	0.085	0.911	5,182.9	0.606	0.608
Singapore	813.2	615.5	0.109	2.618	1,947.4	3.459	2.497
Taiwan	1,830.6	1,956.4	0.006	0.487	1,706.0	0.400	0.362
Indonesia	820.2	926.8	-0.128	0.793	2,005.7	0.201	0.168
Malaysia	782.9	888.9	-0.063	0.545	651.4	0.318	0.325
Philippines	1,267.4	1,320.0	-0.266	1.683	1,485.3	1.169	1.167
Thailand	2,205.4	2,396.4	-0.300	1.122	2,311.4	0.765	0.600
Rest of Asia	1,152.4	779.8	0.372	0.474	2,712.4	0.201	0.233
Other							
Chile	438.3	425.1	0.062	1.171	940.7	0.651	0.612
Mexico	2,374.4	2,670.4	-0.169	1.486	5,244.0	0.470	0.551
CCS	5,034.4	5,170.5	-0.151	1.134	18,928.0	0.269	0.270
RME	4,427.7	5,093.5	-0.306	0.884	7,636.9	0.470	0.446
Total	118,359.8	118,646.8			389,578.8		

Table 5 (continued)

Country	Imports (Millions)	Exports (Millions)	Terms of Trade (Percent)	Welfare (Percent)	Welfare (Millions)	Real Wage (Percent)	Return to Capital (Percent)
MR-4: Millennium Round Combined Liberalization							
Industrialized Countries							
Japan	43,898.2	43,480.6	0.134	1.905	123,690.6	0.563	0.737
United States	66,609.7	66,344.2	-0.066	1.953	177,274.3	0.622	0.668
Canada	9,000.1	9,827.9	-0.256	1.853	13,503.6	0.942	1.039
Australia	6,006.0	5,218.9	0.943	1.163	5,107.1	1.018	0.898
New Zealand	1,855.7	1,414.2	1.994	3.044	2,235.1	1.823	1.563
EU and EFTA	69,228.5	61,710.3	0.708	1.541	168,942.6	0.428	0.458
Developing Countries							
Asia							
Hong Kong	7,559.0	5,298.4	2.039	3.359	4,324.8	3.307	3.250
China	25,970.5	29,968.6	-1.418	1.501	13,599.6	1.336	1.325
Korea	14,382.7	14,642.8	-0.161	2.479	14,107.2	1.843	1.578
Singapore	6,315.9	5,573.1	0.453	5.596	4,161.8	7.158	6.384
Taiwan	11,352.2	10,746.7	0.419	2.784	9,762.5	1.838	1.727
Indonesia	3,951.5	4,026.9	-0.082	1.651	4,175.0	1.080	0.645
Malaysia	6,059.8	6,893.8	-0.728	2.807	3,356.3	3.537	3.489
Philippines	5,665.6	6,695.9	-2.962	5.405	4,769.9	4.148	4.132
Thailand	7,036.3	7,644.1	-0.776	2.621	5,400.8	3.181	1.672
Rest of Asia	13,861.8	16,364.3	-2.648	1.776	10,166.4	1.319	1.399
Other							
Chile	1,423.9	1,428.6	-0.016	2.404	1,930.9	1.527	1.437
Mexico	3,319.0	3,758.5	-0.315	1.841	6,494.3	0.658	0.685
CCS	16,306.4	17,197.5	-0.603	1.412	23,563.8	0.425	0.274
RME	13,950.0	15,875.4	-0.877	1.898	16,388.4	0.903	1.494
Total	333,752.9	334,110.6			612,954.9		

Table 6. Summary Results of the Millennium Round
Change in Imports, Exports, Terms of Trade, Welfare and the Real Return to Capital and Labor
Percent Change and Millions of U.S. Dollars

Country	Imports (Millions)	Exports (Millions)	Terms of Trade (Percent)	Welfare (Percent)	Welfare (Millions)	Real Wage (Percent)	Return to Capital (Percent)
MR-5: Complete Liberalization in All Sectors							
Industrialized Countries							
Japan	133,024.7	131,759.5	0.407	5.772	374,820.1	1.705	2.234
United States	201,847.7	201,043.1	-0.199	5.918	537,194.8	1.884	2.023
Canada	27,273.1	29,781.5	-0.777	5.615	40,919.9	2.856	3.149
Australia	18,200.0	15,815.0	2.858	3.525	15,476.1	3.085	2.722
New Zealand	5,623.4	4,285.4	6.042	9.225	6,773.0	5.525	4.735
EU and EFTA	209,783.3	187,000.9	2.146	4.668	511,947.3	1.297	1.389
Developing Countries							
Asia							
Hong Kong	22,906.0	16,055.8	6.180	10.177	13,105.5	10.022	9.848
China	78,698.5	90,813.8	-4.296	4.549	41,210.9	4.050	4.016
Korea	43,583.9	44,372.0	-0.487	7.513	42,749.0	5.585	4.781
Singapore	19,138.9	16,888.1	1.372	16.958	12,611.5	21.691	19.346
Taiwan	34,400.6	32,565.8	1.269	8.437	29,583.3	5.569	5.234
Indonesia	11,974.2	12,202.7	-0.247	5.002	12,651.6	3.272	1.954
Malaysia	18,363.1	20,890.3	-2.207	8.507	10,170.5	10.718	10.573
Philippines	17,168.5	20,290.7	-8.974	16.380	14,454.2	12.570	12.521
Thailand	21,322.2	23,163.9	-2.353	7.943	16,366.1	9.640	5.066
Rest of Asia	42,005.4	49,588.7	-8.025	5.382	30,807.4	3.998	4.240
Other							
Chile	4,314.8	4,329.2	-0.047	7.285	5,851.1	4.626	4.353
Mexico	10,057.6	11,389.4	-0.955	5.578	19,679.7	1.994	2.075
CCS	49,413.5	52,113.6	-1.826	4.277	71,405.4	1.289	0.831
RME	42,272.9	48,107.2	-2.657	5.751	49,661.7	2.737	4.527
Total	1,011,372.3	1,012,456.4			1,857,439.1		

**Table 7. Millennium Round Liberalization
Percent Change in Exports, Imports, Output, Scale and Employment
Japan**

Product	Exports (Percent)	Imports (Percent)	Output (Percent)	Scale (Percent)	Employment (Percent)	Employment # Workers
Agriculture	6.22	18.80	-1.87	0.00	-1.85	-75703.0
Mining	1.57	1.59	-0.42	0.56	-0.68	-464.2
Food, Beverages & Tobacco	14.92	19.41	-0.61	0.67	-0.86	-28762.8
Textiles	11.93	7.79	0.02	0.48	-0.16	-1195.9
Wearing Apparel	4.63	16.48	-2.10	0.50	-2.30	-31606.0
Leather Products & Footwear	5.05	11.48	-2.25	0.79	-2.95	-3227.3
Wood & Wood Products	7.73	1.42	0.55	0.60	0.07	1296.5
Chemicals	6.63	3.20	0.84	0.52	0.71	10880.1
Non-metallic Min. Products	7.41	2.02	0.83	0.61	0.38	5208.9
Metal Products	7.84	0.68	1.50	0.66	1.00	25089.4
Transportation Equipment	7.71	1.92	2.94	0.61	2.73	15959.5
Machinery & Equipment	5.28	0.84	1.91	0.68	1.42	33395.6
Other Manufactures	4.96	2.97	1.21	0.65	0.66	3421.5
Elec., Gas & Water	1.62	-0.13	0.65	0.60	0.30	10854.8
Construction	9.57	0.87	0.38	0.40	0.25	22699.6
Trade & Transport	10.43	11.31	0.34	0.61	-0.09	-14735.6
Other Private Services	15.21	19.94	0.39	0.52	0.14	24929.5
Government Services	11.92	25.20	0.11	0.15	0.04	1959.4
Average	6.91	8.09	0.54		0.00	0.0

**Table 8. Millennium Round Liberalization
Percent Change in Exports, Imports, Output, Scale and Employment
United States**

Product	Exports (Percent)	Imports (Percent)	Output (Percent)	Scale (Percent)	Employment (Percent)	Employment # Workers
Agriculture	16.23	3.55	3.23	0.00	3.23	132608.1
Mining	2.44	0.61	0.81	0.75	0.08	577.1
Food, Beverages & Tobacco	14.57	11.53	0.92	0.66	0.29	9112.9
Textiles	2.79	9.40	-1.33	0.48	-1.55	-18826.0
Wearing Apparel	7.51	12.59	-3.69	0.87	-4.37	-47604.7
Leather Products & Footwear	4.22	7.15	-5.13	1.36	-6.21	-9042.5
Wood & Wood Products	3.40	1.24	0.53	0.54	0.13	5764.7
Chemicals	5.06	2.58	0.89	0.70	0.27	7792.4
Non-metallic Min. Products	4.28	4.97	0.22	0.53	-0.13	-1019.4
Metal Products	3.91	1.80	0.76	0.67	0.17	4792.7
Transportation Equipment	3.88	1.31	0.86	0.74	0.18	3496.5
Machinery & Equipment	3.65	1.96	0.99	0.57	0.63	18216.2
Other Manufactures	5.88	2.67	0.87	0.60	0.47	8533.7
Elec., Gas & Water	0.31	0.01	0.33	0.35	0.19	8918.9
Construction	10.15	6.16	0.21	0.27	0.10	13048.8
Trade & Transport	9.78	17.91	0.38	0.65	-0.14	-43126.5
Other Private Services	11.02	28.05	0.31	0.66	-0.25	-92051.8
Government Services	20.87	24.07	0.17	0.30	0.00	-1191.1
Average	7.09	6.01	0.47		0.00	0.0

described and as shown in table 4. These estimates of services barriers are intended to be indirect approximations of what the actual barriers may in fact be. Assuming that the ad valorem equivalents of these barriers are reduced by 33 percent, it can be seen in table 5 that global economic welfare rises by $389.6 billion, which exceeds the $210.7 billion welfare increase for manufactures liberalization. All of the countries/regions listed experience positive welfare gains as well as increases in real wages and returns to capital. The United States has the largest welfare gain of $150.0 billion, compared to $103.4 billion for EU/EFTA and $61.6 billion for Japan. For the smaller industrialized and developing countries, the percentage increases in welfare and factor returns are noteworthy.

MR-4: Combined Liberalization Effects (MR-1 + MR-2 + MR-3)— The results for **MR-4** are a linear combination of the other three scenarios. Overall, in table 5, global welfare rises by $613.0 billion. Among the industrialized countries, the United States has a welfare gain of $177.3 billion, EU/EFTA a gain of $168.9 billion, and Japan a gain of $123.7 billion. The percentage welfare gains and increases in returns to factors are sizable in most of the smaller industrialized countries and in the developing countries.

MR-5: Global Free Trade—Since our model is linear, the effects of removal of all tariffs and services barriers would then be some three times the results of MR-4. Thus, in table 6, global free trade would increase global welfare by $1.9 trillion. The welfare gains for the United States are $537.2 billion (5.9 percent of GNP), EU/EFTA, $511.9 billion (4.7 percent of GNP), and Japan, $374.8 billion (5.8 percent of GNP). The gains as a percentage of GNP for the other industrialized countries and the developing countries are also sizable, ranging from 3.5 percent for Australia to 17.0 percent for Singapore.

Sectoral Results

The sectoral results for MR-4 for Japan and the United States are presented in tables 7-8. As was the case for the Uruguay Round scenarios, the negative employment effects, in numbers of workers, for Japan are concentrated in agriculture (-75,703), food, beverages & tobacco (-28,763), textiles (-1,195), wearing apparel (31,606), leather products & footwear (-3,227), and trade & transport (-14,735). The largest employment increases are in metal products, durable manufactures, and construction. For the United States, there are employment declines in textiles (-18,826), wearing apparel (-47,605), leather products & footwear (-9,042), trade & transport (-43,126) and other private services (-92,052). The largest employment increases for the United States are in agriculture (132,608), durable manufactures, and construction. The sectoral employment results for global free trade in Scenario MR-5, which are not shown here, are three times the amounts shown in tables 7-8.

Conclusion

The foregoing computational results suggest that there are substantial benefits to be realized from a new WTO multilateral negotiating round, especially for industrial products and services and for both the industrialized and developing countries. This is the case for the assumed 33 percent reductions in the post-Uruguay Round tariffs and barriers to services, and even more so if there were global free trade.

We should note, as discussed above, that our computational model is based on a comparative static approach, meaning that we move from an initial position to a new equilibrium in which all of the liberalization occurs at one time. That is, we abstract from a variety of dynamic and related effects that may occur through time, especially with the international mobility of real capital, increases in capital accumulation via real investment, and technological improvements. Our results should thus be interpreted as a lower limit to the economic benefits that may be realized from a new WTO multilateral negotiating round and, if it were possible, from a movement to global free trade.[11]

IV. Analysis of Regional Negotiating Options

Both the United States and Japan are engaged in a number of regional arrangements. For the United States, this includes the North American Free Trade Agreement (NAFTA), which became effective in January 1994,[12] and ongoing discussions and negotiations for a Free Trade Area for the Americas (FTAA). Both the United States and Japan are members of the Asia Pacific Economic Cooperation (APEC) forum. In an especially noteworthy change in its trade policy, Japan is currently (January 2001) negotiating a free trade agreement (FTA) with Singapore and is actively discussing similar arrangements with Mexico, South Korea, Chile, and possibly other countries.[13] There has also been some discussion of a so-called ASEAN Plus-3 arrangement in which Japan, China/Hong Kong, and South Korea would join together with the ASEAN nations in a FTA.

Scenarios

In what follows, we use the Michigan Model to investigate the following regional scenarios that involve both the United States and Japan in the case of APEC, as well as Japan's new regional initiatives mentioned above. Japan's FTA initiatives will certainly cover many other issues besides bilateral removal of existing trade barriers. In the absence of detailed information about the different initiatives, it is nonetheless of interest to consider how the preferential trade liberalization per se in the different arrangements may affect the economic welfare of the member and non-member countries. Accordingly, we have used the Michigan Model to carry out the following Regional Agreement (RA) scenarios:[14]

RA-1: *APEC trade liberalization—elimination of all bilateral post-Uruguay Round agriculture and manufactures tariffs and services barriers among APEC member countries.*[15,16]

RA-2: *Japan-Singapore FTA—elimination of all bilateral post-Uruguay Round agriculture and manufactures tariffs and services barriers between Japan and Singapore.*

RA-3: *Japan-Mexico FTA—elimination of all bilateral post-Uruguay Round agriculture and manufactures tariffs and services barriers between Japan and Mexico.*

RA-4: *Japan-South Korea FTA—elimination of all bilateral post-Uruguay Round agriculture and manufactures tariffs and services barriers between Japan and South Korea.*

RA-5: *Japan-Chile FTA—elimination of all bilateral post-Uruguay Round agriculture and manufactures tariffs and services barriers between Japan and Chile.*

RA-6: *ASEAN-Plus-3 FTA—elimination of all bilateral post-Uruguay Round agriculture and manufactures tariffs and services barriers among the ASEAN countries*[17] *plus China/Hong Kong, Japan, and South Korea.*

In each of these cases, our reference point is the post-Uruguay Round, 2005 database described above together with the post-Uruguay Round tariff rates on agricultural products and manufactures and the specially constructed measures of services barriers used in the Millennium Round scenarios in Section III preceding. Four scenarios have been carried out for each of the six arrangements noted: (A) removal of agricultural tariffs; (M) removal of manufactures tariffs; (S) removal of services barriers; and (C) combined removal of agricultural and manufactures tariffs and services barriers. Because of space constraints, we report only the latter combined results, denoted RA-1C, ..., RA-6C. The results of the other scenarios are available on request.

Results

RA-1C: APEC Trade Liberalization—This scenario treats APEC as a FTA and does not take into make allowance for the "open regionalism" that APEC purportedly offers to non-members. If open regionalism were to be pursued, it would mean in effect that APEC liberalization would be extended to non-members who wished to become associated with or to joint APEC. But presumably these non-members would then themselves be required to eliminate their own trade barriers vis-à-vis the APEC members. Since we cannot determine a priori how non-members of APEC would respond, we take the closest approximation to open regionalism to correspond with our global free-trade scenario MR-5 in table 5 above.

In table 9, the complete elimination of (post-Uruguay Round) APEC bilateral tariffs and services barriers increases global welfare by $764.4 billion. Japan's welfare increases by $283.1 billion (4.4 percent of GNP) and U.S. welfare increases by $294.7 billion (2.2 percent of GNP). There is some evidence of trade diversion for EU/EFTA amounting to $7.0 billion and Rest of Asia, $1.0 billion, which reflects trade diversion in manufactures being offset against trade creation in agriculture and services. It is interesting then to compare the bilateral removal of APEC trade barriers with the removal of all global trade barriers in Scenario MR-5 noted above. The welfare gain from global free trade, indicated earlier in table 6, is $1.9 trillion, which compares to a gain of $764.4 billion if all tariffs and services barriers were removed bilaterally among the APEC member countries. The gains for Japan and the United States from global free trade are $374.8 and $537.2 billion, respectively, compared to $283.1 and $294.7 billion, respectively, for complete APEC bilateral liberalization. The detailed sectoral results for Japan, which are not shown here, indicate that, for complete APEC bilateral liberalization, the numbers of workers decline in agriculture, food, beverages & tobacco, wearing apparel, leather products & footwear, and trade & transport services, and increase in all other manufacturing sectors, particularly in metal products, machinery and equipment, and other private services. For the United States, employment declines in most manufacturing sectors, especially textiles, wearing apparel, leather products & footwear, other manufactures, trade & transport, and government services. The main U.S. employment increase is in agriculture.

RA-2C: Japan-Singapore Free Trade Agreement (JSFTA)—As shown in table 10, the combined removal of bilateral tariffs on agricultural products and manufactures and services barriers would increase global economic welfare by $15.4 billion. Japan's welfare rises by $10.9 billion (0.17 percent of GNP), and Singapore's welfare rises by $1.8 billion (2.4 percent of GNP). While not shown here, agricultural liberalization is of no consequence in this case, while manufactures liberalization alone would increase Japan's welfare by $1.0 billion and Singapore's welfare by $176 million. Thus, most of the potential welfare gains would come from services liberalization, $9.8 billion for Japan and $1.6 billion for Singapore. A JSFTA appears to be trade diverting for the other ASEAN economies, as is evident in the declines in economic welfare, real wages, and the return to capital in Indonesia, Malaysia, the Philippines, and Thailand. The other industrialized countries show increases in welfare and a negligible decline in real wages for the United States, Canada, Australia, and New Zealand. The real returns to labor and capital rise by 0.02

Table 9. Summary Results of APEC Liberalization
Change in Imports, Exports, Terms of Trade, Welfare and the Real Return to Capital and Labor
Percent Change and Millions of U.S. Dollars

Country	Imports (Millions)	Exports (Millions)	Terms of Trade (Percent)	Welfare (Percent)	Welfare (Millions)	Real Wage (Percent)	Return to Capital (Percent)
Scenario RA-1C: Complete Elimination of APEC Bilateral Tariffs and Services Barriers							
Industrialized Countries							
Japan	101,907.8	100,500.0	0.269	4.359	283,091.1	1.324	1.747
United States	105,090.3	100,811.6	0.367	3.246	294,663.3	0.918	0.975
Canada	19,801.9	20,886.3	-0.392	4.211	30,690.6	2.165	2.371
Australia	14,755.1	12,191.6	3.163	2.986	13,108.8	2.452	2.100
New Zealand	3,204.8	2,527.8	3.025	6.093	4,473.8	3.856	3.553
EU and EFTA	-339.8	21.3	0.021	-0.064	-7,047.2	0.002	0.016
Developing Countries							
Asia							
Hong Kong	19,128.7	13,615.2	5.263	8.105	10,436.4	8.411	8.304
China	56,333.4	67,387.5	-4.106	2.167	19,635.0	2.823	2.870
Korea	31,764.1	33,001.4	-0.684	5.096	28,996.8	4.081	3.470
Singapore	13,147.1	11,561.9	0.995	11.848	8,811.4	16.206	14.035
Taiwan	28,671.5	26,170.1	1.496	6.323	22,172.0	4.495	3.658
Indonesia	7,886.0	7,725.8	0.239	3.519	8,901.2	2.258	1.655
Malaysia	12,523.0	14,616.8	-1.905	5.318	6,357.2	7.763	7.699
Philippines	12,675.0	14,989.2	-6.415	11.520	10,165.3	9.600	9.709
Thailand	13,865.7	15,059.8	-1.424	5.177	10,665.9	7.202	3.378
Rest of Asia	-666.9	-562.9	-0.126	-0.176	-1,009.8	-0.111	0.019
Other							
Chile	2,036.4	2,152.5	-0.503	3.911	3,141.2	2.399	2.292
Mexico	7,031.2	7,848.4	-0.732	3.945	13,917.2	1.458	1.505
CCS	177.8	40.7	0.025	-0.005	-85.3	0.002	-0.027
RME	2,422.0	1,895.8	0.229	0.387	3,338.6	-0.002	0.399
Total	451,415.4	452,440.6			764,423.7		

Table 10. Summary Results of a Japan-Singapore FTA
Change in Imports, Exports, Terms of Trade, Welfare and the Real Return to Capital and Labor
Percent Change and Millions of U.S. Dollars

Country	Imports (Millions)	Exports (Millions)	Terms of Trade (Percent)	Welfare (Percent)	Welfare (Millions)	Real Wage (Percent)	Return to Capital (Percent)
Scenario RA-2C: Japan-Singapore FTA Elimination of Agricultural and Manufacturing Tariffs and Services Barriers							
Industrialized Countries							
Japan	2,801.7	3,449.6	-0.099	0.167	10,857.4	0.022	0.039
United States	69.3	-118.2	0.016	0.017	1,560.8	-0.002	0.000
Canada	24.2	25.5	0.001	0.016	114.0	-0.001	0.003
Australia	40.8	24.5	0.015	0.028	124.9	-0.004	-0.001
New Zealand	6.8	5.1	0.009	0.025	18.5	-0.004	0.000
EU and EFTA	132.9	-24.8	0.016	0.011	1,249.0	0.000	0.000
Developing Countries							
Asia							
Hong Kong	-18.8	-25.3	0.001	0.007	9.2	-0.129	-0.145
China	-24.1	-27.0	0.007	-0.008	-72.6	-0.003	0.000
Korea	56.1	29.8	0.013	0.009	53.4	0.006	0.004
Singapore	901.0	863.9	0.023	2.431	1,807.8	4.141	3.016
Taiwan	45.2	3.1	0.031	0.018	64.5	-0.010	0.001
Indonesia	-17.1	-30.7	0.022	-0.017	-42.3	-0.019	-0.028
Malaysia	-417.3	-501.4	0.073	-0.335	-401.1	-0.328	-0.390
Philippines	-26.0	-39.0	0.029	-0.026	-22.5	-0.043	-0.047
Thailand	-50.7	-63.6	0.011	-0.014	-27.9	-0.027	-0.058
Rest of Asia	-35.3	-58.0	0.023	0.005	29.7	-0.015	-0.011
Other							
Chile	-3.2	-2.0	-0.005	-0.002	-1.6	-0.005	-0.004
Mexico	22.2	16.0	0.008	0.015	51.7	-0.001	0.002
CCS	-6.0	-14.0	0.002	0.003	52.7	-0.001	0.000
RME	-36.9	-33.7	-0.002	-0.001	-7.0	0.000	-0.009
Total	3,464.8	3,479.8			15,418.6		

and 0.04 percent, respectively, in Japan, and by 4.1 and 3.0 percent, respectively, in Singapore. The sectoral results, which are not included here, indicate that employment rises by relatively small amounts in all sectors in Japan, except trade & transport services. For Singapore, there are relatively substantial employment declines in virtually all manufacturing sectors and increases in employment in trade & transport (20,521) and other private services (5,160). A Japan-Singapore FTA thus appears to shift employment in Japan especially towards durable manufactures and employment in Singapore away from manufactures towards services sectors.

RA-3C: Japan-Mexico Free Trade Agreement (JMFTA)—As indicated in table 11, the combined removal of bilateral trade barriers for agricultural products, manufactures, and services in a JMFTA increases global welfare by $7.3 billion. Japan's welfare increases by $6.3 billion (0.10 percent of GNP) and Mexico's welfare by $1.9 billion (0.54 percent of GNP). The details, which are not reproduced here, indicate that, while removal of agricultural barriers has negligible effects, the gains from removal of manufactures and services barriers are $2.5 and $3.8 billion, respectively, for Japan, and $0.4 and $1.5 billion, respectively, for Mexico. There are indications that a JMFTA would be trade diverting for the United States (-$750 million), Canada (-$33 million), EU/EFTA (-$121 million), and in small amounts for several of the Asian and other Western Hemisphere (CCS) economies. The real returns to labor and capital labor rise by 0.01 and 0.02 percent, respectively, in Japan and by 0.28 and 0.26 percent, respectively, in Mexico. The sectoral results, which are not shown here, indicate relatively small employment declines for Japan in agriculture, food, beverages & tobacco, textiles, wearing apparel, leather products & footwear, and trade & transport services and increases especially in durable manufactures. In Mexico, there are relatively small employment declines in agriculture and all manufactures sectors, and employment increases in trade & transport and other private services.

RA-4C: Japan-South Korea Free Trade Agreement (JSKFTA)—In table 12, a JSKFTA for all sectors combined increases global welfare by $30.3 billion. Japan's economic welfare increases by $27.4 billion (0.42 percent of GNP), and South Korea's welfare increases by $3.2 billion (0.57 percent of GNP). The unreported details for sector liberalization reveal that the bilateral removal of agricultural tariffs has negligible effects. Removal of bilateral tariffs on manufactures increases Japan's welfare by $11.4 billion (0.18 percent of GNP) and reduces South Korea's welfare by -$1.3 billion (-.23 percent of GNP), apparently because of a decline in South Korea's terms of trade associated with bilateral tariff removal. Bilateral removal of services barriers increases Japan's welfare by $15.8 billion (0.24 percent of GNP) and South Korea's welfare by $4.5 billion (0.80 percent of GNP). There is evidence of trade diversion from a JSKFTA for the United States (-$207 million), EU/EFTA (-$214 million), and smaller amounts for several of the Asian developing countries. The real returns to both labor and capital rise negligibly in Japan and by 1.0 percent and 0.88 percent, respectively, in South Korea, and fall in several

Table 11. Summary Results of a Japan-Mexico FTA
Change in Imports, Exports, Terms of Trade, Welfare and the Real Return to Capital and Labor
Percent Change and Millions of U.S. Dollars

Country	Imports (Millions)	Exports (Millions)	Terms of Trade (Percent)	Welfare (Percent)	Welfare (Millions)	Real Wage (Percent)	Return to Capital (Percent)
Scenario RA-3C: Japan-Mexico FTA Complete Elimination of Agricultural and Manufacturing Tariffs and Services Barriers							
Industrialized Countries							
Japan	1,318.9	1,185.1	0.022	0.098	6,343.4	0.014	0.019
United States	-220.5	-192.1	-0.004	-0.008	-750.1	-0.003	-0.004
Canada	-8.5	-9.1	0.001	-0.005	-33.4	-0.002	-0.002
Australia	4.9	3.3	0.002	0.002	8.6	0.001	0.001
New Zealand	1.0	0.7	0.001	0.003	2.4	0.002	0.002
EU and EFTA	-57.2	-37.9	-0.001	-0.001	-120.7	0.000	0.000
Developing Countries							
Asia							
Hong Kong	-8.6	-5.0	-0.003	-0.003	-4.5	-0.003	-0.002
China	0.6	2.8	-0.001	0.000	0.2	0.000	-0.001
Korea	-12.4	-8.1	-0.002	-0.002	-12.7	-0.001	-0.002
Singapore	-17.2	-15.2	-0.001	-0.004	-2.7	-0.001	-0.003
Taiwan	-17.5	-12.0	-0.004	-0.007	-26.2	-0.003	-0.006
Indonesia	0.6	1.0	-0.001	0.002	4.8	0.000	0.001
Malaysia	-13.2	-9.4	-0.004	-0.008	-9.9	-0.003	-0.005
Philippines	-2.4	-1.6	-0.002	-0.001	-0.8	-0.001	-0.001
Thailand	-1.1	0.7	-0.002	0.000	1.0	0.002	-0.001
Rest of Asia	-2.5	-1.4	-0.001	-0.001	-3.2	0.000	0.000
Other							
Chile	1.1	0.4	0.003	-0.001	-0.9	0.000	-0.001
Mexico	947.6	1,022.4	-0.069	0.542	1,911.9	0.280	0.257
CCS	-4.0	-7.0	0.001	-0.001	-21.1	-0.001	-0.001
RME	9.2	7.3	0.001	0.002	15.5	0.000	0.001
Total	1,918.8	1,924.9			7,301.6		

Table 12. Summary Results of a Japan-South Korea FTA
Change in Imports, Exports, Terms of Trade, Welfare and the Real Return to Capital and Labor
Percent Change and Millions of U.S. Dollars

Country	Imports (Millions)	Exports (Millions)	Terms of Trade (Percent)	Welfare (Percent)	Welfare (Millions)	Real Wage (Percent)	Return to Capital (Percent)
Scenario RA-4C: Japan-South Korea FTA Elimination of Agricultural and Manufacturing Tariffs and Services Barriers							
Industrialized Countries							
Japan	9,151.4	8,356.2	0.134	0.421	27,365.1	0.104	0.132
United States	-246.3	-256.5	-0.003	-0.002	-206.6	-0.005	-0.005
Canada	15.2	13.9	0.004	0.005	35.6	-0.001	0.000
Australia	27.5	14.6	0.013	0.012	50.6	-0.002	0.000
New Zealand	4.2	2.1	0.010	0.010	7.2	-0.005	-0.006
EU and EFTA	-256.6	-186.9	-0.001	-0.002	-214.1	-0.002	-0.002
Developing Countries							
Asia							
Hong Kong	9.3	-0.7	-0.002	0.008	10.7	-0.015	-0.016
China	9.3	18.3	0.003	-0.003	-29.5	-0.001	-0.002
Korea	7,552.9	8,474.4	-0.507	0.568	3,232.3	1.006	0.876
Singapore	-97.4	-113.6	0.009	-0.042	-31.2	-0.040	-0.046
Taiwan	-78.2	-60.5	-0.009	-0.033	-116.9	-0.015	-0.024
Indonesia	18.8	13.8	0.009	0.014	34.5	0.000	0.004
Malaysia	-36.0	-35.5	0.001	-0.032	-38.5	-0.020	-0.021
Philippines	-4.6	-7.0	0.001	-0.001	-0.5	-0.005	-0.004
Thailand	-3.3	-5.9	0.001	-0.001	-3.0	0.010	-0.013
Rest of Asia	10.9	-0.1	0.009	0.003	16.8	-0.001	0.001
Other							
Chile	8.4	3.6	0.021	0.015	12.2	0.006	0.003
Mexico	8.3	9.4	0.004	0.005	17.9	-0.001	0.000
CCS	38.1	7.7	0.011	0.003	44.6	0.000	-0.001
RME	64.2	40.0	0.010	0.012	105.3	-0.003	0.007
Total	16,196.1	16,287.3			30,292.4		

of the other countries/regions noted in table 12. The sectoral results, which are not shown here, indicate that there are relatively small employment declines in Japan in agriculture, labor-intensive manufactures, and trade & transport services, and increases in employment in durable manufactures, construction, and other private services. For South Korea, employment falls in chemicals, durable manufactures, and services, except for trade & transport. Employment rises in South Korea's agriculture and labor-intensive manufactures.

RA-5C: Japan-Chile Free Trade Agreement (JCFTA)—A JCFTA covering all sectors is shown in table 13 to increase global welfare by $4.9 billion. Japan's welfare rises by $4.3 billion (.07 percent of GNP) and Chile's welfare rises by $688 million (0.86 percent). While not shown here, the effects of removing bilateral agricultural tariffs are negligible. Bilateral tariff removal for manufactures increases Japan's welfare by $720 million (0.01 percent of GNP) and Chile's welfare by $61 million (.08 percent of GNP). Bilateral removal of services barriers increases Japan's welfare by $3.6 billion (.06 percent of GNP) and Chile's welfare by $630 million (0.78 percent of GNP). There is evidence of small, negative welfare effects due to trade diversion for the smaller industrialized countries and for all of the Asian economies, except Hong Kong. There are negligible increases in the real returns to labor and capital in Japan, while these returns increase by 0.91 and 0.70 percent, respectively, in Chile. The sectoral results, which are not included here, indicate relatively small employment declines for Japan in agriculture, food, beverages, & tobacco, trade & transport, and other private services, and employment increases in all other manufacturing sectors. In Chile, employment falls in mining, all manufacturing sectors, and in services except other private services.

RA-6C: ASEAN Plus-3—Table 14 contains the results of a FTA involving the members of ASEAN together with China/Hong Kong, Japan, and South Korea. Complete removal of all bilateral tariffs on agriculture and manufactures and services barriers increases global welfare by $224.7 billion. Japan's welfare rises by $160.8 billion, and there are welfare increases for the ASEAN members as well as for China/Hong Kong and South Korea. There is evidence of trade diversion for the EU/EFTA (-$2.6 billion), Rest of Asia (-$58 million), and Mexico (-$55 million). In a scenario not shown here, if Hong Kong were to be excluded from this FTA, it would experience a welfare decline of -$366 million. The underlying scenarios, which are available on request, indicate that removal of agricultural tariffs would increase Japan's welfare by $717 million, China's by $1.6 billion, and South Korea's by $429 million. There are pervasive welfare declines, however, especially for agricultural exporting countries. For elimination of tariffs on manufactures, Japan's welfare rises by $89.9 billion, Hong Kong's by $2.3 billion, and Korea's by $9.6 billion. China's welfare declines in this case by -$5.9 billion because its terms of trade deteriorate by 4.4 percent as its export prices fall. The ASEAN members all experience increases in welfare, as do some outside countries, but there is some evidence of trade diversion for EU/EFTA, Rest of Asia, and

Table 13. Summary Results of a Japan-Chile FTA
Change in Imports, Exports, Terms of Trade, Welfare and the Real Return to Capital and Labor
Percent Change and Millions of U.S. Dollars

Country	Imports (Millions)	Exports (Millions)	Terms of Trade (Percent)	Welfare (Percent)	Welfare (Millions)	Real Wage (Percent)	Return to Capital (Percent)
Scenario RA-5C: Japan-Chile FTA Elimination of Agricultural and Manufacturing Tariffs and Services Barriers							
Industrialized Countries							
Japan	558.7	627.3	-0.011	0.067	4,340.9	0.007	0.009
United States	-14.1	-11.5	0.000	-0.001	-46.0	0.000	0.000
Canada	-2.5	-2.4	0.000	-0.001	-4.4	-0.001	0.000
Australia	2.3	1.6	0.001	0.000	1.6	0.000	0.001
New Zealand	0.2	0.1	0.001	-0.001	-0.4	0.000	0.000
EU and EFTA	-47.5	-39.7	-0.001	0.000	-51.8	-0.001	-0.001
Developing Countries							
Asia							
Hong Kong	0.9	-0.1	0.000	0.000	-0.5	0.001	0.000
China	2.1	2.0	0.000	0.000	-4.0	0.000	0.000
Korea	-19.1	-16.1	-0.002	-0.003	-17.9	-0.002	-0.003
Singapore	-0.4	-0.7	0.000	-0.001	-0.8	0.000	0.000
Taiwan	-9.6	-9.1	0.000	-0.002	-7.7	-0.001	-0.001
Indonesia	0.6	0.1	0.001	0.000	-0.7	0.000	0.000
Malaysia	-1.3	-1.3	0.000	-0.002	-2.0	0.000	0.001
Philippines	0.1	-0.2	0.000	-0.001	-0.8	0.000	0.000
Thailand	-0.4	-0.6	0.000	-0.002	-3.6	0.002	0.000
Rest of Asia	0.4	0.2	0.000	0.000	-1.9	0.000	0.000
Other							
Chile	434.8	360.5	0.325	0.857	688.5	0.906	0.698
Mexico	-4.9	-3.7	-0.001	-0.002	-8.2	-0.001	-0.001
CCS	-5.5	-9.7	0.004	0.001	16.0	-0.002	-0.001
RME	7.9	6.3	0.001	0.001	6.5	0.000	0.001
Total	902.7	903.2			4,902.7		

Table 14. Summary Results of an FTA of ASEAN, Hong Kong, China, Japan and South Korea Change in Imports, Exports, Terms of Trade, Welfare and the Real Return to Capital and Labor Percent Change and Millions of U.S. Dollars

Country	Imports (Millions)	Exports (Millions)	Terms of Trade (Percent)	Welfare (Percent)	Welfare (Millions)	Real Wage (Percent)	Return to Capital (Percent)
Scenario RA-6C: Elimination of Agricultural and Manufacturing Tariffs and Services Barriers							
Industrialized Countries							
Japan	133,024.7	131,759.5	0.407	5.772	374,820.1	1.705	2.234
United States	201,847.7	201,043.1	-0.199	5.918	537,194.8	1.884	2.023
Canada	27,273.1	29,781.5	-0.777	5.615	40,919.9	2.856	3.149
Australia	18,200.0	15,815.0	2.858	3.525	15,476.1	3.085	2.722
New Zealand	5,623.4	4,285.4	6.042	9.225	6,773.0	5.525	4.735
EU and EFTA	209,783.3	187,000.9	2.146	4.668	511,947.3	1.297	1.389
Developing Countries							
Asia							
Hong Kong	22,906.0	16,055.8	6.180	10.177	13,105.5	10.022	9.848
China	78,698.5	90,813.8	-4.296	4.549	41,210.9	4.050	4.016
Korea	43,583.9	44,372.0	-0.487	7.513	42,749.0	5.585	4.781
Singapore	19,138.9	16,888.1	1.372	16.958	12,611.5	21.691	19.346
Taiwan	34,400.6	32,565.8	1.269	8.437	29,583.3	5.569	5.234
Indonesia	11,974.2	12,202.7	-0.247	5.002	12,651.6	3.272	1.954
Malaysia	18,363.1	20,890.3	-2.207	8.507	10,170.5	10.718	10.573
Philippines	17,168.5	20,290.7	-8.974	16.380	14,454.2	12.570	12.521
Thailand	21,322.2	23,163.9	-2.353	7.943	16,366.1	9.640	5.066
Rest of Asia	42,005.4	49,588.7	-8.025	5.382	30,807.4	3.998	4.240
Other							
Chile	4,314.8	4,329.2	-0.047	7.285	5,851.1	4.626	4.353
Mexico	10,057.6	11,389.4	-0.955	5.578	19,679.7	1.994	2.075
CCS	49,413.5	52,113.6	-1.826	4.277	71,405.4	1.289	0.831
RME	42,272.9	48,107.2	-2.657	5.751	49,661.7	2.737	4.527
Total	1,011,372.3	1,012,456.4			1,857,439.1		

Mexico. Removal of services barriers increases Japan's welfare by $70.2 billion, China's by $7.6 billion, Hong Kong's by $3.0 billion, Korea's by $7.2 billion, and the ASEAN members' by between $2.0 billion for the Philippines and $3.8 billion for Thailand. There are small welfare declines for Rest of Asia, Chile, and Rest of Middle East. The real returns to labor and capital noted in table 14 rise in Japan by 0.58 and 0.80 percent, respectively, and by sizable percentages in the other member countries of this FTA grouping.

The sectoral results, which are not shown here, indicate employment declines for Japan in agriculture (-31,523), food, beverages, & tobacco (-25,669), textiles (-2,724), wearing apparel (-67,761), leather products & footwear (-6,492), and trade & transport services (-51,285). Employment rises in all other sectors in Japanese manufacturing and services. The sectoral employment effects in China (excluding Hong Kong) are sizable in several sectors. There are declines in textiles (-687,516), wood & wood products (-44,933), chemicals (-359,236), metal products (-55,436), transportation equipment (-141,735), machinery & equipment (-357,464), construction (-614,990), trade & transport (-368,438), and government services (-489,436). There are employment increases in China in agriculture (218,916), mining (92,230), food, beverages & tobacco (148,193), wearing apparel (1,476,032), leather products & footwear (535,672), other manufactures (310,678), and other private services (282,858). For South Korea, there are relatively sizable employment declines in agriculture, durable manufactures, and services, and employment increases especially in textiles, wearing apparel, leather products & footwear, and other manufactures.

Conclusion

Based on the foregoing six scenarios, it appears that there are sizable welfare gains for both Japan and the United States with complete APEC bilateral liberalization, but these gains are considerably smaller than what would be obtained from global free trade. APEC liberalization also would involve some trade diversion especially vis-à-vis the EU/EFTA. The analysis of four FTAs involving Japan with Singapore, Mexico, South Korea, and Chile suggests that Japan would experience most of the gains in welfare compared to these other, smaller economies. But these gains for Japan are relatively small in terms of percentages of GNP and increases in real wages and the returns to capital. The major employment effects in Japan appear to be concentrated in agriculture and labor-intensive manufactures and to some extent in services. The employment effects in the partner FTA countries mirror these employment effects with expansion in agriculture and labor-intensive manufactures and declines especially in durable manufactures. An ASEAN Plus-3 FTA produces sizable welfare increases for the member countries but, in some cases, significant intersectoral shifts in output and employment that could prove disruptive.

The downside of the FTAs is that there are indications of trade diversion in each case, although the global welfare gains are positive. Japan's gains are greater for an ASEAN Plus-3 FTA, but, as in the case of APEC liberalization, these gains are notably smaller than the gains to be had from multilateral liberalization in a new trade round.

Because our computational analysis has been confined to the removal of tariffs on agriculture and manufactures and services barriers, we are not taking into account other features of the FTAs, such as the negotiation of explicit rules and development of new institutional and cooperative arrangements that could be beneficial to the countries involved.[18] These factors do not lend themselves readily to quantification, however. By the same token, we have not made allowance for rules of origin that may be negotiated as part of each FTA and that could be designed with protectionist intentions. It is therefore not obvious that Japan's interests are being well served altogether by its shift towards bilateral and preferential trading arrangements. It also appears that the benefits to Japan's FTA partner countries are limited, and, in some cases, could be disruptive, as workers would be shifted away from durable manufactures and towards agriculture and labor-intensive manufactures. What is clear from our results in the preceding sections is that the successful pursuit of a new round of multilateral trade negotiations promises significant benefits for Japan and for the economies of its major trading partners and the world as whole. There is some danger accordingly that Japan's shift away from multilateralism could jeopardize the realization of the benefits of multilateral liberalization.

V. Conclusions and Implications for Policy

We have used the Michigan Model of World Production and Trade to simulate the economic effects of the trade liberalization negotiated in the Uruguay Round of multilateral trade negotiations that was completed in 1993-94, of a prospective new trade round to be conducted under WTO auspices, and of a variety of regional and preferential trading arrangements. While our focus has been on the United States and Japan, we have also provided results for the effects on the other major trading countries/regions in the global trading system. The overriding conclusion that emerges from our model simulations is that multilateral trade liberalization has positive and often sizable impacts on the economic welfare and real returns to labor and capital in both the industrialized and developing countries/regions covered in the Michigan Model. This is the case both for the Uruguay Round liberalization and for a prospective WTO negotiating round. A second conclusion of our analysis is that regional and bilateral free trade agreements (FTAs) may be welfare enhancing for the member countries involved. But these welfare gains are considerably smaller than those resulting from multilateral trade liberalization, and, in some cases, disruptive employment shifts might occur. It is also the case that the FTAs involve elements of trade diversion and are therefore detrimental to some non-member countries.

While our research is by no means the last word on the subject, our computational results nonetheless strongly support the case for swift multilateral action to be taken by the United States, Japan, and other WTO member countries to move ahead with a new trade round to reduce or remove completely existing tariffs on agricultural products and manufactures as well as barriers to international services transactions.

Notes

[1] The individual countries listed in Table 1 below, and the industries in Table 2, are self-explanatory, as is the European Union (EU). EFTA is the European Free Trade Association and here includes Iceland, Norway, and Switzerland. Rest of Asia is India, Sri Lanka, and Vietnam. CCS is Caribbean, Central and South America, consisting of Argentina, Brazil, Colombia, Uruguay, Venezuela, and the Rest of the Andean Pact. RME is the Rest of the Middle East, consisting of Morocco, Turkey, and the Rest of North Africa.

[2] Intermediate inputs include both domestic and imported varieties.

[3] This source does not provide number-of-firms data for all countries. We have used the number-of-firms data for similar countries in these cases.

[4] We also need data on supply elasticities from ROW, which have been taken from the Michigan Model database.

[5] See Hertel and Martin (1999) and Hertel (2000) for a more elaborate and detailed procedure for calculating year 2005 projections.

[6] See Francois and Strutt (1999) for details on the post-UR tariff rates.

[7] Reductions in post-Uruguay Round agricultural export subsidies will presumably also be negotiated in a new trade round, but they are not included in this scenario.

[8] Because of computer-capacity constraints, Brown and Stern use a 3-sector aggregation consisting of agriculture, manufactures, and services and the same 20-country/region breakdowns as is being used here. They also make allowance for international flows of FDI and increases in capital stocks in response to the multilateral trade liberalization that they analyze.

[9] See Chapter 4 below for a proposal for tariffication in services by Alan Deardorff that is designed to provide the basis for services liberalization in the WTO negotiation.

[10] The potential gains from a new WTO trade round are also analyzed in Hertel (2000), based on the GTAP CGE model, which is a widely used modeling structure. The version used by Hertel assumes perfect competition in all sectors. It also assumes national product differentiation (i.e., the Armington assumption), which may tend to exaggerate terms-of-trade effects.

[11] Brown and Stern have used their 3-sector, 20-country CGE model that incorporates the behavior of multinational corporations (MNCs) and their foreign affiliates and international mobility of FDI-related capital to assess the effects of 33 percent reductions in post-Uruguay Round tariffs and services barriers. Making allowance for imperfect

mobility of real international capital movements and fixed world capital stocks, they estimate that the combined reductions in tariffs and services barriers would increase global welfare by $193.2 billion. The welfare increase for Japan is $3.1 billion and for the United States, $45.8 billion. When allowance is made for increases in the world capital stock of 2 percent in response to the assumed liberalization, the increase in world economic welfare rises to $612.4 billion, with an increase for Japan of $80.2 billion and for the United States, $178.4 billion. International capital mobility combined with an increase in capital accumulation may therefore generate welfare changes that are different in size and geographical distribution as compared to the results generated in the more disaggregated, sectoral version of the Michigan Model used here that abstracts from the behavior of MNCs in response to trade liberalization. Time and resource constraints have thus far prevented Brown and Stern from expanding the sectoral coverage of their FDI model to analyze the more detailed responses to trade liberalization for the world's major trading countries and regions.

[12] See Krueger (2000) for a preliminary assessment of the trade and related effects of NAFTA since its inception in 1994.

[13] See METI, White Papers/Reports (2000a, b, c).

[14] For an earlier computational analysis of an East Asian trading bloc, see Brown, Deardorff, and Stern (1996).

[15] The membership of APEC is as follows: Australia; Canada; Chile; China; Hong Kong; Indonesia; Japan; Korea; Malaysia; Mexico; New Zealand; Philippines; Singapore; Taiwan; Thailand; and United States.

[16] See Chapter 11 below by Taiji Furusawa for a theoretical analysis of APEC's open regionalism and Chapter 12 by Masahiro Endoh for a simulation analysis of whether APEC liberalization will be a building block or stumbling block towards multilateral trade liberalization.

[17] Taken here to include Singapore, Indonesia, Malaysia, Philippines, and Thailand.

[18] The prospective Japan-Singapore FTA is to be referred to as the "Japan-Singapore Economic Agreement for a New Age Partnership." Details of the proposed agreement are set out in METI (2000a).

References

Brown, Drusilla K., Alan V. Deardorff, and Robert M. Stern. 1996. "Computational Analysis of the Economic Effects of an East Asian Preferential Trading Bloc," *Journal of the Japanese and International Economies* 10:37-70.

Brown, Drusilla K. and Robert M. Stern. 2000. "Measurement and Modeling of the Economic Effects of Trade and Investment Barriers in Services," *Review of International Economics*, forthcoming.

Deardorff, Alan V. and Robert M. Stern. 1990. *Computational Analysis of Global Trading Arrangements*. Ann Arbor: University of Michigan Press.

Francois, Joseph and Anna Strutt. 1999. "Post-Uruguay Round Tariff Vectors for GTAP Version 4," processed, Faculty of Economics, Erasmus University, Rotterdam, The Netherlands.

Harrison, W.J. and Ken Pearson. 1996. "Computing solutions for large general equilibrium models using GEMPACK," *Computational Economics* 9:83-127.

Hertel, Thomas W. and Will Martin. 1999. "Would Developing Countries Gain from Inclusion of Manufactures in the WTO Negotiations?" Presented at the Conference on the "WTO and the Millennium Round," Geneva, September 20-21.

Hertel, Thomas W. 2000. "Potential Gains from Reducing Trade Barriers in Manufacturing, Services and Agriculture," *Federal Reserve Bank of St. Louis Review* 82:77-99.

Hoekman, Bernard. 2000. "The Next Round of Services Negotiations: Identifying Priorities and Options," *Federal Reserve Bank of St. Louis Review* 82:31-47.

Krueger, Anne O. 2000. "NAFTA's Effects: A Preliminary Assessment," *The World Economy* 23:761-775.

McDougall, Robert et al. 1998. *Global Trade: Assistance and Protection: GTAP-4 Database*, Purdue University, W. Lafayette, IN.

Ministry of Economy Trade and Industry (METI), Government of Japan, White Papers/Reports. 2000a. "Japan-Singapore Economic Agreement for a New Age Partnership" (http://www.meti.go.jp/english/report/data/gJ-SFTA0e.html).

Ministry of Economy Trade and Industry (METI), Government of Japan, White Papers/Reports. 2000b. "Joint Announcement of the Japanese and Singapore Prime Ministers on the Initiation of Negotiations for Concluding a Bilateral Economic Partnership Agreement, 22nd October in Tokyo" (http://www.meti.go.jp/english/report/data/gJ-SFTA-2e.html).

Ministry of Economy Trade and Industry (METI), Government of Japan, White Papers/Reports. 2000c. "The Economic Foundations of Japanese Trade Policy—Promoting a Multi-Layered Trade Policy," August (http://www.meti.go.jp/english/report/data/g00Wconte.html).

Stolper, Wolfgang and Paul A. Samuelson. 1941. "Protection and Real Wages," *Review of Economic Studies* 9:58-73.

Comment

Keith E. Maskus

I am pleased to have an opportunity to comment on this interesting and cogent analysis of the potential economic effects of various trade liberalization possibilities in the Asia-Pacific region, most of which are under official discussion with varying degrees of priority. The authors first extrapolate forward to 2005 the GTAP-4 database and make it consistent with their modeling structure, in order to derive a benchmark global economy from which trade policies taken subsequently to implementation of the Uruguay Round (UR) may be investigated.

Two key characteristics of the analysis distinguish this paper and drive the results found here. First is the incorporation into the Michigan Model of significant departures from the constant-returns, perfect-competition scenario that limits many other models. Second is the inclusion of *ad valorem* measures of barriers to trade in services. Because those barriers are thought to be so large and inefficient here, their liberalization or removal inevitably generates significant welfare gains.

Regarding the "new trade theory" aspects of the model, the most interesting feature is product heterogeneity attached to firms in the monopolistically competitive sectors. I like this approach very much for it goes beyond the simple Armington framework with single varieties from each country. Rather, individual firms in each country and industry produce differentiated goods that are sold in each country according to a CES utility structure. In this fashion, firm-level entry and exit decisions, along with endogenous effects on costs associated with scale economies, are taken directly into the calculation of welfare impacts from competition. This process permits greater richness in describing the economic impacts that would ensue from trade liberalization. In particular, it seems from the simulations that cutting manufacturing tariffs, already rather low in the included countries and regions, could have large efficiency effects through influencing output scales. Indeed, these impacts are often larger than those found in the more conventional models in use at the World Bank (Hertel and Martin, 1999). This is an interesting finding and could be used to buttress the claims of negotiators that much remains to be accomplished through liberalization of manufactures.

While the inclusion of differentiated products is an important advance, it still requires assuming constant and equal elasticities of substitution across products. This raises two questions for me. First, I suspect that the choice of substitution elasticity at this stage is critical for assessing the distribution of scale effects and trade-diversion impacts across countries. It is impossible to know this in the current paper because the authors do not list their chosen elasticity parameters, nor do they undertake any experimentation of the sensitivity of their results to parameter variations. I can certainly understand this decision, for the paper already contains large numbers of extensive tabular results. However, it would be interesting to know, even if only in a footnote, the extent to which the large impacts of service liberalization are associated with failing to entertain different substitution elasticities in services than in manufacturing. Having no evidence to offer on the subject, I can only conjecture that some kinds of services, such as life insurance and banking, may well be highly substitutable among individual suppliers. At least this notion strikes me as an interesting direction to take the work in the future, particularly if the authors are able to increase the disaggregation of service activities in their model.

A second point is that to maintain constant substitution elasticities before and after a significant trade liberalization makes me wonder if our models fail to account for an important subsidiary effect. Specifically, if the effect of regional free trade areas (FTAs) is to alter critical parameters within a region relative to those outside the region, rather different effects could result. It could well be that the elasticity of substitution between imports and domestic goods, in particular among FTA partners, would rise as a result of better and more certain information becoming available to domestic consumers and firms about the quality characteristics of imported goods. In this scenario, trade liberalization would generate not only entry and rationalization gains, but also a further gain would emerge through reducing imperfectly competitive markups. While it is not immediately clear how one would implement such a story through an endogenous change in substitution possibilities, it could be an important additional impact to consider. For example, thinking like this underlies optimism in the European Union about gains from harmonization of product standards.

Turning to the model in this paper, its rich specification permits welfare impacts from several sources. These include standard efficiency gains from re-allocation of resources, terms-of-trade effects, losses in rents associated with eliminating MFA quotas, and the scale effects from increasing returns. Each of these processes is decisive in different scenarios and their relative importance varies across countries. It is unfortunate, though understandable, that the authors do not have sufficient space in the paper to work out some decomposition exercises so that readers could understand better what is going on in certain scenarios.

For example, the most surprising finding is that the UR commitments on reductions in agricultural tariffs and exports subsidies, if implemented, would reduce global welfare by $26 billion and also the well-being of virtually every country in the model. The authors explain this as the result of relatively larger reductions in export subsidies compared with import tariffs, having a net effect of raising consumer prices on average. It appears that both significant agricultural exporters *and* importers lose from this case, with the main exception being the European Union, the largest single contributor to global inefficiency in this sector! The authors provide some hint at how this would happen by noting that the losses in U.S. welfare stem from a shift in resources out of manufacturing to agriculture, sacrificing scale economies and worsening monopoly distortions in the former sector. Presumably the European Union would gain from such scale effects as agriculture declines. In this context, however, the Japanese welfare loss is mysterious, given the large reduction in agricultural output from the UR. If it comes from a simultaneous increase in consumer price and reduction in producer support, we are left to wonder how such an agreement was ever reached in the first place. Here, then, a decomposition exercise to explore the nature of these effects, and their interaction with other aspects of economic structure, would be instructive.

Most interesting are the simulations of potential liberalization scenarios after the Uruguay Round commitments are phased in by 2005. Anyone could quibble with the authors' decision to use linear extrapolations to update the benchmark model to that year, but other approaches would be at least as arbitrary. Thus, I will accept that benchmark on its merits and address the follow-on experiments.

In considering potentialities for a "Millennium Round" (MR) post-2005, the authors essentially posit an across-the-board 33% cut in tariffs in agriculture, manufacturing, and services. Compared to the prior analysis, the treatment of agriculture, involving no change in export subsidies, is a major difference and perhaps should be made more explicit. If negotiators in the MR choose again to reach an agreement that is inherently inefficient, as they evidently did in the UR, the current calculations could be deceiving. Put another way, the potential for global gains of some $11 billion if negotiators simply cut tariffs is worth noting. However, perhaps an even better scenario to consider would be a combination of tariff and subsidy cuts that would engineer an effective 33% reduction in the consumer-producer price gap in all markets.

Certainly the most remarkable aspect of the simulations, however, is the potential for major gains from services liberalization. At $390 billion per annum, these gains are larger than those from manufacturing and agriculture combined and are sufficiently widespread to procure gains for all countries and regions. It is apparent that the source of these large gains is the highly distorted structure of protection in services, captured by the authors' reliance on huge estimated variations in operating margins across countries. These estimates are fraught with error and should be treated with caution. Moreover, it is a stretch to imagine that fixed entry costs for multinational enterprises may be approximated by the lowest national margin. Even in the absence of restrictive policies that might be relaxed, there are likely to be large differences in such fixed costs depending on market size, distance from headquarters markets, and other factors. Further, I doubt that the impacts of a major cut of 33% in such large tariff-equivalents could reliably be captured in a linear model. I suspect, therefore, that the welfare gains computed by the authors are overstated in static term, perhaps considerably so.[1] Perhaps it is enough simply to remind negotiators of the existing heavy distortions in services.

The various bilateral FTAs modeled in the final section are interesting primarily for their portrayal of different national interests across cases. Note that these FTAs involve complete liberalization, which remains a dubious prospect in agriculture and services. Some anomalies arise, such as the finding that bilateral removal of services barriers between Japan and South Korea raise the latter nation's welfare by more than would complete bilateral liberalization. It would be interesting to hear the authors' explanation for this result, which presumably implies that bilateral liberalization in agriculture and manufacturing would reduce Korean welfare unless there are interesting secondary interactions going on in the economy. Again, this suggests a series of decomposition exercises would be informative. A second is that bilateral agricultural liberalization between Japan and Chile would have negligible effects, which is surprising given the preponderance of Chilean agricultural exports. Perhaps the most unanticipated finding is that all of the bilateral FTAs considered would induce positive global welfare gains. Given prior results, surely this outcome is due to the extensive gains from full liberalization of service barriers, which again remains problematic in terms of what might actually be negotiable.

Overall, I believe the results in this paper should command attention among regional and multilateral trade negotiators. Particular emphasis could be placed on the large and mutual gains from services liberalization. In that context, note that removing restrictions on the international provision of services is akin to deregulation of non-border restraints on other forms of competition, such as the exercise of intellectual property rights. It is conceivable that incorporation of such factors into CGE models of this type could further enrich our understanding of the effects of deregulation and policy harmonization.

Note

[1] At the same time, such gains may be understated in dynamic terms to the extent that services provided by new establishments reduce inter-sectoral production costs and generate other spillovers.

References

Hertel, Thomas W. and Will Martin, 1999, "Would Developing Countries Gain from Inclusion of Manufactures in the WTO Negotiations?" paper presented at the WTO/World Bank Conference on Developing Countries in a Millennium Round, Geneva, 20-21 September.

Comment

Keith Head

In his comment, Keith Head notes that Brown, Deardorff, and Stern (hereafter BDS) conclude their paper saying, "[O]ur computational results . . . strongly support the case for . . . a new trade round to reduce or remove completely existing tariffs . . . as well as barriers to international services transactions." The authors base this strong endorsement of a WTO "Millennium Round" on the results of a computable general equilibrium (CGE) analysis of a number of possible trade liberalization scenarios. Most of the trade economists that I know would favor more trade liberalization before ever reading the BDS paper. In contrast, there is no conceivable paper using CGEs that would sway the mind of the typical anti-globalization protestor. What, then, is the use of CGE modeling exercises such as the one conducted by BDS? I will argue that they are very useful already but could, in principle, be modified to become considerably more useful.

Policy makers (broadly construed to include reporters, civil servants, etc.) constitute possibly the most important audience for this paper's results. But, one wonders, why do they need numerical results on trade-policy scenarios? With our students, we simply argue the near universal gains of exploiting comparative advantage through free trade. Why shouldn't we just reiterate this non-numerical argument? There are three important reasons why the CGE analysis conducted by BDS should be valuable to policy makers.

First, gains from exploiting comparative advantage are just one of the mechanisms through which tariff reductions can influence economic welfare. The BDS model also allows for gains *or losses* associated with changes in terms of trade or changes in scale and variety. Most analytical models treat just one or two such mechanisms at a time. This is the right approach for strengthening our intuition. However, policy analyses need to incorporate every major mechanism in order to attain a reasonable standard of predictive realism.

Second, a quantification of the gains from trade is useful because changes in trade policy consume political resources. Large expected gains are more likely to elicit large effort from policy makers. This claim may seem naïve, but it appears to be the case that the Mulroney government of Canada decided to wage an election on the issue of free trade with the United States in part because of the substantial gains promised by the Cox and Harris (1985) CGE results. The BDS paper reports what seem to be fairly paltry welfare gains from the Uruguay Round. The United States gains $13 billion, but this represents less than a fifth of a percent of U.S. GNP. On the other hand, the numbers reported for future partial or complete liberalizations are an order of magnitude larger. They seem comparable to the gains that would be generated by about three years of strong (but not extraordinary) productivity growth.

Third, CGE results can assist policy makers in selecting from a diverse menu of liberalization alternatives. This paper considers further WTO rounds, bilateral agreements such as Japan and Singapore, and intermediate agreements involving a number of large economies such as APEC. My sense is that policy makers have a natural tendency towards bilateral deals. For one thing, it allows careful partner selection. It is probably no accident that Japan looked towards Singapore for its first bilateral agreement given that a city-state is unlikely to be a major source of politically sensitive agricultural products. In addition, with fewer interests to mollify, parties to a bilateral agreement can move faster towards deeper integration than can the 130 some members of the WTO. This begs the question of whether bilateral and regional agreements have economic benefits to match their perceived political benefits. The results presented by BDS suggest that the temptation of bilateralism should be resisted. They find that multilateral reductions have far greater prospective gains.

Despite these valuable uses, CGE exercises have some serious limitations that leave many economists skeptical of their results. The central problem in my view is one of a false impression of numerical precision. The computer simulation cranks through all its equations, determines a new equilibrium, and calculates a welfare change. For instance, Japan would gain $123.7 billion from another WTO round that reduces tariffs by one third. What is the confidence interval for that prediction? We have very little idea. There are two types of uncertainty affecting the point estimates. First, the model uses specific parameters. Those were usually estimated in other studies. Each estimate has a standard error. In principal one could simulate the BDS model by repeatedly sampling different parameters randomly and thus calculate a standard error for each welfare change. In practice the computational effort involved might not be justified since another more important source of uncertainty would remain. This is what we might refer to as "model uncertainty." Our current understanding of the world economy is so limited that our choice of assumptions is driven more by aesthetic judgments and hunches than sound empirical evidence.

The deployment of the "New Trade Theory" is an example of this difficulty that I would like to explore in some detail. The authors note that "although the New Trade Theory is perhaps best known for introducing new reasons why countries may lose from trade, in fact its greatest contribution is to expand the list of reasons for gains from trade." This gives the impression that there is a single theory to be incorporated. In fact, there are many variations of trade theories incorporating the "new" elements of imperfect competition and economies of scale. The positive and normative predictions of the theory depend acutely on which particular variant is implemented. Models with Cournot oligopoly and segmented markets have profit-shifting effects associated with changes in tariffs. In contrast, models with free-entry monopolistic competition generally do not, since there are no remaining profits to be shifted.

The most commonly used model is probably Krugman's (1980) adaptation of the Dixit-Stiglitz model of monopolistic competition. That model has several features that are relevant for the BDS analysis. First, the firms think of themselves as too small to affect the industry price index. As a result, they perceive a constant price elasticity of demand and set markups accordingly. This assumption implies the absence of a pro-competitive effect of trade; more competition has no effect on price-cost margins. Second the Dixit-Stiglitz model assumes free entry. Combined with the first assumption, this yields the result that output per variety is invariant to trade policy changes. From my reading of their model, BDS do not make these standard assumptions. As a result, their market structure does not correspond to the typical definition of monopolistic competition. This is not necessarily a bad thing since changes in margins and firm scale might well be important consequences of tariff changes (however, Head and Ries (1999) did not find large scale effects Canadian manufacturers as a result of the Canada-U.S. FTA). In any case, as we interpret the BDS results, we must keep in mind that we are looking at the implications of one particular version of New Trade and minor variations on that version could have a major impact on the results. Or they might not; we just do not know.

I am stressing the New Trade Theory implementation issues because I think that they influence two aspects of the BDS results that I found striking. First, although the BDS model has traditional gains from trade associated with differences in factor proportions, their results do not exhibit Stolper-Samuelson effects. That is, in most cases, *both* the abundant and the scarce factor in each country benefit from the simulated trade liberalizations. This is a rather appealing feature for "selling" these results to liberal policy makers who are unlikely to be enthusiastic about efficiency gains that come at the cost of lower real wages. However, one should keep in mind that New Trade models do not always feature such win-win outcomes. Indeed one consequence of increasing returns is a tendency of firms to concentrate in the larger market following tariff reductions. The theory behind this prediction and some empirical evidence from the Canada-U.S. FTA are presented in Head and Ries (2001).

Home-market effects can lead to real wage reductions in small countries in order to maintain competitiveness in those sectors. The surprising thing for me was that the BDS results suggest that Canada, Australia, and New Zealand all stand to gain larger percentage changes in wages and returns to capital than the United States, European Union, and Japan. My guess about what is happening is that the BDS model holds the number of firms in each country constant. This implies that lower tariffs given everyone better access to foreign varieties. This is a bigger deal for small countries, since they produce fewer varieties at home. Also smaller countries obtain better access to large markets and this may increase average scale. I think it would be informative for BDS to report a set of alternative results using the more standard approach to monopolistic competition that is associated with Paul Krugman.

Another valuable feature of CGEs is that they are expandable as more data and newer theories become available. There are three things that I think would add considerably to the realism and interest of CGE models.

1. *Two more primary factors of production:* The Michigan model includes capital and labor but omits land and human capital (skill). Much of the trade between Japan and countries like Canada and Australia probably arises from scarcity of land in Japan. One of the most contentious issues in trade liberalization has always been agriculture. A model without land strikes me as ill-suited to deal with agriculture. An even more controversial aspect of trade liberalization has been the effects on wage inequality. To address these issues, the model needs to incorporate human capital. Data on endowments of both land and human capital are now available. However, it will probably be a much more difficult task to find industry-level factor intensities.
2. *More realistic treatment of labor markets:* Conventional CGE models impose full employment before and after trade liberalization. They defend this approach by saying it reflects interest in the medium-run consequences of liberalization. However, short-run costs are part of a long-run present value analysis. If the gross gains from trade were huge, perhaps one could argue that those costs are negligible. However, modest tariff reductions yield even more modest welfare increases. When economists simply assert that dislocation costs are small enough to ignore, the policy maker is likely to be suspicious. Ideally we would like to consider the dynamic path of adjustment following trade liberalization. In particular, I have in mind workers that must leave one sector but must spend some time searching before they obtain employment in the other sector. I can understand why BDS might be reluctant to incorporate these features. Not only do they require a substantial change in the theoretical structure, but they would also require new parameters (related to the efficacy of search). A recent paper by Davidson, Martin, and Matusz (1999) addresses the issue of how to incorporate unemployment into general equilibrium trade models and the impact this has on the results of liberalization.
3. *"Natural" barriers to trade:* CGE models focus on the trade barriers erected by governments, namely tariffs and various forms of quotas. This is a sensible focus since those are precisely the barriers that we intend to dismantle. However, studies of bilateral trade strongly suggest that in addition to "artificial" barriers, there are even larger "natural" barriers. The most robust result is that bilateral trade is inversely proportional to distance between trading partners. Research by Hummels (1999, 2000) and Rauch (1999) suggests that this negative distance effect comes from freight costs, time costs, and search costs. A second "natural" barrier arises from the diversity of languages. Another robust econometric result is that two countries that share a common language trade much more with each other than pairs that do not. Although these barriers are estimated from variation in bilateral trade patterns, they also affect a country's total

trade since countries are normally close to themselves and use a single language. The implication for CGE models is that even if all artificial barriers are removed, the world will remain quite far from a single, frictionless economy.[1] Taking natural barriers into account may well influence the parameters selected for the model, in particular the elasticity of substitution between domestic and imported goods. More substantively, incorporation of geography and language will allow for a better understanding of the pros and cons of regional liberalization agreements. BDS follow the normal practice among economists of favoring multilateral (WTO-sponsored) liberalization over regional liberalization initiatives (such as NAFTA). However, once one incorporates natural barriers, regional agreements may become more appealing since faraway countries are unlikely to trade large amounts with each other even if artificial barriers were removed.

Most CGE analyses are carried out with the goal of informing policymakers of the gains that they expect from trade liberalization. As with the BDS chapter, they also suggest which policy changes are likely to create larger gains. While there seems to be a clear need for such analyses, I would like to propose an alternative use. CGE models could be used to indicate to empiricists what facts they need to establish. The CGE modeler would do so by varying assumptions to ascertain what critical modeling elements or parameter values are necessary and/or sufficient to make a trade liberalization have certain desirable consequences (welfare improvements for all members, reductions in intra-national inequality, etc.). Identification of the critical assumptions could guide subsequent empirical work. If we knew, for instance, that the crucial New Trade feature that generates welfare improvements is an increase in firm-level scale, then empirical researchers could focus their efforts on estimating the magnitude of such effects. If empiricists amass evidence that such effects are minor or non-existent, then CGE designers would adjust their policy-oriented models accordingly. This collaborative approach would help empiricists to identify critical issues and it would lend greater credibility to CGE results. CGE models might no longer be deemed "theory with numbers" but instead would become something more like "empirics with equilibrium."

Note

[1] Editorial note: Head is correct in noting that real bilateral trade costs are not included explicitly in the BDS model in addition to tariffs and quotas. But, in actuality, existing trade costs are implicitly part of the BDS model and are reflected in the existing trade patterns that enter the database.

References

Cox, David and Richard Harris. 1985. "Trade Liberalization and Industrial Organization: Some Estimates for Canada," *Journal of Political Economy* 93:115-145.

Davidson, Carl, Lawrence Martin, and Steven Matusz. 1999. "Trade and Search Generated Unemployment," *Journal of International Economics* 48:271-299.

Head, Keith and John Ries. 1999. "Rationalization Effects of Tariff Reductions," *Journal of International Economics* 47:295-320.

Head, Keith and John Ries. 2001. "Increasing Returns versus National Product Differentiation as an Explanation for the Pattern of U.S.-Canada Trade," *American Economic Review*, September.

Hummels, David. 1999. "Towards a Geography of Trade Costs," Manuscript available at http://www.mgmt.purdue.edu/faculty/hummelsd/

Hummels, David. 2000. "Time as a Trade Barrier," Manuscript.

Krugman, Paul R. 1980. "Scale Economies, Product Differentiation, and the Pattern of Trade," *American Economic Review* 70:950-959.

Rauch, James. 1999. "Networks Versus Markets in International Trade," *Journal of International Economics* 48:7-35.

CHAPTER 3

Reforming Japan's Agricultural Policies

Yoshihisa Godo

I. Introduction

In the Uruguay Round (UR) negotiations, liberalization of rice imports was a serious problem confronting the Japanese government. Because of policies aimed at achieving self-sufficiency in rice, Japan's rice market had been principally closed to foreign countries for nearly three decades. Despite strong demand for Japan to open its rice market, Japan kept seeking ways to maintain its "self-sufficiency of rice" policy until the last moment of the UR negotiations. Considering that Japan expected to receive large benefits from the successful conclusion of the UR, its attitude on the rice market appeared somewhat incomprehensible, especially to foreigners.

Tariffication by which all existing non-tariff barriers (NTBs) were to be converted into bound duties was a key element involving market access in the Agreement on Agriculture embodied in the UR Final Act in 1994.[1] Yet, in the Agreement, Japan managed to make rice exempt from the tariffication for a six-year grace period from 1995 to 2000, by giving compensation in the form of increased "minimum access" import quotas, from 4 percent of its domestic rice consumption in 1995 to 8 percent by 2000, while the minimum access obligation under the tariffication is graduated only from 3 to 5 percent within the six-year period. In 1999, Japan changed its tactics again, resorting to "dirty tariffication" whereby they imposed an extremely high (de facto prohibitive) tariff rate on rice imports and, as of the year 2000, reduced the minimum-access rice quota to 7.6 percent of its domestic rice consumption.[2]

In this way, the current situation in the Japanese rice market is far from the original purpose of GATT/WTO objectives. Yet, with growing international pressure for free trade, it is unlikely that Japan can maintain such strong protection of rice in the long run. In this sense, a "clean tariff" system—liberalization of imports with a reasonable tariff rate that reflects the exact border price difference and can be used as the basis for subsequent reduction—will soon be demanded in future international trade negotiations.

In consideration of this background, this chapter attempts to answer the following five questions: (1) What kind of political dynamics underlie Japan's rice policy? (2) Why has the Japanese government strongly opposed opening up the rice market (in particular tariffication)? (3) What was the economic impact of the minimum-access rice imports that began in 1995? (4) What will happen in Japan's rice sector if "clean tariffication" is adopted? (5) What is the desirable agricultural policy reform for Japan?

Section II, which follows, provides an overview of Japan's rice policy from the 1960s to 1990s. Section III analyzes the political dynamics of Japanese rice policies by estimating the Producer Support Estimate (PSE), Consumer Support Estimate (CSE), and dead weight loss (DWL).[3] Section IV summarizes findings and considers ways of reforming Japan's agricultural policies.

II. Overview of Japanese Rice Policy from the 1960s to the 1990s

Political Importance of Rice

In spite of its slowly decreasing importance in the agricultural sector, rice still remains the dominant crop in Japan. In 1997, rice accounted for 41.4 percent of total agricultural land use and 38.3 percent of total crop production. Some 2.3 million farmers, 66.8 percent of the total number of farmers, are planting rice.[4] In this way, protecting rice farming is considered almost analogous to protecting farmers in general.

Throughout the postwar era, farmers have been important to politicians as a key voting group. As is the case in Korea and Taiwan, farmers in Japan tend to live in the same place from generation to generation and to interact closely. In addition, the number of registered voters per member of the House of Representatives is small in rural areas and large in urban areas. So, not only ruling parties but also opposition parties find it difficult to oppose farmers' interests.[5]

The emotional reaction of consumers to anything that damages paddy fields is another factor that supports the government's rice-protection policy.[6] Consumer tolerance of agricultural protection is common among affluent economies and Japan is certainly no exception.[7] Moreover, just as in the case of Korea, Japanese consumers often express their belief in the importance of policies pertaining to the self-sufficient production of rice. This is not only because Japanese people are concerned with food security and ecological problems,[8] but also because rice has important social and cultural significance for many Japanese (for example, see Yoshioka (1988)). Of course, consumer sympathy for rice-protection policy is not unconditional. As will be noted below, Japanese citizens, who are tolerant about the rice-protection policy as consumers, resist this protection as taxpayers if the budgetary cost becomes excessively large.[9]

Food Control Law and Food Agency

The Food Control Law, which was originally introduced in 1942, stipulated the rules of rice marketing until 1994. According to this law, the Food Agency, an extra-ministerial bureau of the Ministry of Agriculture, Forestry and Fisheries was in charge of managing all rice distribution. Before 1970, all rice except that for farmers' home consumption (including rice used as gifts to their relatives) was supposed to be purchased and resold by the Food Agency at official prices (the so-called government procurement price and government sale price).

The Food Control Law also imposed meticulous regulations on rice traders. Agricultural cooperatives and their associations were designated as monopolistic, official-rice-collecting agencies. Rice wholesalers and retailers were designated by the Food Agency or the local governors. Even retailer branch allocations and buying routes had to be approved by the Food Agency.

Rice Price Support in the 1960s

From the late 1950s through the 1960s, when the Japanese economy experienced two-digit growth rates, the most serious issue in agricultural policy was the income gap between farm households and urban-worker households. As is often the case in rapid industrialization, agriculture became the lagging sector in the economy. Accordingly, the income level of farm households fell far behind that of urban-working households. This problem reached a politically intolerable level in the late 1950s.

To counteract the increasing income gap, the government implemented a rice-price support policy. Because all rice was then procured by the Food Agency, the producer price could be increased by raising the government-procurement price. In 1960, the government employed a new rice price-determination formula called the "Production Cost Compensation Program," whereby the government-procurement price was determined so as to cover the cost of rice production for which unpaid family labor was calculated based on the wage rate in the manufacturing sector. Under this formula, the government-procurement price increased, leading to rapid rises in wages in the manufacturing sector. Because the government-sale price increased after a few years' time lag, government rice-marketing was operated at a loss. Simultaneously, the border price of rice increased sharply, resulting in an effective embargo on the importing of rice.

Implementation of New Channel of Rice Distribution and Acreage-Control Program in 1970

The national budgetary burden caused by supporting the price of rice peaked in the early 1970s. This coincided with the ending of the two-digit growth of the Japanese economy. In addition, the income disparity between farm households and urban-worker households had almost disappeared by around 1970 as a result of the government's rice-price-support policy and increased income from off-farm employment. Under these circumstances, public opinion turned against the rice policy.[10] The government was under great pressure to cut back the deficit for government rice marketing.

However, because of the farmers' strong resistance, the government could not lower the government-procurement price of rice significantly. Instead, the government launched two measures to reduce the fiscal expenditure on rice marketing. First, it allowed the official rice wholesalers to purchase rice directly from agricultural cooperatives, thus bypassing the Food Agency. This type of rice was called "voluntarily distributed" rice. This new system encouraged production of high quality rice (good tasting rice) that could not be priced adequately in the official grading system. By limiting the volume of the Food Agency's rice trade, introduction of this new channel of rice distribution helped to curb the government expenditure.

Another measure for curbing the national budgetary burden was the acreage-control program. This program can be seen as a government-led rice-production cartel. The government at first set a target acreage that should be diverted from rice planting so as to prevent an excess supply of rice. With the collaboration of agricultural cooperatives, the target acreage was allocated among all the villages in Japan.

Interestingly, this program was conducted according to the administrative guidance of the Ministry of Agriculture Forestry and Fisheries without any legal basis of written law (or legal enforcement).[11] While the Ministry gave financial support to rice farmers according to the acreage diverted from rice planting, it did not fully compensate the reduction of rice income at the microeconomic level. Yet, in the aggregate, the cartel effect of the acreage-control program contributed to the benefit of rice farmers by maintaining high rice prices (numerical evidence is provided in Section III). Thus, persuaded that acreage control was inevitable to protect the total benefit of rice farming, an overwhelming majority of farmers participated in the program. While this acreage-control program was originally introduced in 1970 as an emergency (or impermanent) countermeasure against the excess accumulation of old rice stock, it has continued until the present time. Currently, nearly one-third of the total paddy fields are diverted from rice planting based on the acreage-control program.

Replacement of the Food Control Law by the New Food Law in 1994[12]

By the early 1990s, the provisions of the Food Control Law had become so outdated and unrealistic that even authorized rice dealers were unable to observe the rules. For example, if rice retailers wanted to have a good line of brand rice, they went to a free rice market that the Food Agency did not recognize officially. Simultaneously, a large number of unauthorized rice traders entered the business without the Food Agency's approval and became popular among consumers. In this way, the Food Control Law was destined to be abrogated irrespective of the UR negotiations.

Still, the UR agreement provided a good occasion for abolition of the Food Control Law. In 1994, the same year of the formal signing of the Final Act of the UR at Marrakesh, the New Food Law was established in place of the Food Control Law. Although the government deliberately announced that the new law brought fundamental changes in rice production and the rice market, it was nothing more than ratification of the actual situation. That is, the New Food Law officially recognized the free trade of domestic rice. Yet, the existing rice-distribution system and the controllability of the Food Agency were also maintained under the New Food Law. Agricultural cooperatives retained their monopolistic position in rice collection. In addition, the new Law provided a legal basis for the acreage-control program that had been formerly conducted only according to ministerial guidance.

The UR Agreement and Japan's Rice Market Opening

In December 1991, Arthur Dunkel, the Director General of the GATT, submitted the "Dunkel Final Plan," which was the basis for the UR final agreement. According to the Dunkel draft, all NTBs had to be replaced by tariffs in 1995 and, then, the tariff rate was to be reduced by 36 percent on average with a minimum of 15 percent for individual commodities within a 6-year period from 1995 to 2000. In the case of farm products protected from imports like rice in Japan, tariffs were to be introduced in 1995, with bound tariffs equivalent to the differences between domestic and international prices. Adding to that, a minimum-access obligation was imposed, starting from 3 percent of base-year domestic consumption and rising to 5 percent within a 6-year period.

The Japanese government tried hard to maintain autarky in rice throughout the UR negotiations. This stubborn attitude put Japan in danger of failing to join the final agreement. But immediately before the time limit of the final agreement, the government changed its strategy and made maximum efforts to avoid tariffication on rice imports. Their efforts succeeded in exempting rice from tariffs in a 6-year grace period from 1995 to 2000. As compensation, Japan accepted increased minimum-access imports, starting at 4 percent of domestic consumption in 1995 and rising to 8 percent by 2000.

Japan's refusal of rice tariffication was problematic even among those sympathetic to rice protection. Since the government accepted the larger amount of minimum-access rice imports, the total imports of rice were expected to become larger than in the case of the "Dunkel Final Plan."[13] In other words, if the government really wanted to protect Japan's rice farming, they should have accepted the Dunkel plan.

The question then is why the government so tenaciously refused the tariffication of rice. A likely answer is that the real objective of the government was not to protect Japan's rice farming but to work for the benefit of the Food Agency and the related rice traders. In the case of "clean tariffication," since anyone would be able to import rice so long as they paid the tariffs, the regulatory power of the Food Agency and monopolistic power of the related rice traders would be lost. The expansion of the minimum-access rice imports would benefit the national budget also because the government receives the revenue to the extent of the mark-up on the border-rice price.

In 1999, Japan changed tactics again; it imposed tariffs on rice under the condition of charging an extremely high tariff rate on imported rice (a kind of "dirty tariffication") and curbing the total amount of minimum-access rice imports down to 7.5 percent as of 2000. This can be seen as an opportunistic attitude of the government; they feared that increasing the amount of minimum-access rice imports would depress the domestic rice price with the result that they would lose rice farmers' support for their rice policy.

III. Evaluation of Japanese Rice Policy in Terms of PSE, CSE, and DWL

Definition of PSE and CSE

In this section, the Producer Support Estimate (PSE) and Consumer Support Estimate (CSE) as well as the Dead Weight Loss (DWL) are focused on in order to evaluate the economic effects of rice-protection policies. The PSE and CSE are the indicators that the OECD adopted so as to calibrate the level of support for agriculture (OECD, 1999, pp. 18-22, 84-98). The PSE is defined as the annual monetary value of gross transfers from consumers and taxpayers to agricultural producers, arising from policy measures that support agriculture. Likewise, the CSE is defined as the annual monetary value of gross transfers to (from) consumers, arising from the policy measures. Note that, in the case of protecting farmers at the expense of consumers, CSE is negative while PSE is positive.

Model

The setup of the rice market is specified as follows:

Demand for rice: $q_d = Ap_d^{-\alpha}$

Supply of domestic rice: $q_s = B(1-\theta)p_s^{\beta}$

National budgetary price support[14]: $(p_s - p_d)\, q_s - (p_d - p_w)m = X$

Market equilibrium condition: $q_s + m = q_d$

Subsidy for participants in the acreage-control program: D

where q_d and q_s are quantities of demand and supply, respectively; p_d and p_s are consumer and producer price of rice, respectively; p_w is the world price of rice; θ is the target rate of acreage control (the ratio between the target acreage of diversion and the total acreage of paddy fields); $-\alpha$ and β are price elasticities of demand and supply, respectively; A and B are constants; x is the fiscal expenditure on domestic rice marketing; and m is the volume of rice imports. For reasons of simplicity, D *and* x are assumed to be financed by levying a direct tax on consumers (i.e., rice farmers are assumed to have no tax burden).[15] In this case, the subsidy for participants in the acreage-control program (D) is regarded as the lump-sum income transfer from consumers to rice farmers (thus, resource allocation is not affected by D). θ, x, m and D are determined by the government. p and q are determined at the market equilibrium.

Based on this model, the economic effects of the following four policies are to be analyzed;

Policy (1): fiscal expenditure on domestic rice marketing
Policy (2): subsidies to participants in the acreage-control program
Policy (3): rice-production cartel in the acreage-control program
Policy (4): rice-import prohibition

Note that Policies (1) and (2) need fiscal expenditure and that Policies (3) and (4) do not (the acreage-control program is divided into two policies according to whether fiscal expenditure arises or not). In what follows, Policies (1) and (2) are referred to as "budgetary policies" and Policies (3) and (4) are referred to as "non-budgetary policies."

In order to evaluate those policies, the following four scenarios are simulated.

Scenario 1: All of Policies (1)–(4) are employed; this is the actual case.
Scenario 2: Policies (2)–(4) are employed while Policy (1) is not (x is assumed to be zero).
Scenario 3: Policy (4) is employed while Policies (1)-(3) are not (θ, D and x are assumed to be zero).
Scenario 4: None of Policies (1)–(4) are employed; this is the case of perfect liberalization (θ and x are assumed to be zero; p_d and p_s are equivalent to the world price; m is determined endogenously as $m = Bp_w{}^{\beta} - Ap_w{}^{\alpha}$).

For Scenarios 2 and 3, the equilibrium prices (denoted by p' and p'', respectively) are given by solving the following equations for p' and p'':

$$Ap'^{-\alpha} = B(1-\theta)p'^{\beta} + m$$

$$Ap''^{-\alpha} = Bp''^{\beta} + m$$

Using these prices, producer surplus (denoted by PS) and consumer surplus (denoted by CS; normalized to zero for the case of perfect import liberalization of rice) are as follows (subscripts 1–4 denote the corresponding scenarios):

$$PS_1 = \int_0^{p_s} B(1-\theta)p^{\beta}dp$$

$$CS_1 = \int_{p_d}^{p_w} Ap^{-\alpha}dp$$

$$DWL_1 = (p_s - p_d)B(1-\beta)p_s{}^{\beta} + \int_{p_w}^{p_d} Ap^{-\alpha}dp + \int_0^{p_w} Bp^{\beta}dp -$$
$$\int_0^{p_s} B(1-\theta)p^{\beta}dp - (p_d - p_w)m$$

$$PS_2 = \int_0^{p'} B(1-\theta)p^{\beta}dp$$

$$CS_2 = \int_{p'}^{p_w} Ap^{-\alpha}dp$$

$$DWL_2 = \int_{p_w}^{p'} Ap^{-\alpha}dp + \int_0^{p_w} Bp^{\beta}dp - \int_0^{p'} B(1-\theta)p^{\beta}dp - (p'-p_w)m$$

$$PS_3 = \int_0^{p''} Bp^{\beta}dp$$

$$CS_3 = \int_{p''}^{p_w} Ap^{-\alpha}dp$$

$$DWL_3 = \int_{p_w}^{p''} Ap^{-\alpha}dp - \int_{p_w}^{p''} Bp^{\beta}dp - (p''-p_w)m$$

$$PS_4 = \int_0^{p_w} Bp^{\beta}dp$$

$CS_4 = 0$
$DWL_4 = 0$

Then, the total levels of PSE, CSE, and DWL and their breakdown among Policies (1) - (4) are given as follows:

PSE (total value)=PS_1-PS_4+D
PSE caused by Policy (1) = PS_1-PS_2
PSE caused by Policy (2) = D
PSE caused by Policy (3) = PS_2-PS_3
PSE caused by Policy (4) = PS_3-PS_4
CSE (total value)=CS_1-CS_4 -x -D
CSE caused by Policy (1) = CS_1 -CS_2 -x
CSE caused by Policy (2) = -D
CSE caused by Policy (3) = CS_2 -CS_3
CSE caused by Policy (4) = CS_3-CS_4
DWL (total value)=DWL_1
DWL caused by Policy (1) = DWL_1 -DWL_2
DWL caused by Policy (2) = 0
DWL caused by Policy (3) = DWL_2 -DWL_3
DWL caused by Policy (4) = DWL_3

Besides the absolute levels of PSE, CSE and DWL, their ratios to the total value of rice production or consumption (defined as "PSE ratio," "CSE ratio" and "DWL ratio") are estimated by the following equations:

PSE ratio = PSE/$p_s q_s$
CSE ratio = CSE/$p_s(q_s+m)$
DWL ratio = DWL/$p_s(q_s+m)$

Data

PSE, CSE, and DWL are estimated for all the years between 1960-97 except for 1993, the record-breaking lean year for rice.[16]

α and β are assumed to be 0.2 and 0.4, respectively.[17] The total volume of domestic rice production (q_s), producer's price of rice (p_s),[18] subsidies to participants in acreage control program (D), the target rate of acreage control (θ), the fiscal expenditure for government rice marketing (x), and the total volume of rice imports (m) are available from various publications of the Ministry of Agriculture, Forestry and Fisheries.[19]

The cif price of U.S. rice is estimated as the world price (pw). The average fob price of the U.S. rice is taken from the FAO *Trade Yearbook*. In order to convert the fob price to the cif price, the fob price is multiplied by 1.601, which is derived from the Godo and Owens (1998) case study of the costs of imported rice.

There are two points to be noted about the estimates of the world price (p_w). First, my estimates of the world price may have a bias toward underestimation because low quality rice is included in the *FAO Trade Yearbook*. Second, the world price in 1973-75 was abnormally high because of the worldwide food crisis (figure 1). So, in looking at the estimates of PSE, CSE, and DWL, these three years should be regarded as exceptional.

The values of A, B and p_d are calculated from the following equations:

$$A = \frac{q_s + m}{p_s^{-\alpha}}$$

$$B = \frac{q_s}{(1-\theta)p_s^{\beta}}$$

$$p_d = \frac{(p_w - p_s)m - x}{q_s + m} + p_s$$

Estimation Results of PSE, CSE, and DWL

The results of estimates are shown in figures 2-7. The major findings can be summarized as follows:

1. The PSE, CSE, and DWL ratios are substantial. As of 1997, they were 0.8, -1.0, and 0.3, respectively. These figures imply that Japanese rice production and marketing are strongly influenced by the government in the direction of favoring rice farmers at the expense of consumers and involve a major loss in economic welfare.
2. While the absolute values of the PSE, the PSE ratio, the CSE, and the CSE ratio reached their peaks by the 1980s, the DWL and DWL ratio remained on an upward trend until 1994. This implies that, before 1995, rice policy became less and less efficient even from the viewpoint of rice-income protection. In contrast, the absolute values of these six indicators started decreasing in 1995, corresponding to the beginning of the minimum-access rice imports. Details of the economic effects of minimum-

Figure 1. Comparison of Rice Price

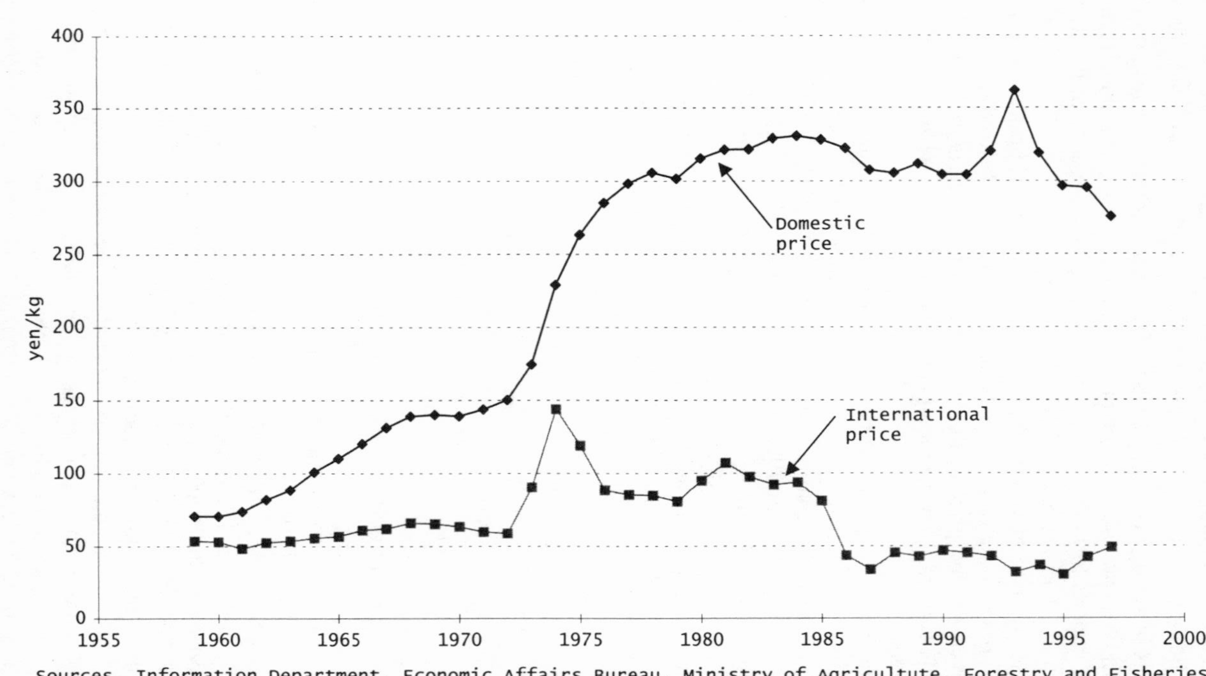

Sources. Information Department, Economic Affairs Bureau, Ministry of Agricultute, Forestry and Fisheries; and Owens (1998); and *FAO Trade Yearbook*.

Figure 2. PSE*

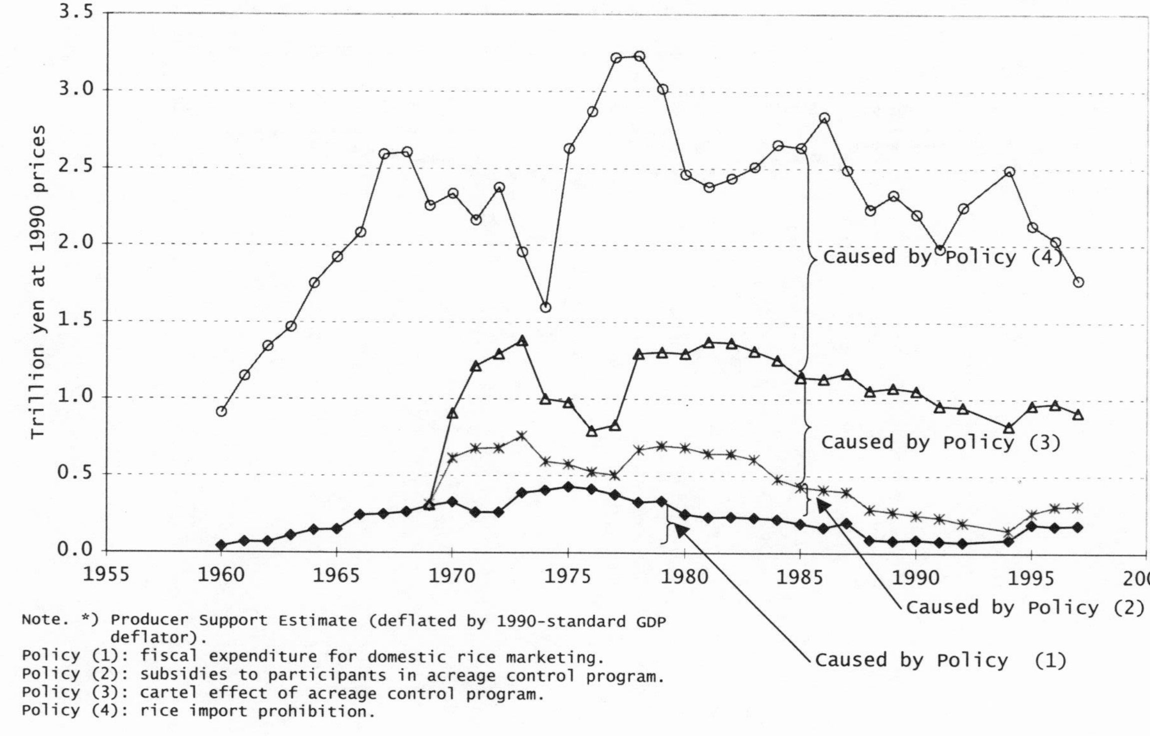

Note. *) Producer Support Estimate (deflated by 1990-standard GDP deflator).

Policy (1): fiscal expenditure for domestic rice marketing.
Policy (2): subsidies to participants in acreage control program.
Policy (3): cartel effect of acreage control program.
Policy (4): rice import prohibition.

Figure 3. PSE Ratio*

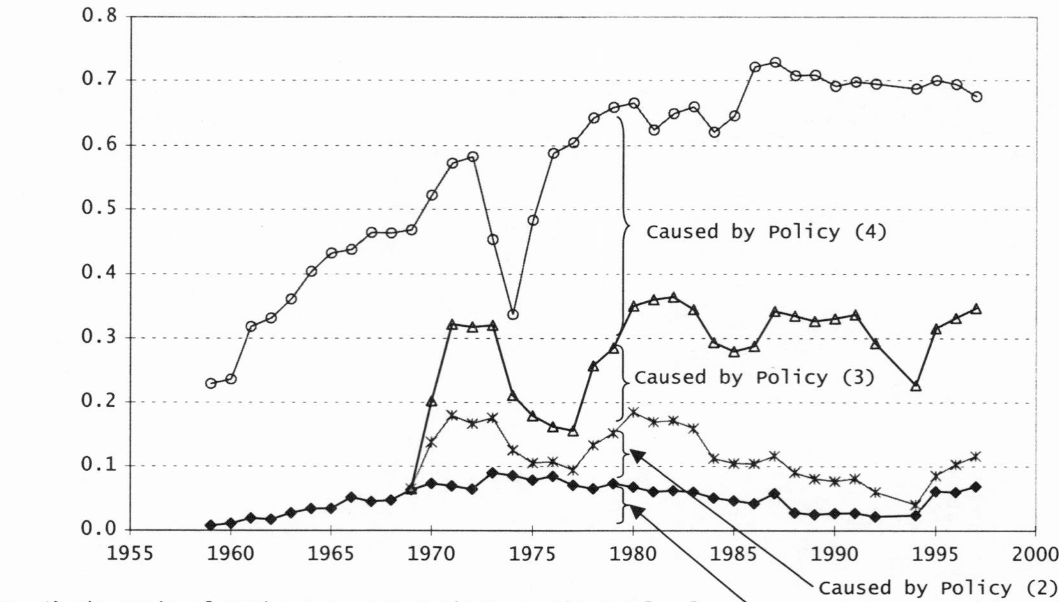

Note. *) The ratio of Producer Support Estimate to the total value of rice production.
Policy (1): fiscal expenditure for domestic rice marketing.
Policy (2): subsidies for participants in acreage control program.
Policy (3): cartel effect of acreage control program.
Policy (4): rice import prohibition.

Figure 4. CSE*

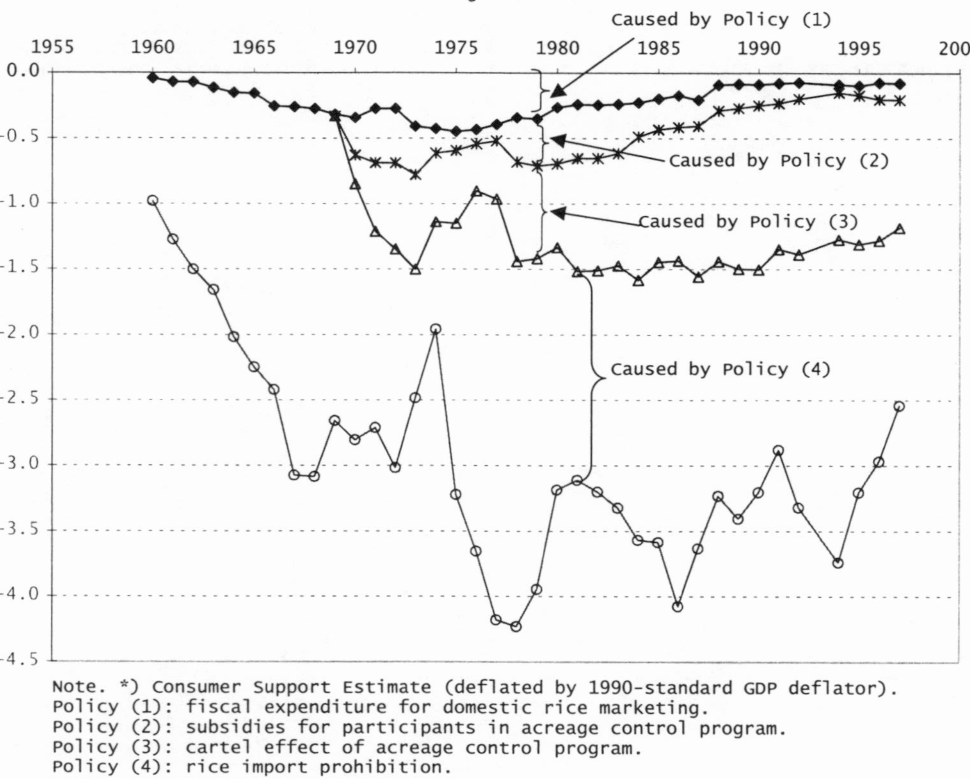

Note. *) Consumer Support Estimate (deflated by 1990-standard GDP deflator).
Policy (1): fiscal expenditure for domestic rice marketing.
Policy (2): subsidies for participants in acreage control program.
Policy (3): cartel effect of acreage control program.
Policy (4): rice import prohibition.

Figure 5. CSE ratio*

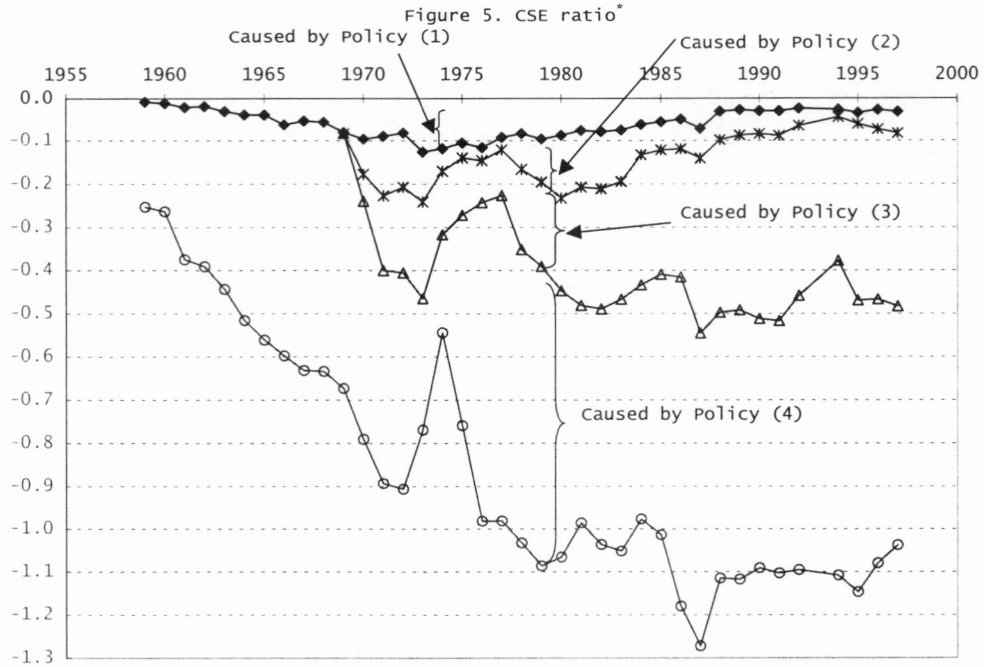

Note. *) The ratio of Consumer Support Estimate to the total value of rice consumption.
Policy (1): fiscal expenditure for domestic rice marketing.
Policy (2): subsidies to participants in acreage control program.
Policy (3): cartel effect of acreage control program.
Policy (4): rice import prohibition.

Figure 6. DWL*

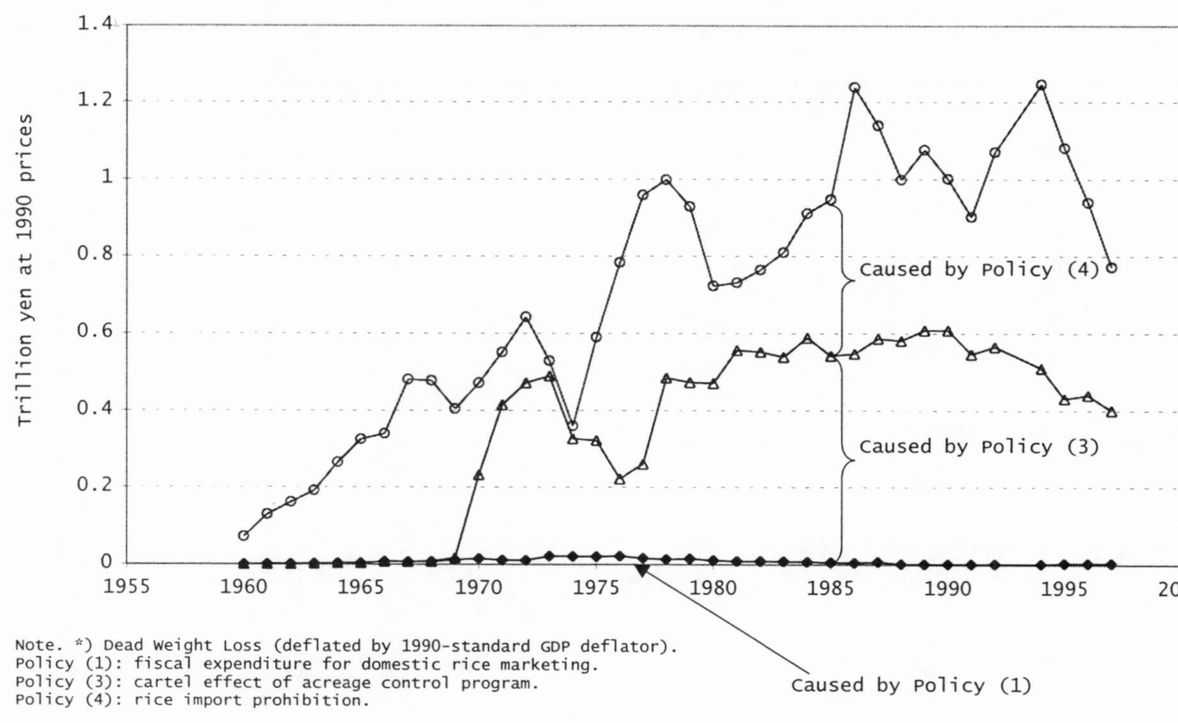

Note. *) Dead Weight Loss (deflated by 1990-standard GDP deflator).
Policy (1): fiscal expenditure for domestic rice marketing.
Policy (3): cartel effect of acreage control program.
Policy (4): rice import prohibition.

Figure 7. DWL Ratio*

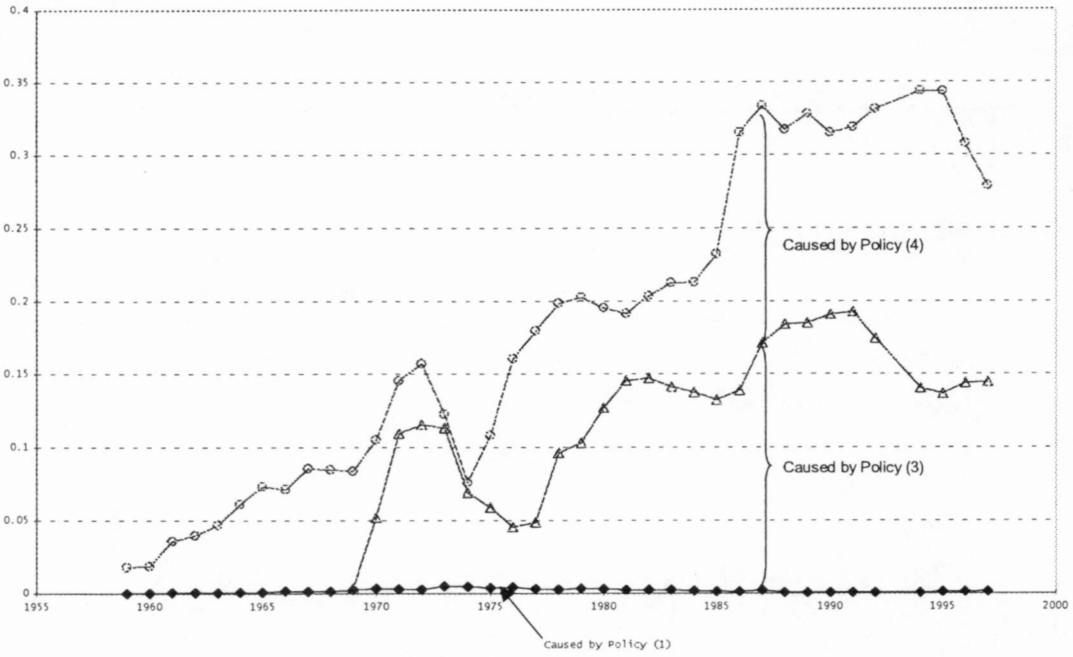

Note. *) The ratio of Dead Weight Loss to the total value of rice consumption.
Policy (1): fiscal expenditure for domestic rice marketing.
Policy (3): cartel effect of acreage control program.
Policy (4): rice import prohibition.

access rice imports are examined in table 1, in which the hypothetical situation of rice-import prohibition for 1995-97 is simulated by setting the value of m to zero). In this sense, the UR agreement relieved the Japanese economy overall from the heavy distortion caused by traditional rice-protection policies.

3. Non-budgetary policies (Policies (3) and (4)) play the predominant roles in the six indicators. Policies (3) and (4) look almost the same in figures 2-7. But considering the possibility that our international rice-price is underestimated, the cartel effect of the acreage-control program should be seen as having the greatest impact on income distribution and economic efficiency. It is especially noteworthy that budgetary policies (Policies (1) and (2)) that often receive popular attention account for only negligible effects in figures 2-7.

In retrospect, Japanese citizens as well as the mass media have seldom recognized and criticized the cartel effect of the acreage-control program while they have repeatedly attacked the fiscal deficit of government rice marketing. This is an interesting contrast with our finding that the economic effect of the acreage-control program is much larger than that of the fiscal deficit of government rice marketing. This suggests that the less visible a political measure is, the less likely it is to confront political resistance. In other words, non-budgetary policies, which do not hurt the national treasury directly, can escape consumer opposition even if those policies impose heavy *real economic* burdens on consumers.

In the context of the international trade negotiations, it should be noted that "clean tariffication" can undermine the price-support effects of the acreage-control program and import prohibition. Once the government tariffies rice imports *cleanly*, the border-to-domestic price gap will continuously decrease according to the sequential reduction of tariff rates. Moreover, since the price elasticity of demand for domestic rice becomes infinite under *clean* tariffication, the cartel effect of the acreage-control program will be nullified. The government would therefore not be able to protect rice income further without expense to the national treasury. This may be the real reason why the Japanese government was so opposed to the Dunkel draft in the UR.

IV. Conclusion

While the original purpose of the Japanese rice protection policy was to reduce the rural-urban income gap that grew sharply during the rapid industrialization of the 1950s, it continued even after the average income of farm households exceeded that of their urban counterparts because of the strong political power of farmers.

Generally speaking, Japanese consumers (and other political groups) have been tolerant about rice-protection policy unless it involved a large budget cost. Using this consumer tolerance, farmers have succeeded in having the government support their income mainly by non-budgetary policies such as the

Table 1. Economic Effects of Rice Imports

	Domestic Rice Production	Foreign Rice Imported[a]	Rice Price[b]	PSE[c]	CSE[d]	DEL[e]	
	.... thousand ton	....	yen/kg	....	trillion yen	....	
1995	10,724	401	296	2.3	-3.4	1.1	Actual Case
1996	10,328	466	295	2.2	-3.1	1.0	
1997	10,004	544	275	2.0	-2.7	0.8	
1995	10,933	0	311	2.4	-3.6	1.2	The Case of Rice Import Prohibition[f]
1996	10,576	0	313	2.4	-3.4	1.1	
1997	10,294	0	296	2.2	-3.0	0.9	

Note. a. Imported as quota of the minimum access.
b. Producer's price.
c. Producer Support Estimate.
d. Consumer Support Estimate.
e. Dead Weight Loss.
f. Simulated by the author.

acreage-control program and import prohibition. In other words, farmers have enjoyed large benefits by charging invisible bills to consumers. The Food Agency and agricultural cooperatives also have utilized the political power of rice farmers to avoid the pressure to downsize their office and employment. This kind of "logrolling" is detrimental to the efficiency and fairness of the Japanese economy overall.

It should be noted that the "clean tariffication" that the WTO authorities have advocated can undermine the rice-income-support effect of these non-budgetary policies. In particular, the "cartel effect" of the acreage-control program would be totally nullified under "clean tariffication." The next round of the WTO negotiations can therefore be seen as the prime opportunity to undermine Japan's traditional political dynamics that underlie its rice-protection policy.

Notes

[1] For details, see International Agricultural Trade Research Consortium (1994).

[2] In 1999, Japan set a specific tariff on rice imports of 351.17 yen per kilogram. This tariff was so high that only a negligible volume of rice was imported beyond the minimum-access quota in 1999. Yet, it should be noted that Japan is not a special case of "dirty tariffication." Many other importing countries employ similarly high "dirty" tariffs on foreign farm products (see, Josling, Tangerman, and Warley, 1996).

[3] Previously, PSE and CSE have been used as the abbreviations of "Producer Subsidy Equivalent" and "Consumer Subsidy Equivalent," respectively. In order to reflect as closely as possible the underlying definitions, it was agreed in 1998 to replace "Subsidy Equivalent" by "Support Estimate" as the names of indicators (OECD, 1999, p.18).

[4] These figures are taken from the 1995 Agricultural Census.

[5] For example, the Japanese Diet adopted unanimous resolutions requiring the government to firmly maintain rice-import prohibitions three times in the 1980s.

[6] A symbolic example is Prime Minister Hosokawa's special press remark on December 15, 1993, at the conclusion of the UR final agreement. Confronting a disquieting political atmosphere, Mr. Hosokawa offered a public apology for his government's failure in maintaining the rice-import prohibition.

[7] It should be noted that consumer tolerance of agricultural protection applies in a variety of circumstances. For example, in the prewar period when the international competitive power of the Japanese manufacturing sector was still weak and dependent largely on cheap labor, any increase in the rice price created severe political pressures. More precise international comparisons about consumer tolerance of agricultural protection policies are given in Hayami (1988) and Honma and Hayami (1986).

[8] Paddy fields in Japan are widely believed to have many ecological benefits such as prevention of floods and soil erosion.

[9] Other political opposition to expenditure on rice policies comes from Ministries other than the Ministry of Agriculture, Forestry and Fisheries. Since those Ministries compete with each other for acquiring budgets from the national treasury, they are intolerant of lavishing money on rice policy.

[10] So-called "3Ks" that hurt the national treasury (3K indicates *Kome* (rice), *Kokutetsu* (national railway), and *Kempo* (national health insurance) were among the most significant issues in the political debates in the 1970s.

[11] As described in the following section, the acreage-control program was written into law in 1994.

[12] The New Food Law was established on December 14, 1994 and became fully effective on November 1, 1995. This section draws on Morita's (1996) study of the New Food Law.

[13] The economic effects of Japan's postponement of tariffication on rice were examined in Hayami and Godo (1998) by means of a simple simulation analysis.

[14] There is no explicit rule about how the revenue from minimum-access rice imports should be used. For reasons of convenience, the revenue is assumed here to be used for domestic rice-price support. Because the total amount of rice imports is very limited so far, this assumption is not critical in the simulation to be done.

[15] Because the Japanese tax system is favorable to farmers, their tax burden is significantly low compared with other types of households (See Ito, 1992, p. 153).

[16] The rice crop was severely affected by adverse weather condition in 1993. While the Food Agency procured 2.6 million tons of foreign rice as emergency imports in 1993-94, consumer confusion was not resolved until the next rice harvesting started in the fall of 1994.

[17] The values of parameters α and β are the same as in Hayami and Godo (1998).

[18] Strictly speaking, p_s is calculated by taking the ratio of the total value of domestic rice production to the total tonnage of domestic rice production (q_s).

[19] The total volume of rice imports (m) is actually zero before 1995.

References

Godo, Y. and L. Owens. 1998. "An Estimation of the Border Price Ratio of Rice in Japan," *The Papers and Proceedings of Economics* (Tokyo: Society of Economics, Meiji Gakuin University).

Hayami, Y. and Y. Godo. 1995. "Economics and Politics of Rice Policy in Japan: A Perspective on the Uruguay Round," in T. Ito and A. Krueger (eds.) *Regionalism versus Multilateral Trade Arrangements*. Chicago: University of Chicago Press.

Hayami, Y. and S. Yamada. 1991. *The Agricultural Development of Japan: A Century's Perspective*. Tokyo: University of Tokyo Press.

Hayami, Y. 1988. *Japanese Agriculture Under Siege: The Political Economy of Agricultural Policies*. London: Macmillan Press.

Honma, M. and Y. Hayami. 1986. "Structure of Agricultural Protection in Industrial Countries," *Journal of International Economics* 20.

International Agricultural Trade Research Consortium. 1994. "The Uruguay Round Agreement on Agriculture: An Evaluation," IATRC Commissioned Paper No 9. St. Paul: University of Minnesota, International Agricultural Trade Research Consortium.

Ito, T. 1992. *The Japanese Economy*. Cambridge: MIT Press.

Josling, T. E., S. Tangerman, and T. K. Warley. 1996. *Agriculture in the GATT.* London: Macmillan Press.

Morita, A. 1996. *New Rice Distribution System and its Effects on Agricultural Protection and Agricultural Cooperatives' Activities.* Tokyo: Nokyo Kyosai Research Institute (in Japanese).

OECD. 1999. *Agricultural Policies in OECD Countries.* Paris: OECD.

Yoshioka, Y. 1988. *Food and Agriculture in Japan.* Tokyo: Foreign Press Center/Japan.

Comment

Will Martin

Godo has given us a very useful paper on Japan's agricultural policies. It contributes to our understanding in three important dimensions: its insights into policy choices in Japan; interpretation of the interaction of Japanese policy preferences with WTO rules; and quantification of the effects of Japan's rice policies.

Explaining Rice Policy Choices in Japan

The discussion of protection policies for rice in Japan focuses strongly on the interest-group model of trade-policy determination. It explains the extraordinary power of rice interests in Japan as deriving in large measure from the strength of community in rice-growing areas, the sympathy for rice producers amongst the urban population, and the policy framework for agricultural policies. The fact that rice production in Japan is an import-competing activity is also seen to be important, given the strong resistance to large budget transfers to the agricultural sector. The ability to use land-area controls was clearly also important in raising prices without budget transfers, although it would be useful to the reader to know what uses have been permitted on the one-third of rice land withdrawn from rice production. Godo also emphasizes the importance of the income gap between rice farmers and urban workers in the 1960s in strengthening support for protection, and the implications of the cost-of-production approach to rice pricing introduced in the 1960s.

To the factors identified in the paper as contributing to agricultural protection, I would add confusion between self-sufficiency and food security. As Sen (1981) has demonstrated, food self-sufficiency is neither necessary nor sufficient for food security at the household level. Lack of food security is essentially a problem of poverty, to which increases in food prices resulting from protection are unlikely to be a useful response, and may be very harmful.

While I agree wholeheartedly with Godo's analysis of the determinants of rice-market protection, it could usefully be placed in a longer-run context. Anderson, Hayami, and Honma (1986) trace the interplay of these forces in Japan back to the opening of the twentieth century and compare them with similar developments in Korea and in Taiwan, China. While protection to rice in Japan was low at the turn of the century, it increased sharply during the interwar period, as is evident in my figure 1. The nominal rate of protection to rice reached 84 percent by 1938. Unfortunately, this rate of protection was exceeded by the early 1960s, as protection rates for rice began their astounding

Figure 1. Nominal Rates of Protection to Rice at the Farm Level

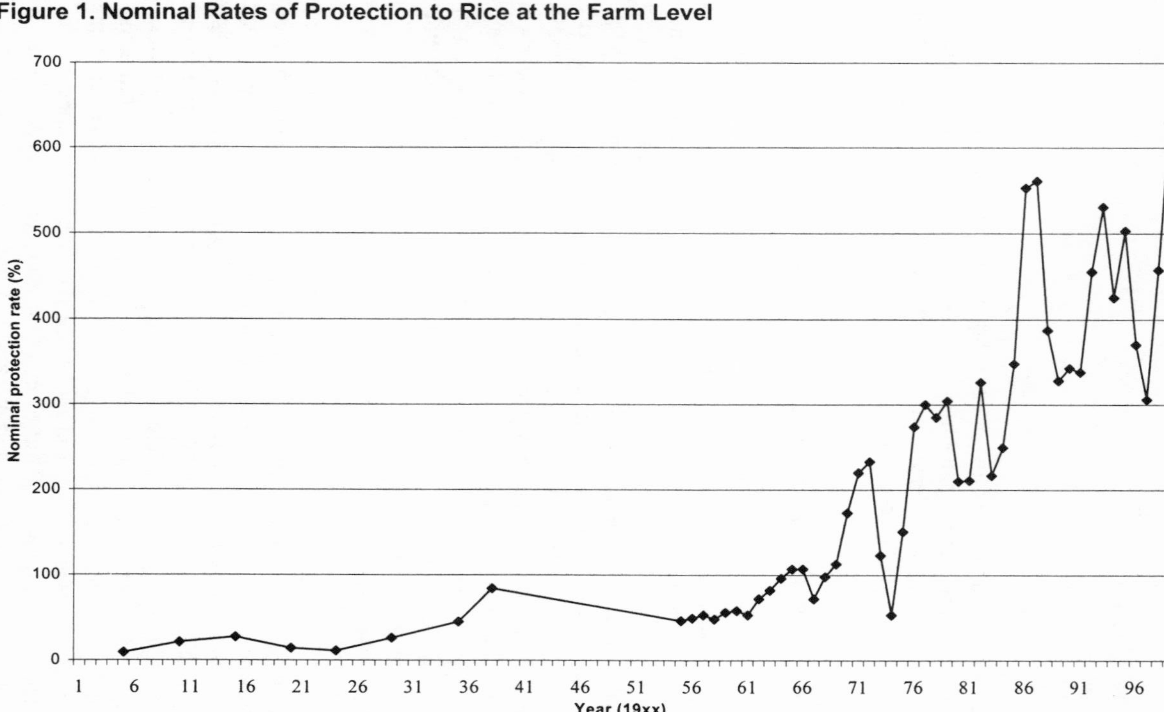

Sources: Anderson, Hayami and Honma (1986) to 1982; OECD (1999) for subsequent years

increases. The constraints on increases to rice protection imposed by budget pressures in the early 1970s, proved to have only a minor effect, as area-reduction constraints were brought into play to increase the gap between domestic and world prices. Nor, unfortunately, does the Uruguay Round Agreement appear to have tamed the forces of agricultural protectionism. While border protection fell in 1996 and 1997, the OECD estimates suggest it rose to the unprecedented level of 630 percent in 1999.

The importance that Godo attaches to the cost-of-production approach to increasing protection resonates strongly with the unrealistic outcomes created by parity-pricing approaches in the United States (Tomek and Robinson, 1981, p. 282). The large distortions created by the cost-of-production for home-market prices in Australia during the 1950s and 1960s (Williams, 1990) also highlight the consequences of using these approaches. While cost-of-production pricing is politically popular, allowing images of *fair* prices to be evoked, it is virtually always misleading—partly because of capture of the calculation methods by vested interests[1] and partly because of the difficulties[2] involved in capturing cost-reducing technical change. Given the relatively rapid rates of technical change in agriculture (Martin and Mitra, 2000), cost-of-production prices for agricultural products quite rapidly become detached from reality.

The Uruguay Round and Japan's Rice Policy

Godo's discussion of Japan's policy choices in the Uruguay Round is extremely interesting. It is clear that Japan paid dearly in the negotiations to establish the Special Treatment policy for rice. Within the sector, it had to accept minimum market access levels of 8 percent instead of the 5 percent that would have been required under the regular rules. Godo suggests that Japan may have accepted this as the price of retaining its state-trading arrangements for agriculture. However, this should not have been necessary. GATT rules on state trading clearly envisage the possibility of having both tariff bindings and state-trading enterprises. Article II of GATT requires that the mark-up charged by state-trading enterprises not, on average, exceed the tariff binding in this situation. Certainly, China has been permitted to retain state trading for agricultural commodities within a trade regime of complete tariffication. It seems more likely that the real goal was the explicitly-stated one of maintaining self-sufficiency.

One other important point that might be made about Japan's agricultural policies and the Uruguay Round is that Japan was willing to make serious commitments on a wide range of the commodities where it converted its non-tariff barriers into tariffs. Hathaway and Ingco (1996) point to commitments on wheat, sugar and dairy products that require substantial reductions in protection from the very high levels prevailing prior to the Uruguay Round. Perhaps these large reductions were part of the beneficial "price" paid for refusing to convert rice protection to tariffs.

Quantifying the Costs of Japan's Rice Policies

The attempt to measure the costs of Japan's rice market policies is an important contribution. However, I have some concerns that relate to the use of *ad hoc* demand and supply curves. This approach has a number of problems. One is that it introduces enormous complexity through the need for integral measures of welfare change. Another is that it does not allow adequate treatment of the welfare effects of land-withdrawal policies. Instead, land withdrawal has been treated as creating a horizontal shift in the supply curve for rice.

The approach of specifying land-area control as creating a leftward shift in an *ad hoc* supply curve seems likely to overstate the costs of this program. It implies that land and other inputs are withdrawn from rice production in fixed proportions, and wasted, or that technological regression requires more of all inputs to produce the same amount of rice. This source of overstatement may be balanced, to some degree, by the use of a very low supply elasticity (0.4). The persistence of measures such as supply control imparts a strong downward bias to the estimates of the supply elasticity for rice on which this selection was based. In the long run, it seems likely that the supply elasticity for an individual crop would be much larger than this, given the long-run possibilities for substitution with other crops.

A better approach to specifying land-area reduction could use dual functional forms of the type suggested by Martin and Alston (1994). This approach greatly simplifies the calculation of welfare change by working from the underlying consumer expenditure and producer-profit functions. It also readily allows land to be treated more appopriately as an input that substitutes for other inputs such as labor and fertilizer. Further, it allows the costs of land withdrawal to be specified in terms of the increased cost of rice production as non-land inputs are substituted for land and the costs in depressed returns to the land taken out of rice production. Only if these two vitally important features of the regime are captured will it be possible to adequately measure the costs of the regime.

Conclusions

Godo's paper provides an extremely valuable contribution to the literature on agricultural policies in Japan. His description of the mechanics of Japan's agricultural policies is extremely useful, and he artfully uses modern theories of interest groups to explain the policy choices made. The discussion of the interaction between policy choices and the Uruguay Round negotiations is also very illuminating. The attempt to measure the costs of rice market interventions is a valuable contribution, but needs further development if it is to provide unbiased estimates of these costs.

Notes

[1] Some of the cost-of-production formulas used for wheat in Australia included the price of land, making the calculation completely circular. Each increase in the price of wheat raised the residual return to land, requiring a further increase in the cost-of-production price.

[2] Even if it were possible to capture adequately the effects of technical change, it seems unlikely that the interest groups involved would want to do so.

References

Anderson, K., Y. Hayami, and M. Honma. 1986. "The Growth of Agricultural Protection," in K. Anderson and Y. Hayami (eds.), *The Political Economy of Agricultural Protection*. Sydney: Allen and Unwin.

Hathaway, D. and M. Ingco. 1996. "Agricultural Liberalization and the Uruguay Round," in W. Martin and L. A. Winters (eds.), *The Uruguay Round and the Developing Countries*. Cambridge: Cambridge University Press

Martin, W. and D. Mitra. 2000. "Productivity Growth and Convergence in Agriculture and Manufacturing," *Economic Development and Cultural Change*, forthcoming.

Martin, W. and J. Alston. 1994. "A Dual Approach to Evaluating Research Benefits in the Presence of Trade Distortions," *American Journal of Agricultural Economics* 76:26-35.

OECD. 1999. *Agricultural Policies in OECD Countries: Monitoring and Evaluation, 1999*. Organization for Economic Cooperation and Development, Paris (and worksheets for 2000).

Sen, A. 1981. *Poverty and Famines: An Essay on Entitlement and Deprivation*. New York: Oxford University Press.

Tomek, W. and K. Robinson. 1981. *Agricultural Product Prices*, 2nd edn. Ithaca: Cornell University Press.

Williams, D. B. 1990. *Agriculture in the Australian Economy*, 3rd edn. Sydney: Sydney University Press.

Comment

Sadao Nagaoka

Yoshihisa Godo has provided us with an excellent political economy perspective on the historical development of the Japanese agricultural protection as well as an informative analytical assessment of its economic consequences. My comments cover both aspects of the paper.

I have two comments on the historical part:

The reader might wonder why "dirty" tariffication was possible, without violating the Uruguay Round (UR) Agriculture Agreement. The Agreement in fact stipulates that the price comparison for deriving the tariff equivalent of the protection should be based on a representative domestic wholesale price and the actual average import price (see articles 2 and 4 of the Attachment to Annex 5 of the Agreement on Agriculture). Since the Japanese consumption and production pattern of rice is highly skewed toward high-quality rice, such price comparison led to a prohibitive tariff rate that consists of both a quality premium and a genuine tariff equivalent. As a result, the reduction of the tariff rate by 15% according to the UR formula in the past six years has not yet made rice import possible.

I agree with Godo that Japanese consumers have been tolerant of agricultural protection, and that they are strongly concerned with food security. However, I am not sure whether they are specifically concerned about maintaining paddy fields or self-sufficiency of rice per se. As Godo says, urban non-farm workers have a strong sense of inequality, since urban farmers often earn higher income than themselves and are wealthier too due to their holdings of land with high value. Thus, the liberalization of the rice market does not seem to be a politically impossible thing to do.

As for the analytical part, I have the following three comments:

In my view, Godo may significantly underestimate the economic cost of the restriction of international trade due to the assumed low domestic supply elasticity of rice. The supply elasticity of 0.4 implies that even if the domestic price of rice becomes one quarter of the current level, its domestic supply level would still exceed half of the current level. As an elasticity of a single commodity, such supply response seems to be artificially low.

I agree with the Will Martin that Godo probably significantly overestimates the effects of the acreage-control program upon the size of the dead weight loss. Godo assumes that this program in Japan caused the proportional leftward-shift of the supply curve. Anecdotal evidence suggests, however, that acreage control has been concentrated on those lands that have better alternative uses, as would be expected when such a program is voluntarily enforced.

In particular, those farmers, who own lands that are singularly suited to rice cultivation, have often chosen not to participate in the program. In addition, those farmers who have participated in the program have often chosen those lands that are suitable for the cultivation of alternative farm products such as vegetables for the lands subject to cutting back from rice cultivation.

On the other hand, in my view, Godo overstates the welfare impact of the minimum access commitments of the UR. Although there has been a significant reduction of the dead weight loss since 1995, it has been primarily due to the large depreciation of the yen from 1994 to 1997, which has reduced the domestic and international price differentials of rice, but not due to the implementation of the minimum-access commitments. In fact, the entire movement of the dead weight loss since 1985 has been significantly determined by the large real exchange rate changes of the yen, but not by the changes in trade-policy instruments. On the other hand, foreign rice aid has accounted for the largest part of the use of the rice imported under the minimum-access commitments. Thus, Godo's assumption that such imports have been domestically used clearly results in the overestimation of the welfare improvement due to the UR Agreement.

Finally, I strongly support Godo's conclusion that clean tariffication is essential not only in reducing trade distortions but also in nullifying the effects of restrictive domestic policy and thus in promoting its reform. One of the central parts of such domestic reform would be to establish a temporary income-support program targeted to severely affected farmers. The tariff revenue would be able to contribute significantly to covering the fiscal cost of such a program, given the large domestic and international price differentials of rice.

CHAPTER 4

Tariffication in Services

Alan V. Deardorff

I. Introduction

The negotiators of the Uruguay Round are to be congratulated for bringing services into the multilateral framework of international trade-policy discipline. This framework, embodied in the WTO, includes trade in services within the General Agreement on Trade in Services (GATS). However, with the benefit of hindsight, it seems to me that they made a serious mistake in the way they designed that framework. Knowing full well that the countries who are members of the WTO would be unwilling to open all services markets fully and immediately, they left it up to the member countries to decide which categories of services would become subject to the discipline of the GATS. But once a country has selected a category of services, the GATS then requires that trade in those services satisfy the requirement of "National Treatment."

The result has been that even the most trade-liberal members of the WTO have accepted this discipline in only a limited number of sectors and modes of supply. Quite naturally, as documented by Hoekman (1996), all countries elected to liberalize only in those service activities where they knew that it would make little difference. These tend to be sectors in which either there is no domestic industry to protect, or in which domestic producers are so clearly dominant that they have no fear of competition from foreign firms. Nor has there been meaningful progress in the years since the WTO went into effect in getting countries to add new service activities to their lists. I will argue (and have argued before—see Deardorff (1994)) that this result was in retrospect inevitable due to the requirement of National Treatment, and that what the GATS should have required instead was only Most Favored Nation (MFN) treatment. To make this meaningful and workable, GATS should have permitted—indeed encouraged—countries to erect new barriers to imports of services that would approximate as closely as possible the tariffs that they continue to have in abundance on imports of goods.

I will call this process the same name, "tariffication," that has been used for what was done in the Uruguay Round for trade in agricultural products. There, starting with a plethora of mechanisms to protect domestic farmers that included tariffs as only one among many policies, countries were persuaded to convert all other barriers to tariffs. The object was to find tariffs that would be no higher than previous trade barriers in the levels of protection that they provided and/or their effects on trade. But in fact, this requirement of tariffication equivalence was hardly honored, and the resulting tariffs protected many sectors far more than the previous arrangements. Nonetheless, tariffication in agriculture can be viewed as a success, for the reason that it turned nontariff barriers into a form of policy that could more easily be understood, quantified, and compared across products and countries. The resulting tariffs can now provide a more useful starting point for future negotiations to bring them down. This is the outcome that I am recommending for trade in services.

My specific proposal is as follows:

Proposal: The terms of the GATS should be re-negotiated to permit countries to comply if they provide MFN treatment of all foreign service providers, not necessarily National Treatment. That is, they would be free to levy taxes on foreign service providers that are different from, and higher than, any taxes that they apply to domestic providers. These taxes must be nondiscriminatory among foreign service providers, being no higher against providers from one WTO member country than from any other. The taxes may be introduced or increased as an explicit part of the process of bringing a designated service sector under GATS discipline. They may be levied on the entire sales of a foreign service provider within a country, and they may be different for different service products so long as the product definitions themselves do not discriminate among national providers. In cases where "sales" is not an appropriate measure of service imports, the taxes can be defined on some other basis, so long as, again, that basis does not implicitly discriminate.

That is the full extent of my proposal. However, the real motivation is not mentioned in it, which is to facilitate the reduction of service barriers over time. Once enough countries have followed this procedure, it should become natural for future rounds of trade negotiation to deal with these taxes on foreign service providers—which I will henceforth call "service tariffs" for simplicity—along with their negotiations on reductions of tariffs on goods. I would therefore hope and expect that this change would lead not only to a considerable increase in the number of service sectors brought under the discipline of the GATS, but also that the barriers themselves would then shrink over time, just as tariffs on goods have been negotiated downwards over the past half century.[1]

In the remainder of this chapter, I will elaborate on this proposal in several ways. In section II, I will extend the arguments in its favor a bit beyond what I have said so far. Then in section III, I will examine what it would mean in economic terms for countries to use taxes on foreign service providers. Since services encompass a diverse set of activities, this will require more than one model. I will first examine a model of services that are produced entirely from inputs that originate outside the importing country—what I will call "remote services." Markets for these, it turns out, behave exactly like goods. Second, I will look at what I will call "on site" services, which are ones that require that some inputs be purchased domestically within the importing country.

The concerns in both cases are: (1) is it really feasible to tax foreign service providers; (2) will the effects of such taxation be analogous to the effects of tariffs; and (3) is it true for services, as it is for goods, that limited trade is better than no trade at all for the importing country? The last of these questions is not as critical as it may sound to the case for my proposal, since the real objective is not just to achieve limited trade in services. Rather, even if it were the case (although we shall see that it is not) that restricted trade in services may be worse than no trade at all, I would still favor permitting it to occur. For I believe that having some trade in place, even if severely limited and even if it is welfare worsening, is desirable from the standpoint of ultimately reducing the barriers to trade.

II. Arguments for Tariffication of Services

Much of the case for tariffication of services, like the case for liberalizing trade in services at all, arises from analogy with trade in goods. After all, we have had long experience, under the GATT, with trade in goods and the effects of reducing tariffs. Much of the theoretical case for doing so has been understood since the time of Ricardo. But the practical case has surely been strengthened by the last half century of trade liberalization in developed countries and, eventually, developing countries as well. As economists we have always known that cutting trade barriers was a positive sum game, but also that it was a game with clear losers. We could not know in advance whether the losers from trade liberalization would have their losses accumulate and their opposition grow as liberalization proceeded, ultimately bringing the process to a halt. Indeed, at several times during the last fifty years, it has looked like that might be happening, most obviously in the early 1980s when the strains of trade were exacerbated by recession, debt crises, and exchange appreciation in the United States, and again in recent months as concerns about "globalization" have attracted whole new groups of opponents of free trade. Nonetheless, the overall lesson of these last fifty years seems clearly to be that an ever-larger portion of the world has come to accept that it is better off with freer trade in goods than without, and the GATT-sponsored process for moving in that direction has been broadly successful. Therefore, a premise of much that I will say below is that the GATS should try to achieve, for services, the same sorts of liberalization that the GATT has achieved for goods.

National Treatment

From that perspective, it is immediately peculiar that the drafters of the GATS should have enshrined National Treatment, not just as the ultimate goal towards which negotiations might be directed, but as the immediate criterion for compliance. After all, in the context of trade in goods, true National Treatment must mean perfectly free trade. That is, if we treat foreign sellers of goods the same as we treat national sellers, then we will not tax imports at all. And yet, the GATT has *never* required that tariffs be zero on any category of trade, except for trade within a preferential trading arrangement that is actually an exception to the GATT rules, rather than a prototype for them.

Of course, free trade is presumably the goal toward which the entire GATT is dedicated, and the purpose of its tariff bindings, together with the requirement that any tariff reductions be done on an MFN basis, was exactly to ratchet the world economy in the direction of free trade. But no one ever suggested, to my knowledge, that the world move immediately to free trade in goods. Why anyone would then think that free trade in services would be achievable in one step is therefore a mystery to me.

I have heard it suggested that my interpretation of National Treatment here is too restrictive. Perhaps National Treatment was never intended to apply at the border, but only to sellers once they were inside a country. The question would then be, once sellers have brought into a country whatever they need for a transaction, do you from then on treat them the same as all "national" sellers regardless of where they came from? By that definition, imported cars are accorded national treatment, even though they bear a tariff, as long as local dealers are treated the same, and bear equally any additional taxes such as sales taxes, independently of where they or their products originated. By that definition I agree that the GATT did require immediate national treatment for domestic sales (but not imports) of goods in the same way that the GATS now requires it for services.

But that, to me, is beside the point. What is important is that the GATT did permit domestic producers some form of continuing protection from competition with foreign-based producers, and this protection, in the form of tariffs, could be very high. The GATS does not provide for any continuing protection at all, and therefore it is hardly surprising that countries have been reluctant to sign on.

Phase-In

One could accept the need to avoid the shock of moving instantly to free trade without accepting the need for erecting a special set of barriers to imports of services, as I am recommending here. After all, negotiated reductions in trade barriers are routinely implemented not all at once but over a gradual phase-in period. Most of the barriers in NAFTA, for example, were scheduled to be eliminated over periods of from five to ten years, and a few were permitted to continue for fifteen. Therefore one might argue that the aims of my proposal could be better achieved by simply permitting the move to National Treatment in services to be accomplished gradually.

There are at least two problems with this, however. First, how do you phase in National Treatment? If foreign service providers are currently simply excluded from the domestic market, how do you permit them to enter while at the same time damping their competitive effects? Entry could be delayed, but that does not make it much less disruptive when it finally happens. Entry could be rationed across firms, allowing in, say, only one per year for a period of time. But selection of the entrants would create discrimination across trading partners, and it would also introduce its own economic distortions across service providers. Finally, entry could be slowed down in a nondiscriminatory way by providing some sort of tax barrier, as I suggest here, and then reducing that tax gradually over time. But that, of course, is just a variant of my own proposal.

The other problem is that any such solution to the phase-in problem retains free trade as the objective that has to be agreed upon to be achieved within a specified time. But as we have seen in goods markets for a great many products, negotiators have not yet accepted any timetable for achieving free trade. While lip service has been given in groups like the forum for Asia Pacific Economic Cooperation (APEC) to achieving free trade within a couple of decades, I doubt that anyone really believes that it will happen. So far, virtually all countries have reserved positive tariffs on many products, and high ones on some, that they have been unwilling to schedule removal of, ever. It seems implausible to me that they would be more forthcoming in markets for services than they have proven themselves to be in markets for goods.

Policy Flexibility

One major advantage of service tariffication, then, is that it will provide a policy tool that can be used to cushion the disruptive effects of trade liberalization, both when sectors are newly liberalized and also at other times when a surge of competition from foreign providers causes damage domestically. Article XIX of the GATT, the Safeguards Clause, already provides for such a cushion for trade in goods, permitting countries to raise tariffs temporarily when a surge of imports causes injury to domestic firms or workers. To provide such protection in services under the existing rules of GATS would be difficult, since foreign providers operate domestically on an all-or-nothing national-treatment basis. It is hard to see how a surge in sales by a group of foreign suppliers could be responded to, except perhaps by limiting any new ones from establishing or, hardly likely, insisting that some existing ones temporarily shut down.

Tariffication, however, provides a ready-made policy for this purpose. The taxes on foreign service providers can in principle be varied as necessary to achieve a limited amount of protection for domestic sellers. Admittedly, this will be hard on the foreign providers, and even the potential for such variation in the taxes will increase their expected costs and put them at a disadvantage. But this problem is familiar from goods markets, and it is surely less extreme than removing their permission to operate at all.[2]

I therefore recommend, as an extension of my proposal, that the GATS be amended to include something analogous to Article XIX, once the concept of service tariffs has been put in place to make it feasible.

Currency for Negotiations

The hope underlying the GATS today is that, even though few service sectors have been scheduled for coverage by the participants, future negotiations will expand the coverage to additional sectors. This is possible, and perhaps even likely. But the negotiations to bring this about will, under current rules, have to be quite different from the negotiations over goods trade in which the GATT has had a half century of experience. There, negotiations typically have involved reducing (bindings on) existing tariffs. Countries could trade off increased openness of particular domestic markets for increased access to particular foreign markets that were of interest to them, in both cases by reducing tariffs. And even though it has never made all that much economic sense, they could balance their own "concessions" by noting the sizes of the tariff reductions themselves and the amounts of trade that were covered by them. Thus the tariff reductions, weighted by amounts of trade, provided a ready measure of what was exchanged in the negotiation, a currency for negotiations serving as a unit of account.

In services under GATS, we do not now have any such tool. Countries are forced to exchange concessions in a very lumpy form, either opening a category of services completely or not. It is therefore going to be very difficult to secure any kind of balance of concessions, without which the negotiations themselves will be cumbersome.

In goods trade, since every country is likely to have comparative advantage in something and therefore is likely to be an exporter of a number of products, all countries typically have something to gain from negotiations to reduce tariffs. That is, each has a group of export sectors where they want improved market access abroad, and they are willing to give up some import barriers to acquire that. However, because the range of service products is much narrower and the technologies for providing them are less diverse, some countries may perceive that they have no comparative advantage at all in any service sectors. If service negotiations are separated from those in goods, such countries may think they have nothing to gain by liberalizing in services. And if liberalization can only take the extreme form of national treatment, then such separation seems likely.

However, with tariffication, the negotiations in services can more easily be conducted alongside, and in conjunction with, negotiations in goods, exchanging service liberalization for goods liberalization and vice versa. This too should make it that much easier to achieve meaningful liberalization, once the service tariffs are initially put in place. Also, the negotiators themselves will be able to quantify what they have accomplished. They will point first to the sizable reductions in service tariffs that are likely to be possible at the start, when tariffication has placed them at prohibitively high levels. Then later they will point to the further reductions in service tariffs weighted by the volumes of service trade, once a meaningful amount of that is underway.

Identifying Foreign Providers

One objection that I have heard to this proposal is that it will be difficult for countries to distinguish foreign service providers from domestic ones in order to know which should be subject to the service tariff. This is not a problem that arises at all for much of trade in goods, since one does not really need to know the national identity of the producer. It is enough that a good crosses a national border in order for it to be subject to a tariff. Of course, in free trade areas like the NAFTA even goods trade is not so simple, and the complications and dangers of rules of origin are not something that one would like to see replicated for trade in services.

However, I do not see that this is a serious problem. Under current rules, those countries that do restrict access to foreign service providers presumably have some way of knowing whom they are keeping out and whom they are letting in. They should be able to apply service tariffs to those previously excluded providers as easily as they can now keep them out of the domestic market.

I would think that it could be left up to the countries themselves to construct their own definitions of foreignness for this purpose, requiring only that their definitions not discriminate across foreign countries and that they not add unnecessarily to the cost of providing the service. As just an example, a foreign service provider might be one whose ownership by domestic residents is less than, say, some set percentage, and this percentage would have to be the same regardless of the foreign nationality, with obvious exceptions for membership in a free trade area or a customs union. National identity for this purpose should *not* depend upon a fraction of domestically sourced inputs, including labor, since doing that would distort input choices in a way that a service tariff is intended to avoid.

III. Analysis of Service Tariffs

Is it really possible to levy tariffs on services? And if so, what effects will they have? Definitive answers to these questions will have to wait for countries actually to attempt to implement such policies, once given the idea and the opportunity. I have little doubt that if governments are permitted to tax a category of foreign firms they will find a way to do it, so my problem is really only to anticipate what might be done and its effects.

For that purpose I will work theoretically through two types of internationally traded services to examine in conceptual terms how these services might be taxed and what effects these taxes might have. In each case, I will not address the problem alluded to above of defining which providers are foreign and which domestic, assuming that this has already been solved.

Standard Remote Services

I start with what I think is the simplest form of internationally traded service, what I will call "remote" services. These are services produced by a foreign firm that uses only foreign inputs (presumably located or based in its home country, although that is not important for the analysis) to provide a product that is purchased by domestic residents (or firms). Being a service, the output takes the form of effecting some sort of change in the purchaser or in their property or environs, and it does not take a physical form that can necessarily be observed crossing the border into the importing country. Effecting the service internationally surely requires the use of some international medium of communication or transportation, just as trade in goods must require transportation, but I will ignore that complication just as we often ignore transportation in analyzing trade in goods.

Several examples of this type of service come to mind. Close to home, a professional consultant may provide services for clients in another country, conveying advice by mail, telephone, or internet. Or they may travel in person to the buying country for a brief visit during which they present their work, as many are doing at this conference. Professionals in all sorts of fields could market their expertise abroad in this way, including medical services, legal services, accounting services, architectural services, and so forth.

Insurance services could equally well be provided in this way, with only the small complication that additional international communication may be necessary at a later time to verify a claim and deliver benefits. But here too, it may be unnecessary for the insurance company to employ any inputs in the importing country, although it may wish to do so in order to provide better service or to help it attract customers. In the latter case, it would fit into my next category of "on-site" services below.

Of the services that I will consider in this paper, remote services differ the least from traded goods. Since the inputs to their production come entirely from outside the importing country, it is just as though they were produced in a factory abroad and transported in. And while it may not be possible to monitor their entry into the country, their value and quantity as an import are likely to be well defined, and comparatively easy to tax. Thus a service tariff in this case is just a tax on the quantity of the service sold. It could even be a specific tariff, since the unit of output of the service is likely to be well defined as well, but it could also be *ad valorem*. That is, the service tariff may collect for the importing country government some set percentage of the market value of the service, and therefore of the revenue from selling it in the domestic market.

Being so similar to a tariff, it is not surprising that the effects of such a tax on a remote service will be identical to the effects of a tariff as well. It seems unnecessary to go through all possible analytics here, but the reader can easily picture the usual cases of supply and demand for a traded service that is either homogeneous or differentiated, and that is imported into a country that is either small or large. The usual results obtain for the tariff compared to free trade: The service tariff will increase the price of the service in the domestic market, both imported and domestically produced, benefiting domestic suppliers, hurting domestic demanders, and lowering the world price if the importing country is large. If the tariff is large enough, it may eliminate imports of the remote service entirely, especially if the service is homogeneous. The net welfare effects are also the usual: A small importing country suffers a net loss of welfare from a tariff, its demanders losing more than its suppliers and its government together gain, but a large country may gain from the terms-of-trade effects of a tariff, and a large country must gain if the tariff is not too large.

More to the point here, however, is another standard result from partial equilibrium tariff analysis: that if any trade occurs in the presence of a tariff, then the importing country is better off (net) than if it did not import at all. This result—that some trade is better than no trade—seems particularly important here, since I am arguing in favor of tariffs on services, not as an alternative to free trade which I regard as unattainable, but as an alternative to the current GATS under which the alternative is often no trade at all.[3] Therefore I illustrate the move from no trade (or a prohibitive tariff) to tariff-encumbered trade in figure 1.

The case shown is a remote service that is differentiated from the domestically produced service of the same industry, with supplies of both services to domestic buyers being upward sloping. The panel on the left shows supply and demand for the domestically produced service, with demand depending on both its own price, p_D, and the price of the imported service, p_M, the level of which is fixed at some p_M^0 for the initial position (the solid curve) of the demand curve. The panel on the right shows the market for the imported service, with price p_M and quantity q_M. Demand for it too depends on both prices, with the position of the demand curve dependent on the intial price of the domestically produced service, p_D^0. Both the demand curve and the supply curve for the imported service are shown with finite vertical intercepts, at $\tilde{p}_M$ and p_M^W respectively, so that imports can be eliminated without their shadow price becoming infinite. The intercept of the supply curve, as the notation suggests, can be thought of as being determined in the world market, and if the importing country is small relative to that, the supply curve could be horizontal at p_M^W. However, I allow for the more general case of a large importing country, which must pay a higher price the more it imports.

The initial equilibrium, with solid lines in both panels, reflects exactly such a no-trade situation, perhaps because imports of the service are simply prohibited or perhaps because a tariff on the imported service already exists at a rate higher than the difference between $\tilde{p}_M$ and p_M^W. Therefore the shadow

Figure 1. From No Trade to a "Tariff" on a Remote Service

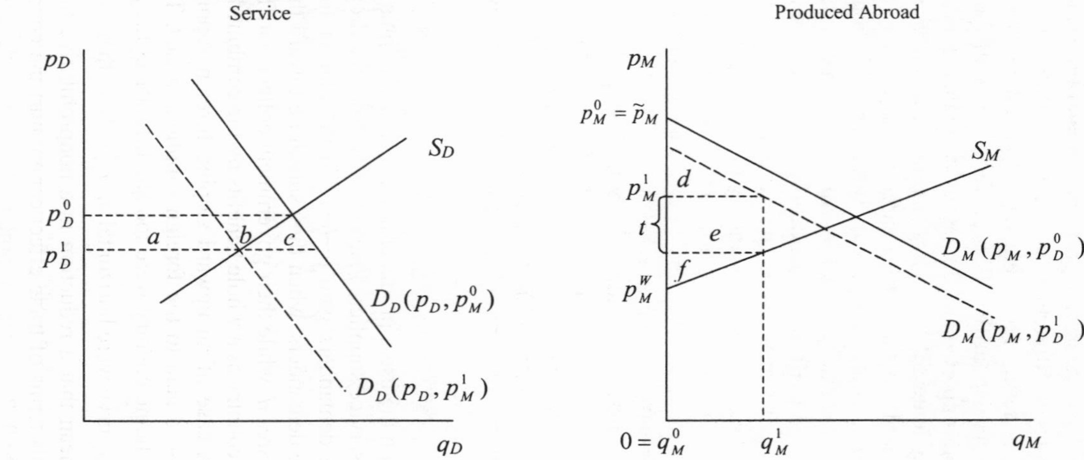

price of the imported service is $p_M^0 = \tilde{p}_M$, which determines the position of the demand curve in the market for the domestically produced service. That, together with its supply curve, determines its equilibrium price as p_D^0, and this then determines the position of the demand curve for the imported service. Clearly, the two equilibria must be simultaneously determined, and the figure merely illustrates what is the solution to a system of simultaneous equations.

Now suppose that imports are permitted, with a positive tariff, or tax, that is too small to eliminate them entirely. The resulting equilibrium is shown by the dashed lines in figure 1, which are again the outcome of a simultaneous system. By lowering the tariff below $\tilde{p}_M - p_M^W$, the price of the imported service is reduced ultimately to p_M^1. That fall in price shifts the demand curve for the domestically produced service down to $D_D(p_D, p_M^1)$ which reduces the equilibrium price of the domestically produced service to p_D^1. That fall in price likewise causes the demand curve for the imported service also to shift downward, to $D_M(p_M, p_D^1)$. The size of the tariff itself that will cause all this to happen is shown as *t*, the vertical distance of p_M^1 above the supply curve, with the quantity of the imported service equaling q_M^1.

The welfare effects of this service trade, compared to its prohibition, can be read from the usual producer and consumer surplus areas on the two panels. Domestic service suppliers lose area $a+b$ from the drop in price, while domestic service demanders gain $a+b+c$. In the market for the imported service, these same demanders, when they substitute toward the cheaper imported service, gain area *d*, while their government collects tariff revenue of *e*.[4] Thus the importing country as a whole benefits by the combined amounts $c+d+e$.

In this case of an upward sloping foreign supply of imported services, there is also a gain to the foreign suppliers, area *f*. This would of course be zero if the home country were too small to affect the price of its imports, and thus the S_M curve were horizontal at p_M^W. Note that while the size of the country may mean that a reduction in a nonprohibitive tariff may lower national welfare, this terms of trade effect cannot hurt the country if it is starting from no trade at all. That is why some trade is better than no trade even for a large country.

Standard On-Site Services

My second category of services is one in which it is necessary for the service provider to have an ongoing presence on or near the site where the service will be provided, so that at least some inputs must be purchased within the importing country's market.[5] The significance of this is twofold. First, by taxing the sales of the imported service with our so-called service tariff, we are no longer really taxing only imported value added. Therefore, the analogy with a goods tariff breaks down slightly, and a distinct analysis is required.

Second, since production of the imported service requires domestic inputs from within the importing country, anything that changes trade, including the service tariff, will affect the domestic market for those inputs. This too could alter the analytical implications of the tariff.

Before proceeding with the analysis, note that this kind of service is much more common than the remote service examined above. Indeed, most international service providers will require some sort of establishment within the importing country from which to operate. In most cases this establishment will make use of at least some domestic labor, in addition to local land and perhaps local capital. Of course, being an imported service will mean that at least some of the inputs also come from abroad, even if only the technology or the brand identity, but also there is often some "headquarter services" as well, provided by the home office. And many imported services use imported intermediate physical inputs as well.

Thus we may think of on-site services as including restaurant and hotel chains such as McDonalds and Hilton, retailers such as Toys R Us and Walmart, and international construction firms such as Bechtel. Many financial firms also fit this mold, as do transportation companies, at least if they are primarily providing transportation within the importing country.

Turning to the analysis, figure 2 extends figure 1 to include interaction with an input market in the domestic (importing) country. This could be any input, but I call it labor, with its price being a wage, w. The top two panels show the same markets for domestically produced and imported services as before, except that the supply curve for the imported service now depends also on the wage in the input market. The figure also includes a lower panel showing the market for labor, with a supply of labor and a demand that depend on the quantity of the imported service being provided, q_M. The initial position of the labor demand curve corresponds to zero imported service supply, since we start as before with no trade in the service. When imports of the service are then permitted, the price of the service falls as before, shifting demand for the domestically produced service downward, and the quantity of the imported service rises, shifting up the demand for labor. The resulting fall in the price of the domestically produced service then shifts the demand for the imported service down as before, and now also the resulting rise in the wage shifts up the supply of the imported service, so that both curves shift in the imported service market to the dashed positions shown.[6]

The effects of tariff-encumbered imports of services are then the same as before, with the addition of an effect on the domestic input market, in this case labor. The price of the input rises, expanding its supply and benefiting its suppliers. The welfare effects are also the same as before, with the addition of the benefit to input suppliers that appears as area $g+h$ in the input market, and a loss to other demanders of the same input given by area g. Since these two net

Figure 2. From No Trade to a "Tariff" on an On-Site Service

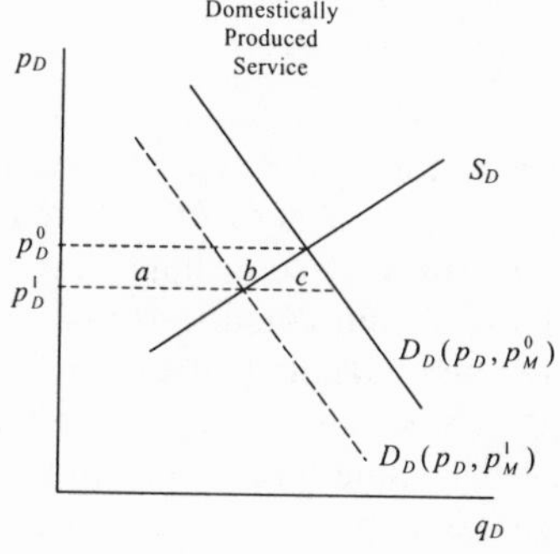

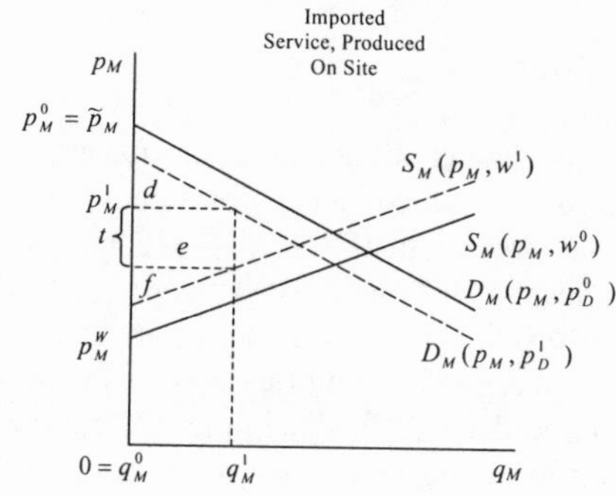

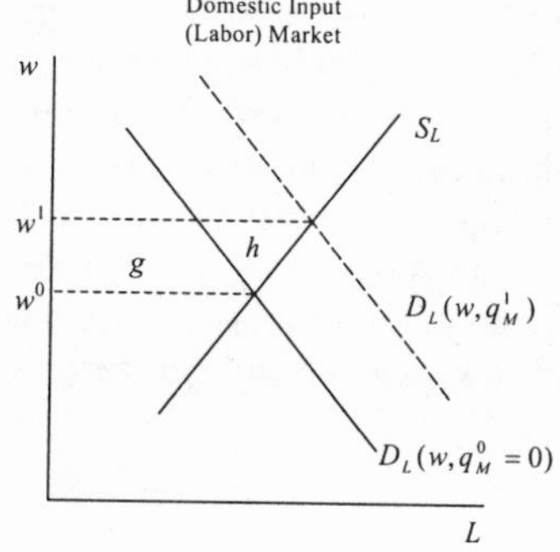

to a benefit h, we can be sure once again that the move from no trade in the service to tariff-encumbered trade is beneficial for the domestic economy as a whole.

IV. Conclusion

In this chapter, I have laid out the case, as I see it, for tariffication of services. I argue that the prospects for achieving significant liberalization of the international provision of services will be greatly improved if something like this proposal is followed. By amending the GATS to permit countries to tax foreign providers of services in a manner that is roughly analogous to tariffs on imported goods, countries will be encouraged to bring most categories of services under GATS discipline. Of course, that discipline will be much weakened by doing this, since the taxes may be set so high that little if any trade will occur. However, once this is done, it will become possible for countries to negotiate reductions in these service tariffs in exactly the same way that they have done for goods over the last fifty years. Considering the amount of time that it has taken to achieve significant liberalization of trade in goods, we should not expect to achieve it in services any time soon. However, by starting the process with tariffication, we place services upon the same well-traveled road that has been followed before, and we can be more confident that the future negotiating process will take us where we want to go, even if we cannot know how soon we will get there.

Notes

[1] See the discussion of measuring services barriers by Drusilla Brown, Alan Deardorff, and Robert Stern in Chapter 2 above and the use of the estimated tariff equivalents for these barriers in their modeling of services liberalization in a new WTO trade round.

[2] A case for safeguards protection is provided in Deardorff (1987).

[3] But not always. As Kyoji Fukao points out in his comment, foreign providers of some services in some countries are currently permitted, in a limited way, in sectors that have not been opened under the GATS. To change to a tariff on these providers will be disruptive, and it may lower welfare, although the gains in facilitating future liberalization may still make this worth doing.

[4] These effects on demanders can best be seen by breaking the changes into two parts, first reducing p_D while holding p_M constant, and then reducing p_M while holding p_D constant. In the first step, demanders gain $a+b+c$, while the demand curve for imports shifts down without affecting welfare there. In the second step, demanders gain consumer surplus d from the fall in price along the new demand curve for imports, while the demand curve in the domestic market shifts down without any further change in welfare there.

[5] Actually, it is the use of local inputs, not the ongoing presence, that is distinctive here, but I could not think of a term to describe this case that emphasized only that.

[6] The rise in the wage, which is the price of the imported service input, may also increase the cost of the domestically produced service, as T. N. Srinivasan points out in his comment. That would cause an upward shift in the SD curve as well, complicating the analysis considerably without (I think) changing the basic conclusion.

References

Deardorff, Alan V. 1987. "Safeguards Policy and the Conservative Social Welfare Function," in H. Kierzkowski (ed.), *Protection and Competition in International Trade*, Blackwell.

Deardorff, Alan V. 1994. "Market Access," in OECD, *The New World Trading System: Readings*, Paris: Organisation for Economic Cooperation and Development, 57-63.

Hoekman, Bernard. 1996. "Assessing the General Agreement on Trade in Services," in Will Martin and L. Alan Winters (eds.), *The Uruguay Round and the Developing Countries*, Cambridge, U.K.: Cambridge University Press.

Comment

T. N. Srinivasan

I have long known Alan Deardorff as one of the ardent crusaders for a liberal world trading order. I was surprised, nay alarmed, when I read in the very second page of his paper that "GATS should have permitted—indeed encouraged—countries to erect *new barriers* to imports of services . . ." (emphasis added). I thought Alan's formidable analytical abilities had suddenly forsaken him! But after reading his paper and his proposal for tariffication of services several times, I was reassured that his ultimate objective is still a liberal trading order in services. But he argues that the adoption of his proposal will facilitate (and perhaps even accelerate the timing of) the achievement of the objective. His reasoning is that GATS, by allowing signatories to exempt a service sector from liberalization altogether, and if they chose to liberalize, requiring them to accord, MFN *and* "full" National Treatment to foreign suppliers of services, in effect pushed many countries not to liberalize. Alan's proposal would allow them to levy a (prohibitive) domestic tax initially, bind it, and later reduce it on a reciprocal basis. He argues that, under his proposal WTO members will no longer have any incentive to exempt any service sector initially from liberalization and over time, to liberalize all sectors. In his view, his proposal is the equivalent to the process of tariffication of the agricultural sector in the Uruguay Round agreement. Further the reciprocal exchange of domestic tax "concessions" on foreign suppliers of services is no different from the traditional mercantilistic process of tariff reduction negotiations with respect to goods trade in the GATT. Thus, the domestic tax on foreign suppliers of services will serve as currency for service negotiations as tariffs have done for goods negotiations.

It seems to me that the negotiating "currency" argument should be sharply distinguished from the argument that gradually reducing tariffs spreads over time the cost of adjustment to the shock of liberalization. The former relies on the 'exchange' value of the currency, that is, through 'concessions' on one's taxes or tariffs on foreign suppliers, one obtains in exchange 'concessions' of others on taxes or tariffs they levy on one's supply to them, be they on exports of one's services or goods. However, if the ultimate objective is free trade in all goods and services, if there are no adjustment costs or large terms of trade effects, the currency would be worthless – a jump to free trade immediately in everything by every country would be the outcome. If this is correct, leaving the terms of trade effects aside as a problem to be addressed by domestic transfers, then spreading the cost of adjustment over time is the only argument for gradually liberalizing tariffs. Then the exchange value of tariffs might come about because of differentials in costs of adjustment across commodities and services. The question then is whether tariffying first, and gradually bringing the tariffs down, is the only, or if not the only, the most desirable, way of spreading adjustment costs. A related, but not identical issue, is one of responding to temporary and reversible shocks. Alan argues that his proposal would permit varying the domestic tax on foreign service supplies (within the agreed bound) to respond to temporary shocks.

Alan addresses the cost of adjustment issue as a problem of phasing in a national treatment (which, I will argue below, is not the analogue of free trade as he suggests). But after dismissing other ways of phasing-in than variants of his proposal, he argues that phasing-in, by definition, implies a terminal date at which free trade would be achieved. Since in agreeing to the gradual liberalization of goods tariffs, no country has committed to achieving free trade ever, there is no reason, in his view, to expect countries to agree to "full" national treatment ever in services. I am not persuaded by this reasoning. Negotiators in any round of multinational negotiations will rationally anticipate that there would be future rounds of negotiations, and that their binding of a tariff in one round only defines the initial level from which it will be negotiated downwards in the next round. I cannot see this process as anything other than implying a rational expectation of, if not a credible commitment to, achieving free trade in the future, albeit through a succession of possibly large numbers of rounds. Finally, there is a non-discriminatory method of phasing-in without having *tariffs initially*. It is its quota analogue – at each round, negotiators agree on a gradual increase in the supply by foreign service producers to the domestic markets, with the rights to supply being auctioned off among suppliers. Once the foreign supplies reach the level that would have prevailed under free trade, any further auctions will yield a zero price for the rights. This procedure also avoids the problem of temporary upsurges in foreign supplies.

Alan seems to succumb to the common misperception that the objective of free trade is the foundation for the disciplines of GATT/WTO. There is in fact no mention of free trade in the GATT. The founding principle of GATT is in fact non-discrimination although, unfortunately, the GATT itself allows derogation of this principle, for example, for free trade areas and customs unions. Article I on MFN ensures that in applying measures at *its border*, a customs jurisdiction treats all suppliers of imports identically. The article on National Treatment ensures, that *domestic* (or inside the border) measures are not used to discriminate among suppliers of imports on the one hand, and on the other, between domestic and foreign suppliers. I am therefore puzzled by Alan's statement: "After all, in the context of trade in goods, National Treatment must mean perfectly free trade." He agrees that this is too restrictive an interpretation of national treatment. But he claims that it is beside his point. That is, in goods trade, domestic producers are offered, under GATT rules, continuing protection through tariffs (albeit subject to agreed bounds) while GATS does not do so for domestic producers of services. This is certainly correct, but as I argued earlier, the lowering of tariffs through reductions in successive rounds of their bound levels is a means of spreading the adjustment costs over time. As such, it is not continuing protection per se, but permitting the use of tariffs as a means of spreading adjustment costs that distinguishes GATT from GATS. Other means than tariffs for spreading adjustment costs, that is to say, phasing in national treatment including, if desired, ways of allowing developing countries a longer phase-in period could be made part of GATS.

Alan argues that since GATS requires full national treatment on any category of services that is opened up, such opening is "lumpy," and a balanced exchange of "concessions" across categories of services becomes very difficult. This difficulty, in his view, is compounded by the fact that the range of service products is narrow. This means that some countries may perceive no comparative advantage at all in any of them. Such countries "may think they have nothing to gain in liberalizing in services." I am surprised that, first of all, Alan ignores welfare gains for small countries from *unilateral* liberalization. Second, as he himself recognizes, the so called "balancing of concessions" in multilateral negotiations has no economic logic to recommend it.

Alan's distinction between imported goods and on-site supply of services by foreigners is over drawn. Imported goods also involve the use of local services (such as transportation and distribution) before they reach their domestic user. Be that as it may, I am not quite sure that the criterion of identifying a foreign supplier of services for levying Alan's tariff through a maximum share of *domestic* ownership would be non-discriminatory across foreign suppliers, unless the incidence of tariff can be presumed to be independent of the percentage of ownership.

Finally, in the second of his two partial equilibrium illustrations of the logic of his proposal, the one dealing with on-site supply of imported services, he does not allow the supply curve of the domestically produced service to shift upwards with an increase in equilibrium wage, while the supply of on-site imported services shifts up. While this simplifies his analysis greatly, it is implausible.

Comment

Kyoji Fukao

Deardorff's argument for tariffication in services is based on the following two grounds. First, the National Treatment discipline of GATS forces member countries to make commitments in a very "lumpy" form, to open their markets completely or not to make any commitment. By introducing "tariffication," member countries will have more flexibility in choice. Further, many countries will make more commitments. Second, by converting all other barriers to tariffs, trade and FDI restrictions will become more transparent. Thus, member countries can use tariff rates as currency of negotiations.

I wish to note first that I do not agree with Deardorff's one basic presumption, which is shown in his theoretical analysis of service tariffs. He seems to presume that no commitment means no trade. And he compares no-trade equilibrium with a tariff equilibrium. But no commitment does not always mean no trade. For example, Japan does not fully guarantee National Treatment in many industries, such as air transportation and insurance. But there are many foreign affiliates within these sectors of Japan. These affiliates do their business and generate profits under discriminatory regulations. If we persuade the Japanese Government to introduce a new sales tax on foreign affiliates, it will be a nightmare for these affiliates. As this example shows, no commitment in GATS schedules does not necessarily mean no trade. If there exists some trade or FDI before tariffication, then tariffication will not always be welfare improving.

Secondly, in order to minimize the negative effect of tariffication, we should permit member countries to introduce tariffs only when the new tariff is equivalent to or lower than existing discriminatory regulations. For this purpose, we need more detailed information than GATS schedules on each country's present regulations. In other words, GATS schedules are not detailed enough. For example, APEC's report, *Guide to the Investment Regimes of Member Economies*, would be a useful source here.

Third, many bilateral investment treaties protect the rights of existing foreign affiliates. National Treatment is sometimes guaranteed for existing foreign affiliates but not for possible future entrants. In such a case, these countries cannot introduce new sales taxes. How then would these countries regulate new entrants after tariffication?

Fourth, Deardorff seems to say that any tax will be fine. But different taxes will have different welfare implications. I would like therefore to know more about which tax is less distorting than other taxes.

Finally, on the mode of supply and Market Access discipline of GATS, Deardorff mainly argues for National Treatment discipline for the cross-border supply mode and the commercial presence mode. I would like to know whether he would like to propose tariffication for other modes of supply such as consumption abroad and presence of natural persons.

CHAPTER 5

Japan, WTO Dispute Settlement, and the Millennium Round

William J. Davey

The new WTO dispute settlement system was a major accomplishment of the Uruguay Round. Compared to the prior GATT system, it is more legalistic, with more stress on compliance with agreed rules. It has been used frequently by WTO Members, who have submitted difficult and sometimes controversial cases to it. Indeed, much of the adverse publicity concerning the WTO in recent years has involved perceptions (sometimes inaccurate) of dispute settlement rulings. While WTO Members have praised the system in general terms, in the 1998-1999 review of the system many changes—most minor, but some fundamental—were proposed. This chapter contains a brief overview of Japan's involvement with GATT/WTO dispute settlement and then catalogs some of the more important issues that may be raised in any near-term WTO negotiations on dispute settlement procedures.[1]

I. Japan and WTO Dispute Settlement

Historically, Japan was viewed as a supporter of a less legalistic approach to dispute settlement in GATT, preferring a system relaying on negotiation and compromise instead of adjudication. This preference was shared by the European Community (EC). However, in the course of the Uruguay Round, both Japan and the EC came to support a more legalistic system, which had been strongly advocated by the United States, in exchange for a requirement in the WTO that WTO Members use the WTO dispute settlement system to resolve all WTO-related disputes. Japan and the EC hoped that a strengthened WTO dispute settlement system would reduce U.S. tendencies toward unilateral actions under Section 301 of the U.S. 1974 Trade Act.

Since the advent of the WTO, Japan has been a more active participant in dispute settlement proceedings than it was in the GATT system. In GATT, Japan requested only two panels—both against the EC and both involving antidumping issues. In the WTO, Japan has requested five panels:

- against discriminatory tax and tariff regimes in the Indonesian automobile sector (with the EC and United States);

- against a discriminatory regime in the Canadian automotive sector (with the EC);
- against a Massachusetts law disadvantaging companies doing business with Myanmar (with the EC);
- against the 1916 U.S. antidumping law (with the EC); and
- against certain U.S. antidumping duties on hot-rolled steel.

In a significant case in 1995 that did not lead to the establishment of a panel, Japan started an action against the United States in respect of its threatened punitive duties on Japanese auto exports to the United States. It is noteworthy that Japan still seems somewhat reticent to bring cases to the point of having a panel established, as evidenced by the fact that outside the antidumping area, it has always had co-complainants (recently the EC).

On the other side of the coin, Japan was the respondent in 10 GATT panel proceedings, including four in the post-1985 period. Those cases were *Alcohol Taxes I*, *Agricultural Quotas (Japan-12)*, *Semiconductors,* and *SPF Lumber*. Japan prevailed in the latter case. So far, in the WTO, Japan has had to defend itself before a panel on three occasions. Of the three, Japan lost two cases (*Alcohol Taxes II* and *Apples*) and won one (*Film*). It has settled several challenges in the consultation stage, most notably a U.S./EC challenge to its failure to afford retroactively the extended copyright protection that the United States and EC alleged was required by the TRIPS Agreement.

Japan has appeared fairly frequently as a third party in WTO proceedings. For example, in the 11 cases where reports had been adopted in 2000 by the Dispute Settlement Body (DSB) (through August), Japan had been a party in one (*Canada Autos*) and a third-party in five others (*U.S. Section 301*, *U.S. FSC*, *Canada Pharmaceuticals*, *Korea Procurement*, *U.S. Copyright*). Of the 16 active cases as of that date, Japan was a party in two (*U.S. 1916 AD*, *U.S. Steel AD*) and a third party in six others (*U.S. Bananas Retaliation*), *EC Bed Linen AD*, *U.S. Lamb*, *Thai AD*, *U.S. Steel AD (Korea)*, *India Autos*). In general, Japan seems to be quite active as a party and third party in cases involving the automotive sector, antidumping measures, intellectual property, and U.S. 301 actions. Indeed, these four categories explain 11 of the foregoing 14 cases.

Overall, Japan has been one of the more active WTO Members in the dispute settlement system. Generally, I think that Japan should view its participation in the dispute settlement system fairly positively. In the cases where it was a complaining party, it generally received satisfactory outcomes—it prevailed against Indonesia and Indonesia has changed its auto regime; it prevailed against Canada in autos and against the United States in the 1916 antidumping case and hopefully there will be implementation in due course. The Massachusetts case was effectively abandoned after the U.S. federal courts (up to the Supreme Court) ruled against the challenged Massachusetts law. The steel antidumping case is pending. Japan's threatened action against the United States in their 1995 auto dispute seemed to be a useful tool in leading to a settlement with the United States that Japan could accept. The existence of the Dispute Settlement Understanding (DSU) rules made it easier for Japan to argue that the United States could not take unilateral action. In the highest profile case against Japan—*Film*—Japan prevailed in a claim by the United States. On the negative side, there were adverse rulings in the *Alcohol Taxes II* and *Apples* cases, as well as a settlement of the copyright dispute, but, in my view, Japan did not have very good defenses in those cases and should not have been surprised that it lost. Overall, Japan has little to complain about in respect of the WTO dispute settlement insofar as it has involved Japan.

Japan was also an active player in the 1998-1999 review of the DSU discussed below. This occurred in part because the Japanese Ambassador in Geneva (Akao) chaired the DSB and the DSU review process during most of 1999 and his deputy (Suzuki) chaired an informal discussion group that led to the proposal made to the Seattle Ministerial that is discussed below.

II. Dispute Settlement Issues in Future WTO Negotiations

At the end of the Uruguay Round, it was decided to have a full review of the DSU before the end of 1998 and to have the WTO Ministerial Conference decide thereafter whether to continue, modify or terminate the DSU. Although virtually all WTO Members participating in the review expressed general satisfaction with the operation of the dispute settlement system, there were many proposals for minor (and some major) changes in the DSU. Some of these changes were included in a proposal made to the Seattle Ministerial Conference. Although they were not adopted since no action on any matter was taken at Seattle, I will describe them separately in this section because there seemed relatively widespread support for them, making their eventual adoption likely.

The Proposed DSU Amendment at Seattle

Although the DSU review formally ended in July 1999, a small group of Members, including the active users of the DSU, continued to work on a package of amendments to the DSU for adoption at the Seattle Ministerial. This work, which was led by Japan, culminated in a proposed amendment cosponsored by Canada, Costa Rica, Czech Republic, Ecuador, the EC and its member States, Hungary, Japan, Korea, New Zealand, Norway, Peru, Slovenia, Switzerland, Thailand and Venezuela.

The principal part of the proposed amendment was a modification of DSU Articles 21.5 and 22 to clarify the relationship between them so as to avoid the problems that arose in the *Bananas* case because of the split between the EC and the United States as to how those articles should be interpreted. In that case, the EC argued that since it had modified its banana regime and there was a disagreement over whether the new regime was WTO-consistent, the United States had to commence an action under Article 21.5 and have a new panel (and possibly Appellate Body) ruling on its new measure. The United States argued that notwithstanding Article 21.5, Article 22 authorized the granting of authority to suspend concessions (i.e., retaliate) under the reverse consensus rules only within 30 days of the end of the period set for implementation and since the EC had not implemented, the United States was entitled to seek and obtain such authority within that period. In the U.S. view, to require it to pursue an Article 21.5 action would prevent it from ever exercising its right to seek authority to retaliate. Ultimately, there was a panel requested by Ecuador under Article 21.5 on whether the new regime was WTO-consistent and an arbitration of the amount of the U.S. retaliation request under Article 22. Both proceedings were conducted by the original panel, and it issued its reports to the parties in both proceedings on the same day and the United States was later authorized to retaliate on the basis of the arbitration report.

As a general proposition, the sponsors of the amendment aimed at establishing a clear sequence of procedures to be followed at the expiration of the reasonable period of time for implementation in the event that there was a dispute over implementation. Since providing for such a sequence required an overall lengthening of the time for completing a typical case and since there was a desire not to lengthen the overall process, a number of adjustments were made in the consultation and panel stages to reduce the time devoted thereto. These changes are set out in more detail below, along with several additional, unrelated changes contained in the proposed amendment.

Changes to DSU Articles 21 and 22

Under the proposed amendment, if a disagreement over compliance arises, the disagreement would be referred to a compliance panel (the Appellate Body, if the underlying panel report had been appealed, or the original panel, if it had not been appealed). The compliance panel is to submit its report within 90 days of the referral and the report is to be adopted at a DSB meeting held 10 days thereafter, absent a consensus to the contrary. If the concerned Member is found not to have brought the measure into conformity, the prevailing party may request authorization to suspend concessions at that same meeting.

Article 22 would be revised to make it clear that a request to suspend concessions can be made only if a Member fails to indicate that it will comply with the DSB recommendations, fails to report that it has implemented, or is found not to have complied by a compliance panel. Thus, it is made clear that if there is a disagreement over implementation, there must be a compliance panel finding of non-implementation before suspension of concessions may be authorized. The period for arbitration of the level of suspension is expanded from 30 to 45 days, and more detail is added as to how the arbitrators are to approach their task of ensuring that the level of suspension does not exceed the level of nullification or impairment. The proposed amendment had two alternative texts dealing with the question of whether a party suspending concessions could change the products subject to the suspension. Under one variant, only adaptations of a technical nature would be permitted; under the other, such changes would be permitted, subject to review by the arbitrator and approval of the DSB (by reverse consensus).

Article 22 would also be amended to add a procedure by which a Member, who had failed to comply with DSB recommendations and was thereafter subject to a suspension of concessions, could implement a new measure and request that the authorization to suspend concessions be terminated. The authorization is to be withdrawn in such cases unless the complaining party objects, in which case the matter is referred to a compliance panel to consider whether the new measure implements the DSB's recommendations. The authorization must be withdrawn and the suspension lifted if the compliance panel finds that the new measure is not WTO-inconsistent and complies with the DSB's recommendations.

The proposed amendment also strengthened the reporting requirements concerning implementation. Given the potential disruption that the DSB could face if the Article 21.5/22 relationship is not resolved, this amendment would be very useful.

Timing Adjustments

The foregoing compliance procedures would enable a determined complainant to obtain authority to suspend concessions about 145 days after the expiration of the reasonable period of time, as opposed (in the view of the United States) to 60 days under the original DSU rules. In order to avoid lengthening the dispute settlement process, the proposed amendment made a number of adjustments to offset the 85 days added at the end of the process. The consultation requirement was cut from 60 to 30 days (saving 30 days), the number of DSB meetings to have a panel established was cut from two to one (saving at least 10 days), the time allotted for a panel's preparation of the interim report was cut by two weeks (saving 14 days), the time for the interim review process was cut from 5 weeks to 20 days (saving 15 days), and the period between the circulation of the report to the parties and to WTO Members generally was cut by 18 days. Thus, there was an overall time savings of 87 days. As a practical matter, it is unlikely that the new time limits will be respected in all cases (indeed they often will not be). But I see no harm in establishing hard-to-reach goals for the system (as long as they are understood to be goals), particularly if such time limits are necessary to an agreement on clarifying the Article 21/22 relationship.

Third-party Rights

In the third major change proposed, the rights of third parties would be significantly expanded. At present, they receive the first round of party submissions and attend a special session of the panel devoted to hearing their oral statements. Under the proposed revisions, third parties would receive all submissions to a panel prior to the issuance of the interim report and would be able to attend all panel sessions with the parties.

Other Proposed Changes

There were a number of other changes proposed, including a strengthening of the requirement to notify settlements, a provision allowing parties to agree to extend any time limit in the DSU, a requirement that public versions of submissions must be made available within 15 days (no time is now specified), and the substitution of the word "shall" for "should" in two provisions according differential treatment to developing countries.

Current Status of the Proposed Amendments

As noted above, no action was taken on the proposed amendments at the Seattle Ministerial, although it appears that they had reasonably broad support. There remain two major sticking points. First, there are some concerns about the shortening of the consultation and panel stages. These concerns are largely felt by developing countries and the proposal would arguably give them as much or, in the case of time for filing a respondent's brief or commenting on the interim report, more time than at present. The problem is that in some cases, they would need the agreement of the other party, which is to give sympathetic consideration to their position. This is, of course, less certain than a provision that clearly grants developing countries additional time if they desire it.

Second, the United States and the EC are not in agreement over whether and how a Member who has suspended concessions should be able to change the product list on which concessions are suspended. This disagreement has become more serious in recent months because recent U.S. legislation requires U.S. authorities to change such product lists every six months (the so-called "carousel" provision). The United States is expected to do so in the *Bananas* and *Hormones* cases in the near future, and the EC has already initiated dispute settlement proceedings in respect of the legislation itself.

The disagreement over the carousel provision makes it very unlikely that any of the proposed changes will be adopted in the near future. However, the fact that they are mostly agreed does make it more likely that they will be included in any future reform proposals. In this regard, it is important to recall that under the WTO Agreement, to amend the DSU requires a consensus decision of the Ministerial Conference or General Council and the amendment has immediate effect. Thus, an amendment could be implemented quite quickly if there were the will to do so.

Additional Reform Proposals for Consideration

Whatever may become of the Seattle proposal to amend the DSU, there are a number other reforms that should be considered for the long term. There are four issues in particular that merit serious discussion: (1) the need to improve remedies in the WTO system; (2) the need to move toward permanent panelists; (3) the need to improve the transparency of the system and related access issues; and (4) the need to improve the capacity of developing-country Members to participate more effectively in the system. In the formal DSU review, these issues were only introduced in a very general manner.

Improving Remedies in the WTO System

Overall, the record of compliance by WTO Members with DSB recommendations is relatively good. So far, there have been only two, long-term instances of non-compliance—the *Bananas* and *Hormones* cases. Retaliation has been authorized in those cases, but it has not led to compliance.

In considering remedies in the WTO system, it is important to recall that they are prospective—whether in the form of compensation or retaliation. In addition, it is important to consider their two principal aims—to restore the balance of concessions that was upset when one Member violated its obligations; and to give that Member an incentive to comply. The current problem with achieving the first aim—rebalancing—is that if retaliation is authorized, rebalancing takes place at a lower level of trade liberalization that had been agreed to. It would be desirable if a remedy could be devised that would not lead to that result. One could consider monetary payments or requiring the payment of compensation through a reduction in other tariffs or trade restrictions maintained by the non-complying Member.

In respect of the second aim—incentive to comply—there are two issues—timing and level of compensation or retaliation. At present, because remedies are prospective, there is an incentive initially to delay the time at which point they might be implemented, such as by seeking a long reasonable period of time for compliance and then forcing the victor to go through an Article 21.5 panel (and Appellate Body) proceeding. Moreover, if the threat of retaliation does not work, it is possible that the actual existence of retaliation will become viewed as the status quo and a long-term solution, even though the WTO rules in theory require compliance. This fear that retaliation will lose effect over time explains in part the U.S. desire to implement a carousel provision as described above. A preferable solution may be to create incentives for early compliance, such as by providing that any retaliation will be calculated as from six months after the report finding a violation is adopted or by providing for increasing retaliation over time.

These issues will require careful thought. While retaliation seems to work when threatened by a large country against a smaller one, and has worked as between two large countries, it may not be an effective remedy for a small country (even if it can target sensitive large-country sectors such as copyright holders). Moreover, the *Bananas* and *Hormones* cases show that it is not always effective between the large players. Its inefficacy and the unfavorable position in which it leaves developing countries may soon combine to create a serious credibility problem for the system that must be confronted.

Establishing a Permanent Panel Body

One of the proposals made in the DSU review was to form a permanent panel body, like the Appellate Body, from which all panelists would be drawn. This idea was not given serious consideration in the review, but it seems inevitable that the WTO system will move in this direction. Most panelists serve only once or twice. Yet as cases become more complex, particularly in respect of procedural aspects and the evaluation of evidence, experience is evermore necessary. A panel body would have a host of advantages: it would speed the process since the time now taken for panelist selection would be avoided and scheduling delays would be less common. The use of a standing body would mean that panelists would likely know each other and be able to establish an effective working relationship immediately. Panelists would have greater expertise on procedural issues and could more easily meet at short notice to deal with preliminary issues. Consistency of approach and results would be more easily achievable.

There are of course a few disadvantages. From the Members' perspective, there would be more expense. Nowadays most panelists are not paid (except to reimburse travel and living expenses). The choice of the members of the panel body would be difficult given the importance of their role. Depending on how Members handled the selection process and the importance given to nationality, there could be a politicization of the system. Moreover, the use of professional panelists would mean that delegates and government officials would be much less involved in the process than at the moment, which would mean that there would be less contact with the realities of governments and trade negotiations. In the end, however, these disadvantages do not seem so great, especially given that the same concerns exist in respect of the Appellate Body. Yet, in its case, they do not seem to have prevented its emergence as an effective institution.

Transparency and Access to the WTO Dispute Settlement System

There have been complaints, particularly by non-governmental organizations (NGOs), that the WTO dispute settlement system lacks transparency and does not permit sufficient access for non-Members. In this regard, the United States has proposed that dispute settlement proceedings be open to the public, that submissions be made public and that non-parties be permitted to file "friend-of-the-court" submissions to panels. While these proposals were discussed in the review, there was considerable opposition to them. Many developing country Members view the WTO system as exclusively intergovernmental in nature and hesitate to open it to NGOs. In their view, if a NGO wants to make an argument to a panel, it should convince one of the parties to make it and if no party makes the argument, those Members would view that as evidence that the argument is not meritorious. Moreover, they view such openness as favoring the positions espoused by western, developed country NGOs, which they view as likely not to be in their interest. Other Members argue that the credibility of the system would be much enhanced if it were more open and that openness would have no significant disadvantages. Given popular fears of globalization and the WTO's connection therewith, such increased credibility is viewed as essential to ensure the future effectiveness of the WTO itself, as well as the dispute settlement system.

In this regard, it is noteworthy that the Appellate Body recently ruled that it and panels have the right to accept non-requested submissions from non-parties (such as NGOs). It remains to be seen how frequently panels will exercise this right, although one may anticipate that panels will accept such submissions, at least once procedures are worked out in respect of timing, etc. Unfortunately, it is not clear how such procedures will be put in place.

On balance, I think that it is clearly in the interest of the system to become more transparent. In the end, the system has nothing to hide in the way in which decisions are made and the basis on which they are made. Indeed, all of the arguments of the parties and the reasoning of the panels and Appellate Body is made public when the reports are circulated to WTO Members. The openness issue is essentially a matter of timing. I see no gains to the system in delaying access to the parties' arguments, whereas there is much to be gained, at least symbolically, by openness. I also see no downside in allowing NGOs or others to file amicus briefs with panels and the Appellate Body, so long as parties are assured that they will have a chance to respond to any arguments or facts so submitted on which a panel or Appellate Body intends to rely. It is a question of whether one can trust the good judgment of the panels and the Appellate Body to handle such filings responsibly and I think that they can be so trusted.

Developing Countries and Dispute Settlement

Developing countries have been more involved in the WTO dispute settlement system than they were in the GATT system—both as complainants and respondents. The principal issue of interest to developing countries in the DSU review concerned the resource difficulty that many developing countries face when they participate in the dispute settlement system. For the moment, the DSU Article 27.2 addresses this problem by requiring the WTO Secretariat to provide legal assistance to such countries, which it does through two staff lawyers in the Technical Cooperation Division and through the use of lawyers (typically ex-Secretariat employees) who are hired on a consultancy basis to provide assistance on a regular (e.g., one day a week) or case-specific basis. The Secretariat also conducts a number of training courses that either include or are exclusively focused on dispute settlement. Recently, UNCTAD announced plans for a training program on dispute settlement in the WTO and elsewhere for developing countries. At the Seattle Ministerial, a group of developed and developing countries announced the creation of an Advisory Centre on WTO law, which would be an international intergovernmental organization providing legal assistance to developing countries in respect of WTO matters. While the training programs will be valuable in the long run, for the immediate future, the Centre seems to offer the best hope for a significant improvement in dealing with inadequate developing country resources.

Note

[1] Other discussion of dispute settlement is to be found below in Chapter 13 by Robert Stern, Chapter 14 by Gary Saxonhouse, and Chapter 16 by Robert Howse.

References

For more information on the various WTO dispute settlement cases referred to, see the WTO's website (www.wto.org) where all WTO and GATT dispute settlement reports are available, as well as an overview of activities to date in the WTO dispute settlement system. For Japan's view of the DSU and specific dispute settlement cases, see MITI's Report on the *WTO Consistency of Trade Policies by Major Trading Partners* (issued annually)(the 2000 report is available at www.miti.go.jp/report-e/gCT00coe.html).

The proposed changes to the DSU at Seattle were contained in WT/MIN(99)/8 & Corr. 1, which are also available on the WTO website.

On remedies, see Joost Pauwelyn, "Enforcement and Countermeasures in the WTO: Rules are Rules—Toward a More Collective Approach," *American Journal of International Law*, vol. 94, no. 2, p. 335 (April 2000).

CHAPTER 6

Antidumping as Safeguard Policy

J. Michael Finger, Francis Ng, and Sonam Wangchuk

I. Introduction

Political reality suggests that any government that attempts to establish or maintain an open import regime must have at hand some sort of pressure valve—some process to manage occasional pressures for exceptional or sector-specific protection. Since the 1980s antidumping has served this function. An antidumping petition is the usual way in which an industry beset by troublesome imports will request protection—to say the same thing from the other side, an antidumping investigation is the usual way that the government will consider a request for protection.

In this chapter we treat antidumping from the general safeguard perspective. We begin with a discussion of how the safeguard instrument has evolved in the GATT/WTO system—through the post Uruguay Round period in which antidumping has become the most commonly used instrument of import politics for developing countries as well as developed. Looking at the record of antidumping cases since the Uruguay Round, we demonstrate, for example, that the developing countries now use the instrument even more intensely than the traditional users, Australia, Canada, the European Community and the United States. We then review the usefulness of antidumping as a general safeguard instrument and provide some suggestions as to the characteristics of a more sensible safeguard instrument—one which provides a means for a government to manage pressures for protection in a way that: (a) helps it to reach economically sensible answers as to when to impose new protection; and (b) supports rather than undercuts the politics of openness. We conclude that antidumping does not serve this function well.

II. GATT Experience

While the GATT is best known as an agreement to remove trade restrictions, it includes a number of provisions that allow countries to impose new ones. Among them, Article VI allows antidumping and countervailing duties, XVIII allows restrictions to defend the balance of payments or to promote industry development. Article XX lists ten broad categories, e.g., restrictions necessary to protect human, animal or plant life or health.[1]

Renegotiation

As reciprocal negotiation was the initial GATT mode for removing trade restrictions, it is no surprise that renegotiation was the most prominent provision for re-imposing them. The 1947 agreement gave each country an automatic right to renegotiate any of its reductions after three years (Article XXVIII), and under "sympathetic consideration" procedures, reductions could be renegotiated more quickly. Even quicker adjustment was possible under Article XIX. In instances of particularly troublesome increases of imports, a country could introduce a new restriction and then afterwards negotiate a compensating agreement with its trading partners.[2] The idea of compensation was the same here as with a renegotiation, to provide on some other product a reduction that suppliers considered equally valuable.

In the 1950's the GATT was amended to add more elaborate renegotiation provisions. Though the details were complex, the renegotiation process, in outline, was straightforward:

- A country for which import of some product had become particularly troublesome would advise the GATT and the principal exporters of that product that it wanted to renegotiate its previous tariff reduction.
- If, after a certain number of days, negotiation had not reached agreement, the country could go ahead and increase the tariff.
- If the initiating country did so—and at the same time did not provide compensation that exporters considered satisfactory—then the principal exporters were free to retaliate.
- All of these actions were subject to the most-favored-nation (MFN) principle; the tariff reductions or increases had to apply to imports from all countries.[3]

Emergency Actions

Article XIX, entitled "Emergency Actions on Imports of Particular Products," but often referred to as the escape clause or the safeguard clause, provided a country with an import problem quicker access to essentially the same process. Under Article XIX:

- If imports cause or threaten serious injury to domestic producers, the country could take emergency action to restrict those imports.[4]
- If subsequent consultation with exporters did not lead to satisfactory compensation, then the exporters could retaliate.

The GATT asked the country taking emergency action to consult with exporting countries before, but allowed the action to come first in "critical circumstances." In practice, the action has come first most of the time.[5]

History shows that during GATT's first decade and a half, countries opening their economies to international competition through the GATT negotiations did avail themselves of *pressure valve* actions (figure 1). These actions were in large part renegotiations under Article XXVIII, supplemented by emergency actions (restrict first, then negotiate compensation) under the procedures of Article XIX.[6] Over time, the mix shifted toward a larger proportion of emergency actions.

By 1963, fifteen years after the GATT first came into effect, every one of the 29 GATT member countries who had bound tariff reductions under the GATT had undertaken at least one renegotiation—in total, 110 renegotiations, or almost four per country.

In use, Article XIX emergency actions and Article XXVIII renegotiations complemented each together. Nine of the 15 pre-1962 Article XIX actions that were large enough that the exporter insisted on compensation (or threatened retaliation) were eventually resolved as Article XXVIII renegotiations. Article XXVIII renegotiations, in turn, were often folded into regular tariff negotiations. From 1947 through 1961, five negotiating rounds were completed; hence such negotiations were almost continuously under way.

Negotiated Export Restraints

By the 1960s, formal use of Article XIX and of the renegotiations process began to wane. Actions taken under the escape clause tended to involve negligible amounts of world trade in relatively minor product categories.[7] Big problems such as textile and apparel imports were handled another way, through the negotiation of "voluntary" export restraint agreements, VERs. The various textile agreements beginning in 1962, provided GATT sanction to VERs on textiles and apparel. The same method, negotiated export restraints, or VERs, were used by the developed countries to control troublesome imports in several other important sectors, e.g., steel in the United States, autos in the European Union.

Except for those specially sanctioned by the textile arrangements, VERs were clearly GATT-illegal.[8] However, while VERs violated GATT legalisms, they accorded well with its ethic of reciprocity:

- They were at least in form, *negotiations* to allow replacement of restrictions that had been negotiated down. Negotiation was also important to prevent a chain reaction of one country following another to restrict its imports as had occurred in the 1930s.
- A VER did provide compensation, the compensation being the higher price that the exporter would receive.
- In many instances the troublesome increase of imports came from countries that had not been the "principal suppliers" with whom the initial concession had been negotiated. These new exporters were displacing not

Figure 1
Renegotiations, Emergency Actions and VERs

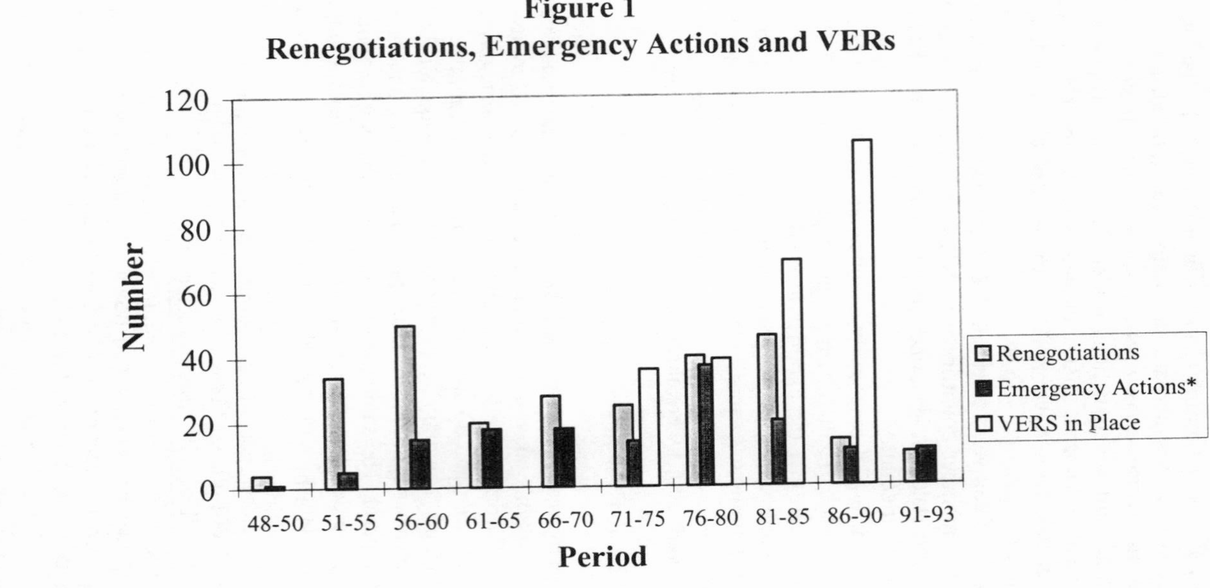

only domestic production in importing countries, but the exports of the traditional suppliers as well. A VER with the new, troublesome, supplier could thus be viewed as defense of the rights of the principal suppliers who had paid for the initial concession.

- The reality of power politics was another factor. Even though one of GATT's objectives was to neutralize the influence of economic power on the determination of trade policy, VERs were frequently used by large countries to control imports from smaller countries.

As the renegotiation, emergency-action mechanism was replaced over time by the use of VERs, VERs also gave way to another mechanism—antidumping. There were several reasons behind this evolution:

- the growing realization in developed countries that a VER was a costly form of protection,[9]
- the long-term legal pressure of the GATT rules,
- the availability of an attractive, GATT-legal, alternative.

The Uruguay Round agreement on safeguards explicitly bans further use of VERs and, along with the Agreement on Textiles and Clothing, requires the elimination of all such measures now in place.

Antidumping

Antidumping was a minor instrument when GATT was negotiated, and provision for antidumping regulations was included with little controversy. In 1958, when the contracting parties finally canvassed themselves about the use of antidumping, the resulting tally showed only 37 antidumping decrees in force across all GATT member countries, 21 of these in South Africa (GATT 1958, p. 14). By the 1990s antidumping had become the developed countries' major safeguard instrument. Since the WTO Agreements went into effect in 1995, it has gained increasing popularity among developing countries. The scale of use of antidumping is a magnitude larger than the scale of use of renegotiations and emergency actions have ever been (figure 2).

Once antidumping proved itself to be applicable to any case of troublesome imports, its other attractions for protection seeking industries and for governments inclined to provide protection were apparent:[10]

- Particular exporters could be picked out. GATT/WTO does not require multilateral application.
- The action is unilateral. GATT/WTO rules require no compensation or renegotiation.
- In national practice, the injury test for antidumping action tends to be softer than the injury test for action under Article XIX.
- The rhetoric of foreign unfairness provides a vehicle for building a political case for protection.

Figure 2
Renegotiations, Emergency Actions, Antidumping Initiations and VERs

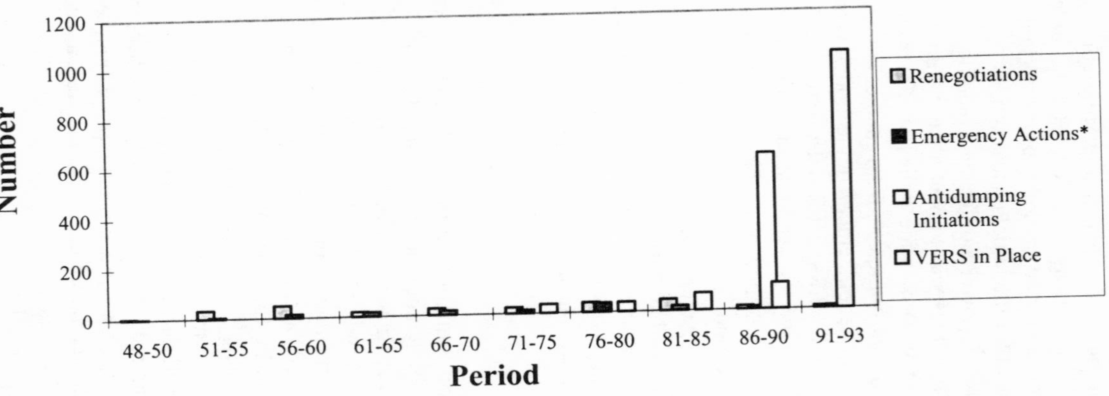

- Antidumping and VERs have proved to be effective complements; i.e., the threat of formal action under the antidumping law provides leverage to force an exporter to accept a VER.[11]
- The investigation process itself tends to curb imports. This is because exporters bear significant legal and administrative costs, importers face the uncertainty of having to pay backdated antidumping duties, once an investigation is completed.
- There is no rule against double jeopardy. If one petition against an exporter fails, minor respecification generates a new valid petition.

III. Post-Uruguay Round Use of Antidumping

This section provides a brief factual presentation of which economies are the most frequent perpetrators of antidumping cases and which economies the most frequent victims. It begins with no hypothesis, its purpose is more to raise questions than to answer them.

Perpetrators

Since the WTO Agreements went into effect in 1995, more than 50 developing countries have informed the WTO of their antidumping regulations, 28 have notified the initiation of antidumping cases. Figure 3 plots the number of antidumping initiations by developed and by developing countries over the past 15 years. Developing countries since the Uruguay Round (in 1995-99) have initiated 559 cases, developed countries 463 cases (table 1). Even transition economies have entered in, 4 cases by Poland, 2 by the Czech Republic and 1 by Slovenia.

The EU and the United States have initiated by far the largest numbers of cases. These economies are, however, the world's largest importers. Hence we provide in tables 2 and 3 two measures of frequency of use of antidumping: the number of cases initiated, and the number of cases *per dollar of imports*.

The latter measure we present as an index. As the United States is the country most associated with antidumping, we set the index of antidumping cases per dollar of imports to 100 for the United States and scale other values from there.

By cases per dollar of imports, the United States has been one of the least intense users of antidumping. Countries such as Japan that have *never* initiated an antidumping case are among the least intense users.

Perhaps the most worrisome information in table 2 is that the most intense users of antidumping are developing countries. South Africa, 89 cases; Argentina, 89 cases; India, 83 cases; and Brazil, 56 cases are high on the list by simple number of cases. By the alternate measure, Brazil's intensity of use is *five times* the U.S. intensity—India's *seven times*, South Africa and Argentina's *twenty times* the U.S. figure.

Figure 3. Antidumping Initiations by Developed and Developing Economies, 1986-99

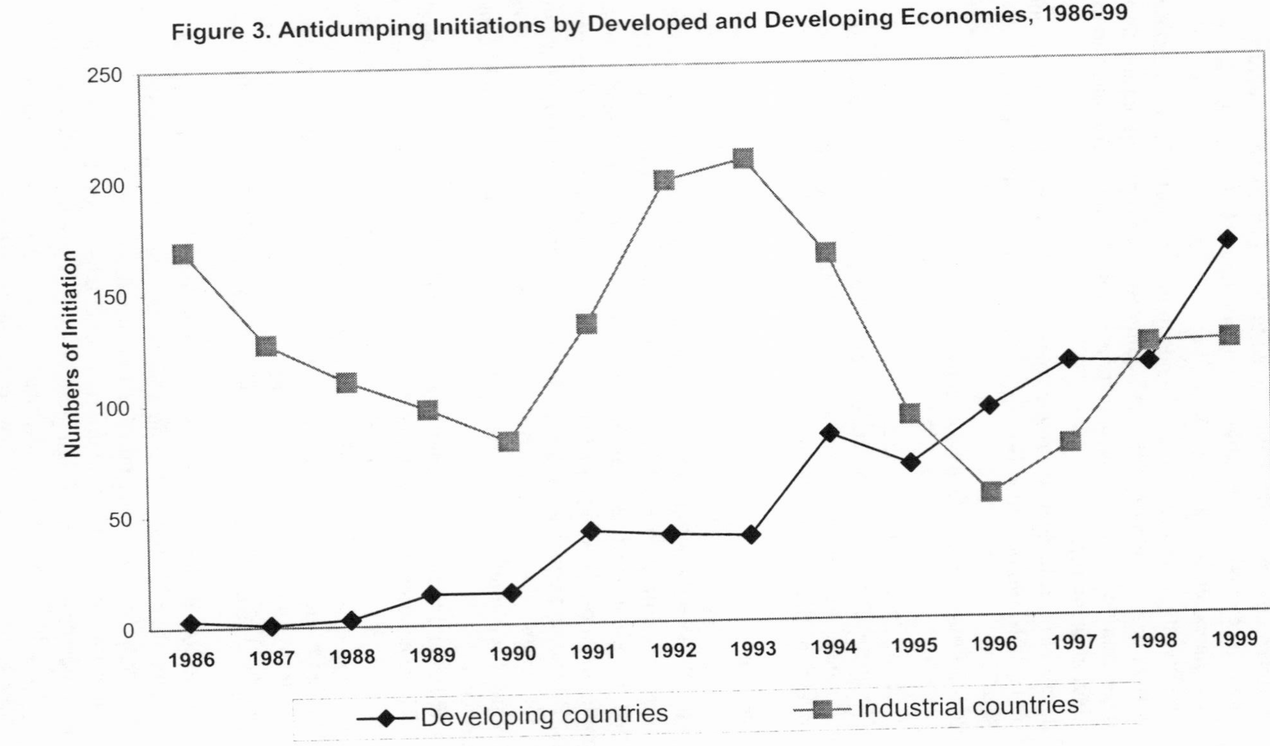

Table 1. Numbers and Percentages of Antidumping Initiations by Country Group, 1995-99

Against By	Industrial Economies[a]	Developing Economies[b]	China, PRC[c]	Transition Economies[d]	All Economies
	Numbers of Antidumping Initiations				
Industrial Economies	127	274	54	62	463
Developing Economies	178	282	82	99	559
Transition Economies	3	1	1	3	7
All Economies	308	557	137	164	1029
	Percentages of Antidumping Initiations				
Industrial Economies	27	59	12	13	100
Developing Economies	32	50	15	18	100
Transition Economies	43	14	14	43	100
All Economies	30	54	13	16	100

Notes:

a Include United States, Canada, Australia, Japan, New Zealand, Iceland, Norway, Switzerland, and 15 European Union members.

b All other economies excluding industrial economies and transition economies.

c Exclude Hong Kong, China; Macau, China; and Chinese Taipei.

d Include 27 transition economies in Eastern Europe and Central Asia

Table 2. Antidumping Initiations Per U.S. Dollar of Imports by Economy, 1995-99

Country/Economy Initiating	Against All Economies	
	No. of Antidumping Initiations	Initiations per U.S. dollar Index (USA=100)
Argentina	89	2125
South Africa	89	2014
Peru	21	1634
India	83	1382
New Zealand	28	1292
Trinidad & Tobago	5	1257
Venezuela	22	1174
Nicaragua	2	988
Australia	89	941
Colombia	15	659
Brazil	56	596
Panama	2	431
Israel	19	418
Chile	10	376
Indonesia	20	330
Mexico	46	290
Egypt	6	278
Turkey	14	204
Korea	37	185
Canada	50	172
Guatemala	1	168
Costa Rica	1	144
Ecuador	1	140
European Union	160	130
Philippines	6	113
United States	136	100
Malaysia	11	97
Slovenia	1	66
Poland	4	65
Czech Republic	2	45
Singapore	2	10
Thailand	1	10

Table 3. Antidumping Initiations Per Dollar of Imports by Country Group, 1995-99

Against	All Economies	
By	No. of Antidumping Initiations	Initiations per U.S. dollar Index (USA=100)
Industrial Economies	463	116
Developing Economies	559	184
Transition Economies	7	23
All Economies	1029	140

Per dollar of imports, the United States is not a high user of antidumping. Each of the other developed country users (table 2) is above the United States. Moreover, the number of cases per dollar of imports is lower for the United States than for *all* developed countries *combined*, including non-users such as Japan.

Victims

Table 4 provides summary information about which countries are most often the victim of antidumping cases. Table 5 provides country-by-country information, not only the number of antidumping cases against each country, but also a measure of how many cases against a country per dollar of exports. The measure of how intensely a country's exports are targeted by foreign antidumping cases is scaled to the figure for Japan.

Perhaps the most striking finding in table 5 is that the transition economies are the ones with the highest intensity of antidumping cases against them. Tables 6 and 7 profile the relative intensity of initiations against different groups of countries. Transition-economy exporters are the most intensely targeted, developed economy exporters the least intensely. As compared to developed economy exporters, developing economy exporters (including Chinese) are almost three times more intensely targeted.

Developing economy antidumping enforcement is as much aimed at developing economy exporters as is developed economy enforcement. Developing economy exporters do not get a break from developing economy antidumping authorities. Developing economy antidumping cases pick out developing economy exporters to the same degree as do developed economy exporters.

Table 4. Numbers of Antidumping Initiations by Victim Country Group, 1995-99[a]

By Against	All Economies	Developing Economies	Transition Economies	Industrial Economies
	Number of Antidumping Initiations			
Industrial Economies	308	178	3	127
Developing Economies	557	282	1	274
China, PR	137	82	1	54
Transition Economies	164	99	3	62
All Economies	1029	559	7	463
	Percentage of Antidumping Initiations			
Industrial Economies	100	58	1	41
Developing Economies	100	51	0	49
China, PRC	100	60	1	39
Transition Economies	100	60	2	38
All Economies	100	54	1	45

Source: Adapted from WTO documents G/L and G/ADP series, 1995-2000.

Notes:

[a]For country/economy classifications, see table 1.

Table 5. Antidumping Initiations per U.S. Dollar of Exports by Victim Economy, 1995-99

Against ↓	Initiations by All Economies	
	No. of Antidumping Initiations	Initiations per U.S.$ Index (Japan=100)
Armenia	1	6777
Georgia	1	3909
Kyrgyzstan	1	3737
Tajikistan	1	3153
Azerbaijan	1	3118
Yugoslavia	5	3059
Kazakhstan	11	2588
Former Yugoslav Rep of Macedonia	3	2313
Ukraine	25	2095
Bosnia-Herzegovina	1	1880
Latvia	3	1818
Egypt	6	1608
Bulgaria	6	1287
Uzbekistan	3	1274
Belarus	6	1255
Cuba	2	1247
Romania	10	1154
Lithuania	4	1107
India	38	1079
Honduras	1	1077
Paraguay	1	917
Zimbabwe	2	889
Moldova, Rep. Of	1	852
Bolivia	1	837
South Africa	20	809
Brazil	41	788
Trinidad & Tobago	2	783
China, PRC	137	776
Estonia	2	749
Indonesia	36	691
Croatia	3	628
Portugal	3	621
Spain	19	609
Korea	75	564
Turkmenistan	1	562
Russian Federation	41	558

Against ↓	Initiations by All Economies No. of Antidumping Initiations	Initiations per U.S.$ Index (Japan=100)
Chile	9	554
Costa Rica	2	513
Slovak Republic	5	512
Thailand	30	509
Turkey	13	502
Hungary	9	499
Macau, China	1	474
Poland	12	448
Pakistan	4	438
Bahrain	1	424
Chinese Taipei	47	386
Hong Kong, China	11	381
Uruguay	1	379
Greece	2	378
Netherlands	17	330
Argentina	8	313
Austria	6	267
Colombia	3	265
Denmark	5	240
Czech Republic	6	240
Venezuela	5	231
Vietnam	2	223
Slovenia	2	222
Malaysia	16	199
Finland	4	197
Italy	22	195
Sweden	7	188
Mexico	20	188
Germany	44	182
Peru	1	179
Ireland	3	177
Israel	4	177
Iran	3	159
United Kingdom	19	157
New Zealand	2	144
Belgium	7	142
France	15	134
European Union 2[b]	179	106
United States	66	105
Japan	44	100

Against ↓	Initiations by All Economies No. of Antidumping Initiations	 Initiations per U.S.$ Index (Japan=100)
Philippines	2	82
Saudi Arabia	4	66
Algeria	1	64
Australia	3	56
Singapore	6	48
Canada	10	46
Switzerland	3	36
Norway	1	21
European Union 1[a]	6	7
Liechtenstein	1	.[c]
All Above Countries	1203	268

Notes:

[a] European Union 15 members as a whole.

[b] European Union as a whole plus EU individual members.

[c] Export data not available

Table 6. Comparing the Intensity of Antidumping Initiations 1995-99 across Different Groups of Economies

Victim Initiator	Developed Economies	Developing Economies	China, PRC	Transition Economies	All Economies
Developed Economies	55	131	199	285	100
Developing Economies	52	147	240	403	100
Transition Economies	71	101	989	168	100
All Economies	54	138	230	294	100

Table 7. Antidumping Initiations per Dollar of imports—Relative Intensities Against Different Groups of Exporting Economies[a]

Initiated against By	Industrial Economies	Developing Economies	China, PRC	Transition Economies	All Economies
Argentina	61	147	625	194	100
Australia	54	194	161	1190	100
Brazil	64	90	819	1986	100
Canada	64	209	262	2897	100
Chile	35	93	289	6997	100
Colombia	20	182	703	2532	100
Costa Rica	0	310	0	0	100
Czech Republic	144	0	0	0	100
Ecuador	0	238	0	0	100
Egypt	0	55	0	1062	100
European Union[b]	22	150	681	517	100
Guatemala	0	253	0	0	100
India	61	103	724	703	100
Indonesia	40	150	277	1600	100
Israel	105	88	765	0	100
Korea	77	109	295	763	100
Malaysia	75	116	0	1422	100

Initiated against By	Industrial Economies	Developing Economies	China, PRC	Transition Economies	All Economies
Mexico	36	196	621	13535	100
New Zealand	28	354	337	0	100
Nicaragua	0	203	0	0	100
Panama	0	226	0	0	100
Peru	9	181	1250	1557	100
Philippines	29	120	596	2219	100
Poland	34	220	1184	336	100
Singapore	0	212	0	0	100
Slovenia	0	0	0	613	100
South Africa	48	189	448	1539	100
Thailand	0	0	0	5522	100
Trinidad & Tobago	0	365	1536	0	100
Turkey	31	375	1360	0	100
United States	61	133	186	672	100
Venezuela	32	161	30770	7866	100
All Above Economies	52	143	280	324	100

Notes: For country/economy classifications, see Table 1.

[a] Number of antidumping initiations against the country group per dollar of imports from the group, scaled to the figure for initiations against imports from all economies; e.g., Argentina, per dollar of imports had 6.25 times more antidumping initiations against China PR than against all countries.

[b] Exclude EU intra trade.

IV. Antidumping Methodology Since the Uruguay Round Agreement

The surge of antidumping usage in the 1980s brought forward a wave of legal and economic analyses of antidumping methodology.[12] Antidumping arms protection-seeking interests with the emotionally compelling argument that foreigners are behaving unfairly. This work focused on two points:

- The administrative methodology was biased—inclined to find dumping when a fair accounting even of pricing below cost would not.
- The social justification—that antidumping extended to transactions from outside the national borders the same discipline that anti-trust law applied to internal transactions.

The definitive analysis of the latter point was an extensive review by the OECD of antidumping cases in Australia, Canada, the European Union and the United States. The review found that 90 percent of the instances of import sales found to be unfair under antidumping rules would never have been questioned under competition law, i.e., if used by a domestic enterprise in making a domestic sale. Much less than ten percent of the antidumping cases would have survived the much more rigorous standards of evidence that applies under competition law.[13]

As this mass of criticism came forward, defenders of antidumping shifted to a more political argument, based on a sense of legitimacy—rules of the game—rather than efficiency. Some sources of seller advantage should not be allowed—e.g., subsidies, selling from a "sanctuary" or protected home market and other government-provided advantages—even if they did not result in consumers being harmed by restraints on competition.[14]

Brink Lindsey (1999) of the Cato Institute has provided a damning analysis of these arguments. He reviewed 141 company-specific dumping determinations by the U.S. Commerce Department, 1995-98, to ascertain the methods used, identify the source of their findings of dumping, and to evaluate the compatibility of the actual determination of dumping with the rhetoric of what justified it. He investigates at two levels:

- Are antidumping determinations as actually conducted effective methodologies to identify the pricing practices of price discrimination and selling below cost?
- Are these pricing practices reliable indicators of the alleged market distortions that justify import restrictions?

In simpler words:

- Does the process bring forward the evidence it alleges?
- Does the evidence prove that the crime was committed?

The evidence Lindsey marshals soundly supports a negative answer to both questions.

On detecting discrimination between home market and export price—and hence a direct indication of selling from a sanctuary market—Lindsey points out that price comparisons are almost never made. Virtually all cases are based on artificial indicators of what the home-market price might (or should) be. Lindsey's findings on this point are in table 8.

From here, Lindsay went on to investigate the impact of various adjustments that the Commerce Department routinely makes to the price information provided by exporters. He did this—generally speaking[15]—by obtaining from exporters the complete information they had submitted to Commerce, then recalculated dumping margins from the entire data set, e.g., the data set, including the sales that Commerce threw out as "below cost."

Among the telling points Lindsey documents is the extent to which constructed-cost methodology overstates profit rates. In no instance for which he found comparable data was the profit rate used in the Commerce calculation less than *twice* the actual rate of profit in the US industry. In no other instance was it less than *three times* as high.[16] He also documents an investigation in which the dumping margin is increased by a factor of *three* when Commerce screened out as "below cost" some of the prices on home-market sales supplied by the exporter, others in which there would have been no dumping margin without the adjustments.

As to the results of a dumping investigation supporting the conclusion of the exporter enjoying a sanctuary home market, the first point Lindsey makes is that such investigations hardly ever provide price comparisons. "Data" on selling below cost is based on questionable measures of cost, and even if it were accurate cost data, it does not demonstrate that the same low prices were available in the home market.[17] The evidence leaves much more than a reasonable doubt that the alleged sanctuary situation.

Lindsey adds supplementary evidence against the sanctuary allegation. For example:

- he finds no correlation between dumping margins and foreign tariff rates, and
- the U.S. government's own "official" tabulation of foreign import restrictions lists significant restrictions in only two of the instances that he covered.[18]

In sum, Lindsey's findings establish that the Uruguay Round Agreement did not change the nature of antidumping practice. The evidence against the exporter is mostly constructed (value). If the exporter does not supply data from which the investigating agency can perform the construction, the accusation from the companies seeking protection then becomes the evidence—the "facts available."

V. Misunderstandings about Antidumping

Dealing sensibly with antidumping as trade policy requires first that it be dealt with for what it is—a wide-reaching instrument for restricting. Thus, two of

Table 8. Methodologies and Outcomes of U.S. Antidumping Investigations, 1995-98

	Number of determinations			Average dumping
Methodology	Total	Affirmative	Affirmative as percent of total	margin (percent) affirmative determinations only
U.S. prices to home-market prices	4	2	50	7.36
U.S. prices to third-country prices	1	0	0	-
U.S. prices to mix of third-country prices, above cost third country prices and constructed value	2	2	100	7.94
U.S. prices to mix of home-market prices, above cost home-market prices and constructed value	31	25	81	17.95
Constructed value	20	14	70	35.07
Nonmarket economy	47	28	60	67.05
Facts available	36	36	100	95.58
Total	141	107	76	58.79

Source: Adapted from WTO documents G/L and G/ADP series, 1995-2000.

Washington's most skilled international trade lawyers begin their advise on how to deal with such instruments in the following way:

> "From the perspective of a U.S. industry seeking protection, [trade laws] simply represent different ways of reaching the same goal—improvement of the competitive position of the complainant against other companies. Exporters should disregard any moralistic claims associated with trade litigation ('dumping,' 'subsidies,' 'unfair' access to raw materials, cheap labor, etc.) and view it from the same perspective—how will the dispute affect their competitive position in the US market." (Horlick and Shea, 2000, p. 1)

Sensible as it sounds, this is not the typical attitude. The following three incidents, drawn from the experiences of the authors of this paper, portray more typical views:

- The chairperson, director of the local chamber of industries, opened a one-week seminar on antidumping by exhorting his colleagues on the benefits of integrating the local economy into the world economy, cajoled them against the dangers of their traditional protectionist sentiments, and urged them to pay attention to the possibilities offered by this modern, WTO-sanctioned instrument, antidumping.
- A deputy minister of a small country descried his situation as follows. "In our country, farmers grow chickens. If you want chicken for dinner, you go to the market and you buy a chicken. In the United States, farmers do not grow chickens, they grow chicken parts. Because people in the United States are afraid of cholesterol, they prefer white meat, so it sells at a good price. The legs, the dark meat, they export to our country, at a price lower than what our farmers usually get for a chicken. That's dumping, isn't it, so shouldn't we take action?"
- Since 1990, an industrializing Asian country has conducted a number of antidumping investigations. Several of these investigations concerned imports of industrial inputs such as steel or chemicals. After receiving a petition from another such domestic industry, the country's international trade commission examined the petitions, found them to be complete and the information in them to be accurate. The government then imposed a preliminary antidumping duty. User industries complained about the higher costs imposed on them, and eventually convinced the government that the jobs and output that would be lost by user industries exceeded what would be saved in the industry that had sought protection. The government then lifted the antidumping duty and closed the case.This decision left the Commission in a quandary. The (preliminary) antidumping investigation had proceeded by the letter of the WTO agreement, had come out affirmative. Yet imposing an antidumping action did not seem to be the correct

thing to do. The Commission called in several outside experts to help them to review their investigation procedures.

The point of these stories is that the WTO antidumping agreement is not economic advice. It is about when an import restriction is *permitted*, not about when one is *recommended.* Antidumping's rise to prominence had nothing to do with the logic of a sensible pressure valve instrument. The political struggle that shaped it was over more vs. less import restrictions, not over what makes for sensible economic policy.

The government in the third incident above made the correct decision, the decision that took into account the impact of an import restriction on *all* domestic interests. Yet the government was uncomfortable with its decision, both because it was not one dictated by GATT/WTO rules, and because following GATT/WTO rules had not convinced the domestic users to accept the hardship an import restriction imposed on them.

VI. A Better Safeguard Mechanism

The key issue is the impact on the local economy. Who in the local economy would benefit from the proposed import restriction, and who would lose? On each side, by how much? It is therefore critical that the policy process by which the government decides to intervene or not to intervene gives voice to those interests that benefit from open trade and would bear the costs of the proposed intervention. Such a policy mechanism would both: (a) help the government to separate trade interventions that would serve the national economic interest from those that would not; and (b) even in those instances in which the decision is to restrict imports, support the politics of openness and liberalization.

Antidumping fails to satisfy either criteria. As economics, it looks at only half of the economic impact on the domestic economy. It gives standing to import-competing, domestic interests, but not to domestic users, be they user enterprises or consumers. As politics, it undercuts rather than supports a policy of openness by giving voice to only the negative impact of trade on domestic interests and by inviting such interests to blame their problems on the "unfairness" of foreigners.

The key characteristic of a sensible safeguard procedure is that it treat domestic interests that would be harmed by an import restriction equally with those domestic interests that would benefit. The "morality" of the foreign interest is irrelevant—the issue is the plus and minus on the domestic economy. Operationally, this suggestion means simply that what is done in an "injury test,"—identification of impact on import-competing interests—is repeated for users of imports. The mechanics involve the same variables: impacts on profits, output, employment, etc. and the same techniques to quantify them.

VII. Conclusion

Antidumping is by far the most prevalent instrument for imposing new import restrictions. As a "pressure valve" to maintain an open trade policy, it has serious weaknesses. Burgeoning use by developing economies demonstrates how dangerous it can be. Even so, the WTO community continues to take up antidumping as if it were a specialized instrument. As long as the rest of us continue to deal with antidumping within the apparent technical conception that its users have created, we will continue to lose.[19]

Notes

[1] A complete list, with information on frequency of use, is provided in Finger (1996).

[2] The early GATT rounds were collections of bilateral negotiations, but tariff cuts had to be made on a most-favored-nation (MFN) basis (i.e., applicable to imports from all GATT members). A renegotiation was not with the entire GATT membership, but only with the country with whom that reduction was initially negotiated, plus any other countries enumerated by the GATT as "principal suppliers."

[3] Renegotiation procedures are basically the same now—under the Uruguay Round Agreements—as they were then.

[4] The Uruguay Round agreement on safeguards (but not the initial GATT) requires a formal investigation and determination of injury. It allows however a provisional safeguard measure to be taken before the investigation is completed.

[5] GATT 1994, p. 486. The Uruguay Round Safeguards Agreement modified the emergency action procedure in several ways. Among these,

- no compensation is required or retaliation allowed in the first three years that a restriction is in place.
- no restriction (including extension) may be for more than eight years, (ten years by a developing country).
- all measures of more than one year must be progressively liberalized.

[6] Though, as figure 1 shows, the mix shifted over time toward a larger proportion of emergency actions.

[7] Statistics for 1980 show that actions taken under Article XIX covered imports valued at $1.6 billion while total world trade was at the same time valued at $2.0 trillion. Sampson (1987, p. 145).

[8] GATT (1994, p. 494).

[9] For example, Hufbauer and Elliott (1994) found that of the welfare loss placed on the U.S. economy from all forms of protection in place in the early 1990s, over 83 percent of that loss came from VERs.

[10] The process by which the scope of antidumping was expanded is examined in Finger (1993, Ch. 2).

[11] Over 1980-1988, 348 of 774 United States antidumping cases were superseded by VERs (Finger and Murray, 1993). July 1980 through June 1989, of 384 antidumping actions taken by the European Community, 184 were price undertakings. (Stegmann, 1992).

[12] Boltuck-Litan (1991) and Finger (1993) pulled together much of the criticism, both legal and economic. The first criticisms came from legal analysis, e.g., Dickey (1979).

[13] OECD Economics Department 1996, p. 18. The country studies were eventually published in Lawrence (1998).

[14] Lindsay (1999, pp. 2ff.) provides a good discussion as well as quotations from and references to antidumping defenders.

[15] See Lindsey for specifics.

[16] Lindsey, Table 4.

[17] Lindsay, p. 10, documents instances where, had the cost comparison been against *variable* cost there would have been no dumping margin—even using Commerce "cost" data.

[18] *The National Trade Estimates Report*, issued annually by USTR.

[19] We offer another conclusion that is not supported by the material in the paper: any economics treatise on antidumping that begins by defining "dumping" is part of the problem, not part of the solution.

References

Boltuck, Richard and Robert Litan (eds.). 1991. *Down in the Dumps: Administration of the Unfair Trade Laws*. Washington, D.C.: Brookings Institution.

Dickey, William L. 1979. "The Pricing of Imports into the United States," *Journal of World Trade Law*, 13:238-56.

Finger, J. Michael and Tracy Murray. 1993. "Antidumping and Countervailing Duty Enforcement in the United States," Ch. 13 in Finger (1993).

Finger, J. Michael and K. C. Fung. 1993. "Will GATT Enforcement Control Antidumping?" World Bank, Policy Research Working Paper Number 1232.

Finger, J Michael. 1993. *Antidumping: How It Works and Who Gets Hurt*. Ann Arbor: University of Michigan Press.

Finger, J Michael. 1996. "Legalized Backsliding: Safeguard Provisions in the GATT," in Martin and Winters (1996).

GATT Secretariat. 1994. *The Results of the Uruguay Round of Multilateral Trade Negotiations: The Legal Texts*. Geneva: GATT.

Horlick, Gary N. and Eleanor Shea. 2000. "Dealing with US Trade Laws: Before, During and After," in Bernard Hoekman and Philip English (eds.) *Developing Countries and the Next Round of WTO Negotiations*, World Bank, forthcoming.

Hufbauer, Gary Clyde and Kimberley Ann Elliot. 1994. *Measuring the Costs of Protection in the United States*. Washington, D.C.: Institute for International Economics.

Lawrence, Robert Z. (ed.). 1998. *Brookings Trade Forum 1998*. Washington, D.C.: Brookings Institution.

Lindsey, Brink 1999. "The US Antidumping Law: Rhetoric versus Reality," Cato Insitute, Washington, D.C. Trade Policy Analysis No. 7, August 16. (http://www.freetrade.org/pubs/pas/tpa-007es.html)

Martin, Will and L. Alan Winters (eds.). 1996. *The Uruguay Round and the Developing Countries.* Cambridge: Cambridge University Press.

OECD, Economics Department. 1996. *Trade and Competition, Frictions After the Uruguay Round (Note by the Secretariat)*. Paris: OECD.

Mastel, Greg. 1998. *Antidumping Laws and the U.S. Economy*. Washington, D.C.: M. E. Sharpe for the Economic Stategy Institute.

Sampson, G. 1987. "Safeguards." in J. Michael Finger and Andrej Olechowski (eds.), *The Uruguay Round, A Handbook for the Multilateral Negotiations*. Washington, D.C.: World Bank.

CHAPTER 7

Intellectual Property Issues for the United States and Japan: Disputes and Common Interests

Keith E. Maskus

I. Introduction

The protection of intellectual property rights (IPRs) remains at the forefront of international policy deliberations. Many developing nations are in the process of designing and implementing new regimes as required by the WTO Agreement on the Trade-Related Aspects of Intellectual Property Rights (TRIPS). Under TRIPS a number of disputes about IPRs have been the subject of panel decisions, with those disputes often arising between developed countries. Intellectual property laws and judicial interpretation of those laws continue to evolve in the developed nations as the dictates of technological change and competition place stresses on standard forms of protection. Furthermore, IPRs are integral to issues concerning the international provision of public goods. The controversies they engender are likely to increase in number and intensity, even as TRIPS becomes an accepted set of multilateral rules.

The United States and Japan share a broad commonality of interests in shaping the evolution of global IPRs over the medium term. The United States is the world's largest net supplier of intellectual creations and Japan takes a similar role with respect to transferring technologies to the industrializing nations of Asia. Thus, both nations should see enhanced abilities of their creative firms to earn higher returns on the international exploitation of new technologies and products as global standards are tightened.

However, there are interesting and important differences of opinion between the two nations. First, each country continues to complain about certain aspects of the other country's intellectual property regime, despite considerable convergence in those regimes since 1994. Second, the United States has recently taken actions that may reasonably be described as overly protectionist on any utilitarian grounds (Maskus, 2000a) and it is doubtful that Japan would wish to emulate these standards. Indeed, each country can learn from the other as it wrestles with the tradeoff between innovation and diffusion that is inherent in IPRs. Moreover, developing nations may look to both models as they consider their own standards. For example, Japan's growth performance since the second world war may be attributed in part to its intellectual property system, which favored learning and diffusion over fundamental invention. Thus, developing countries may wish to model their systems more closely on the Japanese example.

II. Bilateral IPRs Issues

Overall there has been marked convergence in intellectual property standards between Japan and the United States since 1994. For example, as a component of the Japan-U.S. Framework Talks, in 1994 the two countries signed a pair of agreements that committed both sides to changes in their patent systems (Suzuki, 1997). As a result, Japan began permitting patent applications to be filed in English, ended third-party opposition proceedings prior to patent grant, accelerated patent examination procedures to obtain a disposition on applications within 36 months, and eliminated the threat of dependent-patent compulsory licenses except where anticompetitive practices may be demonstrated. Japan adopted a revised patent law in 1999 that made it easier for plaintiffs to prove patent infringement in courts and gave judges more discretion over setting damages. The Japan Patent Office (JPO) is also working to reduce the examination period to 12 months by the end of the year 2000 (USTR, 2000).

For its part, the United States changed the term of patent protection from 17 years from the grant date to 20 years from the initial filing date. Japan had complained further about the lack of an early publication system, which permitted the practice of "submarine patents," discussed below. In 1999 the United States enacted legislation for publication with 18 months of applications that had been filed abroad as well as in the United States. However, the law provides filers the choice of preventing early disclosure if the applications are made only in the United States. This partial resolution of the problem remains a sticking point.

Implementation of the TRIPS requirements led to further convergence in intellectual property protection (Suzuki, 1997). Japan added certain rights to its patent and copyright laws, while extending the term of patent protection. Japan also clarified procedures for receiving utility model grants, removing the examination requirement and shortening protection to six years. This latter change placed the utility model system on a par with that in Germany and France; the United States has no such system. Finally, in response to an adverse WTO ruling in 1997, Japan provided retroactive copyright protection for pre-existing sound recordings in order to provide a full 50-year term, an issue of considerable interest to the United States.

Both Japan and the United States have signed the Copyright Treaty and the Performances and Phonograms Treaty, concluded under the auspices of the World Intellectual Property Organization (WIPO). In preparation for ratification of the Copyright Treaty, the Diet revised Japan's copyright law in 1999 to include criminal penalties for producing and distributing devices designed to circumvent copyrights in electronic transmissions (USTR, 2000).

Recent judicial decisions in Japan have further strengthened intellectual property protection and increased its harmonization with U.S. practices (Takenada, 1997). For example, in a recent case the Osaka High Court elucidated a doctrine of equivalents, much like that recognized in U.S. courts, in finding for a plaintiff in a patent case.[1] This ruling significantly extended the range of equivalency that could be found to constitute infringement relative to prior Japanese procedure. As such it reflects a significant increase in patent scope. In another case, the Tokyo High Court took the unprecedented step of overriding a decision of the JPO in finding an issued patent to be invalid.[2] In another, the Japanese Supreme Court adopted the first sale doctrine, as developed by U.S. courts.[3] This doctrine limits the patentee's right to exclude parallel imports of products that it legally puts on the market to cases in which the patent owner imposes a territorial restriction on its buyers. In applying the U.S. permission of territorial restrictions, this decision sharply increased protection against parallel imports of patented goods into Japan.

Despite this tendency toward convergence, there remain differences in the national systems. In their most recent reports on foreign trade barriers, the trade authority of each country lists perceived problems with the intellectual property regime of the other. Following is a brief overview of these problems with accompanying commentary.

Japanese Concerns about the U.S. System

In its review of American trade policies, the Ministry of International Trade and Industry (MITI) lists several problems with the U.S. intellectual property regime (MITI, 2000). One objection is that the United States uniquely retains its "first to invent" patent system, while the rest of the world follows a "first to file" system. The United States prefers to maintain this approach in the belief that it rewards the ultimate inventor and also promotes voluntary disclosure of research results prior to patent filing by scientists and inventors. Indeed, it is primarily university researchers and small inventors who argue for retention of this system. However, the Japanese—and other—governments are concerned that the American approach raises a threat of uncertainty for their firms. Specifically, in conjunction with the partial absence of early disclosure and the prior practice of beginning a patent term on the date of grant rather than filing, the U.S. system permitted the existence of "submarine patents." In this situation, an applicant could indefinitely delay processing of its application and have the patent granted after a rival firm merchandised the same technology, often much later.

The United States has moved partially to rectify this problem by providing the limited early disclosure mentioned above and beginning the term of protection from the filing date, as required by Article 33 of TRIPS. However, this change in procedure does not apply to patent applications submitted before

June 7, 1995, raising the continuing specter of hidden patents coming to light. Moreover, the U.S. Patent Reform Act of 1999 relaxed many of the limitations on patent term extensions, suggesting that confidential patent applications, particularly in the pharmaceutical and biotechnology sectors, could remain hidden and potent for some time. An additional problem with the first-to-invent system is that rivals often must invest considerable sums in determining the identity of the first inventor. This can be particularly costly when a new invention must attain license rights from a number of prior inventors of overlapping technologies.

It has been observed frequently that the U.S. Patent and Trademark Office (USPTO) is increasingly overwhelmed with patent applications, making adequate examination procedures difficult (Maskus, 2000a). This problem, stemming in part from an onslaught of applications for business-methods patents in internet distribution technologies, is thought to result in patents issued in error due to the failure by examiners to take prior art into account. Indeed, examiners tend to rely on listings of prior art solely in the applications themselves rather than engage in an independent search. Such a system could be rectified by an adequate opportunity for re-examination permitting third parties to contest validity of patents. However, the U.S. system places severe limitations on the rights of third parties to challenge patents (Janis, 2000). In the U.S. Patent Reform Act of 1999, Congress failed to relax these limitations in any significant way and continued to deny third parties any appeal of re-examination findings issued by the USPTO. Thus, this system erects barriers to rival inventors who believe that patents have been issued in error.

The Japanese government retains some concerns over the operation of Section 337 of the U.S. Tariff Act of 1930. Numerous procedures for enforcing this law were found to be in violation of national treatment obligations by the GATT in 1989.[4] Virtually all of the discriminatory elements of the law were removed in the Uruguay Round implementation legislation in 1995. However, the U.S. International Trade Commission even today could effectively discriminate against imports in the designation of its "target date" for final determination in each investigation, for no such date exists in cases involving domestic infringement. The EU requested consultations on this issue in January 2000 and Japan is monitoring the progress of the case (MITI, 2000).

Finally, the Japanese government contends that the existence and use of Special 301 in U.S. trade law poses dangers of unilateral assertion of intellectual property standards in ways that could be inconsistent with multilateral norms.

U.S. Concerns about the Japanese System

As recently as 1999 Japan remained on the Special 301 "Watch List" issued by USTR, but did not appear on it in 2000. However, the United States continues to complain about the narrow scope and interpretation of Japanese patent claims, the practice of "patent flooding" around invention patents, the slow pace of patent litigation in Japanese courts, the inability to compel effective compliance with discovery procedures, and inadequate safeguards for confidential information produced in discovery (USTR, 2000; Suzuki, 1997). The introduction of a doctrine of equivalents into Japanese jurisprudence, as mentioned earlier, could overcome objections regarding narrow patent claims (Katoh, 1997). Patent flooding is facilitated by various characteristics of the Japanese patent system. Some of these characteristics have been removed or modified, such as pre-grant opposition and low filing fees. Japan is modifying others, including ineffective judicial remedies and compulsory cross-licensing. Nonetheless, as one observer noted, the massive numbers of patent applications in Japan compared to the United States reflects, to an important extent, the nature of intense competition for small-scale innovation in Japan (Katoh, 1997). In that context, it is debatable whether continual broadening of patent scope is in Japan's interest, a point to which I return in a later section.

According to USTR, Japan has made considerable progress in reducing copyright piracy. The United States calls for Japan to amend its Civil Procedures Act to award punitive damages rather than actual damages and to provide for effective evidence collection (USTR, 2000). It also urges Japan to strengthen its anti-circumvention law for devices aimed at defeating copyrights on the internet.

It should be noted that, at least in one area of copyrights, Japan has stronger standards than does the United States. In particular, Japan provides extensive moral rights for authors and artists, whereas the United States does not. This difference stems from Japan's tradition of emulating German and French intellectual property law, which distinguishes between an author's "personal rights" (moral rights) and his "economic rights" (copyrights). The U.S. tradition of treating IPRs as utilitarian devices recognizes only the latter rights.

The U.S. government acknowledges the revisions made in 1997 to Japan's Trademark Law, which accelerated the registration of rights, strengthened protection of well-known marks, and increased penalties for trademark infringement (USTR, 2000). However, USTR claims without explanation that protection of well-known marks remains weak, an interpretation that is rejected by one Japanese expert (Katoh, 1997).

A continuing irritation to the U.S. government is Article 82(2) of Japan's Constitution, which requires that all court proceedings be open to the public. This requirement erects a roadblock to maintaining confidential trade secrets in seeking intellectual property protection. The United States considers this situation to be unacceptably weak and urges Japan to reform its protection of trade secrets, which would require Constitutional amendment. The Japanese government responds that its system is in compliance with TRIPS Article 42, which requires a means to protect confidential information except where it would be contrary to existing constitutional requirements.

The United States continues to press Japan to increase its number of intellectual property lawyers and judges in order to make litigation more effective and expeditious. In response, Japan has instituted additional training programs and new legal curricula focusing on IPRs. However, Japan has a long way to go to catch the United States. As of 1997, Japan had 16, 368 lawyers (13 per 100,000 population) in comparison with the U.S. supply of 906,611 lawyers (340 per 100,000). The United States had 15 times as many judges (Millhaupt, 2000), with the discrepancy in the area of intellectual property presumably being even larger.

In reviewing this history it is fair to say that while both nations continue to strengthen their protection of intellectual property, there has been substantive convergence of Japanese standards to U.S. norms. Surely this reflects the evolution of Japan from a technology follower to a nation with enterprises that innovate on a global scale (Maskus and McDaniel, 1999). Both countries have mature regimes and the differences between them are, in the main, small irritants rather than major conflicts.

Nonetheless, Japan's system retains features that make it less protective than the American regime, which has been described as "protectionism unchained" (Maskus, 2000a). The wisdom of the U.S. system may be questioned on the grounds of, *inter alia*, its recognition of broad patents on biotechnological inventions and research tools, awarding of business-methods patents with non-existent standards for non-obviousness, and privatization of data already in the public domain through the protection of databases. Japanese authorities should think carefully about whether its system should emulate these standards.

III. Interests in TRIPS Implementation

Developing countries were supposed to meet their obligations under TRIPS (except in the area of pharmaceutical and biotechnology patents) by the beginning of 2000, though many have been unable to implement all dimensions of the required standards. The least-developed countries have until the year 2005 to do so. Thus, the short-term policy challenge is to monitor and influence the extent of implementation.

Short-term and Long-term Effects of Stronger Standards

Both the United States and Japan have export interests in seeing stronger standards implemented and enforced in developing countries, with Japan's concerns arising particularly in East Asia. The United States remains, by far, the largest net recipient of royalties and license fees earned on intellectual property (Maskus, 2000a). While Japan is a net payer of such fees overall, it earns substantial amounts from its licensing of intellectual property in the newly industrializing economies. Japan also transfers considerable amounts of technology to developing Asia through both exports of capital goods and investment in manufacturing facilities. The economic returns to such activities should rise sharply as stronger IPRs are implemented.

To see this, consider an updating of the results in McCalman (2001), who analyzed 1988 bilateral patent statistics for 29 countries. He assessed the implicit price of technology transfers through patent portfolios as how that price is influenced by patent rights. In particular, he inferred econometrically the value of patent rights in each country by relating local parameters to the decision to patent. McCalman employed the Ginarte-Park (1997) index of patent rights to capture the patent changes TRIPS requires country by country. For example, many developing countries must improve enforcement, remove working requirements, provide for reversal of burden of proof, and lengthen patent duration. These components are identified in the patent index and their impact on patent value could be estimated with dummy variables. The resulting coefficients were applied to bilateral patent stock ownership to compute the anticipated rise in patent rents. This is inherently a static calculation based on an unchanged 1988 patent portfolio.[5]

Table 1 lists selected estimates that I have modified from his computations, using GDP deflators and exchange rates to update the figures to millions of 1995 dollars. As may be seen, the United States would be a net recipient of higher patent rents on its 1988 international portfolio from all countries, with a total net inward transfer of $5.7 billion. This figure may be compared to total U.S. net receipts of royalties and license fees in 1995 of approximately $20 billion. Germany and Switzerland also would be net recipients among the countries listed. While patents owned by Americans in Japan would have higher value of some $690 million, Japan would actually be a net recipient from all other countries combined. Japan's inward transfers are particularly large from the two Asian developing economies represented, Korea and India. This finding reflects the large net ownership by Japan of patents registered in Korea and India (in comparison with the reverse ownership), combined with the significant strengthening of patent regimes that would be required of those nations relative to their 1988 systems.

These figures suggest that the short-run impact of TRIPS would be to transfer considerable ownership rents to firms in developed countries, especially the United States but including Japan as well.[6] Over the long term, however, TRIPS may be expected to increase international flows of high-technology trade, FDI, and licensing (Maskus, 2000a). On past trends, Japan should be a major participant as an exporter of technology through these channels, particularly to industrializing East Asia. In this context, there is both a direct impact of stronger IPRs on technology transfer and an indirect impact through subsequent growth increases, which would rebound into higher demand for U.S. and Japanese products.

While any such calculations are speculative, consider the implications of the econometric results reported in Maskus (2000a). In Table 2 I make an educated guess about the expected increases in the Ginarte-Park patent index that

Table 1. Estimated Bilateral Net Rent Transfers from TRIPS Patent Standards ($millions in 1995 prices)

	Country of Residence of Patent Holder												
Country of Patent Location	US	JP	GE	UK	SW	CA	AU	KO	ME	BR	IN	OT	Total
USA (US)	--	-690	-212	-521	-132	-1199	-102	-197	-480	-767	-240	-1198	-5738
Japan (JP)	690	--	115	20	21	-56	15	-92	-15	-70	-86	10	552
Germany (GE)	212	-115	--	-257	-57	-46	-19	-48	-28	-128	-127	-648	-1261
UK (UK)	521	-20	257	--	33	-10	5.7	-17	-10	-44	-48	30	698
Switzerland (SW)	132	-21	57	-33	--	-8.8	-1.4	-12	-6.8	-33	-37	-96	-60
Canada (CA)	1199	56	46	10	8.8	--	3.5	-3.4	-5.5	-11	-5.1	7	1305
Australia (AU)	102	-15	19	-5.7	1.4	-3.5	--	-12	-3.5	-16	-17	-6	44
Korea (KO)	197	92	48	17	12	3.4	12	--	-0.1	-0.3	-0.5	48	429
Mexico (ME)	480	15	28	10	6.8	5.5	3.5	0.1	--	-0.01	0.01	18	567
Brazil (BR)	767	70	128	44	33	11	16	0.3	0.01	--	0.09	191	1260
India (IN)	240	86	127	48	37	5.1	17	0.5	-0.01	-0.09	--	80	641
Others (OT)	1198	-10	648	-30	96	-7	6	-48	-18	-191	-80	--	1564
Total	5738	-552	1261	-698	60	-1305	-44	-429	-567	-1260	-641	-1564	0

Source: Author's updates of calculations in McCalman (2001).

Table 2. Estimated Effects of TRIPS Patent Regulations on International Activity ($millions in 1995 prices)

Country	*GP1*	*GP2*	*Manufacturing Imports*	*(%)*	*High-Tech Mfg. Imports*	*(%)*	*Manufacturing Asset Stocks*	*(%)*	*Unaffiliated R&L Fees*	*(%)*
China	2.00	3.25	16,020	(15)	2,693	(12)	657	(19)	na	(na)
Korea	3.94	4.30	2,072	(2)	446	(2)	188	(6)	271	(48)
Thailand	2.24	3.25	6,384	(11)	1,390	(8)	1,017	(33)	na	(na)
Indonesia	2.27	3.25	3,163	(21)	318	(8)	861	(91)	79	(226)
India	1.17	3.25	6,552	(43)	653	(32)	573	(57)	260	(929)

Source: Author's computations from Maskus (2000), modifying results from Maskus and Penubarti (1995), Maskus (1998), and Yang and Maskus (2000).

would prevail after TRIPS implementation in selected Asian nations. Some of these increases are large relative to prior protection levels (compare GP2 with GP1 for India, for example), suggesting that the results of econometric estimation should be treated with caution.

The underlying econometric models found that, particularly in large developing economies, the impacts of stronger patent rights on manufacturing imports from all countries and FDI and licensing flows from the United States would be statistically and economically significant. For example, the trade model suggested that Chinese imports of manufacturing goods would rise by $16 billion, or 15 percent of 1995 manufacturing imports. Imports of high-technology goods would rise by 12 percent. The stock of FDI assets owned in manufacturing by American multinational enterprises would rise by $657 million, or 19 percent of its 1995 level. Other flows may be read in similar fashion. The implausibly large proportional increases in FDI assets in Indonesia and licensing fees in Indonesia and India stem from the large simulated increase in patent protection in those countries, combined with high estimated elasticities across developing nations.

These figures suggest that U.S. firms could enjoy considerable increases in demand for goods and technology in large developing economies as a result of TRIPS. Assuming these estimates hold also for Japanese activity, which is at least as large as American activity in these countries, the same may be said for that nation's firms. Thus, over the longer term, TRIPS promises export gains and cost reductions through FDI. Moreover, such increases in technology absorption in developing economies may be expected to raise their growth performance. For example, Maskus (2000a) computed that China's average TFP growth could rise from 3.5% to 4% or higher as a result of the higher imports of machinery and FDI.

Subtleties in Implementation

Despite this long-term commonality of interests, it is likely that the United States would place greater emphasis than Japan on implementation of strong intellectual-property standards in developing countries. In part, this difference in views could be strategic in that American firms on average have more global technology to protect than do Japanese firms. Moreover, the extensive production networks Japan has built in Eastern Asian countries could benefit from easier learning and diffusion possibilities, subject to observing minimum TRIPS standards, than would be available if protective American standards were established widely.

In part, it also could reflect recent history, in that Japan's patent system in place from the 1950's until 1994 embodied features that promoted diffusion and incremental innovation, with a positive impact on TFP growth (Maskus and McDaniel, 1999). With that background, Japanese officials might be expected to be more sympathetic with a phased implementation of successively stronger standards as spelled out in Maskus (2000a). In particular, Japan's positive history with utility models provides a useful model for technology-follower nations as they select new patent regimes. Japan also seems more willing to undertake the best-efforts technology-transfer commitments reached in TRIPS on the part of developed economies.

More broadly, the task in selecting IPRs standards in developing countries is to promote dynamic competition and information diffusion through the use of fair means. Thus, for example, countries might be expected to adopt narrow patent claims, pre-grant opposition, early disclosure, limited use of compulsory licenses, exclusion of computer programs from patentability, and permission of reverse engineering of computer programs. Not all of these policies would be in Japan's economic interests on a sectoral basis. Patents for computer programs and video games might be of particular interest for Japan's information-technology sector. Again, however, given its extensive international production and design networks, there may be some interest in avoiding patents outside the developed countries in order to promote interoperability among national affiliates and associated programming enterprises. This observation is consistent with Japan's copyright law, which is silent on the issue of reverse engineering of computer programs, thereby permitting it under a "private use" defense. Japan's patent law also recognizes a free right to use patented material for experimental and research purposes.

Issues for TRIPS Revision

As has been noted elsewhere, TRIPS itself is subject to revision through commitments to revisit certain issues, though extensive changes are unlikely (Maskus, 2000b). Two issues of particular relevance arise. First, countries are committed to review the operation of Article 27 regarding exemptions from patent protection for certain biotechnological inventions and required protection for plant varieties. Both the United States and Japan have dynamic interests in strong protection for biotechnology and plant varieties; indeed, Japanese residents applied for more plant variety registrations in 1996 than did American residents (Maskus, 2000a). Thus, they might be expected to present a unified front on this issue.

However, proposals to strengthen these provisions even further are met with suspicion in developing countries, which see patents in biotechnology and plant breeding systems as damaging for their industrial and farming interests. To the extent that Japan and the United States seek to push this agenda they would need presumably to provide greater market access, particularly in agriculture, in compensation. It remains to be seen whether such a linkage is feasible.

Second, discussions are under way at the WTO regarding extension of the special protection for geographical indications in wines and spirits to further sectors. There is scope for agreement here as a number of developing countries would like to protect their own food products with distinctive geographical indications. Japan also could benefit from specified protection for sake and varietal fruits, among other products.

IV. Interests beyond TRIPS

The TRIPS Agreement continues to be implemented internationally and its basic structure is unlikely to be changed in the foreseeable future. However, a number of broader questions arise in the intellectual property context that countries need to consider. I provide a brief overview of three such issues here; all are far more complicated than this treatment can convey.

First, among industrialized nations Japan adopted strong intellectual property standards relatively recently. For example, pharmaceutical products have been patented only since the late 1970s and its patent rules regarding scope and opposition were reformed in 1994. Software patents are also relatively recent, though in wide use and, according to USTR, there are still difficulties in its recognition of well-known trademarks.

The essence of IPRs is to create market power in order to encourage innovation. In this regard, Japan has layered strong standards onto an economy that many consider to suffer from weaknesses in both static and dynamic competition. Where barriers to entry of new domestic enterprises and of incoming FDI are significant, the strengthening of IPRs could stifle competition at least as much as it promotes technical change.

Thus, there is an intimate connection between IPRs and competitive processes. While Japan has extensive guidelines in place regarding the competitive abuses of IPRs, its competition authorities may need to be vigilant in monitoring and disciplining anti-competitive arrangements arising from the nexus of intellectual property protection and private market restraints. American antitrust officials cannot escape this connection either. The Federal Trade Commission and the Anti-Trust Division of the Justice Department increasingly are faced with complex decisions regarding the exercise of market power through patent pooling and vertical acquisition of technologies.[7]

These problems increasingly will reach across borders over time. TRIPS Article 40 recognizes the right of countries to discipline anti-competitive abuses of IPRs within their borders, subject to transparency and consultation requirements. However, in my view this provision will prove inadequate to deal with cross-border licensing restraints, pooling agreements, and mergers associated with IPRs. Accordingly, in my view, it is time to begin multilateral and plurilateral consideration of the basic framework of an international competition agreement.

Second, important questions emerge in the interface between IPRs and environmental regulation. A considerable problem for the WTO regards how to deal with policies that could restrict trade in genetically modified organisms (GMOs), the development of which is directly tied to IPRs. Both Japan and the United States are active in producing new GMOs in agriculture and pharmaceuticals, so their industries share a common interest in limiting trade barriers.

Nonetheless, TRIPS itself squarely introduces conditions of production into the disciplines of the multilateral trading system. Thus, the interplay between patent protection for GMOs and trade restraints becomes an urgent issue for multilateral consideration.

Finally, Japan and the United States share an interest in securing multilateral adherence to the WIPO Copyright Treaty and Performances and Phonograms Treaty. These treaties should help protect producers and performers whose work is disseminated electronically but also should permit nations to strike an adequate balance between information generation and fair use (Maskus, 2000b). The importance to both countries of electronic commerce in promoting international exchange of information services makes recognition of rights and obligations within this medium a critical issue for the evolution of IPRs. Note further that there is a strong linkage between ensuring such protection and providing a nation's citizens access to the internet through effective telecommunications linkages. Thus, for example, the recent U.S.-Japan Agreement on Telecommunications Access Fees extends the opening of this market in Japan (USITC, 2000). Beyond these agreements, Japan and the United States could consider collaboration in developing standards for international information on centralized clearing of copyrights on the internet (Rutchik, 1997).

V. Concluding Remarks

The United States and Japan share a broad commonality of interests in securing global protection of their intellectual property. Indeed, a collaboration of private IPRs interests in those countries and the European Union was influential in pushing the TRIPS agenda in the first place. Moreover, recent legislative reform and judicial opinions have moved the Japanese system closer to that of the United States.

Nevertheless, their regimes retain important differences, which are the basis of some bilateral contention. Arguably, the views of the two countries differ as well regarding the strength of TRIPS implementation in developing countries. Finally, fissures could emerge from variable regulation of competitive abuses that might surface from the international exploitation of IPRs. Thus, there is reason to think carefully about the medium-term future of global intellectual property protection and the role these countries will play in advancing it.

Notes

[1] *Genentech Inc. v. Sumitomo Seiyaku K.K.*, 29 March 1996.

[2] *Fujitsu Ltd. v. Texas Instruments*, 10 September 1997.

[3] Judgment of the Supreme Court, 1 July 1997.

[4] United States—Section 337 of the Tariff Act of 1930, complaint by the European Economic Community, adopted 7 November 1989, BISD 36S/345.

[5] Currently there are far more patents owned internationally, suggesting that the figures presented are significant underestimates of potential rent flows.
[6] Put another way, TRIPS may be considered an outstanding exercise in strategic trade policy on the part of the United States.
[7] Author's conversation with Justice Department officials, August 17 2000.

References

Ginarte, Juan Carlos and Walter G. Park. 1997. "Determinants of Patent Rights: A Cross-National Study," *Research Policy* 26:283-301.

Janis, Mark D. 2000. "*Inter Partes* Patent Re-examination," *Fordham Intellectual Property, Media, and Entertainment Law Journal* 10:481-499.

Katoh, Masanobu. 1997. "New and Unresolved U.S.-Japan Intellectual Property Issues," paper prepared for the conference, "Intellectual Property in Japan," Japan Information Access Project, Washington, D.C.

Maskus, Keith E. 1998. "The International Regulation of Intellectual Property," *Weltwirtschaftliches Archiv* 134:186-208.

Maskus, Keith E. 2000a. *Intellectual Property Rights in the Global Economy*. Washington, D.C.: Institute for International Economics.

Maskus, Keith E. 2000b. "Intellectual Property Issues for the New Round," in Jeffrey J. Schott (ed.), *The WTO after Seattle*. Washington, D.C.: Institute for International Economics.

Maskus, Keith E. and Christine McDaniel. 1999. "Impacts of the Japanese Patent System on Productivity Growth," *Japan and The World Economy* 11:557-574.

Maskus, Keith E. and Mohan Penubarti. 1995. "How Trade-Related Are Intellectual Property Rights?" *Journal of International Economics* 39:227-248.

McCalman, Phillip. 2001. "Reaping What You Sow: An Empirical Analysis of International Patent Harmonization," *Journal of International Economics*, forthcoming.

Millhaupt, Curtis J. 2000. "Law, Judicial Systems, and Economic Growth: Notes on the Uneasy Case of Japan," paper prepared for the World Bank Summer Research Workshop on Market Institutions, Washington, D.C.

Ministry of International Trade and Industry. 2000. *2000 Report on the WTO Consistency of Trade Policies by Major Trading Partners*. Available at www.miti.go.jp.

Rutchik, Gregory A. 1997. "Protecting Copyrightable Works in Japan in the Digital Age," paper prepared for the conference "Intellectual Property in Japan," Japan Information Access Project, Washington, D.C.

Suzuki, Kunizo. 1997. "Unresolved U.S.-Japan Intellectual Property Issues: Will 1997 be a Landmark Year?" paper prepared for the conference "Intellectual Property in Japan," Japan Information Access Project, Washington, D.C.

Takenada, Toshiko. 1997. "Harmonizing the Japanese Patent System with its U.S. Counterpart through Judge-Made Law: Interaction between Japanese and U.S. Case Law Developments," paper prepared for the conference "Intellectual Property in Japan," Japan Information Access Project, Washington, D.C.

United States International Trade Commission. 2000. "United States-Japan Agreement on Telecommunications Access Fees to Reduce Costs and Likely Increase Competition," *International Economic Review*, USITC Publication 3354, August/September, 1-2.

United States Trade Representative. 2000. *National Trade Estimates Report on Foreign Trade Barriers: 2000*. Available at www.ustr.gov.

Yang, Guifang and Keith E. Maskus. 2000. "Intellectual Property Rights and Licensing: An Econometric Investigation," *Weltwirtschaftliches Archiv*, forthcoming.

CHAPTER 8

Prospects for Investment Negotiations in the WTO*

Fukunari Kimura

I. Introduction

Just after WWII, the International Trade Organization (ITO) was about to be established together with the International Monetary Fund (IMF) and International Bank for Reconstruction and Development (IBRD) for the new order of the world economy. It is well known that the ITO was supposed to take care of the liberalization of both trade and investment. However, the ITO did not unfortunately come into reality due to the failure of ratification by the U.S. Congress and other reasons. It is not therefore a new claim at all that the liberalization of international transactions should include the liberalization of investment. But since then, it has proven difficult to establish an international policy discipline of investment-related policies at the multilateral level.

There are many arguments, both academic and nonacademic, that can be offered to support the liberalization of investment. As the globalization of firms' activities proceeds, foreign direct investment (FDI) has become one of the major channels to enhance the efficiency of worldwide resource allocation. Lipsey, Blomstrom, and Ramstetter (1998) estimated that roughly 6% of world GNP was generated by foreign affiliates of MNEs in 1990. More recently, UNCTAD (2000b, pp. 3-4) estimates that this ratio went up to about one-tenth in 1999 and the gross product of all transnational corporations (TNCs) was roughly a quarter of world GNP in 1997. Among OECD member countries, more than 25% of the value added in manufacturing sector was generated by affiliates of foreign firms in the mid-1990s in the following countries: Ireland (66.4%), Hungary (62.4%), Canada (50.9%), the United Kingdom (33.2%), Netherlands (29.7%), and France (28.8%).[1] Table 1 presents rough estimates of the significance of affiliates of Japanese and U.S. firms in the East Asian developing countries. In addition, it is estimated that in recent years about one-third of world trade is intra-firm trade.[2] It is abundantly clear accordingly that FDI is of major importance in the world economy.

Table 1. The Significance of Affiliates of Japanese and U.S. Firms in East Asian Countries (1996) (%)

	Value Added		Employment		Exports		Imports	
	Affiliates of Japanese Firms	Affiliates of U.S. Firms	Affiliates of Japanese Firms	Affiliates of U.S. Firms	Affiliates of Japanese Firms	Affiliates of U.S. Firms	Affiliates of Japanese Firms	Affiliates of U.S. Firms
Korea	0.46	0.49	0.33	0.17	6.95	n.a.	6.34	n.a.
Hong Kong	5.24	1.91	2.66	3.18	17.02	17.17	16.38	n.a.
Singapore	11.90	7.69	4.73	5.68	33.17	55.13	33.38	n.a.
Malaysia	4.61	4.68	2.67	1.62	13.11	18.47	15.19	n.a.
Thailand	4.54	1.89	0.89	0.26	33.28	n.a.	29.76	n.a.
Philippines	1.56	2.60	0.34	0.24	13.98	31.02	9.70	n.a.
Indonesia	1.12	2.61	0.26	0.06	11.33	18.93	15.26	n.a.
China	0.42	0.26	0.05	0.02	3.82	5.32	4.51	n.a.

Affiliates of Japanese firms: Affiliates abroad with more than 10% Japanese ownership (except those whose parent firms are in finance & insurance or real estates). Data for 1996 F/Y.

Affiliates of U.S. firms: Affiliates abroad with more than 50% American ownership (neither parents nor affiliates are banks). Data for 1996.

Note that the ratio of returned questionnaires is as low as 59.1% for the data of affiliates of Japanese firms.

The definition of "value added": "sales minus purchases" for affiliates of Japanese firms, and "gross product" for affiliates of U.S. firms.

Value added and exports/imports for affiliates of Japanese firms are estimated by using the data for total NIEs and total ASEAN4.

Source: MITI (1999), U.S. Department of Commerce (1998), and IMF (2000).

Furthermore, since 1998, we have been experiencing an unprecedented FDI boom. According to estimates by UNCTAD (2000b, p. 289), total outward FDI in the world increased from $391 billion in 1996 to $687 billion in 1998, and reached $800 billion in 1999. A large part of the increase has come from a boom in cross-border mergers and acquisitions within Europe and across the Atlantic Ocean, which has been drastically changing the map of corporate firms in developed countries. In reaction to the fear of marginalization from the world investment boom, a large number of less developed countries (LDCs) have become positive or even aggressive for hosting FDI.

Because many FDI-related policies are intertwined with domestic policies, it is not easy to establish a general policy rule for investment at the multilateral level. However, considering the recent and ongoing globalization of economic activities, liberalization of FDI needs to be pursued. Of course, we must take into account possible needs for infant industry promotion and effective competition policy. If we can take proper care of market failures due to liberalization though, most economists would support the general direction of liberalization.

However, in reality, FDI-related policies in many countries are often poorly defined and implemented. Even the essential elements of international policy principles such as the most-favored-nation (MFN) principle and the national treatment (NT) principle are not systematically carried out. Transparency may be lacking and an effective dispute settlement mechanism may not even exist in many cases. LDCs in particular have imposed a variety of FDI-related policies, some of which are highly distortive. Two such policies relate to the entry and exit of affiliates of foreign firms and the activities of affiliates after entry, including performance requirements. Investment policies include those that are designed both to restrict FDI or to promote FDI, and many of these policies distort the market. In addition, the lack of policy discipline generates incentives for rent-seeking activities by bureaucrats/politicians of host countries and oligopolistic investors.

Under the Uruguay Round (1986-1994), there were extensive discussions of investment-related policies that culminated in the Agreement on Trade-related Investment Measures (TRIMs) in Annex A of the Marrakesh Agreement. The Agreement specifies that TRIMs must follow the national treatment principle (GATT Article III) and the ban on quantitative restrictions (Article XI) and attaches a list of illustrative measures inconsistent with GATT obligations. Although the TRIMs obligation has contributed to the removal of several restrictive policies such as local content requirements, it covers only a small subset of investment-related policies after all.

Following the Uruguay Round, the Organization for Economic Co-operation and Development (OECD) tried to take an initiative in establishing investment rules. The negotiation for the Multilateral Agreement on Investment (MAI) started in May 1995. The draft version of the MAI consisted of three pillars: investment liberalization, investment protection, and a dispute-settlement mechanism. The participation of LDCs was supposed to follow after the agreement was reached among developed countries. The negotiation, however, did not proceed well. The participating OECD countries could not reach agreement in the initially planned period of two years and an extended one-year period. The negotiations were subsequently abandoned and have not resumed since then.

The WTO organized a Working Group on the Relationship between Trade and Investment in December 1996 and started background studies on investment. Reports of the Working Group to the General Council of the WTO were submitted in 1997, 1998, and 1999. They were not, however, penetrating reports in the sense that they only summarized the discussions on the relationship between trade and investment, and abstained from arguing a possible role of the WTO in establishing investment policy rules.

In the WTO Ministerial Meeting in Seattle in December 1999, there was not enough time to discuss whether or not investment rules should be included in a new negotiating round. Meetings of the Working Group on trade and investment have been held in 2000, but no conclusion has been reached yet. Countries with a positive attitude for negotiating multilateral investment rules include the European Union (EU), Japan, Korea, Hungary, Chile, and Switzerland. On the other hand, India, Pakistan, Malaysia, Egypt, and some others are strongly opposed. It seems clear that FDI is asymmetric in nature. Investors are predominantly corporate firms from developed countries, and there is a need especially for LDCs to carry out substantial policy reform once investment rules are imposed. This asymmetry sometimes makes LDCs schizophrenic about investment rules. They would like to host FDI while at the same time they want to maintain policy discretion.[3]

The United States has been somewhat reluctant about including investment negotiations in the WTO, especially after experiencing the anti-globalization protests by labor unions and environmental NGOs. This disinclination partly comes from the fact that the United States already has high-level bilateral investment treaties (BITs) with a number of LDCs and thus does not readily need multilateral agreements. In fact, U.S. firms are sometimes enjoying preferential status over firms of other nationalities. Another concern of the U.S. Government is that multilateral rules may require local U.S. governments to change their FDI-related policies. There has also been some skepticism in academic writings about the need to pursue multilateral investment rules at least in the short run even though investment liberalization might well be an important issue on the policy agenda in the future.[4]

Thus, the immediate prospects for multilateral investment rules are not very promising. I believe however that trade economists have a mission to promote investment liberalization. I would argue that distortions due to the lack of investment-policy principles are important, and we should at least establish a minimal set of policy disciplines including the MFN and NT principles and transparency requirement on FDI-related policies in the framework of the WTO.

In what follows, I review in Section II the background of FDI-related policies particularly in LDCs and discuss the possible economic/politico-economic justification for multilateral investment rules. Section III examines the FDI-related policies currently conducted by a number of countries and claims that those policies are often distortive in nature. I also argue that the endorsement of policy discipline may solve some existing problems. Section IV discusses the reasons why the MAI failed and tries to draw lessons from this failure. Section V reviews the current situation of BITs and discusses a possible relationship with multilateral agreements. Section VI discusses TRIMs and other efforts by the WTO to deal with investment. The last section summarizes what I believe economists should do regarding investment issues.

II. Economic Justification of Multilateral Investment Rules

The theoretical support of FDI liberalization is straightforward. The removal of distortive FDI-related policies basically enhances the efficiency of static and dynamic resource allocation and is thus welfare improving. Along the intuition of MacDougall's model without market distortions (MacDougall (1960)), both investing and host countries enjoy welfare gains unless there exists a strong terms-of-trade effect, though, of course, some of the economic agents in both countries may be worse off without proper income redistribution. FDI is not a simple movement of colorless capital but comes with the movement of firm-specific assets. Therefore, we often emphasize the benefits from the transfer of technology, managerial ability, and other firm-specific assets, both internal and external to the market. Starting from this benchmark intuition, FDI-related policies, either restricting or promoting FDI, must be justified as anti-distortionary policies to cancel out market distortions.[5]

Although the theoretical intuition appears robust, the formal empirical evidence that FDI is beneficial is somewhat fragile. There have been a number of simulation attempts to measure the effect of FDI using applied general equilibrium models. Most of the studies, however, have not been successful in taking the special characteristics of FDI into account. Some crude empirical studies including Borensztein, De Gregorio, and Lee (1998) have tried to connect FDI with growth performance, but the relationship does not seem very robust. There is a literature documenting that affiliates of foreign firms are generally more productive and pay higher wages than local indigenous firms,[6] but we are not sure whether hosting FDI helps indigenous firms grow or not. Actually, micro studies such as Harrison (1996) rather find a negative impact of hosting FDI on local industries at least in the short run. To promote the liberalization of FDI, we, trade economists, must present more convincing evidence.

Starting from the non-discrimination principle as the rule of thumb, we obviously need some special consideration for LDCs. It was not until the 1980s that LDCs overcame their hostile sentiments against multinational enterprises (MNEs). Now policymakers in LDCs understand that hosting FDI is largely beneficial for economic development. But still, MNEs are in many cases too large, too advanced in technology and managerial ability, and too sophisticated an entity for many LDCs. It is thus natural for them to seek some sort of backup by proper competition policy to counteract possible anti-competitive conduct by MNEs. In addition, policymakers in LDCs naturally take into consideration the influence of hosting MNEs when they construct industrial promotion policies. When they would like to foster their own infant industry, they may want to restrict FDI. Or, when they would like to utilize MNEs for accelerating industrialization, they would rather promote FDI by providing preferential arrangements. The attitude of policymakers in LDCs toward FDI is often mixed, confused, and self-contradictory. But in any case, it is natural for them to desire to maintain policy discretion on FDI.

There is a question then of how far the WTO policy discipline, particularly the nondiscrimination principle, should immediately apply to LDCs and on what aspects temporary exempion from the principle should be allowed. As for the MFN principle, it is difficult to think of a case in which the diversion should be granted. For the purpose of infant industry promotion, LDCs may want to limit the number of foreign firms to enter the market or to receive preferential arrangements. Even in such a case, nothing prevents LDCs from selecting foreign firms in a transparent, nondiscriminatory procedure such as competitive bidding. As for the NT principle, on the other hand, there is more room for temporary exemption. Particularly in the case of FDI-related policies to regulate entry, provision might be made for limited discretionary treatment for LDCs as we grant "special and differential (S&D) treatment" in commodity-trade liberalization.[7] In the case of FDI-related policies after entry, however, there may be less justification for differential regulations between indigenous firms and foreign firms. Because indigenous firms are often weak and fragile compared with affiliates of MNEs, there could be a case in which temporary policies disadvantageous for affiliates are justifiable as anti-distortionary policies. However, such discriminating policies after entry may generate larger frustration of foreign companies than policies on entry.[8]

Some of the performance requirements imposed by LDC governments raise issues beyond the MFN and NT principles, suggesting a delicate problem of demarcation between international commercial policy and domestic policy. Once we stop confining our scope to the liberalization of "trade-related" policies and consider investment liberalization in general, we have to redefine a new borderline between pure domestic policies and international commercial policies under the WTO. Considering the heterogeneity of economic institutions across countries and multiple purposes of domestic policies as opposed to simply efficiency-oriented international policy discipline, we must certainly grant more room for policy discretion in general investment liberalization. However, some essential codes such as investment-facilitating institutional convergence should not face much resistance.

So far our discussion has been limited to the implications of FDI-related policies for efficient resource allocation in a narrow sense. In addition, we should not underestimate the politico-economic implications of FDI-related policies. Discretionary FDI-related policies provide opportunities for rent-seeking activities by both investing foreign firms and hosting governments and may bring about the formation of undesirable politico-economic coalitions. Immature governance in LDCs and the oligopolistic character of MNEs may well enhance the danger of such political economy. It may even divert the effort of liberalization in a skewed direction and interfere with the development of transparent and accountable governance and competitive business practices. If so, the establishment of international discipline for FDI-related policies is the best solution to avoid such potentially damaging outcomes.

In summary, the establishment of comprehensive policy discipline for FDI-related policies requires careful consideration on the borderline between pure domestic policies and international commercial policies. However, it should be possible to reach a consensus on such policy principles as MFN, NT, transparency requirements, and restrictions on some obviously distorting performance requirements. Both the efficiency and the political-economy arguments support the multilateral effort of specifying and enforcing a certain level of policy discipline, while at the same time making some allowance for modest special treatments for LDCs.

III. FDI-related Policies in LDCs

Presently at the multilateral level, there is little policy discipline imposed on individual country FDI-related policies. The TRIMs and the GATS (General Agreement on Trade in Services) take care of some limited aspects of investment-related policies, but there do not exist any global policy rules covering FDI as a whole. Some regional preferential arrangements and bilateral investment treaties (BITs) include investment rules, but they do not apply on an MFN basis. No rule means no effective dispute settlement mechanism. As a result, the policy environment related to FDI is far from the ideal of non-discrimination and transparency, particularly in LDCs.

Since a serious negotiation on multilateral investment rules has not yet commenced, there does not even exist a clear definition of investment-related policies. There is no consensus on the scope of issues, for example, such as whether to include portfolio investment and other capital flows in addition to FDI,[9] and where we should set the borderline between pure domestic policies and investment-related policies under the international policy rule. However, there have been a few plurilateral attempts to classify investment-related policies and to list each country's policies by the category. The Association of Southeast Asian Nations (ASEAN) Secretariat compiled investment-related policies for nine member countries (Brunei, Indonesia, Laos, Malaysia, Myanmar, the Philippines, Singapore, Thailand, and Vietnam) "in the effort to enhance transparency and to make the ASEAN investment environment better known to investors" (The ASEAN Secretariat (1998, p. 1)). Table 2 presents the ASEAN classification of investment-related items. "Relevant legislation" and "applications" present laws and government agencies in charge of incoming FDI, which indicates that each country has a different administrative struc-

Table 2. The Classification of Investment-related Policies by the ASEAN Secretariat

Relevant legislation
Investment act
Companies act/factory act
Other legislation
Minimum investment level
Applications
Agency involved in administering investment application and granting incentives
Conditions
Special services
Investment fields/sectors
Fields/sectors
Restrictions
Foreign equity policies
Incentives
Corporate income taxes
Exemption from or reduction of taxes on imported capital goods
Exemption from or reduction of taxes on imported raw materials
Other incentives
Foreign loan
Taxation
Corporate tax
Value added tax/sales tax
Withholding tax
Personal income tax
Other taxes
Financial regulations
Borrowing
Foreign exchange
Source of financing
Special regulation
Employment of foreign workers
Conditions for approval of foreign employees
Work permit
Land ownership
Acquisition of land and building (for business and residential purposes)
Restriction

Source: Adapted from the ASEAN Secretariat (1998).

ture. "Investment fields/sectors" and "foreign equity policies" summarize regulations on incoming FDI in terms of industrial sectors and capital shares. "Incentives" include preferential treatments for investment as well as those in exchange of obeying performance requirements. "Taxation" and "financial regulations" itemize general conditions for both local indigenous and foreign-owned firms as well as differential treatments for the latter. "Employment of foreign workers" and "land ownership" list regulations often claimed as restrictive by foreign-owned firms.[10]

Actual conditions for FDI depend not only on formal laws and regulations but also on operations and discretionary judgment by administrators. Thus, one effective way of picking up possible problems for the policy environment for FDI is to listen to the complaints of foreign investors. The Business Council on Facilitation of Trade and Investment in Japan is a coordinating body of about 150 industrial/business associations and helps Japanese firms exchange views on trade- and investment-related issues in their international operations. Every year, it lists issues and problems that Japanese firms face in their activities in foreign countries and publishes them in a report entitled *Barriers to Trade and Investment* in both Japanese and English. Because this is a list of requests by private companies, some claims are naturally biased toward individual firms' interests, rather than the public interest with regard to desirable investment-policy discipline. In addition, companies often adapt themselves to the existing distorted policy environment and are perhaps earning some gains out of the distortion itself. Hence, we must read the list with caution. Nevertheless, most of the complaints and requests are useful to identify hidden problems and evaluate the real cost of regulations.

Table 3 presents the classification of issues as well as the number of issues pointed out by Japanese firms (Business Council on Facilitation of Trade and Investment (2000a, 2000b)). The figures do not necessarily indicate the degree of seriousness or unfairness of issues. The larger the presence of Japanese firms, the more issues are naturally raised. However, we can still obtain a rough idea of major barriers Japanese investors are facing and consider what can be solved by establishing international policy discipline. In addition, notice that neither an effective dispute settlement procedure nor a county-to-country problem-resolving mechanism takes care of most of these issues. This is because no policy discipline is endorsed in the international community.

It is useful to explicate some of the details noted in Table 3, as follows.

"#1: Restrictions on entry and foreign ownership" and "#4: Withdrawal regulations" in table 3 present a large collection of requests by Japanese firms for removing or easing regulations on entry and exit, including foreign ownership restriction. Entry restrictions seriously affect the activities of foreign firms, and those restrictions do not often seem to be based on sensible infant-industry-promotion policies that are in the host country's interest. Another problem is that these restrictions are often not clearly written or announced so that ad-hoc decision making by administrators becomes crucial and sometimes

Table 3. Barriers to Trade and Investment Listed by Japanese Firms

		ASEAN	Brunei	China	Hong Kong	India	Indonesia	Korea
#1	Restrictions on entry and foreign ownership			11		4	10	5
#2	Regulations concerning domestic production ratios and local procurement ratios			5		5	3	
#3	Export requirements			5		1		1
#4	Withdrawal regulations			5		2	1	
#5	Restrictions in parts industry policies			1				
#6	Preferential policies for foreign capital			6		2		
#7	Procedures for the operation of the Foreign Affiliate Law			1				
#8	Investment recipient organization					1	1	
#9	Export-import regulations; tariffs; customs clearance	7	1	35	1	11	14	11
#10	Regulations on activities in free trade areas and others			6		1	5	
#11	Recovery of profit and technical fees; demands for technological transfer			3		6		3
#12	Exchange controls			7		5	1	2
#13	Finance			7		7	4	2
#14	Taxation			18		13	12	4
#15	Price control						1	
#16	Employment			11		6	9	3
#17	Infringement of intellectual property rights			6	1	1	4	4
#18	Demands for technology transfer			2		2		
#19	Industrial specifications and standards			6	1	1	1	2
#20	Monopoly							
#21	Land-holding restrictions			2		1	1	
#22	Environmental pollution, waste disposal			1		1		
#23	Systems, practices and administrative procedures			22		4	6	6
#24	Underdeveloped legal systems, sudden changes			10		2	2	1
#25	Government procurement					7		
#26	Other			9	3	15	7	2
	Total	7	1	179	6	98	82	46

Table 3 (continued)

		Malaysia	Myanmar	Pakistan	Philippines	Singapore	Taiwan	Thailand
#1	Restrictions on entry and foreign ownership	9		1	4		2	2
#2	Regulations concerning domestic production ratios and local procurement ratios	3		1	2		1	3
#3	Export requirements				2		3	
#4	Withdrawal regulations							
#5	Restrictions in parts industry policies	1						1
#6	Preferential policies for foreign capital				1	1		
#7	Procedures for the operation of the Foreign Affiliate Law							4
#8	Investment recipient organization		1		1			7
#9	Export-import regulations; tariffs; customs clearance	14	3	4	12	1	13	9
#10	Regulations on activities in free trade areas and others	1					1	1
#11	Recovery of profit and technical fees; demands for technological transfer	2			1			
#12	Exchange controls	7	6	1	2		3	4
#13	Finance	3		1	4		3	4
#14	Taxation	4	3	3	9	1	5	12
#15	Price control							1
#16	Employment	7	4		4	6	7	5
#17	Infringement of intellectual property rights	3	1	1	3	5	6	10
#18	Demands for technology transfer	1						
#19	Industrial specifications and standards	2		1	1	2	4	2
#20	Monopoly	1						
#21	Land-holding restrictions	1	1		1	2		1
#22	Environmental pollution, waste disposal	1	1		3	1		4
#23	Systems, practices and administrative procedures	5	2	2	4	1	3	7
#24	Underdeveloped legal systems, sudden changes	1	3	3	2		1	1
#25	Government procurement	4		1				
#26	Other	5	8		5	2	4	6
	Total	75	33	19	61	22	56	84

Table 3 (continued)

		Vietnam	Australia	N.Z.	P.N.G.	NAFTA	Canada	Mexico
#1	Restrictions on entry and foreign ownership	1	2				1	2
#2	Regulations concerning domestic production ratios and local procurement ratios	3				4		1
#3	Export requirements	2						1
#4	Withdrawal regulations							
#5	Restrictions in parts industry policies	1						2
#6	Preferential policies for foreign capital	1					1	
#7	Procedures for the operation of the Foreign Affiliate Law	2						
#8	Investment recipient organization	1						
#9	Export-import regulations; tariffs; customs clearance	16	5	1		3	3	7
#10	Regulations on activities in free trade areas and others	1						1
#11	Recovery of profit and technical fees; demands for technological transfer	1					1	
#12	Exchange controls	5			1			1
#13	Finance	4						1
#14	Taxation	8	5	1	1		8	12
#15	Price control							
#16	Employment	5	4	1			6	4
#17	Infringement of intellectual property rights	1	1	1				
#18	Demands for technology transfer	4						
#19	Industrial specifications and standards	1	1	1			4	1
#20	Monopoly							
#21	Land-holding restrictions	3	1		1			
#22	Environmental pollution, waste disposal	1					1	1
#23	Systems, practices and administrative procedures	7					1	5
#24	Underdeveloped legal systems, sudden changes	6					1	4
#25	Government procurement		1				1	
#26	Other	7	2		1	1	4	3
	Total	81	22	5	4	8	32	46

Table 3 (continued)

		U.S.A.	MERCOSUR	Argentina	Brazil	Chile	Peru	Russia
#1	Restrictions on entry and foreign ownership	2			3	1		1
#2	Regulations concerning domestic production ratios and local procurement ratios	4	2	1	3			
#3	Export requirements			1	1			
#4	Withdrawal regulations							
#5	Restrictions in parts industry policies							
#6	Preferential policies for foreign capital							1
#7	Procedures for the operation of the Foreign Affiliate Law							
#8	Investment recipient organization							2
#9	Export-import regulations; tariffs; customs clearance	23	1	6	14	1	3	14
#10	Regulations on activities in free trade areas and others	1		1	3			
#11	Recovery of profit and technical fees; demands for technological transfer		1		4			
#12	Exchange controls				4			8
#13	Finance	2		1	2			5
#14	Taxation	6		4	6	2	2	14
#15	Price control							
#16	Employment	8			10		1	2
#17	Infringement of intellectual property rights	9		1			1	3
#18	Demands for technology transfer	1			1			
#19	Industrial specifications and standards	5	1				1	16
#20	Monopoly	1			1			
#21	Land-holding restrictions							
#22	Environmental pollution, waste disposal	2		1	1			
#23	Systems, practices and administrative procedures	2			1	1		12
#24	Underdeveloped legal systems, sudden changes				4	2		11
#25	Government procurement	6						2
#26	Other			1	10			7
	Total	72	5	17	68	7	8	98

Table 3 (continued)

		EU	Austria	Belgium	U.K.	Denmark	Finland	France
#1	Restrictions on entry and foreign ownership							
#2	Regulations concerning domestic production ratios and local procurement ratios	3			1			
#3	Export requirements							
#4	Withdrawal regulations							
#5	Restrictions in parts industry policies							
#6	Preferential policies for foreign capital							
#7	Procedures for the operation of the Foreign Affiliate Law							
#8	Investment recipient organization							
#9	Export-import regulations; tariffs; customs clearance	15		2	2			1
#10	Regulations on activities in free trade areas and others							
#11	Recovery of profit and technical fees; demands for technological transfer							
#12	Exchange controls	1			3			
#13	Finance							
#14	Taxation	4	1	3	3	2	1	5
#15	Price control				1			
#16	Employment		3	3	5	1	1	7
#17	Infringement of intellectual property rights	1			3			
#18	Demands for technology transfer							
#19	Industrial specifications and standards	16			1			1
#20	Monopoly				1			
#21	Land-holding restrictions							
#22	Environmental pollution, waste disposal	6						1
#23	Systems, practices and administrative procedures	5			4			
#24	Underdeveloped legal systems, sudden changes	1			1			
#25	Government procurement							
#26	Other	1			3			2
	Total	53	4	8	28	3	2	17

Table 3 (continued)

		Germany	Greece	Ireland	Italy	Luxembourg	Netherlands	Portugal
#1	Restrictions on entry and foreign ownership							
#2	Regulations concerning domestic production ratios and local procurement ratios							
#3	Export requirements							
#4	Withdrawal regulations							
#5	Restrictions in parts industry policies							
#6	Preferential policies for foreign capital		1		1			
#7	Procedures for the operation of the Foreign Affiliate Law							
#8	Investment recipient organization				1			
#9	Export-import regulations; tariffs; customs clearance				1			1
#10	Regulations on activities in free trade areas and others							
#11	Recovery of profit and technical fees; demands for technological transfer							
#12	Exchange controls							
#13	Finance	1			1			
#14	Taxation	7	2		5	1	1	
#15	Price control							
#16	Employment	7	4	2	6	3	4	6
#17	Infringement of intellectual property rights							
#18	Demands for technology transfer							
#19	Industrial specifications and standards	1					1	
#20	Monopoly							
#21	Land-holding restrictions							
#22	Environmental pollution, waste disposal	1	1		1			
#23	Systems, practices and administrative procedures	4	3		5		1	
#24	Underdeveloped legal systems, sudden changes		1					
#25	Government procurement							
#26	Other	1						
	Total	22	12	2	21	4	7	7

Table 3 (continued)

		Spain	Sweden	Switzerland	Turkey	Belarus	Burgaria	Czech
#1	Restrictions on entry and foreign ownership							
#2	Regulations concerning domestic production ratios and local procurement ratios				1			
#3	Export requirements							
#4	Withdrawal regulations	1						
#5	Restrictions in parts industry policies							
#6	Preferential policies for foreign capital							2
#7	Procedures for the operation of the Foreign Affiliate Law							
#8	Investment recipient organization							
#9	Export-import regulations; tariffs; customs clearance	2			4		2	1
#10	Regulations on activities in free trade areas and others							
#11	Recovery of profit and technical fees; demands for technological transfer							
#12	Exchange controls				3			1
#13	Finance							
#14	Taxation	1	1		1			
#15	Price control							
#16	Employment	6	2		2		1	3
#17	Infringement of intellectual property rights			1				
#18	Demands for technology transfer							
#19	Industrial specifications and standards		1		1			1
#20	Monopoly			1				
#21	Land-holding restrictions							1
#22	Environmental pollution, waste disposal							1
#23	Systems, practices and administrative procedures	3			2	1		5
#24	Underdeveloped legal systems, sudden changes				1		1	3
#25	Government procurement							
#26	Other				2			4
	Total	13	4	2	17	1	4	22

Table 3 (continued)

		Hungary	Poland	Romania	Slovakia	Slovenia	Ukraine	Yugoslavia
#1	Restrictions on entry and foreign ownership		1					
#2	Regulations concerning domestic production ratios and local procurement ratios	1	1					
#3	Export requirements							
#4	Withdrawal regulations							
#5	Restrictions in parts industry policies							
#6	Preferential policies for foreign capital	2	1	2	1			
#7	Procedures for the operation of the Foreign Affiliate Law							
#8	Investment recipient organization	1						
#9	Export-import regulations; tariffs; customs clearance	3	3	2	3	1		1
#10	Regulations on activities in free trade areas and others				1			
#11	Recovery of profit and technical fees; demands for technological transfer							
#12	Exchange controls	1	1					
#13	Finance	1	1					
#14	Taxation	2	2	4	2			
#15	Price control							
#16	Employment	1	2	1	3			
#17	Infringement of intellectual property rights							
#18	Demands for technology transfer							
#19	Industrial specifications and standards		1		1		1	
#20	Monopoly							
#21	Land-holding restrictions	1	1					
#22	Environmental pollution, waste disposal	1			1			
#23	Systems, practices and administrative procedures	5			1		1	
#24	Underdeveloped legal systems, sudden changes	3	3	1				
#25	Government procurement							
#26	Other	2	3		1			
	Total	24	20	10	14	1	2	1

Figures in the table indicate the number of issues raised by Japanese firms.
Figures do not necessarily indicate the degree of seriousness or unfairness of issues.
Source: Constructed from Business Council on Facilitation of Trade and Investment (2000a, 2000b).

can generate room for rent-seeking activities. Restrictions on exit often take the form of cumbersome, time-wasting procedures and do not seem to be economically rational in many cases. Although these restrictions have gradually been removed in a number of LDCs recently, they are often used to force foreign companies to accept performance requirements such as local content and export requirements, which complicates the process of liberalization. A fundamental problem is that the non-discrimination principle and transparency requirements are not endorsed at the multilateral level as a rule of thumb and thus these restrictions are left altogether for policy discretion.

"#2: Regulations concerning domestic production ratios and local procurement ratios," "#3: Export requirements," and "#5: Restrictions in parts industry policies" are on regulations after entry or performance requirements, which do not conform to the national treatment principle in many cases. These include requirements on domestic production, local procurement, and exports and are quite often linked with some incentives such as tariff reduction. Again, there is much room for discretionary practices by administrators in host countries. Therefore, the endorsement of non-discrimination and transparency principles would again be helpful to solve these problems. Some of the regulations must be removed anyway under the obligation of the TRIMs Agreement in the case of the WTO member countries.[11] In cases of North American countries and the European Union, most of the complaints by Japanese firms point out operational uncertainty or inconvenience on the rule of origin related to preferential regional arrangements.

"#6: Preferential policies for foreign capital" and "#10: Regulations on activities in free trade areas and others" include complaints on sudden removals of investment incentives after entry. Of course, policy changes are often necessary from the viewpoint of host countries, but a problem is that such changes are sometimes not announced beforehand or are not communicated even in written form. Transparency is again the issue here.

"#9: Export-import regulations; tariffs; customs clearance" is on trade regulations, some of which are closely related to the operation of MNEs. Preferential treatment for MNEs often takes the form of trade policy; a typical example is a tariff-rebate system for imported parts and components when the product is exported. Many complaints by Japanese firms cite operational uncertainty and inconvenience as well as sudden changes in policies and administrative procedure. Non-discrimination and transparency are again the issues to be solved. In addition, some claims are related to preferential trade arrangements, examples of which are issues related to CEPT (Common Effective Preferential Tariffs) in ASEAN countries, the rule of origin in NAFTA, and preferential arrangements for some specific non-member countries by the EU. Problems on antidumping are also listed in the case of the United States and EU.

"#11: Recovery of profit and technical fees; demands for technological transfer," "#12: Exchange controls," "#13: Finance," and "#14: Taxation" are on profit recovery, exchange controls, finance, and taxation. Many issues pointed out here are inherent in the immaturity of economic institutions and governance, not directly subject to policy discipline. However, these include some of the key issues to activate the commitment of foreign firms in their territory, examples of which are restrictions on foreign currency exchange or profit repatriation, the treatment of royalty fees, inefficient administrative procedures for financial transactions, and troublesome taxation procedures. Some claims are related to investment protection and the national treatment principle, and multilateral policy discipline may work for those problems to some extent. We often observe a complicated combination of performance requirements and preferential taxation treatment, which possibly results in inefficiency as well as leeway for rent-seeking activities.

"#16: Employment" includes problems of both local labor and foreign labor. Again, many points listed here are not necessarily the issues of policy discipline but come from institutional arrangements. However, non-discrimination and transparency are again important to solve some of the issues. Similar patterns are observed for "#21: Land-holding restrictions" and "#25: Government procurement."

"#7: Procedures for the operation of the Foreign Affiliate Law", "#8: Investment recipient organization," "#23: Systems, practices, and administrative procedures," "#24: Underdeveloped legal systems, sudden changes," and "#26: Other" are related to the quality of governance and legal systems. Together with the lack of an effective dispute settlement mechanism, transparency and accountability of policy implementation tend to be lost, with attendant potential for rent-seeking activities.[12]

Overall, the cost of nonexistence of multilateral investment rules may be substantial, even though it is difficult to quantify in empirical studies. Taking into account an extremely skewed pattern of FDI destination across LDCs, we must conclude that FDI is very sensitive to a host country's policy environment. In the era of globalization, channels of international transactions are diversified, and the liberalization of FDI seems to be a natural step next to commodity trade liberalization.[13] An urgent issue is to set up a minimal set of multilateral discipline on FDI-related policies. This must include: (1) the confirmation of the non-discrimination principle, i.e., the MFN and NT principles; (2) phasing out distortive performance requirements; (3) enhancing transparency of policy implementation; and (4) setting up an effective dispute settlement mechanism. The establishment of multilateral policy discipline will be an important step in creating a more efficient regime of global commercial policies and also have immediate effects in removing or mitigating some of the distortions. Going that far should be much less controversial than intellectual property issues, or even less ambitious than the liberalization of services, in terms of the interface between domestic and international commercial policies.

IV. Lessons from the Failure of MAI

The MAI negotiation was an ambitious effort. In addition to standard provisions on investment protection, the draft of the MAI included core principles of liberalization: the NT and MFN principles; transparency requirement; and the prohibition of performance requirements with a wide coverage. Furthermore, it contained a strong dispute settlement mechanism.

If we wish to proceed with investment negotiations in the WTO, we must seriously review what happened in the collapse of MAI negotiation. Bhagwati's 1998 newspaper article published just after the withdrawal of France from re-negotiation is a good starting point. He wrote that the MAI was unbalanced in three ways. First, it failed to claim that preferential arrangements for FDI are as distortive as restrictions for FDI. Second, it advocated the rights of MNEs, but not their obligations. Third, it made little concession to the political environment of host countries. Then he continued that there were more powerful reasons why the investment issue should be dropped altogether from the WTO agenda. He claimed that the negotiation must inherently include controversial issues, and thus the WTO may enter into a politically supercharged domain, ending up with endangering the real mission of the WTO, i.e., to free trade. He added that the WTO already has gone too far on intellectual property protection (IPP) and that the tensions on labor and environmental issues would be enhanced. Then he concluded that "with IPP and MAI both in, it would be hard to refute the charge that what is good for 'capital' at the WTO is not good for 'labour' or for 'nature'."

After looking at mass turmoil in Seattle and Washington, D.C., Bhagwati's concerns are real. Nonetheless, in my judgment, trade economists should make more of an effort to disseminate the idea that FDI liberalization is important, rather than simply putting on the brake in response to politico-economic pressures. When we call for commodity free trade, we say that free trade is good not only for exporters but also for the majority of people, including consumers in importing countries. Why don't we claim that the liberalization of FDI is good not only for 'capital' but for the majority of people in both investing and hosting countries? We are not at all against a large number of conscientious NGO activists supporting 'labor' (though not for the protectionists' purposes) or 'nature'!

We must of course pay much more attention to LDCs. Developed countries should be generous to LDCs to give them sufficient time for seeking their own industrial development. If competition policy helps LDCs to overcome the traditional fear of MNEs, we must support their effort for institution building. This should not necessarily hinder the establishment of the investment-policy principle and setting of the long-term targets.

When going beyond the liberalization of border policies, we inevitably face difficult issues of how far international policy discipline should affect policies traditionally regarded as "pure domestic." This issue will potentially connect with a more fundamental issue on the relationship between national sovereignty and international organizations. From the viewpoint of international laws, Kotera (2000) has pointed out that the draft of the MAI included a seriously arguable point on the dispute settlement mechanism. That is, the MAI tried to provide binding arbitration of disputes between states or between an investor and a participating government.[14] Kotera claims that this sort of arrangement would intrude upon national sovereignty more than the WTO dispute settlement procedure. The WTO only deals with disputes between states, not those between a state and a private company. In addition, because a treaty arrangement among states is the legal foundation of the WTO, it does not force a state to follow its decisions even if it leaves room for possible retaliation. It simply says that "prompt compliance with recommendations or rulings of the dispute settlement body is essential in order to ensure effective resolution of disputes to the benefit of all Members" (Article XXI of Annex 2 of the Marrakesh Agreement). The MAI had much stronger compulsory power because a state representative had to sit at an arbitration table, whether the claimant was a state or a private firm and the decision was going to be binding. Such an arrangement would provide strong judicial power to an international body and would not be compatible with the structure of the WTO. The nature of the dispute settlement mechanism is one of the key issues to be decided as to whether investment-rule negotiations can have wide support or not.

While the negotiation over the MAI collapsed, the draft of the MAI is a useful starting point when we begin to discuss investment rules in other policy forums.[15] We thus need more careful discussion of the MAI draft in order to use it as a concrete benchmark.

V. Connection with Bilateral Investment Treaties (BITs)

Comprehensive investment-related policy rules at the multilateral level have not been established, but there are already a number of arrangements at the bilateral and regional level. According to UNCTAD (2000b, p. 6), there were 1,856 BITs in the world at the end of 1999.

At the bilateral level, treaties of friendship, commerce, and navigation (FCN) were traditionally concluded mainly between developed countries and covered a wide range of bilateral economic, cultural, and political cooperation, including investment protection. No new FCN treaties have been concluded since the 1960s though. Bilateral investment treaties (BITs) began to be formed in the late 1950s and have recently been popular. Table 4 shows the number of BITs being signed each year. West Germany, Switzerland, and other European countries were forerunners while the United Kingdom and the United States followed in the 1980s. BITs were traditionally concluded between a developed country and an LDC, but BITs between LDCs are also increasing recently (see the row of "Others").[16]

The contents of BITs are mainly for investment protection. However, some BITs include articles promoting FDI liberalization such as national

Table 4. The Number of Bilateral Investment Treaties Being Signed (as of September 1997)

	-1959	1960-64	1965-69	1970-74	1975-79	1980-84	1985-89	1990-94	1995-	Total
Germany	2	21	16	7	6	10	11	24	26	123
United Kingdom					7	16	18	31	18	90
Switzerland		11	8	9	5	2	7	27	16	85
France		1		7	13	10	7	23	13	74
Netherlands		1	3	9	3	3	11	20	9	59
Belgium and Luxembourg		1	1	2	5	6	12	10	7	94
Italy			4		2		12	22	10	50
United States						5	5	23	7	40
Spain							2	21	16	39
Sweden			3		3	5	2	15	7	35
Denmark			4			1	4	18	5	32
Finland						3	4	15	5	27
Greece		1*			1		1	14	6	23
Austria					1	1	6	11	11	30
Norway		1				2	1	9	2	15
Australia							1	10	4	15
Canada							1	6	14	21
Portugal						1*	1	15	9	26
Japan					1	1	1	1	1	5
Iceland								1		1
New Zealand							1		1	2
Others		1		1	7	11	23	177	106	323
Total	2	36	40	35	54	76	131	493	293	1162

* indicates a BIT with Germany.

Adapted from MITI material.

treatment before and after entry and a ban on performance requirements. In particular, recent BITs by the United States include the prohibition of performance requirements.[17] The United States also has high-level investment arrangements with Canada and Mexico under the NAFTA scheme. This is actually one of the reasons why the United States is not very positive about multilateral investment negotiations particularly when the proposed investment rules do not seem to reach to a high level. A problem though is that the liberalization of investment at the bilateral or regional level is not conducted according to the MFN principle.

Japan has not been an active player in BITs. As of April 2000, there were only six effective BITs (with Egypt, Sri Lanka, China, Turkey, Hong Kong, and Bangladesh) and two BITs (with Pakistan and Russia) signed but not yet effective. The Japanese Government has recently recognized the importance of BITs and has started negotiating with Korea, Viet Nam, Mexico, and Mongolia, possibly to be followed by negotiation with Indonesia. The negotiation with Korea is particularly a politically symbolic one for regional cooperation, seeking a high-level BIT.

When BITs are working in the direction of FDI liberalization, we must appreciate them in general. But it is unfortunate if the existence of BITs discourages some countries from establishing multilateral policy discipline. In addition, as Kotera (1999) has pointed out, once we start a multilateral investment negotiation, we must carefully consider the consistency between the multilateral rule and BITs. When a BIT has a higher standard of liberalization obligation than the multilateral rule, we may need to introduce a special arrangement similar to Article XXIV of GATT for commodity trade. The treatment can be different depending on whether the BIT is concluded before or after the establishment of a multilateral rule. In addition, we may need to build a system minimizing the risk of "forum shopping" in dispute settlements.

VI. The TRIMs Agreement and Beyond

The TRIMs negotiation was an epoch-making effort to establish policy discipline on investment, but the scope was narrowly confined from the beginning. The starting point was to examine the operation of GATT articles related to the trade restrictive and distorting effects of investment measures. Thus, "the focus of the negotiations was to be the adverse trade effect of investment measures and not the legitimacy of the measure per se" (Grimwade (1996, p. 326)). The scope of the TRIMs Agreement was limited to investment measures related to trade in goods, and the logical structure was constructed in the spirit of reaffirming the implementation of GATT Article III (national treatment) and Article XI (general elimination of quantitative restrictions).

The Annex of the TRIMs Agreement presents an illustrative list of TRIMs that are inconsistent with the GATT obligation. It includes: (1) local content requirements; (2) trade balance requirements; (3) import restriction through foreign exchange control; and (4) export restriction. Other parts of the Agreement reaffirm the commitment to obligations on transparency/notification and the application of the GATT dispute settlement mechanism.

The TRIMs Agreement obviously takes care of a very small subset of policy discipline on investment. However, it has already had some real impacts. The Agreement requires member countries to notify all nonconforming TRIMs within 90 days and to eliminate them within two years in the case of a developed country, five years in the case of a developing country, and seven years in the case of a least-developed country (TRIMs Article V). This means that original-member developing countries had to eliminate nonconforming TRIMs by the end of 1999, although they were able to request an extension of the transition period by demonstrating particular difficulties. Table 5 lists the notified nonconforming TRIMs.[18] The ban on TRIMs is affecting LDC policies particularly in the automobile industry.

When the contents of the TRIMs Agreement were virtually completed in October 1991, the time framework of removing nonconforming TRIMs was set rather strictly in exchange for narrowing the scope. Because the TRIMs Agreement was included in the single-undertaking portion of the Marrakesh Agreement, LDCs perhaps signed on it without much serious thought. However, LDCs later realized that it was a serious commitment with an enforceable dispute settlement mechanism and the transition period of five years was rather short. As shown in table 5, a number of LDCs are now submitting extension requests to the WTO. The WTO announced that these requests will be examined in the Council for Trade in Goods,[19] which means that some sort of compromise would be sought.

If we can expand the scope of investment rules in the next multilateral negotiating round, we must reconsider a proper time framework for removing barriers, particularly for LDCs. The TRIMs Agreement was perhaps asking LDCs to remove nonconforming TRIMs too quickly, and the negotiation process of the transition-period extension was not well specified. In the case of trade in goods, member countries are first requested to switch nontariff barriers (NTBs) to transparent tariffs and then lower tariffs gradually. LDCs are not forced to remove all barriers in a period as short as five years. Actually, even developed countries have not eliminated all NTBs and tariffs yet. Thus, it seems reasonable to specify "dirty" and "clean" investment measures and to conduct a sort of "purification" as a first step. Then we had better take a comprehensive approach for special and differential (S&D) treatment for LDCs, including various types of liberalization obligations.

VII. Conclusion

In my view, the establishment of multilateral investment rules is a natural step beyond commodity free trade and is essential to the world economy with rapidly globalizing firms' activities. In the current regime without multilateral policy discipline, there are significant market distortions, particularly in LDCs,

Table 5. Trade-related Investment Measures Notified to WTO

	Local content requirements	Trade balance requirements	Import restriction through foreign exchange control	Export restriction
Argentina	Am(e)	Am(e)		
Bolivia				O
Barbados	Ag			
Chile	Am(e)	Am(e)		
Colombia	Am, Ag(e)	Am, Ag(e)		
Costa Rica	O			
Cuba	Am, O			
Cyprus	Ag			
Dominican Rep.	O	Ag, O		
Ecuador	Am			
Indonesia	Am, Ag, O			
India	O			Am, Ag, O
Mexico	Am(e)			
Malaysia	Am(e)			
Pakistan	Am(e), O			
Peru	Ag			
Philippines	Am(e)		Am(e)	
Uganda*	O	O		
Romania	Am(e), O(e)			
Thailand	Am, Ag, O			
Uruguay			Am	
Venezuela	Am			
S. Africa	Am, Ag, O			
Egypt	?	?	?	?
Nigeria	?	?	?	?

Am: TRIM in automobile industry
Ag: TRIM in agriculture
O: TRIM in other fields
(e): Extension request submitted to WTO
*: Uganda is classified as a least-developed country, and thus the TRIM obligation will be effective on Jan. 1, 2002.
Source: Adapted from MITI (2000, p. 167).

which are harmful to both investing and host countries. The endorsement of the minimal set of policy disciplines, including the non-discrimination principle (MFN and NT), gradual removal of distortive performance requirements, transparency requirements, and decent dispute settlement procedure is essential. In this effort, we should of course consider special and differential treatment for LDCs.

To make the argument more convincing, we, trade economists, have much to do. First, we must tell a more convincing story about the importance of multilateral investment rules. In the political economy of international negotiations, MNEs in developed countries are obvious supporters of investment liberalization. However, it does not mean that they are the only beneficiaries of liberalization. We must convince the general public that both investing and host countries can enjoy welfare improvement in most cases. As well as theoretical justification, strong empirical support is needed. In particular, it is important to accumulate studies on the quantification of investment-liberalization effects.

Second, we have to prepare backstops for possible market failures accompanied with investment liberalization. As for the S&D treatment for LDCs, we must develop a comprehensive approach, including various types of measures not conforming to the principles but being allowed temporarily. In addition, if necessary, the institution building for competition policy in LDCs should be supported through international policy coordination or technical assistance.

Third, we should discuss more fully the scope of the WTO. One issue is the interface between international commercial and "pure" domestic policies. As the globalization of economic activity proceeds, the interface has inevitably become blurred. However, we should not say that everything is related to international commercial policies and thus should be under the international policy discipline. Another issue is the legal background of the WTO. The WTO is not a "super-government" in the sense that the EC Commission is. It is not directly legitimized by the sovereignty of people but is supported as an international treaty among sovereign states. Taking a virtually effective dispute settlement mechanism into consideration, the scope of the WTO may need to be set rather conservatively. It is further important to undertake education of the public and to provide intellectual antidotes to the rhetoric of the anti-globalization hardliners.[20]

Fourth, if it is really difficult to initiate investment negotiations as Bhagwati has claimed, we may need to consider alternative channels. One possibility is to proceed with investment liberalization by using other negotiating forums such as GATS and TRIMs, even if the scope is limited. In this case, we must carefully examine the possibility of undesirable sequencing problems and try to minimize distortions. As stressed by Hoekman and Saggi (1999), FDI in services sectors may effectively be taken care of by the GATS. However, distortions related to manufacturing FDI are too important to be left aside. Setting up multilateral policy discipline on overall FDI policies seems to be a more coherent way to proceed in the globalization era.

Notes

[*] Earlier versions of this paper were presented at conferences held at Keio University in May 2000 and at the University of Michigan (Ann Arbor) in October 2000. The author would like to thank Robert Stern, John Ries, and other participants in the conferences for helpful comments and suggestions.

[1] From Fukasaku and Kimura (2001, Table 1).

[2] Fukasaku and Kimura (2001) discuss the magnitude of intra-firm trade based on data of the United States and Japan.

[3] In addition, India claims that the liberalization of labor movements must be discussed if we are to proceed to liberalize investment. For the detail of India's claim, see WTO (2000a).

[4] See, for example, Hoekman and Saggi (1999).

[5] Hoekman and Saggi (1999) discuss in detail the cases in which FDI-related policies are justifiable as anti-distortionary policies.

[6] See, for example, Aitken, Harrison, and Lipsey (1995), Globerman, Ries, and Vertinski (1994), and Doms and Jensen (1998).

[7] As for the S&D treatment for LDCs, see Hoekman and Kostecki (1995, Chapter 10 and Annex 6).

[8] Some countries provide for foreign investment incentives that are more favorable than for domestic indigenous firms. Because the NT principle usually requires a policy environment for foreigners "no worse than" that for domestic economic agents, the above case is not treated as a violation of the NT principle. However, economic theory suggests that such policy would also distort a market in general.

[9] The MAI tried to define investment in a wider sense including FDI, portfolio investment, and other investment. This move was paralleled by the IMF's attempt to expand its mandate to capital-account liberalization in 1997. However, since the Asian economic crisis started, a number of economists think that FDI should be separated from other types of investment. For discussion of the treatment of short-term capital flows, see Fischer et al. (1998) and IMF (1999). As for the possible scope of "investment" in the WTO rules, WTO (2000b) provides a good starting point for discussion.

[10] More detailed information on investment-related policies of Asian countries and others can be obtained from JETRO (various years) and JMCTI (various issues).

[11] See Section VI of the TRIMs Agreement.

[12] Furthermore, there are also a number of cases involving FDI-related policies that are not consistent with the MFN principle. For example, the zoning system in Thailand is applied to firms from Japan and other countries while U.S. firms do not have to follow it because of the U.S.-Thai bilateral investment treaty. There are also a number of unconfirmed claims of MFN-inconsistent implementation in China. There does not, however, exist any international legal basis to criticize such practices.

[13] Hoekman and Saggi (1999) claim that distortions related to FDI in the manufacturing sector can be minimized by trade liberalization, and thus we had better concentrate on policies on FDI in services sectors in the short run. However, our review of issues and problems in LDCs suggests that the reform of policies for manufacturing FDI is also urgent.

[14] See Witherell (1996) and OECD (1997).

[15] Actually, the draft of the MAI has already influenced some negotiations on investment such as the Japan-Russia bilateral agreement and the ASEAN Investment Area.

[16] UNCTAD is actively providing technical assistance as well as match-making services for LDCs to conclude BITs. One of the recent campaigns by UNCTAD with the support of the Government of Japan and the United Nations Development Programme (UNDP) was a two-week conference held in Sapporo, Japan in June 2000, where 12 LDCs initialed 22 BITs (UNCTAD (2000a)).

[17] See UNCTAD (1999, p. 119) for the contents of the BIT between the United States and Bolivia, for example.

[18] In addition, Brazil, Canada, and India were claimed to have nonconforming TRIMs in the automobile industry, and the cases went to the WTO Dispute Settlement procedure. Brazil actually removed the TRIM at the end of 1999.

[19] According to *Nihon Keizai Shinbun*, May 9, 2000.

[20] One of the typical stance of hardliners is found in *Foreign Policy*'s article entitled, "The FP Interview: Lori's War" (No. 118, Spring 2000: 28-55). We really need greater efforts to disseminate reasonable economic thought to the general public such as by Deardorff and Stern (2000) and the ACIT (Academic Consortium on International Trade) activities (http://www.spp.umich.edu/rsie/acit) are trying to do.

References

Aitken, Brian, Ann Harrison, and Robert Lipsey. 1995. "Wages and Foreign Ownership: A Comparative Study of Mexico, Venezuela, and the United States," NBER Working Paper 5102.

ASEAN Secretariat. 1998. *Compendium of Investment Policies and Measures in ASEAN Countries.* Jakarta: ASEAN Secretariat (December).

Bhagwati, Jagdish. 1998. "Letters to the Editor: Powerful Reasons for the MAI to Be Dropped Even from WTO Agenda," *Financial Times*, October 22.

Borensztein, E., J. De Gregorio, and J.-W. Lee. 1998. "How Does Foreign Direct Investment Affect Economic Growth?" *Journal of International Economics* 45:115-135.

Business Council on Facilitation of Trade and Investment (Japan). 2000a. "Barriers to Trade and Investment in European Countries," March 24, in Japanese. (Available at http://www.jmcti.org.)

Business Council on Facilitation of Trade and Investment (Japan). 2000b. "Barriers to Trade and Investment in Asia-Pacific Economies," August 30, in Japanese. (Available at http://www.jmcti.org. The English version is also available for APEC member countries/economies.)

Deardorff, Alan V. and Robert M. Stern. 2000. "What the Public Should Know about Globalization and the World Trade Organization," Research Seminar in International Economics, School of Public Policy, The University of Michigan, Discussion Paper No. 460 (July).

Doms, Mark E. and J. Bradford Jensen. 1998. "Comparing Wages, Skills, and Productivity between Domestically and Foreign-Owned Manufacturing Establishments in the United States," in Robert E. Baldwin, Robert E. Lipsey, and J. David Richardson (eds.), *Geography and Ownership as Bases for Economic Accounting.* Chicago: University of Chicago Press.

Fischer, S. et al. 1998. *Should the IMF Pursue Capital Account Convertibility?* Essays in International Finance No. 207 (May), International Finance Section, Princeton University.

Fukasaku, Kiichiro and Fukunari Kimura. 2001. "Globalization and Intra-firm Trade: Further Evidence," forthcoming in Peter Lloyd, Herbert Grubel, and Hyun-Hoon Lee (eds.), *The Frontiers of Intra-industry Trade Research*, New York: Macmillan.

Globerman, Steven, John C. Ries, and Ilan Vertinsky. 1994. "The Economic Performance of Foreign Affiliates in Canada," *Canadian Journal of Economics* 27: 143-156.

Grimwade, Nigel. 1996. *International Trade Policy: A Contemporary Analysis.* London: Routledge.

Harrison, Ann. 1996. "Determinants and Effects of Direct Foreign Investment in Cote d'Ivoire, Morocco, and Venezuela," in Mark Roberts and James R. Tybout (eds.), *Industrial Evolution in Developing Countries: Micro Patterns of Turnover, Productivity, and Market Structure.* Oxford: Oxford University Press.

Hoekman, Bernard and Michel Kostecki. 1995. *The Political Economy of the World Trading System: From GATT to WTO.* Oxford: Oxford University Press.

Hoekman, Bernard and Kamal Saggi. 1999. "Multilateral Disciplines for Investment-related Policies?" Mimeo. (January).

International Monetary Fund (IMF). 1999. "Country Experiences with the Use and Liberalization of Capital Controls." Mimeo.

International Monetary Fund (IMF). 2000. *International Financial Statistics*, June.

Japan External Trade Organization (JETRO). (various years). *JETRO Toushi Hakusho (JETRO Whitepaper on Investment).* Tokyo: JETRO. In Japanese.

Japan Machinery Center for Trade and Investment (JMCTI). (various issues). *Ajia Toushi Kanren Seido News (News on Investment-related Policies in Asian Countries).* Tokyo: JMCTI. In Japanese.

Kotera, Akira. 1999. "Toushi Ruuru Sougo Kan no Seigousei (On the Consistency among Investment Rules)." Mimeo. In Japanese.

Kotera, Akira. 2000. *WTO Taisei no Hou Kouzou (The Legal Structure of the WTO System).* Tokyo: University of Tokyo Press. In Japanese.

Lipsey, Robert E., Magnus Blomstrom, and Eric D. Ramstetter. 1998. "Internationalized Production in World Output," in Robert E. Baldwin, Robert E. Lipsey, and J. David Richardson (eds.), *Geography and Ownership as Bases for Economic Accounting.* Chicago: University of Chicago Press.

MacDougall, G.D.A. 1960. "The Benefits and Costs of Private Investment from Abroad: A Theoretical Approach," *Economic Record* 26:13-35.

Ministry of International Trade and Industry (MITI), Government of Japan (GOJ). (various years). *Fukousei Boueki Houkoku-sho (Report on the WTO Consistency of Trade Policies by Major Trading Partners).* Tokyo: Tsuushou Sangyou Chousa Kai. In Japanese. The English version is published every year.

Ministry of International Trade and Industry (MITI), Government of Japan (GOJ). 1999. *Dai 27 Kai Wagakuni Kigyou no Kaigai Jigyou Katsudou (The 27th*

Survey on the Foreign Activities of Japanese Firms). Tokyo: Ministry of Finance Printing Office. In Japanese.

Organization for Economic Cooperation and Development (OECD). 1997. "MAI, The Multilateral Agreement on Investment." MAI home page, http://www.oecd.org/publications/pol-brief/1997/9702-pol.htm.

United Nations Conference on Trade and Development (UNCTAD). 1999. *World Investment Report 1999: Foreign Direct Investment and the Challenge of Development*. New York and Geneva: United Nations.

United Nations Conference on Trade and Development (UNCTAD). 2000a. "22 Bilateral Investment Treaties Signed at Sapporo (Japan)." June 29. http://www.unctad.org/iia/Press/pr2848en.htm.

United Nations Conference on Trade and Development (UNCTAD). 2000b. *World Investment Report 2000: Cross-border Mergers and Acquisitions and Development*. New York and Geneva: United Nations.

U.S. Department of Commerce (Economics and Statistics Administration/ Bureau of Economic Analysis). 1998. *U.S. Direct Investment Abroad: Operations of U.S. Parent Companies and Their Foreign Affiliates, Preliminary 1996 Estimates*.

Witherell, William H. 1996. "An Agreement on Investment," *The OECD Observer* 202:6-9.

World Trade Organization (WTO) (Working Group on the Relationship between Trade and Investment). 2000a. "Communication from India." WT/WGTI/W/86, June 22.

World Trade Organization (WTO) (Working Group on the Relationship between Trade and Investment). 2000b. "Communication from Japan: Definition of "Investment" in the WTO Rules on Investment." WT/WGTI/W/92, October 24.

CHAPTER 9

Trade and Competition at the WTO: Competition Policy for Market Access Development

Jiro Tamura

I. Introduction

Globalization brings with it many new challenges, and in the field of world trade, the challenge of gaining market access[1] in the new global economy calls for a consistent rethinking of strategy. In free market economies, the respective agencies advocate measures to improve the conditions for its nation's exports and investment in the world's markets. For developing countries, market access has been associated with large foreign multinational firms attempting to enter the domestic market. Today, we see how market access is becoming more and more essential to all players, both developing and developed, of global trade. It is now time to take stock of the progress that has been made in implementing market access, regulating restrictive business practices, and enforcing and maintaining free and fair competition. Despite the unfruitful WTO Ministerial Conference in Seattle, globalization continues at a perpetually increasing pace. Market access is likely to be considered as a possible issue of debate at the next round of talks. This paper seeks to review the elements of competition enforcement in Japan and to identify the inseparable relationship between competition policy, which ensures market access, and free trade. It will argue how attempts on various levels, domestic, unilateral, bilateral, and multilateral, are all indispensable in approaching this issue of market access. A proposal addressing possible options on acquiring better market access from a multilateral level will precede the conclusion.

II. Market Access as a Trade Issue?

A student of Japanese trade and competition policy is most familiar with cases in Japan where stronger legal actions could have been implemented, but were not. The failure to fully utilize available resources seems to be a major problem in the implementation of competition law. Added, in the field of global competition, there are cases where available legal actions have been examined and applied, yet the core issue itself was not adequately addressed. In other words, the problem lies not only in the questionable application of the law or the absence of it, but in its implementation and the depth and effectiveness of a law or regulation in addressing an issue. In this case the issue would be market access. The U.S. Japan Film case[2] is an example of a case, which vividly portrayed the inseparable relationship between domestic competition policy, market access, and trade. The case also showed the limits of the WTO in dealing with the issue of market access.

In promoting free trade and market access, GATT has removed tariffs and non-tariff barriers on the governmental level to the bare minimum. Non-tariff barriers are strongly related to the legal system of one country and the accessibility of the market.[3] The barriers can be basically divided into two categories: government regulations and private restrictive business practices.

The first category of barriers results from government regulations restricting the number of new entries into the market. Restrictions must be a "government" regulation in order to be resolved by the WTO. The second category of barriers is created by the actions of private industry or non-government related organizations. These may occur easily as a result of, or under the influence of a government measure but are basically the independent actions of private businesses.

Since the jurisdiction of the WTO only covers government regulations, the WTO is not the venue for nations wishing to raise complaints regarding private restrictive business practices. Yet cases arise where the origin of certain practices, either government or private industry, is not definitively clear. In the Film Case,[4] the United States based its arguments on the claim that the Japanese government collaborated with private businesses. The involvement of the government was, and still is necessary in order for private restrictive business practices to be considered at the WTO. In other words, the WTO can only deal with government measures. At present, in order to make a case against certain actions of private businesses at the WTO, the direct relationship between the government and anticompetitive measures must be established.

The panel in the Film Case ruled in favor of Japan, but left many issues unresolved. Should actions of private businesses that hinder market access fall within the jurisdiction of the WTO? If not, how should these actions hindering market access be addressed?

In addition to the appeal at the WTO, the United States had also submitted a case under section 301 of the U.S. Trade Act[5] against Japan. Moreover, Kodak's appeal to the Japan Fair Trade Commission (JFTC) further shows the seriousness, with which the United States considered the problems of competition conditions and the closed nature of Japan's market. The inability of the WTO to squarely and thoroughly deal with trade and competition issues exposes its limitation and leaves behind a necessary debate on to what extent the organization seeks to improve market access for the purpose of free trade.

The Film Case shows that the ability of the WTO in resolving market access barriers that are not of government origin is extremely limited. Yet as previously mentioned, it is often difficult to define which actions exactly fall under government measures. When measures are not technically authored by the government, but are tolerated or even encouraged by the government, it becomes a thin line deciding whether or not a measure is a government measure. The attention is then mistakenly focused on the job of determining the identity of the measure. The burden of the aggrieved party to provide enough evidence to establish the direct relationship between the government and the alleged measure is considerably heavy, for such measures are not taken as official administrative measures. Should a panel decide that certain measures are not government actions, but are the actions of private businesses, the issue no longer falls within the scope of the WTO panel. Yet unfavorable market access conditions remain. The WTO looks at non-tariff measures affecting market access to determine first whether it is a government measure or not, but existing restrictive practices of private businesses are not being addressed. This is an issue in need for a hurried solution. If no resolution is reached, this will negatively affect the image of the WTO as a non-partisan trade organization committed to removing trade barriers, questioning its objective of attaining free trade and competition.

III. Antimonopoly Issues Affecting Market Access in Japan

The Film case gives an impression of a tight relationship between the Japanese government and the private industry. And without the jurisdiction over restrictive business practices, the WTO cannot do much to alleviate the situation. Yet multilateral agreements are not the only means to treat market access issues. A look at the history of Japanese competition law shows that the enforcement of Japanese antimonopoly law (AML) against cartels, boycotts, and trade association contributes to market accessibility.

The history of the provisions of unreasonable restraint of trade[6] and trade associations[7] indicates its effectiveness to a certain degree towards actions that limit competition among competitors but exposes its limitation in its attempts at removing market barriers. Yet guaranteeing free market access is an essential element of, and at the foundation of competition laws.[8]

In Japan, rules regulating and limiting cartels, boycotts, and trade association activities are spelled out respectively in sections 3, 8, and 19 of the AML. Though one would not say there are a large number of cases, which have set precedents and have clarified these sections, guidelines compliment the law and make up for the shortage in these cases. A cartel is prohibited by the latter part of section 3 of the AML[9] as an "unreasonable restraint of trade." Section 2.6 of the AML defines an "unreasonable restraint of trade" as

> Such business activity, in which enterprises by contract, agreement, or any other concerted activity mutually restrict or conduct their business activities in such a manner as to fix, maintain, or increase prices, to limit production technology, products, facilities, customers, or suppliers, thereby

> causing, contrary to the public interest, a substantial restraint of competition in a particular field of trade.[10]

One of the major problems concerning this act was whether or not it was applicable only to concerted activities among directly competing enterprises or to concerted activities among non-competing enterprises as well; the problem directly relating to the interpretation of the term "a particular field of trade."

Cartels are prohibited as a form of unreasonable restraint of trade, but there is dispute among legal specialists as to whether or not vertical agreements are subsumed under the unreasonable restraint of trade section. The position of the JFTC regarding this issue still remains unclear. How vertical restraints will be interpreted, whether as an unreasonable restraint of trade or not, is crucial for it affects the enforcement of cartels.

Cartel regulation overall has carried out its function within AML objectives, however, if other business restrictive practices are not controlled, even the most strict enforcement against cartels will not produce significant positive competition effects. For example, if the regulation of boycotts is not strictly enforced, market access problems will still remain. A strong enforcement against cartels while allowing boycott activities dismisses the objective of regulating cartels.

In Japan, a boycott violates section 19 of the AML,[11] which prohibits firms from engaging in "unfair trade practices." Though there have been very few instances where boycotts were regulated directly as boycotts, since the conclusion of the 1990 Structural Impediments Initiative (SII),[12] Japan has made its effort to strengthen the enforcement of the AML, especially in regulating boycotts. As a result, among other measures, the JFTC released a guideline in 1991 entitled the Antimonopoly Act Guidelines Concerning Distribution Systems and Business Practices.[13]

In addition, the JFTC has made it clear that boycotts among competitors, trading partners, or boycotts by trade associations are subject to the application of section 3 as an "unreasonable restraints on trade," if "substantial restraint on competition" is evident. The guideline suggests that the JFTC is determined to strengthen its enforcement against boycotts as they recognize how boycotts can significantly impede market access for new firms. However, an issue yet to be addressed is that the JFTC seems to consider the total business capacity as an important factor in determining unreasonable restraint of trade cases. It appears that the JFTC is more likely to enforce the law in cases involving large enterprises that have the capacity or more likely potential to cause substantial restraints on competition.

Section 8 of the AML regulates the activities of trade associations and it is applied to cartels and boycotts engaged through trade associations. Although this kind of enforcement may seem practical considering the important role trade associations play in the Japanese economy, questions on the enforcement's effectiveness in terms of ensuring free market access still exist. In Japan, a trade association is seen as an independent legal entity, distinct from the members that of which the association is composed of, and the application of AML is lenient towards trade associations compared to that towards individual enterprises. Deemed as an independent legal entity, the activities of trade associations are always regulated as a group activity. Even though each individual member should be punished in cases involving concerted actions, section 3 is not applied if it is conducted within a trade association, which means that surcharges based on section 7.2 cannot be imposed, lessening the deterrent against such violations.[14] Common criticism is directed at the JFTC for not adopting effective regulation towards trade associations given the opportunity to do so.

Though Japan's AML itself is as strong and strict as that of the United States, the lack of enforcement allows undesirable circumstances to continue. In contrast to the Film Case where the WTO lacked the law, and thus the jurisdiction over restrictive business practices, the case here is not the problem of the inexistence of the law itself, but the way in which the law is enforced. With further enforcement of AML by the JFTC on a domestic level, added the jurisdiction over private restrictive business practices of an international organization on a multilateral level, market access issues can be better addressed. In attaining the objectives of free and fair trade, in which free market access is indispensable, the solution lies not in one particular method but in a combination of attempts on a unilateral, bilateral, and multilateral level.

IV. International Efforts on Market Access

The limitation of the GATT and the GATS (General Agreement on Trade in Services) with respect to market access is due to their limited scope in addressing private restrictive business practices. Bilateral and other efforts have been made but international efforts have been substantially weakened by the lack of progress at the multilateral level. The following describes some of the international efforts in competition law enforcement. But even these efforts have yet to assure market access. Effort through the WTO is a necessary and effective component of the international framework in creating and protecting market access. Attempts that have been made thus far, on the domestic or unilateral level, on the bilateral level, and on the multilateral level, are as follows.

Firstly, seeking an appropriate, transparent, and non-discriminatory application of domestic competition law would be a preliminary effort that can be, and often is, taken on the domestic level. It is effective against obviously discriminatory cases such as when more strict conditions and investigations are set for the distribution system of import goods, and against cases where respective domestic competition law agencies are lenient towards the systemization of distribution for domestic versus foreign industries.

An example of a unilateral approach would be the application of section 301 of the U.S. Trade Act, which addresses the tacit approval of restrictive business practices by a foreign government or agency. This was an approach taken by the United States in the early stage of the U.S. Japan Film Case.

Secondly, as an approach on the bilateral level, competition issues can be dealt through and between the respective agencies of nations. Presently, the most widely used approach towards competition is the common application of competition law created through bilateral agreements. Since the United States EC Agreement of 1991, we have seen the increase of U.S. centered bilateral agreements. With the objective of preventing trade frictions concerning market access between countries, bilateral agreements have been reached, i.e. the 1976 U.S. Germany Agreement, the 1982 U.S. Australia Agreement, and the 1995 U.S. Canada Agreement. Recently, the 1991 U.S. EC Agreement and the 1995 U.S. Canada Agreements have placed a special emphasis on the cooperation in the effective enforcement of competition law. Within these bilateral agreements, there are a number of stipulations such as the negative comity, the positive comity, and enforcement cooperation.

Negative comity is where investigations of an apparent violation and its impending results negatively influence benefits that are important to that country. It is in short a method of avoiding conflict. It is directly related to the debate on extraterritoriality, the application of domestic law outside a nation's territory. Positive comity is where anticompetitive practice is damaging to one party and a request for enforcement is submitted through the respective agencies of the second party. With positive comity, signatories may share information, collaborating on a single investigation, rather than conducting two separate investigations each of which would be based on the different competition laws of the two nations.[15] The necessity of cooperation is seen in a positive comity, particularly in regard to the treatment of confidential information. The publication of such confidential information is strictly prohibited; however, according to the 1994 U.S. International Antitrust Enforcement Assistance Act[16] (IAEAA), information gathered through investigations according to a bilateral agreement may be made available to foreign agencies.

Bilateral agreements, though commonly used, have their limitations in that the policies of the nations are likely to be different and the anticompetitive behavior being controlled or limited will also affect each nation differently. And when disputes are not resolved, retaliatory actions or the threat of them, such as the luxury tax on import autos between the United States and Japan in 1995, could be detrimental to both parties. Seen in such a light, multilateral approaches may be of more effectiveness in assisting the future development of competition law.

Thirdly, moving on to some approaches at the multilateral level, several obligatory minimum rules have been established. These include the system for competition law in the OECD Recommendation for Hardcore Cartels (1998),[17] the WTO Reference Paper on Basic Telecommunications, and the EC Experts Group (1995).[18] The European Competition Law, a transnational standardized application and enforcement of competition law, is an ideal solution for unifying and harmonizing a nation's substantive law. However, there are countries that still lack competition laws, and even among those with developed competition laws, the standards vary. At this point, establishing a common competition law would not be a realistic alternative to consider.

Perhaps the most significant step in addressing international antitrust problems multilaterally was taken by the OECD. The OECD promotes a three-step process based upon "notification, consultations, and exchange of information,"[19] which helps foreign enforcement officials gather information required to determine whether or not a violation has occurred. The principle of the OECD trade and competition policy "appears to be that through notification and consultation…countries [are] allowed to discuss problems in their incipiency before conflicts and costs escalate."[20] Yet multilateral agreements are by their nature more complex than bilateral agreements, primarily because there are greater and wider interests involved depending on the number of nations taken into consideration. And needless to say, interests differ between developing and industrialized countries. Even so, we must realize that globalization has increased the need for the standardization of rules governing competition.

Furthermore, as an effort for the multilateral framework, the International Antitrust Code Working Group[21] has proposed a draft international antitrust code. Although the implementation of an international code is considered by many to be years away, proposed codes have started the process of international analysis and debate that could lead to a common code or at least to a more uniformed provision in each nation's code.

Many are quick to turn down the option of approaching market access issues and this antitrust (competition) issue on a multilateral level, assuming the only approach to be setting a minimum standard rule. Yet the establishment of a set of minimum standard rules is not the one and only effective measure in approaching the problem of market access on the multilateral level. The following sections will examine the present situation within the WTO,[22] and will analyze why and how the issue of market access should further be dealt with on the multilateral level.

V. The Possibilities of a Multilateral Competition Framework in the WTO

The objective of obtaining market access, as suggested from the previous two sections, can be better served through jurisprudence over restrictive business practices and other anticompetitive behavior, both at the level of a multilateral organization, and through stronger enforcement by the respective domestic agencies. There are multilateral agreements that seek to address problems of competition. As we take a close look at the articles of the GATS, we can see that it has a slight head start over the GATT regarding competition issues.[23] Yet, the degrees to which these two agreements tackle competition issues differ, and we need to examine why this disparity exists. Competition should be an agenda, not only for trade in services but for trade in goods as well.

The GATS contains articles that are related to competition law. They are the articles dealing with Domestic Regulation (article 6), Recognition (article 7), Monopolies and Exclusive Service Suppliers (article 8), Business Practices (article 9), General Exceptions (article 14), and the Security Exception of (article 14.2 in Part 2).[24] Market access is found in article 16 and National Treatment in article 17 of Part 3. The core issue dealt within the GATS concerns promoting deregulation and competition. In other words, the GATS undoubtedly places one focus on competition. The many articles that are related to competition show that the components of competition law are important and indispensable in the area of services.

The ultimate purpose of competition law is to distinguish the anticompetitive measures of enterprises in assuring free and fair competition. This should not only be an issue dealt within the GATS, but should also be a component of the GATT as well. Discussions on issues related to competition law, especially concerning market access in the GATT should seriously be considered.

The purpose of the GATS is to liberalize and to magnify services trade by creating an international legal framework. The GATS is a remarkable multilateral agreement, which provides enforceable rules in service-related trade. However, at this stage of development, where market access is not necessarily guaranteed, it is quite a challenge for the present GATS to achieve its purpose of liberalizing and magnifying service trade. Clearly, the components of competition law are essential to facilitate the efforts of reaching the agreement's objectives. The same can be said with the GATT. Market access is a core issue, not only for service-related trade, but also for trade in goods.

In order to secure the freedom of market entry and exit in the GATS, it is necessary to implement the character components of competition law and its understanding and interpretation to the term "business practice" of article 9. We should determine whether certain terms are indeed components of competition law. Left ambiguous, these terms such as "certain business practices" will be used at each party's discretion to meet its own needs. In short even the GATS does not provide a complete apparatus for the purpose of attaining market access. Yet the very fact that the GATS contains ideas dealing with market access and other elements of competition law cannot be ignored. And this should be considered when discussing competition-law related issues within the WTO framework. It is also worth noting that there are other agreements in addition to the GATS which contain competition related ideas.

In the TRIPS agreement,[25] elements of competition appear under Article 8 on the Control of Anticompetitive Practices in Contractual Licenses. Article 40.1 states that some licensing practices or conditions pertaining to intellectual property rights "which restrain competition may have adverse effects on trade and may impede the transfer and dissemination of technology."[26] Article 40.2 provides that Members may "adopt...appropriate measures to prevent or control such practices."[27] The fact that competition-related issues are portrayed in the GATS and TRIPS questions if it is appropriate to treat competition separately for GATT. And because, as discussed in section 3, domestic competition policy and or law is crucial in attaining market access, such provisions must be included in the GATT for it to effectively attain its objective of free and fair trade.

VI. Proposal for the WTO

The future and direction of the topic of trade and competition at the WTO is currently under much heated debate.[28] There are several issues within trade and competition that the WTO is not equipped to handle but are nonetheless within the organization's framework. These issues are close to reaching the limits of what the international society permits. In the Film Case, the United States initially argued that Japan, by allowing problems of competition to exist, thereby denied access to its market. However, the United States came to the conclusion that it would be extremely difficult to bring such an allegation before the WTO and that solving the problems bilaterally would be more effective. As a result, the debate on competition policy was not brought to the WTO. Yet, if the debate on competition policy is not brought to the multilateral forum, problems of unilateral measures are likely to increase.

The WTO needs to promote the creation of a facility dealing with trade and competition in a way beneficial to both industrialized and developing countries. However, even among industrialized nations, the views towards various behaviors addressed by competition policies differ. Many developing nations lack competition law, and without a standardized set of rules, it would be difficult for a panel to settle a dispute concerning market access or any other competition-related issue. But that being the case does not mean that problems of competition should not be handled by the WTO. This is an unresolved question left after the Film Case. Added to raising the awareness concerning this issue, the WTO can also work to ensure the transparency of various business practices in different countries.

Even though a consensus on a universal competition law may not be reached, an organization that makes transparent the approach of each country towards competition is of great value in terms of market access. What is effective is not the abstract reports and reviews on trade policy, but the more specific exchanges of information.

One example would be to set up a "Competition Committee" to handle problems regarding trade and competition issues. The committee would monitor and report the situation of authorities concerning the application of competition law. Its purpose would be to maintain and promote the international competition mechanism by monitoring anticompetitive activities.

When problems concerning competition arise, the Committee would require the agency representing a country's competition policy to explain and provide an outline of the competition policy of that country. This would allow countries without competition law to have a venue to discuss and deal with problems of trade and competition. For countries equipped with competition law, it would provide a forum to address market-access issues, and for those without competition law, it would provide a foundation on which further competition policies can be built. The Committee would provide opportunities for questions and answers when competition law is applied to countries. Realistically speaking, without an approved minimum standard, the competition committee would not have any enforcement and binding power, but it is nonetheless a way of investigating how a particular case would be handled by a country. Even without a standardized competition policy, pressure from an international observer overseeing competition providing a forum for debate, and providing greater transparency on various levels will no doubt be useful. A multilateral approach along with other approaches to competition would create an effective interim system. The exchange of information among the respective authorities of member nations and the Competition Committee is also in line with the objective of converging competition policies in future forums.

The discussion of the Competition Committee would not be complete without mentioning the areas of concern that the idea brings to the table. Firstly a clear definition of the relationship of the Committee to the Dispute Settlement System is required. This is necessary to ensure an understanding that the Committee will work together with, rather than substitute certain roles of the Dispute Settlement Panel. How the Committee will develop down the line is a question left for the future, but its purpose should be more than a mere forum for the exchange of ideas and opinions. Thus the Committee will need to develop its expertise in the field of competition law. Another debatable issue is the effect the Committee would have on the entire WTO organization. The merits and demerits of dealing with the private sector, as opposed to restricting the organization's boundaries to government measures, require further debate.

The WTO contributes greatly to the protection of the export markets of its member nations. If the present system continues to function, handling only those measures created by the government and not those of private businesses, we face the danger of losing sight of the most important goal of enlarging world markets through free trade. The importance here is keeping a focus on the original and foremost goal of ensuring the means to open and create accessibility to the markets of the member nations.

The manner in which export markets have been protected directly links to the effectiveness of the multilateral trading system. The opening and globalization of the market is not only the aim of industrialized nations but the hopes of developing nations as well. The reduction of tariff barriers and the elimination of non-tariff barriers are for no other purpose than to create an open and accessible market. Within multilateral agreements, the rules of the WTO apply only towards government measures, but a consensus in striving to prevent non-government measures involving restrictive business practices from interfering market access is naturally to be expected. However, the lack of agreement regarding this is due to the fact that the debates on competition policy have been led by industrialized nations. In other words, not all nations have a sufficient understanding of this goal. If more countries are able to understand the new role of competition policy in representing the interests of both developing and industrialized countries, perhaps more progress in the discussion can be seen.

VIII. Conclusion

Though progress on market-access issues has been delayed due to the failure of the WTO Ministerial Conference in 1999, the extra time allows a more in-depth analysis of market- access issues before the next round of talks. Though most experts would agree that a variety of approaches in treating market access issues offers the most flexible and available means conducive to each country's needs, whether that range of options should be increased to allow multilateral organizations such as the WTO to have authority over private restrictive business practices, in addition to its authority over government measures, and other trade and competition issues, is a subject that requires further discussion and debate. Yet when options through unilateral and bilateral agreements have been exhausted, the availability of a multilateral framework to discuss competition issues allows another supportive measure. How anti-competitive issues are treated in the GATS and TRIPS agreements but not in the GATT suggests the need for further development on the topic of market access within the framework of the WTO. This suggests, that even though a universally common standard of competition law may not be realistic to consider at this point in time, other efforts, such as the establishment of the Competition Committee are worthy of consideration. And progress made in examining this issue of market access will be in the mutual interest of both industrialized and developing countries, for without market access, free and fair trade will never be attained in its true context.

Notes

[1] See Masu Uekusa, Nihon No Sangyou Kouzou (Japan's Industry Structure), YUHIKAKU (1995) See also Masayoshi Maruyama, Nihon Shijou No Kyousou Kouzou (The Structure of Competition in the Japanese Market), SOUBUNSHA (1994).

[2] Panel Report on Japan—Measures Affecting Consumer Photographic Film and Paper 31 March 1998 WT/DS44/. See also Jiro Tamura, "WTO ni okeru Boeki to Kyousou no yukue (The Future Direction of Trade and Competition at the WTO)" Nihon Kokusai Keizaihougaku Nenpou No. 8 September (1999).

[3] See "Communication by the European Community and Its Member States" WT/WGTCP/W/62 March 5 (1998) "Communication from the United States" WT/WGTCP/W/66 March 26 (1998) "Report of the Working Group on the Interaction between Trade and Competition Policy to the General Council" WT/WGTCP/W/2 December 8 (1998).

[4] *Id.*

[5] The U.S. Trade Act of 1974 provided the U.S. President with tariff and nontariff trade barrier negotiating authority for the Tokyo Round of multilateral trade negotiations. It also gave the President broad authority to counteract injurious and unfair foreign trade

practices. Section 201 of the Act requires the International Trade Commission to investigate petitions filed by domestic industries or workers claiming injury or threat of injury due to expanding imports. Investigations must be completed within 6 months. If such injury is found, restrictive measures may be implemented. Action under Section 201 is allowed under the GATT escape clause, GATT Article 19. Section 301 was designed to eliminate unfair foreign trade practices that adversely affect U.S. trade and investment in both goods and services. Under Section 301, the President must determine whether the alleged practices are unjustifiable, unreasonable, or discriminatory and burden or restrict U.S. commerce. If the President determines that action is necessary, the law directs that all appropriate and feasible action within the President's power should be taken to secure the elimination of the practice. URL: http://agriculture.house.gov/glossary/trade_act_of_1974.htm P.L. 93-618.

[6] Section 2.6 of the AML defines unreasonable restraint of trade as an agreement or arrangement among enterprises to the effect that they mutually refrain from competing with each other with regard to a product or service. See Mitsuo Matsushita, International Trade and Competition Law in Japan, Oxford University Press (1993) trade associations at 91-92 and at 302-303 restraint of trade: cartels at 136: control of at 87-88; international contracts at 163.

[7] Supra note 6.

[8] Shiteki dokusen no kinshi oyobi kousei torihiki no kakuho ni kansuru houritsu (Law Concerning the Prohibition of Private Monopoly and the Maintenance of Fair Trade), Law No. 54 (1947) See also Jiro Tamura, "Hantorasuto Hou niokeru Tozen Ihou to Gouri no Gensoku no Kankei (The relationship between the *illegal per se* of AML and the *rule of reason*)," Hougakukenkyu (Keio University Law Review) 62nd Vol. No.12, and "Ryutsu Seigen Koui ni tai suru Nichibei Dokusenkinshihou no Tekiyou (The U.S. and Japan Antitrust Law on Competition Restraints in Distribution)," Hougakukenkyu (Keio University Law Review) 68th Vol. No. 3 (1995).

[9] There are two other provisions in the AML, which are relevant to the prohibition of a cartel: Section 8.1 (i) -(iii) and Section 6.1. Supra note 7 "Definition of a Cartel" at 136.

[10] See Matsushita supra note 6 "Definition of a Cartel" at 136.

[11] See Matsushita supra note 6.

[12] Talks where the closed nature of the Japanese market and the keiretsu structure became the center of the issue.

[13] See Masayoshi Maruyama, The Japanese Distribution Handbook, Chicago, Probus Pub. Co. See also OECD: A Study on the Distribution System in Japan (1992).

[14] Ideally, in cases where cartel behavior is found among individual firms, they should be dealt with, as a Section 3 violation, and at the same time, Section 8 should be applied to regulate the group activity as well, in order to ensure the freedom of each individual member.

[15] Masahiro Murakami, "Kyousouhou no Kokusaiteki Shikkoutaisei: Nikokukankyoutei no Yakuwari (The Role of Bilateral Agreements: The International Enforcement System of Competition Law)," Boeki To Kanzei Vol. 47 No. 4 at 80 (1998).

[16] International Antitrust Enforcement Assistance Act of 1994. The U.S. Congress adopted the IAEAA to improve [its] ability to obtain evidence located abroad in antitrust investigations. Under the agreement, the respective enforcement agencies will be able to share information obtained in the course of the agencies' investigations. The agencies also may provide each other with investigative assistance in order to obtain information, evidence, or testimony for use in antitrust matters. See http://www.ftc.gov/opa/1997/9704/iaeaa.html.

[17] OECD, New Release "Hard Core Cartels" SG/COM/NEWS (98) 33 March 30, 1998.

[18] Report of the Group of Experts "Competition Policy in the New Trade Order: Strengthening International Cooperation and Rules" July, 1995.

[19] OECD, Competition and Trade Policies: Their Interaction (1984) para. 356.

[20] *Id.* Para. 393.

[21] See "Antitrust: Justice Official Predicts Scant Prospect of International Code," BNA International Business & Finance Daily, Feb 8 (1994).

[22] WTO "The Fundamental WTO Principles of National Treatment, Most-Favoured-Nation Treatment and Transparency," WT/WGTCP/W/114, April 14 (1999).WTO "Report (1998) of the Working Group on the Interaction Between Trade and Competition Policy to the General Council," WT/WGTCP/2, Dec 8 (1998).

[23] Yoko Sazanami and Toru Nakakita, WTO De Naniga Kawattaka (What Changed at the WTO?), Nihon Hyoron Sha (1997) at 69.

[24] Hiromi Yamaura, "GATS Services Kyoutei no Seiritsu to sono Igi (The Establishment of the GATS Services Agreement and its Meaning)," Boeki to Kanzei September, (1994) at 46-48.

[25] Trade Related Aspects of Intellectual Property Rights: the intellectual property rules of the GATT agreement that established the principles, enforcement, and maintenance of intellectual property rights.

[26] Nihon Kokusaimondai Kenkyuujo, WTO at 735-737.

[27] *Id.*

[28] Brian Hindley "Competition Law and the WTO: Alternative Structure for Agreement" Bhagwati/Hudec Ed. Fair Trade and Harmonization Vol 2 (1996); See supra note 21. See also Petersmann Ed. International Trade Law and the GATT/WTO Dispute Settlement System (1997).

Part Two: Trade and Environment; Regionalism

CHAPTER 10

Eco-Labelling, Environment, and International Trade*

Kenzo Abe, Keisaku Higashida, and Jota Ishikawa

I. Introduction

In recent years, the concern for the environment has been growing, and protection of the environment is one of the main issues being discussed around the world. In this connection, eco-labelling programs are a set of measures to protect the environment, although there are other kinds of measures such as taxes, subsidies, and standards that are also used. In the past decade, eco-labelling programs have been disseminated since Germany first introduced the eco-label called "Blue Angel" in 1977. Now more than 26 countries/regions, including developing countries such as India, Brazil, and Zimbabwe, have introduced similar programs. A non-profit association of eco-labelling organizations around the world was also founded in 1994 called the Global Eco-labelling Network (GEN).[1] The purpose of the association is "to improve, promote, and develop the eco-labelling of products and services". This suggests that eco-labelling may be expected to be an effective measure to protect the environment.[2]

Eco-labelling programs provide consumers with information on the environmental burdens of products. They may thus affect the behavior of consumers, in particular, who are aware of the importance of the environment. Those consumers tend to purchase environmentally preferable products, which can be identified through the eco-label on the products. Thus, eco-labelling programs will increase demand for environmentally preferable products, and will change resource allocation so as to protect the environment.

Eco-labelling programs are basically voluntary. They establish the environmental criteria that labelled products should satisfy. In this sense, they are similar to standards. The difference between eco-labelling programs and environmental standards is whether the measure is compulsory or voluntary. Eco-labelling programs being voluntary measures allow firms to choose whether or not they affix eco-labels on their products. Environmental standards being compulsory measures mean that firms cannot sell their products in a market without complying with those standards.[3] The nature of the eco-labelling programs and the diffusion of them in many countries, however, raise new questions related to their effectiveness and trade effects.

First, the effects of eco-labelling programs are not altogether apparent. They affect resource allocation indirectly through a change in consumer behavior. Some consumers are very conscious of the environment, while others are not. Consumer sensitivity to the environment is essential for eco-labelling programs to be effective.

Moreover, eco-labelling may involve a limited number or percentage of firms in a voluntary scheme. Since introduction of the eco-labelling program may be of benefit to a small number of firms who have attained the label, it may result in enhancing the power of firms in setting prices and thus alter industry market structure. Thus, we cannot simply predict the effects of eco-labelling on resource allocation and welfare, assuming a competitive market.

Second, most eco-labelling programs are established independently in each country. The criteria of awarding eco-labels are usually developed and adopted by domestic parties. Then, the criteria may be determined, intentionally or unintentionally, in favor of domestic firms. If domestic firms can adopt the eco-label more easily than foreign firms due to the criteria established, this may cause undesirable trade effects or trade frictions.

In this respect, transparency is very important to avoid unnecessary international frictions. Colombia, Pakistan, Hong Kong China, Korea and others have remarked that "the key way to minimize the negative trade effects of eco-labelling is to ensure transparency in the processing and application of eco-labels, that interested parties could participate in their development" (WTO 1998a). Eco-labelling procedures tend to be open to public participation, including environmentalists, consumers, industry, trade unions, and foreign interest groups. For example, in a Japanese eco-labelling scheme, called Eco-Mark, there is a 60-day public-review process.

Mutual recognition of criteria may also reconcile differences in country-based criteria. "The concept of equivalencies in the context of eco-labelling implies that when comparable environmental objectives can be achieved in different ways, taking into account the specific environmental conditions of each country, different criteria can be accepted as a basis for awarding eco-labels" (Vossenaar 1997, p. 31). If both importing and exporting countries have their own eco-labelling schemes and they have accepted different criteria to each other, this is referred to as mutual recognition. Analyzing environmental criteria leading to mutual recognition is one of the purposes of GEN. This issue has also been discussed in the Committee on Trade and Environment (CTE) of the WTO.[4]

Finally, the use of Life-Cycle Approaches (LCA) in eco-labelling programs is designed to evaluate the overall environmental effects of products, including trade effects. The key feature of LCA is to take into consideration all life stages of the product, and it is sometimes called a "cradle to grave" approach. Generally life cycle assessment covers five phases of the life cycle of products: (1) acquisition of raw materials; (2) process and production; (3) distribution; (4) use; and (5) disposal. The International Organization for Standardization (ISO) has developed international guidelines for LCA and almost all of the work has been completed (ISO 1997, 1998, 2000a, 2000b, 2000c). LCA may in theory therefore be an ideal way to assess the overall environmental effects of products.

In terms of practical use, however, there are a lot of difficulties.[5] First, there does not exist any clear analytical methodology for LCA. Even experts and scientists cannot identify the clear boundary of the phases of the life cycle and the impacts in each life phase. Second, it is difficult for LCA to take into account such non-environmental factors as resource allocation. Therefore, introduction of eco-labelling schemes based on LCA may lead to inefficient resource allocation and the degradation of the environment. Third, the public may be irritated if a new LCA is developed and the criteria of eco-labelling programs are changed frequently.

Moreover, the eco-labelling programs based on LCA have to consider issues of international trade. In an open economy, a producing country (exporting country) may be distinguished from a consuming country (importing country). However, the use of LCA in eco-labelling schemes theoretically considers all life stages, including acquisition of raw materials, production of materials, and fabrication of products. In the absence of international methodologies and standards, "LCA systems could deliberately and unwittingly become barriers to the entry of foreign products,"[6] since eco-labelling schemes may reflect the environmental conditions and preferences of the importing country.

This aspect of eco-labelling programs is also discussed in relation to the Agreement on Technical Barriers to Trade (TBT Agreement) at the WTO. Both developed countries and developing countries have argued whether eco-labelling schemes fall under the TBT Agreement. This issue has become complicated due to LCA. As for the product-related process and production methods (PPMs), countries have already reached an agreement that they are covered by the TBT Agreement. However, they have not yet agreed whether the non-product related PPMs fall under the TBT Agreement.[7]

In connection with the point above, the concept of "like product" is also in dispute. If the TBT Agreement allows for the concept of "like product" to be extended to cover non-product related PPMs, exporting countries may not be able to set environmental standards based on their own environmental preferences, but may have to adjust their standards to those of importing countries. Therefore, many developing countries have objected to non-product related PPMs to be allowed by the TBT Agreement.

At the present stage, the full use of LCA may be unrealistic, even impossible. "The most interesting use of LCA is for the identification of significant environmental impacts in the various phases of the life cycle in order to guide the development of criteria that mirrors those impacts" (Neitzel 1997, p. 242).

We have briefly reviewed some important issues regarding eco-labelling schemes, but it is difficult to find any rigorous analyses of the effects of these schemes. The most noteworthy studies include OECD (1997) which investigated some practical effects of eco-labelling schemes operating in OECD countries, and Zarrilli et al. (1997), who surveyed the general issues relating to eco-labelling and international trade for a number of eco-labelling programs.

In what follows in this chapter, we discuss the effectiveness of eco-labelling schemes and their impacts on consumer behavior, the environment, international trade, and investment. We then present a simple oligopoly model of eco-labelling schemes in an international economy. The eco-labelling scheme to be analyzed is assumed to be voluntary and may discriminate against foreign producers. We analyze the effects of an introduction of domestic or foreign eco-labelling programs on the profits of firms and on the environment. We also consider the issue of recognition of foreign eco-labelling schemes. Even with a simple model, our results are complex and depend, in particular, on the change in competitive pressure in the market and the origin of the environmental damages.

Section II following considers the pros and cons of eco-labelling schemes and mutual recognition in terms of the effect on consumer behavior. The effects of eco-labelling programs on the environment and international trade are described in sections III and IV, respectively. In section V, we consider the effects on investment in environmentally sound technology (EST) by firms. In section VI, we briefly describe a theoretical model to analyze the effects of eco-labelling in an international setting, which is fully presented in appendix. Section VII provides some concluding remarks.

II. Effects on Consumer Behavior

The purpose of eco-labelling schemes is to influence consumer behavior by affixing eco-labels to environmentally preferable products and services. In other words, the objective is to induce consumers to buy products that have less negative impacts on the environment than other products. Eco-labelling schemes, however, have intended effects as well as unintended side-effects. In this section we provide a brief review of these effects and extend them to the case of mutual recognition.

First, we consider the effects expected by an introduction of eco-labelling programs. We can infer whether or not eco-labelling programs have changed consumer behavior by looking at the change in market share of labelled products and unlabelled products. The share of labelled products has increased since the introduction of eco-labelling schemes in many countries. For example, with regard to 'Blue Angel' in Germany: "For recycled paper products, an increase in market share of eco-labelled products was observed as follows: in 1993, 64 percent for sanitary paper products compared to 32 percent in 1986; and respectively 24 percent for administrative paper products compared to 13 percent" (OECD 1997, p. 53). Moreover, for varnishes and coatings, market shares of unlabelled products have fallen.

It should be noted that a small share of labelled products does not necessarily mean failure of an eco-labelling scheme. The criteria for assigning eco-labels have been revised at intervals. For example, in Eco-Mark in Japan, the criteria for load-stabilizing devices for energy conservation were abolished and the criteria for paper for communication were revised in May 2000. Some eco-labelling schemes may set the criteria so that the share of labelled products is small to induce firms to compete for labels.

Second, eco-labelling schemes make consumers more environmentally conscious. If eco-labelling schemes did not exist, consumers could not know the information about environmentally unfriendly products, and therefore they could not know how their consumption may damage the environment.

As for the unexpected or negative effects of eco-labelling programs, first, consumers may be confused if they face many kinds of eco-labels. That is, the oversupply of eco-labels may hinder consumption of environmentally friendly products. According to polls conducted in Germany, the share of people who consider the Blue Angel in purchasing products has decreased. A 1990 survey carried out for Tesco, a British market chain, may be another example of the confusion of consumers, in which only about 10 percent of consumers bought labelled products although about 50 percent of consumers said that they were willing to pay extra for labelled-products. Neitzel (1998a, p. 17) noted that "the Blue Angel program has to accept the competition raised by other environmentally-related labelling activities. This "labelling market" should be evaluated and compared by independent bodies—the only solutions how to solve confusion are well prepared information campaigns to achieve correct understanding."

A second negative effect is that consumers are skeptical of environmental claims on eco-labelling in general. This may be another explanation for the results in the survey quoted above. As already mentioned, almost all eco-labelling schemes have not been able to take into consideration non-product related PPMs. Consumers know this and may thus question eco-labels. If non-product related PPMs in eco-labelling are not used, "it may be very difficult to convince the public about the life cycle approach of a particular scheme" (Neitzel 1998b, p. 4).

Third, "consumers may use labelled products without the necessary care to avoid environmental effects in the use phase" (Neitzel 1998a, p. 15). Consumers may not completely understand the meaning of eco-labels. Eco-labels are assigned, taking some life stages into account. Therefore, if consumers use and dispose of the labelled products that are environmentally unfriendly at the other life stages, the eco-labelling schemes may be counterproductive.

Therefore, we cannot tell definitely whether or not the original purpose of eco-labelling schemes has been attained since there are both positive and negative effects. There are, however, some factors that may serve to make eco-labelling schemes function properly.

The first is a consumer-information campaign or consumer education. Neitzel (1997) emphasized the importance of this scheme with an example of campaigns about how to use washing machines in an environmentally sound way. From this campaign, it is clear that the campaigns do affect consumer behavior. He concluded that "the future review of environmental labeling criteria programs shall include improved and optimized consumer information and tools on how to wash environmentally sound" (p. 248). In Japan, many institutions, such as the Hyogo Environmental Advancement Association, have campaigned for the consumption of labelled products.

The second factor relates to retailers or "professional purchasers" (Neitzel 1998a, p. 12). Eco-labelling does not affect consumer behavior directly. "However, eco-labels may affect them significantly when retailers want to stock products with eco-labels "(OECD 1997, p. 6).

The third factor is government procurement. According to OECD (1997), total public-sector procurement in Canada is more than $75 billion per year. In the United States and Japan, governments, institutions, and universities have been important sources for labelled products. Since the amount of government procurement, including local governments, is very large, their behavior affects the share of labelled products.

Let us finally examine the effects of mutual recognition arrangements on consumer behavior. If mutual recognition is established between two countries, the share of the products awarded eco-labelling will increase in the importing country since eco-labels become affixed to imported products. This gives rise to a price effect: "Egypt noted that mutual recognition could, for example, result in an integration of markets and the establishment of a lower equilibrium price for the labelled product. This would encourage environmentally motivated consumers to switch from unlabelled goods and generate a positive income effect in developing countries, thus increasing their capability to improve the environment" (WTO 1995). Because of the increase in labelled products and the fall in their price, consumers buy more labelled products. They may also become more environment-conscious since they are able to acquire the information on the environment of the exporting countries.

On the other hand, consumers may be confused and become skeptical more than before insofar as there are two or more different criteria to be determined that are presently equivalent. Or they may use and dispose of the labelled products with less care than before since the labelled products in the market increase, possibly leading to consumers mistakenly believing that products in the particular category have become more environmentally friendly.

The point then is that mutual recognition has both positive and negative effects. Therefore it is very important that eco-labelling schemes are enforced with other appropriate complementary schemes as mentioned above.

III. Effects on the Environment

In this section, we concentrate on the effects of introduction of eco-labelling schemes and mutual recognition of them on the environment. According to a survey conducted by the Federal Environmental Agency of Germany, 56% of 296 companies are of the opinion that the "Blue Angel" is "very beneficial" or "beneficial" to the environment. However, OECD (1997, p. 38) noted that "most eco-labelling programs are relatively new and their environmental effectiveness has not been evaluated. Also, the environmental benefit of eco-labelled products is difficult to differentiate from the environmental benefit achieved through other environmental measures".

Only with respect to certain products is it possible to estimate the effect of eco-labelling schemes. For example, in the Nordic Swan program, a study conducted in 1995 showed that "the eco-labelling of fine paper had resulted in an 11 percent reduction in sulphur emissions from Swedish pulp and paper mills, a 21 percent reduction in COD emissions and a 50 percent reduction in AOX emissions" (OECD 1997, p. 48).

We can infer the environmental effects of eco-labelling programs by analogy with the effects on consumer behavior, although accurate evaluation of the effects will depend on surveys to be carried out in the future. If consumers can know the accurate impact on the environment by consuming the products and change their behavior in favor of the environment by the introduction of a eco-labelling scheme, eco-labellings will be useful schemes for conservation. However, if consumers are confused and become skeptical because of the increase in the number of eco-labelling schemes, they may deteriorate the environment rather than conserve it.

A similar analogy holds on the effect of mutual recognition. Moreover, we should not overlook another essential point about mutual recognition, which is related to LCA. Generally existing eco-labelling schemes have excluded only the non-product related PPMs. Hence they cannot reflect the impacts both in the acquisition and the production phases. This incomplete consideration of LCA in conjunction with mutual recognition may expand the negative effects. On the other hand, if each eco-labelling scheme takes into consideration the environmental impacts that cannot be identified in the product itself based on its own damages and preferences, mutual recognition works in favor of the environment, since the eco-labelling schemes give producers both in exporting and importing countries proper incentives to improve the environment. The standardization of LCA has almost been completed in ISO, although Neitzel (1998b) has pointed out that the lack of standardization tools has made it difficult to achieve mutual recognition.

IV. Effects on International Trade

WTO members have discussed the trade effects of eco-labelling schemes at CTE meetings. They have focused on whether or not eco-labelling schemes give rise to technical barriers to trade (TBT). Canada, the EC, Argentina, India, the ASEAN countries, the United States and others have noted that "the recent increase in the use of eco-labelling schemes raised concerns about transparency, unfair burdens and high competitive costs on foreign producers of like products—eco-labelling schemes could lead to protectionist abuse" (WTO 1995). In March 1998, Colombia presented a document (WTO 1998b), which showed that some environmental measures adopted by particular developed countries, such as eco-labelling or packaging regulations, have negative effects on its exports in spite of the introduction of strict environmental standards in Colombia. Moreover, Colombia insisted that "despite this effort towards environmental protection, Colombia's flower sector had encountered difficulties with market access due to the fact that private organizations in certain importing countries had promoted a campaign to denigrate Colombian flowers" (WTO 1998a). Colombia demonstrated this effect using data comparing the percentage change in volume of flower exports to the whole world with that to Germany (WTO 1998b). Korea, Pakistan, and Egypt also noted that in some cases developing country exporters must bear "5 to 20 per cent of additional costs on exported products" (WTO 1998a) in the existence of an eco-labelling scheme in the importing country.

OECD (1997, p. 38) has mentioned four possible points on whether circumstances potentially leading to trade concerns exist "in the absence of evidence of specific trade effects:"

(1) the number of eco-labels developed for product groups of particular export interest to developing countries;

(2) the eco-label criteria based on life-cycle analysis;

(3) the proportion of eco-labelled products manufactured or produced in foreign countries and in particular developing countries; and

(4) the proportion of foreign licensees who have obtained an eco-label for their products.

We consider the Blue Angel as an example. The criteria of the Blue Angel do not generally include the non-product related PPMs. Moreover, foreign producers form about 13 per cent of the total of producers awarded the label. This number underestimates the actual ratio of foreign producers since there exist cases in which domestic retail chains apply for the label on foreign products that they import. Thus, at the present stage, the first point can be considered as the best explanation for eco-labelling schemes having negative trade effects.

The industries that raise concerns about trade effects are especially textiles and paper products. The EU eco-label criteria for textile industries include the environmental impacts from the use of pesticides in growing cotton, the harmful process during the production of polyester, and the use of harmful substances during the processing, making up, and finishing of products. It is difficult for producers in developing countries to comply with these criteria. The criteria for paper products in several eco-labelling schemes include the requirements on the ratio of recycled paper and that of renewable resources, which can be technical trade barriers.

The key point is to what extent the criteria are based on LCA. If the criteria include the environmental impacts in the acquisition and production phases, they can easily become points in dispute. The reason is that, although the environmental impacts from the same production method are different between the exporting country and the importing country, which leads to the difference of strictness of environmental standards, the criteria usually reflect the impact in the importing country. Scarlett and Morris (1996) have referred to this fact and attributed it to political processes, in which stakeholders in the importing country have an advantage over those in the exporting country.

Now considering mutual recognition, there are two positive effects. First, if mutual recognition is established between countries, the cost of complying with the criteria falls, since the cost of meeting the different criteria required by different schemes is likely higher than that of meeting only one set of criteria.

Second, if mutual recognition is established with the full LCA, it achieves efficient resource allocation. The reason is as follows. With the full LCA, the environmental impacts in the acquisition and production phases are respected not only in the importing country but also in the exporting country. Although mutual recognition in all categories between any two eco-labelling schemes cannot be attained in the short term, there are two alternatives to consider. First, as in the case of Nordic Swan, which is an eco-labelling program common to Sweden, Norway, Finland, and Iceland, the criteria should be set so that a product is awarded the label if the method of producing the product complies with all relevant provisions in the legislation/laws of the place/country of production, since those laws reflect the preference for the environment in the place/country. Second, as noted by Neitzel (1998b), the criteria should include the requirements on non-product related PPMs according to specific international, or regional agreed certification systems, only if they are available. Sustainable forest certification organized by the Forest Stewardship Council and Codex Alimentarius, with complete texts on food labelling, are among them.

V. The Effects on Investment

The introduction of eco-labelling schemes may have both positive and negative effects on investment in environmentally sound technologies (EST).

The positive effect is as follows: the producers with labelled products profit more than those with unlabelled products since the eco-label puts a premium on the products. This market condition gives rise to the competition for eco-labels. Producers have to invest more in EST to put an eco-label on their products. According to a survey in Germany in 1998, "76% of companies believe that the eco-label has increased competition for environmental innovation in their branch" (Neitzel 1998a, p. 12).

On the other hand, "technical options and innovations, which may be a breakthrough for future developments, and which may require support from labelling activities, may be restricted by LCA because of status-quo scenarios and present data" (Neitzel 1997, p. 242). Moreover, when new criteria are being developed, producers of eco-labelled products may "try to ensure that criteria favor the current technology" (Scarlett and Morris 1997, p. 32) they have, which also may distort the direction of innovation.

In terms of the international aspects, there are two factors that may distort innovation: one is about transparency and the other relates to non-product related PPMs. If the decision-making process is not transparent, it costs much time and money for the producers in the exporting country to collect the information, which hinders them from investing in EST. Furthermore, if it is very difficult for the producers to comply with the criteria for the non-product related PPMs, they may also give up innovation.

Mutual recognition accelerates the positive effect since potential entrants to the market of labelled products increase and reduce the negative effect in terms of the international aspect. This permits the producers to collect the information and comply with non-product related PPMs more easily.

One point should be noted on mutual recognition according to GEN (1999), which is that mutual recognition is attained more easily when "the exporting country's environmental criteria are similar to the importing country's program requirements." We may say that the more similar technologies the two countries have, the more similar requirements the eco-labelling schemes of those countries become. Therefore technology transfer from developed countries to developing countries plays an important role in mutual recognition. At CTE meetings, several countries have pointed this out. For example, Egypt recommended that "developing countries should be provided with technical assistance to improve environmental performance" (WTO 1998b).

VI. A Theoretical Analysis of Eco-labelling

To analyze the relationship between eco-labelling and international trade, we construct a simple oligopoly model in which there exists trade between domestic and foreign countries. Since the full description of the model and analysis is given in Appendix, we briefly describe the model and discuss the essence of its implications in this section.

The model has the following specific features. First, domestic and foreign firms compete in quantities with Cournot conjecture. The oligopolistic framework is adopted, because eco-labelling could lead to some market power as was mentioned above. With respect to the supply side, we also assume for simplicity that the numbers of firms are fixed; all firms are identical; marginal costs are constant; and the domestic market is supplied by all firms but the foreign market by only foreign firms.

Second, to capture the characteristic that eco-labelling is voluntary and open to any producers, we assume that the number of firms that obtain eco-labels is endogenously determined such that the profits between those firms that will obtain eco-labels and those that will not obtain eco-labels are equalized. However, to reflect another characteristic that eco-labelling may discriminate against foreign producers, it is assumed that the domestic eco-label is available to only the domestic firms. The reason why we impose such an extreme assumption is to examine whether foreign firms could gain regardless of such an unfair program.

Third, to reflect the effect of eco-labelling on consumer behavior, we assume that once the eco-labelling is introduced, consumers are decomposed into two groups: those who consume only the labelled good (and never consume the unlabeled good any longer) and those who are indifferent between the labelled and unlabelled goods.[8] That is, the eco-labelling divides a market into two markets: the unlabelled-good market and the labelled-good market.

Fourth, the production (or consumption) emits pollution that is proportional to the output (or consumption) level and damages the environment. Both domestic and foreign firms can abate the emission by incurring an extra marginal cost (MC). This MC is related to the emission level. The higher the MC, the lower the emission level per unit. When eco-labelling is introduced, the government sets a certain target level of emission per unit. Those firms which intend to obtain the eco-label have to incur an extra MC to attain the target level.

In the model, we consider and compare the following four cases. In Case 0, there is no eco-labelling. In Case 1, only the domestic country introduces eco-labelling. In Case 2, both countries independently establish eco-labelling schemes, while in Case 3, the domestic country recognizes the foreign label. We are particularly interested in the effects on the domestic economy of the introduction of eco-labelling and the domestic recognition of the foreign eco-label.

The basic results obtained in the model are as follows. First, the effects of eco-labelling on domestic emission crucially depend on whether the pollution is emitted during production or consumption. In particular, the introduction of eco-labelling or the recognition of the foreign eco-label could increase the local emission level. When only the domestic country introduces eco-labelling, the domestic emission falls if pollution is emitted during consumption but could rise if it is emitted during production (see Proposition 1). When the domestic eco-labelling increases domestic emission in this case, the emission per unit of production of the firms with the eco-label becomes less, but the total domestic production becomes larger. That is, the direct effect of eco-labelling (i.e., the decrease in the emission per unit of production) is dominated by the indirect effect (i.e., the increase in total domestic production). Moreover, the recognition of foreign eco-labelling may raise the domestic emission (see Propositions 2 through 4). This is basically because the recognition leads the foreign firms with the foreign label to enter the domestic labelled-good market and hence the number of domestic firms that obtain the eco-label falls. In an extreme case, no domestic firm will obtain the eco-label and the labelled good is supplied by the foreign firms alone.

Second, even if the foreign firms cannot obtain the domestic eco-label, this does not necessarily mean that the foreign firms lose from it. Moreover, the domestic firms may not benefit from such eco-labelling. When only the domestic country introduces eco-labelling, there are three possible outcomes: all firms lose or gain from the domestic eco-labelling; and the domestic firms gain while the foreign firms lose (see Proposition 1). The reason why these three cases are possible is that the domestic eco-labelling basically leads to two opposing effects on profits. The introduction of the domestic eco-labelling makes the market that each firm faces smaller but the competitive pressure in each market weaker. Since the market power for the foreign firms rises, the domestic eco-labelling is not necessarily bad for foreign firms.

The following should be noted with respect to the result that no firm may gain from eco-labelling. This result suggests a reason why the government needs to initiate eco-labelling. In fact, there are three types of eco-labels.[9] Type I is criteria-based, third-party certification programs. Type II is information self-declaration programs. Type III is quantified product information label programs, using preset indices. One may argue that type II is sufficient as eco-labels. However, our analysis shows that no firm may have an incentive to introduce Type II or the emission levels set by a firm or an industry may not be socially optimal. Furthermore, some third party such as the government may be necessary for monitoring.

VII. Concluding Remark

In this chapter, we have provided a comprehensive description of the effects of eco-labelling programs and have constructed a simple theoretical model to analyze the effects of these programs. As there are positive and negative aspects for eco-labelling programs, our theoretical model also reveals various consequences of them. At present, we may say that we should carefully evaluate the introduction and mutual recognition of eco-labelling programs. They may degrade the environment instead of improving it. In terms of trade effects, however, the eco-labelling programs may not hurt foreign firms. It may be too much to say that eco-labelling programs become trade barriers.

While we have focused on the effects of eco-labelling programs in this chapter, it would be useful to compare eco-labelling programs with other policy instruments such as standards. Since eco-labelling programs are voluntary, they may distort the firms' optimal decisions less than compulsory policy instruments. On the other hand, the eco-labelling programs may not be as effective as compulsory measures. Further analysis is needed therefore to provide a more authoritative evaluation of eco-labelling programs.

Appendix

In this appendix, we present a simple international oligopoly model that can specifically take account of the following characteristics of eco-labelling:

- Eco-labelling is voluntary and open to any producers.
- Eco-labelling may discriminate against foreign producers.
- Eco-labelling affects consumer behavior.

We are particularly interested in the effects on the domestic economy of the introduction of eco-labelling and the domestic recognition of the foreign eco-label.

The Basic Model

We begin with the case where there is no eco-labelling. This case is referred to as Case 0. To avoid unnecessary complication, we impose several assumptions. There are n^d domestic firms and n^f foreign firms. All firms are identical and the numbers of firms are fixed. Firms produce a homogeneous good with constant marginal cost (MC), which is assumed to be zero. The production (or consumption) emits pollution that is proportional to the output (or consumption) level and damages the environment. Both domestic and foreign firms can abate the emission by incurring an extra MC. This MC is related to the emission level. The higher the MC, the lower the emission level per unit. There are two segmented markets, domestic and foreign. To mainly focus on the domestic market, however, we assume that the domestic market is supplied by both domestic and foreign firms, while the foreign market is supplied by only foreign firms. The firms compete in quantities with Cournot conjecture in each market.

The inverse demand function of the domestic markets is given by[10]

$$P = 1 - X \tag{1}$$

where P and X are, respectively, the price and the total demand. *Variable profits from the domestic market* for the domestic firm (firm d) and the foreign firm (firm f) are, respectively, given by

$$\pi^d = Px^d, \quad \pi^f = Px^f, \tag{2}$$

where x^i is the supply of firm i ($i = d, f$).

We can then determine the Cournot equilibrium in the domestic market:[11]

$$x_0^d = x_0^f = \frac{1}{n^d + n^f + 1}, \quad P_0 = \frac{1}{n^d + n^f + 1}, \quad \pi_0^d = \pi_0^f = \frac{1}{\left(n^d + n^f + 1\right)^2}. \tag{3}$$

In the following, we consider three cases to examine the effects of eco-labelling on the domestic economy.[12] In Case 1, only the domestic country introduces eco-labelling. In Case 2, both countries independently establish eco-labelling systems. In Case 3, the domestic country recognizes the foreign eco-label which is not recognized in Case 2.

Introduction of Domestic Eco-labelling

In Case 1, eco-labelling is introduced in the domestic country alone. The domestic government sets a certain target level of emission per unit. Those firms which intend to obtain the eco-label have to incur an extra MC, c^d, to attain the target level. To capture the feature of discrimination against foreign producers, however, we assume that the eco-labelling is available only to the domestic firms. It is also assumed that any firm can produce only one type of good, i.e., either the labelled good or the unlabelled good.[13]

To reflect the effect of eco-labelling on consumer behavior, following Mattoo and Sigh (1994), we assume that once the eco-labelling is introduced, consumers are decomposed into two groups: those who consume only the labelled good (and never consume the unlabelled good any longer) and those who are indifferent between the labelled and unlabelled goods. The share of the former consumers is λ, which is assumed to be constant. That is, the domestic inverse demand for the labelled good and that for the unlabelled good are, respectively, given by[14]

$$P^l = 1 - \frac{X^l}{\lambda}, \quad P^u = 1 - \frac{X^u}{1-\lambda}. \tag{4}$$

In the following analysis, we focus on the parameter values under which $P^l > P^u$ always holds.

To capture the voluntary feature of eco-labelling, we assume that the number of domestic firms that obtain eco-labeling, n^{dl}, is endogenously determined such that the profits are equalized among all the domestic firms. Different target levels of emission per unit (i.e., different values of c^d) lead to different numbers of firms that obtain the label. The (variable) profits of the domestic firm with the label are given by

$$\pi^{dl} = \left(P^l - c^d\right) x^{dl}. \tag{5}$$

The domestic equilibrium in Case 1 is as follows:[15]

$$x_1^{dl} = \frac{\lambda\left(1-c^d\right)}{n_1^{dl}+1}, \quad P_1^l = \frac{1+n_1^{dl}c^d}{n_1^{dl}+1}, \quad \pi_1^{dl} = \frac{\lambda\left(1-c^d\right)^2}{\left(n_1^{dl}+1\right)^2}, \tag{6}$$

$$x_1^{du} = x_1^f = \frac{1-\lambda}{n_1^{du}+n^f+1}, \quad P_1^u = \frac{1}{n_1^{du}+n^f+1},$$

$$\pi_1^{du} = \pi_1^f = \frac{1-\lambda}{\left(n_1^{du}+n^f+1\right)^2}. \tag{7}$$

Specifically, we consider two cases. One is the case where the domestic firms are divided into two groups, those with the eco-label and those without the eco-label. The other is the case where all domestic firms obtain the eco-label.[16] We have:

$$\pi_1^{dl} = \frac{\lambda\left(1-c^d\right)^2}{\left(n_1^{dl}+1\right)^2} = \frac{1-\lambda}{\left(n_1^{du}+n^f+1\right)^2} = \pi_1^{du} = \pi_1^f \tag{8}$$

in the former case and

$$\pi_1^d = \frac{\lambda\left(1-c^d\right)^2}{\left(n^d+1\right)^2} > \frac{1-\lambda}{\left(n^f+1\right)^2} = \pi_1^f \tag{9}$$

in the latter.

The domestic prices of both labelled and unlabelled goods are higher than the domestic price without eco-labelling. With respect to the effect on profits, the following three cases could arise:

(1) All firms lose from domestic eco-labelling.
With $n^d = n^f = 10$, $\lambda = 0.5$, and $c^d = 0.533333$,
$n_1^{dl} = 6$ and $\pi_0^i = 0.0022675 > 0.00222222 = \pi_1^{dl} = \pi_1^{du} = \pi_1^f$, *I=d, f*.

(2) All firms gain from domestic eco-labelling.
With $n^d = n^f = 10$, $\lambda = 0.5$, and $c^d = 0.166667$,
$n_1^{dl} = 9$ and $\pi_0^i = 0.0022675 < 0.00347222 = \pi_1^{dl} = \pi_1^{du} = \pi_1^f$.

(3) The domestic firms gain while the foreign firms lose.[17]
With $n^d = n^f = 10$, $\lambda = 0.8$, and $c^d = 0.25$,
$n_1^{dl} = 10$ and $\pi_1^f = 0.0016528 < \pi_0^i = 0.0022675 < \pi_1^{dl} = 0.003719$.

The reason why three cases are possible is that the domestic eco-labelling leads to two opposing effects on profits. It makes the market that each firm faces smaller but the competitive pressure weaker. It should be noted that although the foreign firm cannot obtain the domestic eco-label, the foreign firm could benefit from the domestic eco-labelling system.

We now consider the effect of the domestic eco-labelling system on environmental damage. Since we are primarily concerned with the domestic economy, we focus on the local pollution. When the pollution is emitted during production, the total emission in the domestic country is given by

$$E^p = \beta(0)\, n^{du} x^{du} + \beta\left(c^d\right) n^{dl} x^{dl}; \quad \beta'(\cdot) < 0, \tag{10}$$

where β measures the level of emission per unit of production. β decreases as the MC of abatement rises. When it is emitted during consumption, on the other hand, the total emission is given by[18]

$$E^c = \gamma(0)\left(n^{du} x^{du} + n^{fu} x^{fu}\right) + \gamma\left(c^d\right) n^{dl} x^{dl} + \gamma\left(c^f\right) n^{fl} x^{fl}; \quad \gamma'(\cdot) < 0. \tag{11}$$

where γ measures the level of emission per unit of consumption.

Since the domestic prices of both labelled and unlabelled goods are higher than the domestic price without eco-labelling (i.e., $P_0 < P_1^u < P_1^l$), $E_0^c > E_1^c$ clearly holds. However, whether or not E^P declines is ambiguous. For example, suppose that $n^d = n^f = 10$, $\lambda = 0.8$, and $c^d = 0.25$. As we have seen above, all domestic firms obtain the label in this case (i.e., $n_1^{dl} = n^d = 10$). Then $E_0^p = \beta(0) n_0^d x_0^d = \beta(0) \times 0.4761904$ and $E_1^p = \beta(0.25) n_1^d x_1^{dl} = \beta(0.25) \times 0.545454$. If $\beta(0)$ and $\beta(0.25)$ are close enough, thus, $E_0^p < E_1^p$ holds. Although all domestic firms produce the labelled good, the domestic eco-labelling system makes the total domestic emission higher.[19] This is because the emission per unit of production becomes less, but the total domestic production becomes larger. This case is likely to arise when c^d is small and λ is large.

Proposition 1 *Suppose that only the domestic country introduces eco-labelling. All domestic consumers face higher prices. The foreign firm does not necessarily lose. All firms could gain or lose at the same time. The foreign firms alone are hurt only if all domestic firms obtain the label. The domestic emission is mitigated if the pollution is emitted during consumption but may be magnified if it is emitted during production.*

Recognition of Foreign Eco-labelling

We next consider Case 2 where the foreign country also introduces the eco-labelling system. To obtain the foreign eco-label, the foreign firm has to incur an extra MC, c^f. However, the foreign eco-label is not recognized in the domestic country. That is, the domestic consumers cannot distinguish the foreign labelled good from the foreign unlabelled good and hence regard the foreign labelled good as the unlabelled good. We assume $c^d = c^f = c$ for simplicity.

The domestic equilibrium is given by

$$x_2^{dl} = \frac{\lambda(1-c)}{n_2^{dl}+1}, \quad P_2^l = \frac{1+n_2^{dl}c}{n_2^{dl}+1}, \quad \pi_2^{dl} = \frac{\lambda(1-c)^2}{\left(n_2^{dl}+1\right)^2}, \tag{12}$$

$$x_2^{fl} = \frac{(1-\lambda)\left\{1-\left(n_2^{du}+n_2^{fu}+1\right)c\right\}}{n_2^{du}+n^f+1}, \quad x_2^{du} = x_2^{fu} = \frac{(1-\lambda)\left(1+n_2^{fl}c\right)}{n_2^{du}+n^f+1},$$

$$P_2^u = \frac{1+n_2^{fl}c}{n_2^{du}+n^f+1}, \tag{13}$$

$$\pi_2^{fl} = \frac{(1-\lambda)\left\{1-\left(n_2^{du}+n_2^{fu}+1\right)c\right\}^2}{\left(n_2^{du}+n^f+1\right)^2}, \quad \pi_2^{du} = \pi_2^{fu} = \frac{(1-\lambda)\left(1+n_2^{fl}c\right)^2}{\left(n_2^{du}+n^f+1\right)^2}. \quad (14)$$

To compare Case 1 and Case 2, suppose $n_1^{dl} = n_2^{dl}$ for the moment. We have two cases: one with $n_1^{dl} < n^d$ and the other with $n_1^{dl} = n^d$. In the former case, we have $\pi_1^{du} < \pi_2^{du}$, because those foreign firms that obtain the foreign eco-label have to incur the higher MC to produce the labelled good. That is, the foreign eco-labelling system affects not only the competition in the foreign markets but also that in the domestic markets.

As a result, n^{dl} falls (i.e., $n_1^{dl} > n_2^{dl}$). This, in turn, raises the price of the domestic labelled good and decreases its total supply. It should be noted that the supply and profits rise for each domestic firm that still obtains the eco-label.[20] As all domestic firms obtain the same profits, π^{du} and hence π^{fu} actually increase. The price of the unlabelled good becomes higher. E^c is reduced. This reduction is due not only to the decreases in the demands for both goods but also the supply of the foreign good with the foreign eco-label. Since $n^{dl}x^{dl}$ falls and $n^{du}x^{du}$ rises, E^p is likely to increase. Thus, the recognition of the foreign eco-labelling may affect the domestic environment reversely.

When $n_1^{dl} = n^d$ initially holds, n^{dl} may or may not fall. If it falls, the effects are the same as the case with $n_1^{dl} < n^d$. If n^{dl} does not change, there is no effect on the domestic market of the labelled good. With respect to the market of the unlabelled good, P^u and π^{fu} rise and π^{fl} falls. E^c falls but E^p does not change.

Proposition 2 *Suppose that the foreign country also introduces the eco-labelling system, which is not recognized by the domestic country. Then* π^{fu} *increases, but* π^{fl} *decreases.* n^{dl} *either decreases or remains unchanged. When* n^{dl} *falls, all domestic firms gain and the domestic emission decreases if the pollution is emitted during consumption but is likely to increase if it is emitted during production. When* n^{dl} *remains constant, the profits of all domestic firms remain unchanged, and the domestic emission falls if the pollution is emitted during consumption but does not change if it is emitted during production.*

We next consider Case 3 where the domestic country recognizes the foreign eco-label. We assume for simplicity that n^{fl} remains constant (i.e., $n_2^{fl} = n_3^{fl} \equiv n^{fl}$).[21] Then the equilibrium in Case 3 is given by

$$x_3^{dl} = x^{fl} = \frac{\lambda(1-c)}{n_3^{dl} + n^{fl} + 1}, \quad P_3^l = \frac{1 + \left(n_3^{dl} + n^{fl}\right)c}{n_3^{dl} + n^{fl} + 1},$$

$$\pi_3^{dl} = \pi^{fl} = \frac{\lambda(1-c)^2}{\left(n_3^{dl} + n^{fl} + 1\right)^2}, \tag{15}$$

$$x_3^{du} = x^{fu} = \frac{1-\lambda}{n_3^{du} + n^{fu} + 1}, \quad P_3^u = \frac{1}{n_3^{du} + n^{fu} + 1},$$

$$\pi_3^{du} = \pi^{fu} = \frac{1-\lambda}{\left(n_3^{du} + n^{fu} + 1\right)^2}. \tag{16}$$

To compare Case 3 with Case 2, suppose $n_3^{dl} = n_2^{dl}$ for the moment. π^{du} and π^{fu} rise but π^{dl} falls, because the total number of firms in the domestic market of the labelled good increases and that of the unlabelled good decreases.

Again, we examine the two case: $n_2^{dl} < n^d$ and $n_2^{dl} = n^d$. With $n_2^{dl} < n^d$, n^{dl} clearly falls. We first show:

Lemma 3 *If* $n_2^{dl} \geq n^{fl}$*, then the decrease in* n^{dl}*,* $-\Delta n^{dl}$*, is less than* n^{fl}*.*

Proof: Suppose in contradiction that $-\Delta n^{dl} \geq n^{fl}$. Then $\pi_3^{dl} \geq \pi_2^{dl}$ and $\pi_3^{du} < \pi_2^{du}$ hold, because the domestic firm does not need to incur c anymore when it decides not to obtain the label. Since $\pi_2^{dl} = \pi_2^{du}$ and $\pi_3^{dl} = \pi_3^{du}$ hold in equilibrium, this is a contradiction. (Q.E.D.)

The lemma implies $n_3^{dl} + n^{fl} > n_2^{dl}$. Thus, $\pi_3^{dl} = \pi_3^{du} = \pi_3^{fu} < \pi_2^{du} = \pi_2^{dl} = \pi_2^{fu}$ holds. π^{fl} is likely to increase. Both P^l and P^u fall. E^c becomes higher, but E^p may or may not become higher.

It should be noted that if $n_2^d \leq n^{fl}$, the domestic labelled good may be completely replaced by the foreign one, i.e., $n_3^{dl} = 0$ may hold. The larger n^{fl} is, the more likely this is to occur. If this is the case, P^l decreases while P^u may increase. When it does increase, π^{du} and π^{fu} also increase. The effect on E^p is ambiguous. E^c increases if P^u does not rise but may decrease if P^u rises.

With $n_2^{dl} = n^d$, the recognition of the foreign label may not decrease n^{dl}. If this is the case, P^l falls but P^u rises. The recognition reduces π^{dl} but raises π^{fu}. Since the output of each domestic firm falls, E^p falls. The effect on E^c is not clear.

Proposition 3 *Suppose that the domestic country now recognizes the foreign eco-label that has not been hitherto recognized. The price of the labelled good falls.* n^{dl} *either decreases or does not change. With* $n_3^{dl} = 0$, *the effects on the profits and emission level are ambiguous. With* $0 < n_3^{dl} < n^d$, *the domestic firms lose and the domestic emission rises if it is emitted during consumption. With* $n_3^{dl} = n^d$, *the domestic firms lose and the domestic emission falls if it is emitted during production.*

We can compare Case 1 with Case 3. This corresponds to the situation in which the domestic country recognizes the foreign eco-label as soon as it is established. Again, n^{dl} either decreases or does not change. The following three cases are possible. First, $n_3^{dl} + n^{fl} = n_1^{dl}$ holds if $n^{fl} \leq n_1^{dl} < n^d$. That is, the number of foreign firms that obtain the eco-label is equal to that of the domestic firm that stops obtaining the eco-label. If this does not hold, $\pi_3^{dl} = \pi_3^{du}$ does not hold, either. With $n_3^{dl} + n^{fl} = n_1^{dl}$, the foreign eco-labelling does not affect the prices and profits in both markets. Although E^c is not affected at all, E^p obviously goes up.

Second, if $n_1^{dl} < n^d$ and $n_1^{dl} < n^{fl}$, then $n_3^{dl} = 0$. In this case, the price of the labelled good falls while that of the unlabelled good rises. Although no domestic firm obtains the label, the domestic firms gain. The effect on the emission is ambiguous whether the pollution is emitted during consumption or production.

Lastly, n^{dl} may remain unchanged with $n_1^{dl} = n^d$. In this case, the price of the labelled good falls, but that of the unlabelled good rises. The domestic firms lose. Since the output of each domestic firm declines, E^p falls. The effect on E^c is not clear.

Proposition 4 *Suppose that the domestic country recognizes the foreign eco-label once it is established.* n^{dl} *either decreases or does not change. With* $n_3^{dl} = 0$, *the price of the labelled good falls, the price of the unlabelled good rises, the domestic firms gain, but the effect on the domestic emission is ambiguous. With* $0 < n_3^{dl} < n^d$, *there are no effects on the prices and profits at all. The domestic emission does not alter if it is emitted during consumption but rises if it is emitted during production. With* $n_3^{dl} = n^d$, *the domestic firms lose and the domestic emission declines if it is emitted during production.*

Notes

* We wish to thank Stephen Salant, John Whalley, T. N. Srinivasan, and seminar participants at Otaru University of Commerce, Research Institute of Economy, Trade and Industry, and University of Western Ontario for their helpful comments. All remaining errors are, of course, our own responsibility.

[1] http://www.gen.gr.jp/whats.html

[2] There are many international organizations that discuss eco-labelling programs themselves, or their relation to international trade. These include the WTO, OECD, Codex Alimentarius Commission, International Trade Center (ITC), United Nations Conference on Trade and Development (UNCTAD), United Nations Environment Programme (UNEP), United Nations Industrial Development Organization (UNIDO), and International Organization for Standardization (ISO).

[3] For the classification of environmental policies, see Oates and Baumol (1975). Bensako (1987) and Oates et al. (1989) analyze standards.

[4] See WTO (1996).

[5] For example, it is difficult to know how long consumers may use and how they dispose of the products. For details, see Scarlett and Morris (1996) and Neitzel (1997).

[6] WTO (1995).

[7] According to GEN (1999), criteria or requirements in the manufacturing process that have no impact at the product use or disposal stages are referred to as requirements arising from non-product related PPMs. In an environmental context, non-product related PPMs normally refer to situations where the environmental damage caused by the PPM is not transmitted by the product itself. In the WTO context, non-product related PPM requirements may become a fundamental challenge to the basic GATT/WTO concept of like products.

[8] We simply assume the demand structures without specifying the preferences underlying them. Our demand structures may be somewhat extreme because those consumers who are concerned about the environment will not consume the unlabelled good with eco-labelling. A more realistic situation is that the consumption choice between labelled and unlabelled goods is endogenously determined depending on the price difference of those two goods. We deal with this case elsewhere [Abe et al. (2000)]. But even with these more realistic preferences, we conjecture that the main results are still valid. Mattoo and Singh (1994) also impose the same assumption in their analysis. Our discussant, Stephen Salant, wonders why consumers cannot infer that the product must be produced using an environmentally unfriendly technology without eco-labelling. He argues that if they can, those consumers who care about the environment will not consume the product even without eco-labelling. With respect to this point, some informational aspect of eco-labels should be emphasized. Consumers usually know very little about processes and production methods (PPMs). For example, most consumers did not know much about genetically modified organisms (GMO) until quite recently. The presence of eco-labels themselves often provides consumers with information on PPMs.

[9] For details, see Markandya (1997).

[10] The essence of the main results will not change even if the demand is not linear.

[11] Subscript j denotes Case j in the following.

[12] We will not specify any welfare function in our model. Thus, the welfare-effects of eco-labelling are not examined. Our concern is how we should evaluate environmental damage [for this point, see Sen (1995), for example]. In particular, the pollution could be transboundary in the framework of an open economy. In this case, the degree of damages caused by cross-border pollution is crucial for the result. However, it is not easy to measure that degree. Thus, we focus on the local emission level.

[13] This may be because of the presence of fixed costs.

[14] Superscripts l and u, respectively, denote "with" and "without" the eco-label in the following.

[15] The domestic eco-labelling does not affect the foreign market at all in this case, because the two markets are segmented and MCs are constant.

[16] Also, no domestic firm may have an incentive to obtain the eco-label, but this case is not interesting.

[17] With $n^d = n^f = 10$, $\lambda = 0.8$, and $c^d = 0.5$, we have $n_1^{dl} = 10$ and $\pi_0^i = 0.0022675 > 0.0016528 = \pi_1^{dl} = \pi_1^f$. Thus, if $c^d < 0.5$, then $n^d = n_1^{dl}$ and $\pi_1^{dl} > \pi_1^f$.

[18] c^f will be defined later.

[19] The total world emission becomes less, because the domestic eco-labelling system does not affect the foreign market.

[20] We can verify that the price rises if and only if the output and profits rise. This is valid even with more general demand and cost structures. For details, see Ishikawa (1997).

[21] This could be the case if the domestic markets are very small relative to the foreign ones. Even if n^{fl} is endogenously determined, the essence of the following analysis will not change.

References

Abe, K., K. Higashida, and J. Ishikawa. 2000. "Eco-labelling under International Oligopoly", mimeo.

Bensako, D. 1987. "Performance versus Design Standards in the Regulation of Pollution", *Journal of Public Economics* 34:19-44.

GEN. 1999. GEN discussion paper on enhanced co-operation, http://www.gen.gr.jp/.

Ishikawa, J. 1997. "Diagrammatic Demonstration of the Cournot Equilibrium", *Japanese Economic Review* 48:90-100.

Markandya, A. 1997. "Eco-labelling: An Introduction and Review", in S. Zarrilli et al. (eds.), *Eco-labelling and International Trade*. London: MacMillan Press.

Mattoo, A., and H. V. Singh. 1994. "Eco-labelling: Policy Considerations," *Kyklos* 47:53-65.

Neitzel, H. 1997. "LCA and Eco-labelling: Application of Life Cycle Assessment in Environmental Labeling, German Experiences," http://www.blauer-engel.de/.

Neitzel, H. 1998a. "20 Years of Experiences of the German Environmental Labeling Scheme: 'Blue Angel'," given at the Consumer's Choice Council Conference, "Labelling for a Sustainable and Just World." http://www.blauer-engel.de/.

Neitzel, H. 1998b. "Applying Non-product Related Criteria in Eco-labelling: Some Controversies and Experiences," *Gate Magazine* 98/2.

Oates, W. E., and W. J. Baumol. 1975. "The Instruments for Environmental Policy," in E. Mills (ed.), *Economic Analysis of Environmental Problems*. New York: Columbia University Press.

Oates, W. E., P. R. Portney, and A. M. McGartland. 1989. "The Net Benefits of Incentive-based Regulation: a Case Study of Environmental Standard Setting," *American Economic Review* 79:1233-42.

OECD. 1997. "Eco-labelling: Actual Effects of Selected Programs," OCDE/GD(97) 105.

Scarlett, L., and J. Morris. 1996. "Green Groceries: Consumers, Product Labels and the Environment," http://www.rppi.org.

Sen, A. 1995. "Environmental Evaluation and Social Choice," *Japanese Economic Review,* 46:23-37.

Vossenaar, R. 1997. "Eco-labelling and International Trade: The Main Issues," in S. Zarrilli et al. (eds.), *Eco-labelling and International Trade*. London: Macmillan Press.

WTO. 1995. CTE Bulletin No.6.

WTO. 1996. CTE Bulletin No.8.

WTO. 1997. "Eco-labelling: Overview of Current Work in Various International Fora," WT/CTE/W/45, WTO.

WTO. 1998a. CTE Bulletin No.23.

WTO. 1998b. "Environmental Labels and Market Access: Case Study on the Colombian Flower-growing Industry," WT/CTE/W/76, G/TBT/W/60 (Colombia).

Zarrilli, S., V. Jha, and R. Vossenaar (eds.). 1997. *Eco-labelling and International Trade*. London: Macmillan Press.

Comment

Stephen W. Salant

This is certainly the first paper that I have ever read on eco-labelling, and apparently it is among the first such analyses to be formulated. The authors are to be thanked not only for their pioneering effort but also for the clarity with which they have expressed themselves both in the paper and in their oral presentation of its principal results.

Given that theirs is among the first papers on this subject, I think the most constructive role I can play as a discussant is to focus on the assumptions underlying their analysis and to suggest directions for further research. In the process, I hope to indicate how the welfare effects of eco-labelling might be evaluated and to point out an argument for eco-labelling as a supplement to Pigouvian emissions taxes.

The authors envision a world where firms produce at constant marginal cost. A clean technology has a smaller emission per unit of output than a dirtier technology. If a firm chooses a clean technology, its constant marginal cost is strictly larger. Although emissions presumably cause social damage, the damage function is never specified. This is one of the reasons why the authors can conduct no welfare analysis. A second reason is that the authors report consumer demand curves rather than the preferences underlying them. When all products are unlabelled, consumers have a downward-sloping linear demand. When products are labeled, however, the underlying two groups of consumers respond differently. A fraction λ of the market (call them the greens) refuses to purchase an unlabelled product no matter how inexpensive it is; the remaining fraction $1-\lambda$ of the market (call them the browns) will buy whatever product is cheaper.

The browns are entirely conventional. But the greens are among the strangest consumers I have encountered in an economic model. First, consider the depth of their powers of inference in one context juxtaposed with its shallowness in another. When eco-labelling is available, the greens are capable of inferring that a product must have been produced using a dirty technology if it bears no label. But when eco-labelling is unavailable to any firm, they are *incapable* of making a similar inference even though it is then plainly in *every* firm's interest to use a dirty technology.

But it is their preferences and not their erratic ability to draw inferences that I find striking. Greens abhor consuming products produced with a dirty technology even if the consumption good is indistinguishable (to someone who did not know its lineage) from a good produced with a clean technology.

There are two reasons why spelling out the green's preferences is important. First, welfare analysis cannot be conducted unless this is done. More important, however, is that a second externality exists which would become obvious if their preferences were expressed explicitly. The technology choice of the firm from which they purchase evidently matters to these consumers. Why? As economists, we are taught not to ask such questions about preferences. Preferences, we like to say, are given and it is *our* job merely to characterize and promote allocations which are efficient relative to these given preferences. That some of these given preferences belong to extremists of one form or another (be they racists and anti-Semites on the one hand or greens and sweatshop opponents on the other hand) should not, we are told, trouble us. Not to treat these preferences even handedly is to impose our own value judgment. This is a standard assumption and, however tempting, this is not the place to question it. So let's take these preferences as given.

It follows that, even if the markets were competitive and even if Pigouvian taxes on emissions communicated to the firms through emissions taxes the marginal social damage associated with an additional emission in the solution to the planning problem, nonetheless this efficient solution could not be supported as a competitive equilibrium! Suppose for example that, because of the concerns of the greens, the efficient solution involved at least some firms switching to the clean technology and providing their product to the green consumers even though actual social damage from the emissions was nonexistent (suppose, for concreteness, that emissions involved harmless water vapor). Then no Pigouvian emissions tax by itself could support this efficient solution as a competitive equilibrium. A large Pigouvian tax on emissions would be necessary to induce any firms to utilize the clean technology; but a Pigouvian tax of zero would be needed to generate the correct outputs from firms using the two technologies. One instrument cannot handle two margins. What is needed to handle the second externality is a second instrument. In some cases, eco-labelling could fill the role of supplementing Pigouvian taxes on emissions.

Of course, the assumption that green consumers would refuse to purchase the product of a dirty technology *no matter how small* its price seems to me very unrealistic. But a second externality would still exist even if a less extreme assumption had been made instead. For, as long as greens care *at all* about the technology used to produce a good rather than merely caring about its price and characteristics as a consumer good, then the greens' preferences reflect a second externality and a second instrument is needed to restore efficiency.

I encourage the authors in their future work to evaluate the welfare consequences of using eco-labelling not only separately but in conjunction with Pigouvian emissions taxes—and not only in an imperfectly competitive environment but also in a competitive environment. In order to evaluate these welfare consequences, the authors will have to specify a social damage function and will have to be explicit about the preferences of both groups of consumers.

COMMENT

John Whalley

It is my great loss that I am unable to be with you at this admirable conference that Bob Stern and his colleagues have organized. Though close by (just across the border) it is out of my reach at present due to disc herniation in my back. Medical advice has been to avoid "total body vibration" for a while (meaning cars and planes!), and so I have had to approach this paper with caution given the potential of this topic, and trade and environment issues in general, to get people vibrating.

The authors very usefully set out the broad contours of the "eco-labelling" issue noting that it has been a central topic of conversation in the Committee on Trade and Environment (CTE) in the WTO. They give the German "Blue Angel" scheme as an example; a scheme which designates certain products as environmentally preferred. They then later in the paper present some simple analytics which show that such schemes generally raise prices, and can still help foreign firms even if their products are non-qualifying.

My comments are threefold:

1. The author's are not to be faulted in using a term that is widespread in the literature, "eco-labelling." But I think a broader term, such as "eco-retailing" might be more appropriate to the debate since much of what concerns people goes beyond labelling per se. There are, for instance, proposals in some European countries to limit packaging of products by value (to, say, 15% of the retail price). There are other proposals that manufacturers of products be required to accept packaging returned to them from customers via retailers and wholesalers. The thesis is that product distribution and retailing are environmentally unsound; there is not enough information, there is too much packaging, and consumption activity in general is in conflict with sound environmental management.
2. With this broader statement of the issue, my view is that economists have much to contribute by pointing out the basic economics involved. Many environmental concerns reflect externality problems of various kinds, and (in my view) eco-retailing restrictions are typically poor instruments to use to address them. Packaging limitations, for instance, not only do not deal with congestion problems; they can worsen them through extra trucks on the road with packaging materials; to say nothing of worsened air quality through added emissions. Many features of these schemes are thus seemingly inefficient upon a second's reflection. Why return packaging all the way to original producers? Why not dispose of it where unwrapping occurs, and bill someone (the producer?) for it.

3. These "eco-retailing" issues often arise because of market failures elsewhere, and attempting indirect remedy through regulation is a second best procedure. Thus local (household) garbage disposal is generally unpriced. Studies indicate that even a small charge of a few cents per bag of household garbage results in a surprisingly large reduction in garbage (the theory seems to be that people sprinkle some of their garbage on their lawn!). The point, however, is that with appropriate pricing on garbage collection much of the pressure for packaging limitation schemes as part of "eco-retailing" would weaken.
4. The developing countries in all of this have perhaps the most to lose. Product identification schemes, qualification for which is difficult, make it harder for them to penetrate markets. Packaging returned from Germany to shippers in Laos rather than Italy adds a significantly differential cost burden. Developing countries have been the group reluctant to negotiate on the trade and environment issue in the WTO, but presumed to be willing to discuss these issues. I personally don't see why they should be any more willing to discuss here than elsewhere on trade and environment, unless they receive a major more than offsetting concession.
5. I have said little about the analytics in the paper. These strike me as intuitive and reasonably straightforward. Product restrictions raise prices. Foreign suppliers who do not qualify have reduced volumes, but higher prices; giving an ambiguous outcome. At the same time, there would seem to be analytics one could produce going the other way. Thus, if consumers are genuinely uninformed (or if information gathering is costly) a mandatory labelling for which the producer is liable if incorrectly displayed could, it would seem, be welfare improving. As is often the case with our analytics, the initial assumptions will lead to the result. I will look forward to the richer version of an already strong paper that might go in such directions.

CHAPTER 11

Preferential Trade Arrangements vs. Open Regionalism: A Theoretical Analysis of APEC

*Taiji Furusawa**

I. Introduction

Substantial multilateral trade liberalization has been accomplished through the eight rounds of GATT negotiations since the World War II. As the number of contracting parties increases and the negotiation agenda becomes diverse, however, it becomes more and more difficult to proceed further with multilateral negotiations over international trade and other related issues.[1] Difficulty in multilateral negotiations may spur a surge of regional economic integration. Economic integration of the European Community has been deepened to form the European Union (EU). The Canadian-U.S. free trade area extends its membership to Mexico to become the North American Free Trade Agreement (NAFTA). These Preferential Trade Arrangements (PTAs) are permitted through GATT Article XXIV as an exception to its Most Favored Nation (MFN) principle. Each member country of a PTA is required to completely eliminate tariffs for almost all goods imported from other member countries, but is allowed to set positive, discriminatory tariffs against nonmember countries.

Because of its discriminatory nature, it is ambiguous whether or not PTAs are welfare enhancing from the global point of view. Welfare implications of PTAs were originally brought to our attention by Viner (1950), who identified a favorable "trade creation effect" of PTAs and an adverse "trade diversion effect." Whether or not a PTA is welfare enhancing depends largely on which of these two effects outweighs the other. This criterion remains practically valid when we assess welfare consequences of a particular PTA, even though Ohyama (1972) and Kemp and Wan (1976) show that there always exist internal transfer and external tariff profiles such that neither member countries nor nonmember countries will be worse off with the formation of the PTA. Krugman (1991), for example, shows that as the number of PTAs that constitute the world increases, the trade-creation effect comes to dominate the trade-diversion effect. He reports a simulation result that the welfare of each country is minimized if the world is divided into three equal-sized blocs. Grossman and Helpman (1995) and Levy (1997) examine the incentive to form a PTA in political economy models. Levy especially asks whether the PTA formation is detrimental to multilateral trade liberalization. Bagwell and Staiger (1997a,b) also investigate how the formation of a PTA affects multilateral tariff cooperation. The analysis of PTAs in relation to multilateral trade liberalization is particularly important since PTAs that harm multilateral trade liberalization efforts are not desirable from the viewpoint of the world welfare.[2]

Another type of regional economic integration came into existence in 1989. Unlike PTAs under the GATT Article XXIV, the Asia Pacific Economic Cooperation (APEC) forum launched in 1989 adopts open regionalism as its fundamental principle. Among several possible definitions of open regionalism, I focus on the aspect of offering unconditional MFN, which is the most prominent feature of APEC.[3] That is, open regionalism refers to a principle of regional arrangements such that any internal agreement is extended to nonmember countries. Because of this inherent feature of openness, regional economic integration is complementary to global trade liberalization if it adopts the principle of open regionalism. Therefore, whether or not a trading bloc adopts open regionalism crucially affects global welfare.

I examine the choice between a preferential arrangement and open regionalism when countries form a trading bloc.[4] When member countries of a PTA reciprocally reduce internal tariff rates while keeping their external tariff rates at relatively high levels, it may not be best for them to eliminate internal tariffs completely. This is because they can mitigate the trade-diversion effect by setting relatively low, but positive internal tariff rates. Even though preferential arrangements are preferable in the aspect of keeping positive external tariffs, the inability to adjust internal tariff rates in an optimal manner can lower member countries' individual welfare. Open regionalism is more desirable in this aspect, since member countries are allowed to set internal tariff rates at any desired levels. However, member countries under open regionalism must also reduce the tariff rates to nonmember countries even though nonmember countries do not reduce their tariff rates in return. Because of this lack of reciprocity, cooperation within the trading bloc may well be limited. Together with the limitation of extending the market power to nonmember countries, open regionalism is made relatively unattractive to member countries.

Whether a PTA is preferred or open regionalism is adopted cannot be determined *a priori*. In a simple three-country model, I examine the incentive of member countries to adopt open regionalism when they engage in economic integration. I find that they always choose not to adopt open regionalism. Indeed, I show that if the status quo tariff rates are large enough, it is possible for PTA member countries to select the best tariff profile that maximizes their social welfare in the absence of any constraint on the feasible tariff profiles. This result, however, is not universally true. In the Concluding Remarks, I discuss a possible extension of the model, so that politically motivated governments of member countries adopt open regionalism when they are economically integrated.

In the next section, I set out a simple three-country model and derive some preliminary results. Then, in Section III, I derive the optimal tariff profile for member countries when they are economically integrated without any constraint. Section IV and V investigate the optimal tariff structure when countries adopt a PTA and when they adopt open regionalism in the formation of trading blocs, respectively. Section VI compares these two types of regional economic integration and concludes that member countries prefer PTAs to trading bloc under open regionalism. Some concluding remarks follow in Section VII. I relegate the rigorous, mathematical presentation of the model to the Appendix.

II. The Model and Preliminary Results

There are three countries, Country 1, Country 2, and Country 3. Each country is endowed with three goods, Good 1, Good 2, and the numeraire good. I assume that Country 1 is a natural exporter of Good 2 and a natural importer of Good 1, whereas Country 2 is a natural exporter of Good 1 and a natural importer of Good 2. They may also trade the numeraire good. Country 3 is a natural exporter of Goods 1 and 2, and a natural importer of the numeraire good.

Country 1's import demand for Good 1 and Country 2's import demand for Good 2 are represented by a common function $m(p)=1-p$. Export-supply functions are defined with the usage of the function $x(p)=p$. I assume that both Country 1's export supply of Good 2 and Country 2's export supply of Good 1 are defined by $ax(p)$, where $a\in(0,1)$ is a parameter that represents the mutual dependence between Country 1 and Country 2. Country 3's export supplies of Good 1 and Good 2 are individually represented by the common function $(1-a)x(p)$.

Country 1 imports Good 1 from Country 2 and Country 3, whereas Country 2 imports Good 2 from Country 1 and Country 3. Country 3, on the other hand, only imports the numeraire good. I assume that each country imposes tariffs only on its imports of the non-numeraire goods. In this setting, therefore, only Countries 1 and 2 impose import tariffs. I consider economic integration between these two symmetric countries, 1 and 2. Let τ_i and τ_i^*, for $i=1,2$, represent the specific tariff rates that Country i imposes on its imports from the partner country and from Country 3, respectively. I assume that all tariff rates are the same before the economic integration. I call this common rate $\bar{\tau}$.

Once Country 1's internal and external tariff rates τ_1 and τ_1^* on the imports of Good 1 are given, the price for Good 1 in each country is determined so as to clear the world market. Similarly, the market clearing prices for Good

2 are obtained given Country 2's tariff rates τ_2 and τ_2^* on the imports of Good 2. Since the import-demand function is decreasing in the importing country's price while the export-supply function is increasing in the exporting country's price, an increase in any tariff rate on any good raises the price of the good in question in the importing country and lowers the price in the exporting country that is faced with that particular tariff.

Country 1 and Country 2 derive surplus from exporting and importing the non-numeraire goods, whereas Country 3 derives only the surplus from the export since all it imports is the numeraire good. The surplus from the import for either Country 1 and Country 2 is defined to include tariff revenues, and can be written as a function of the internal tariff rate, external tariff rate, and the parameter that measures the mutual dependence of member countries. We express this function as $M(\tau,\tau^*,a)$, where τ and τ^* represent the internal and external tariff rates, respectively. Similarly, we can write the surplus from the export for each member country as $X(\tau,\tau^*,a)$.

Since import restrictions induce the improvement of the terms of trade at the costs of creating distortions, the surplus from the import $M(\tau,\tau^*,a)$ increases as τ and τ^* increases when they are small. Indeed, I can show that in this specific model, $M(\tau,\tau^*,a)$ is maximized when $\tau = \tau^* = 1/3$. On the other hand, the surplus from the export $X(\tau,\tau^*,a)$ decreases in τ since the export price to the partner country falls if the partner country increases the internal tariff rate. However, the member country's surplus from the export increases if the partner country raises the external tariff rate τ^*. An increase in the partner country's tariff raises the demand for the good exported to that partner country. The exporting member country derives more surplus from the export as the export price rises as a result.

Social welfare for Country 1 and Country 2 can be represented by $w_1 = M(\tau_1,\tau_1^*,a)+X(\tau_2,\tau_2^*,a)$ and $w_2 = M(\tau_2,\tau_2^*,a)+X(\tau_1,\tau_1^*,a)$, respectively. The best response to the partner country's tariff rates is given by the tariff rate profile (τ,τ^*) that maximizes its own social welfare. Thus, each member country chooses $(\tau,\tau^*)=(1/3,\ 1/3)$ so as to maximize the surplus from the import. I assume that the initial tariff rates are less than or equal to this common tariff rate, i.e., $\overline{\tau} \le 1/3$.

Due to the symmetry, it is natural to assume that Countries 1 and 2 set the same tariff rate profile (τ,τ^*) after they are economically integrated. I define the social welfare function, common to both member countries, under the condition that they individually select the same tariff profile (τ,τ^*) by

$$W(\tau,\tau^*,a) = M(\tau,\tau^*,a)+X(\tau,\tau^*,a).$$

III. Unconditional Economic Integration

If there is no regulation for regional economic integration, Countries 1 and 2 select the tariff rates so as to maximize $W(\tau,\tau^*,a)$ when they are economically integrated. To derive the tariff profile (τ,τ^*) that maximizes $W(\tau,\tau^*,a)$, we consider separately the optimal internal tariff rate τ for a given external tariff rate τ^* and the optimal external tariff rate for a given internal tariff rate. The former relationship is depicted by the τ-line and the latter is represented by the τ^*-line in figure 1. Notice that both the τ-line and τ^*-line are positively sloped. Let us consider the τ-line, for example. If τ^* increases, the pre-taxed world price of the imports from Country 3 decreases. Consequently, each member country benefits from importing less from the partner country and importing more from Country 3. This shift in the source of the import can be accomplished by an increase in the internal tariff rate τ. That is why the τ-line is positively sloped.

Another prominent feature of the τ-line is that τ takes a negative value when τ^* is small. Let us consider the extreme case where $\tau^* = 0$. If τ also equals zero, there is no discrepancy among domestic prices across countries and hence there exists no distortion at all. But then, the member countries have an incentive to "exploit" Country 3 through the improvement of their terms of trade against Country 3. Lowering the common internal tariff rate below zero achieves this goal, since it shifts the source of imports from Country 3 to the partner country. Now, as τ^* increases, the optimal internal tariff rate increases as I have explained above. However, it remains negative until τ^* reaches the critical level $1/(3+a)$.

As figure 1 shows, $W(\tau,\tau^*,a)$ is maximized at $(\tau,\tau^*)=(0,1/(3+a))$, the intersection between the τ-line and τ^*-line. Thus, the internal tariff is completely eliminated, while the external tariff rate is set at $1/(3+a)$ if Countries 1 and 2 are economically integrated.

What is striking is the fact that the internal tariff is completely eliminated in the unconstrained economic integration. This result is not remarkable at all if member countries do not import any good from Country 3, i.e., $a=1$ in this model. Free trade is Pareto optimal in two-country trade models. Unless $a=1$, however, member countries import goods from Country 3 and they impose positive tariffs on those imports. In such cases, each member country can import the good at a lower price from Country 3 than from the partner country if the internal tariff rate is zero. Thus, member countries have an incentive to

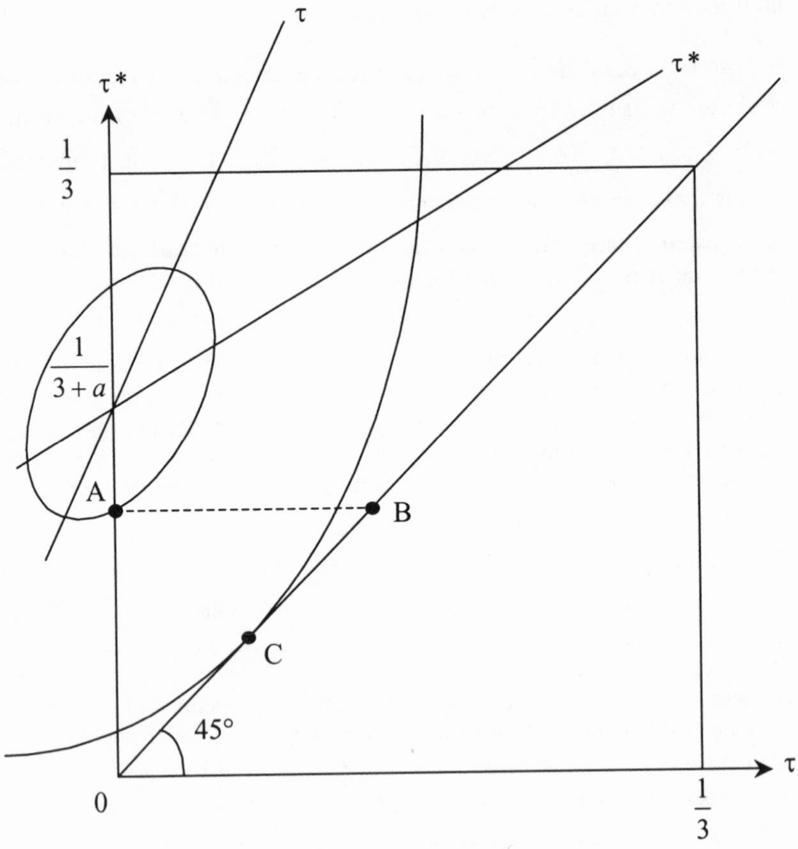

Figure 1. Cooperative Tariff Profiles

raise the internal tariff rate from zero in order to shift the source of imports to Country 3. Despite this incentive, member countries set their internal tariff rate at zero. The incentive to raise the internal tariff is offset by the incentive to "exploit" Country 3 by lowering the internal tariff.

Moreover, as the member countries become more dependent on each other, i.e., as a increases, the external tariff rate decreases.

Proposition 1. If there is no regulation for regional economic integration, the member countries completely eliminate the internal tariff while they select a positive external tariff rate.

IV. Preferential Trade Arrangements

If Countries 1 and 2 adopt a PTA, they must eliminate the internal tariff completely, while they must select the external tariff rate such that it does not exceed the status quo tariff rate $\bar{\tau}$. As figure 1 indicates, the resulting tariff profile depends on whether or not $\bar{\tau}$ exceeds $1/(3+a)$.

If $\bar{\tau} \geq 1/(3+a)$, the member countries attain the unconditionally optimal tariff profile $(0, 1/(3+a))$ under the PTA. Social welfare for member countries unambiguously improves as a result. The impact on Country 3's welfare can be assessed by looking at the effect on its export price for the non-numeraire goods. Now, the domestic prices for the non-numeraire goods in member countries drop as both τ and τ^* decrease. Although a decrease in τ^* tends to increase Country 3's export price, the change in τ^* is small relative to the change in τ, so that this effect does not outweigh the effect on the domestic price in the member countries. Therefore, Country 3's export price, which is the domestic price in the member countries minus the external tariff rate, falls and its social welfare declines, as a result of the PTA between Countries 1 and 2.

Next, consider the case where $\bar{\tau} < 1/(3+a)$. In this case, the internal tariff drops to zero, while the external tariff remains to be $\bar{\tau}$. In figure 1, this change is represented by a movement from B to A. The figure also depicts a member country's indifference curve that passes through A.[5] This curve is horizontal on the τ-line and is vertical on the τ^*-line. As we can guess from this observation, the slope of the indifference curve at A is positive and point B is outside of this indifference curve, which means that the PTA enhances the member countries' social welfare.[6] What is the impact of the PTA on the nonmember country's social welfare? Since τ drops from $\bar{\tau}$ to zero while τ^* remains at $\bar{\tau}$, the domestic prices for the non-numeraire goods in member countries fall and so does Country 3's export price. Thus, Country 3's welfare declines by the PTA between Country 1 and Country 2.

Proposition 2. Member countries of a PTA reduce the external tariffs if the status-quo tariff is sufficiently large. Social welfare for the member countries rises, whereas social welfare for the nonmember country falls, as a consequence of the PTA.

V. Open Regionalism

Member countries of a trading bloc that adopts open regionalism select a non-discriminatory tariff rate so as to maximize the individual country's social welfare. The optimal non-discriminatory tariff rate τ that maximizes $W(\tau,\tau,a)$ is given by the tangency between an indifference curve and the 45-degree line in figure 1. At the tangent point C, the non-discriminatory tariff rate τ equals $(1-a)/(3-a)$. Notice that this tariff rate decreases as a increases. If a is small, trade with the nonmember country is relatively more important than internal trade. Since the nonmember country will not reduce its own tariff rate in return (indeed the nonmember country is assumed not to impose a tariff on its imports of the numeraire good in this model), the member countries select a relatively high tariff rate to exercise their market power. If a is large, on the other hand, the weight on the internal trade is high, and hence the member countries considerably reduce the tariff rates.

Since an agreed-upon tariff rate should not exceed $\bar{\tau}$, the cooperative tariff rate under open regionalism is given by

$$\tau^c(\bar{\tau},a) \equiv min\left\{\bar{\tau},\frac{1-a}{3-a}\right\}.$$

Notice that regional free trade is not chosen unless $a=1$.[7] Moreover, if $\bar{\tau}$ and a are so small that $\bar{\tau} \leq (1-a)/(3-a)$, there is no room for regional trade liberalization. Under open regionalism, regional trade liberalization is more likely to take place if the dependence between member countries is large.

As for welfare consequences, it is obvious that the formation of a trading bloc is beneficial to member countries since they can always choose to maintain the status-quo tariff profile $(\bar{\tau},\bar{\tau})$. Thus, as far as $\bar{\tau}>(1-a)/(3-a)$, Countries 1 and 2 reduce both internal and external tariff rates, which benefits both countries. What about the impact on Country 3's social welfare then? The bloc formation lowers the domestic price for the non-numeraire goods in member countries as in the case of PTAs. Under open regionalism, however, the external tariff rate drops as much as the internal tariff rate. As a consequence, Country 3's export price rises so that Country 3 benefits from the bloc formation by Countries 1 and 2 if they adopt open regionalism.

Proposition 3. If the status-quo tariff rate is sufficiently large, countries reduce the non-discriminatory tariff rates when they are economically integrated under open regionalism. Social welfare rises for both member and nonmember countries as a result of the economic integration. Moreover, the deeper the mutual economic dependence between member countries, the lower the agreed-upon tariff rate.

VI. Comparison between the Two Types of Regional Economic Integration

This section investigates whether or not countries adopt open regionalism when they form a trading bloc. The previous sections reveal that in either regime, the cooperative tariff profile varies with the status-quo tariff rate $\bar{\tau}$.

If $\bar{\tau} \geq 1/(3+a)$, the PTA can select the most favorable (to member countries) tariff profile $(0,1/(3+a))$. Therefore, the member countries prefer the PTA to the trading bloc that adopts open regionalism in this case.

Let us next consider the case where $\bar{\tau} < 1/(3+a)$. Here, the tariff profile under the PTA is $(0, \bar{\tau})$, whereas it is $(\tau^c(\bar{\tau},a), \tau^c(\bar{\tau},a))$ under open regionalism. If $\bar{\tau}$ is relatively high such that $(1-a)/(3-a) \leq \bar{\tau} \leq 1/(3+a)$, $\tau^c(\bar{\tau},a)$ is equal to $(1-a)/(3-a)$. In figure 1, the tariff profile under open regionalism is depicted as point C, while a typical tariff profile under the PTA can be represented by point A since $\bar{\tau} \geq (1-a)/(3-a)$ in this case. As the figure shows, point A lies within the indifference curve that passes through C. Indeed, the tariff vector under the PTA must always lie within the indifference curve that passes through C. Therefore, we find that member countries will not adopt open regionalism even in this case. Finally, if the status quo tariff rate is so small that $\bar{\tau} < (1-a)/(3-a)$, $\tau^c(\bar{\tau},\alpha)$ is equal to $\bar{\tau}$ so that the trading bloc will not be formed if they are supposed to adopt open regionalism. Even in this case, the PTA can successfully reduce the internal tariff rate, which is beneficial to member countries as we have seen in Section IV.

Proposition 4. Member countries of a trading bloc always prefer the PTA to the bloc that adopts open regionalism. Open regionalism will never be adopted in the economic environment that we consider.

VII. Concluding Remarks

Under a PTA, member countries of a trading bloc are allowed to discriminate tariffs on the basis of its membership. This feature makes PTAs more preferable than trading blocs that adopt open regionalism. However, they must completely eliminate the tariffs for almost all imported goods under a PTA, which makes PTAs less preferable. I have shown in a simple three-country model that member countries will not adopt open regionalism when they are economically integrated.

This result, however, is not universally true. Indeed, my analysis indicates some directions of extending the basic model, so that in a richer setting member countries adopt open regionalism. Here, consider the case in which the government of each country is politically motivated, and each government of a trading bloc puts more weight on the well-being of the import-competing industries. In that case, the τ-curve shifts to the right while the τ^*-curve shifts up from the respective counterparts when the governments are benevolent social welfare maximizers. Figure 2 indicates the situation in which the two governments are politically motivated. The optimal tariff-rate profile, represented by point A, is not attainable under a PTA even if the status-quo tariff rate is large. The PTA tariff-rate profile is depicted as point B at which an indifference curve is tangent to the vertical axis. The tariff-rate profile under open regionalism, on the other hand, is shown by point C. As figure 2 indicates, member countries adopt open regionalism in this situation, where complete elimination of internal tariffs is quite unfavorable to the politically motivated governments.

Appendix

In this Appendix, I show the rigorous presentation of the three-country model that I consider in this chapter. Each consumer's preferences can be characterized by a quasi-linear utility function that is separable for the three goods: Good 1, Good 2, and the numeraire good. I assume that the numeraire good linearly enters the utility function, and the countries are endowed with a large amount of the numeraire good, so that we can proceed with partial equilibrium analysis for the non-numeraire goods.

Country 1 imports Good 1 from Country 2 and Country 3, whereas Country 2 imports Good 2 from Country 1 and Country 3. These two countries share the same import-demand function $m(p) = 1 - p$ for their respective imports of the non-numeraire goods. Export-supply functions for the non-numeraire goods exported from a member country, Country 1 or Country 2, and the nonmember country, Country 3, are given by $ax(p)$ and $(1-a)x(p)$, respectively, where $x(p) = p$.

Now, consider the market-clearing conditions. Due to the symmetry, I need only consider the market-clearing condition for a representative non-numeraire good. Let τ and τ^* denote the internal and external tariff rates imposed on the imports from the member country and Country 3, respectively. Letting p denote the domestic price in the importing country, we have

$$m(p) = ax(p - \tau) + (1 - a)x(p - \tau^*).$$

The market clearing domestic price can be derived explicitly as

$$p(\tau, \tau^*) = \frac{1 + a\tau + (1-a)\tau^*}{2}. \tag{1}$$

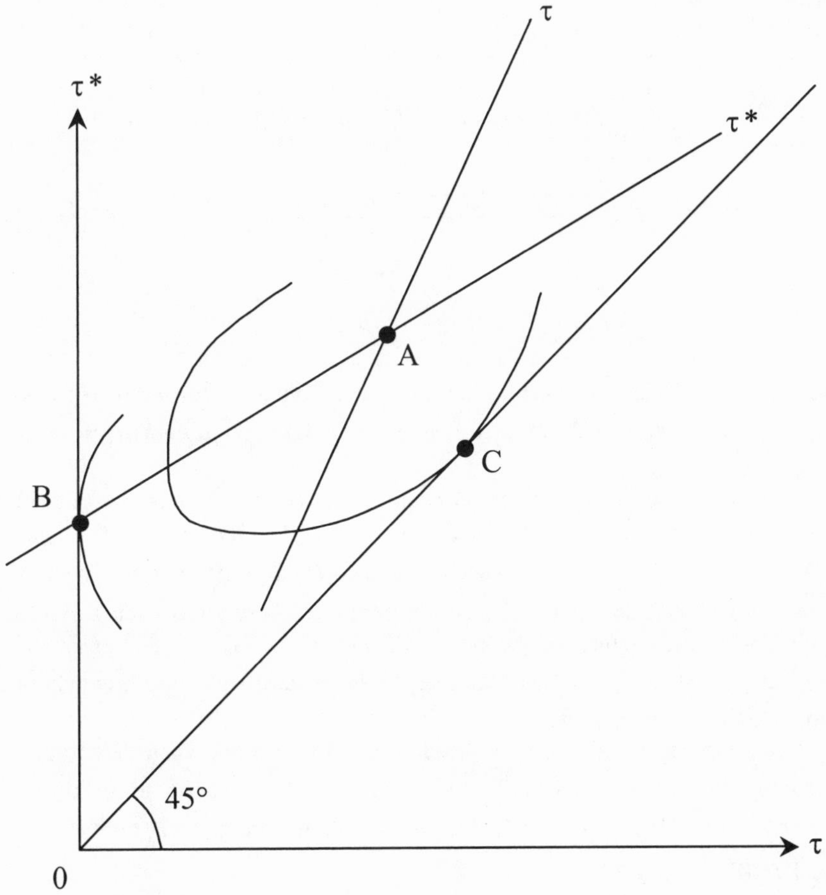

Figure 2. Politically-Motivated Governments

The surplus from the import inclusive of tariff revenues and the surplus from the export can be computed as

$$M(\tau,\tau^*,a)=\int_{p(\tau,\tau^*)}^{1} m(p)dp+a\tau x(p(\tau,\tau^*)-\tau)+(1-a)\tau^* x(p(\tau,\tau^*)-\tau^*)$$

$$=\frac{[1-a\tau-(1-a)\tau^*]^2}{8}+\frac{a\tau[1-(2-a)\tau+(1-a)\tau^*]}{2}$$

$$+\frac{(1-a)\tau^*[1+a\tau-(1+a)\tau^*]}{2},$$

$$X(\tau,\tau^*,a)=\frac{a[1-(2-a)\tau+(1-a)\tau^*]^2}{8},$$

respectively. Social welfare for Country 1 and Country 2 can be represented by $w_1=M(\tau_1,\tau_1^*,a)+X(\tau_2,\tau_2^*,a)$ and $w_2=M(\tau_2,\tau_2^*,a)+X(\tau_1,\tau_1^*,a)$, respectively.

The best response to the partner country's tariff rates is given by the tariff rate profile (τ,τ^*) that simultaneously satisfies $D_1M(\tau,\tau^*,a)=0$ and $D_2M(\tau,\tau^*,a)=0$. It is easy to see that such optimal tariff rates are given by $\tau=\tau^*=1/3$ and do not depend on the partner country's tariff rates. Hence the Nash tariff rates, common to Countries 1 and 2, are given by $(\tau^N,\tau^{N*})=(1/3,1/3)$. I assume that the initial tariff rates are less than or equal to the Nash tariff rates.

If Countries 1 and 2 are not faced with any constraint when they form a trading bloc, they select the tariff rates τ and τ^* so as to maximize $W(\tau,\tau^*,a)\equiv M(\tau,\tau^*,a)+X(\tau,\tau^*,a)$. It follows from $D_1W(\tau,\tau^*,a)=0$ and $D_2W(\tau,\tau^*,a)=0$ that

$$\tau=\frac{(1-a)[(3+a)\tau^*-1]}{4-a-a^2}, \tag{2}$$

and

$$\tau^*=\frac{1+a+a(3+a)\tau}{(1+a)(3+a)}, \tag{3}$$

respectively. Figure 1 depicts these relationships: The τ-line represents (2) while the τ^*-line shows (3). As the figure shows, (2) and (3) are simultaneously satisfied at $(\tau,\tau^*)=(0,1/(3+a))$.

Next, consider the PTA between Country 1 and Country 2. It is obvious that if $\bar{\tau}\geq 1/(3+a)$, Countries 1 and 2 choose unconditionally optimal tariff profile $(\tau,\tau^*)=(0, 1/(3+a))$ when they form a trading bloc. The member countries' social welfare unambiguously rises. The impact on Country 3's welfare can be assessed from the effect on its export price for the non-numeraire goods. As can be seen from (1), the domestic prices for these goods in the importing countries decrease as a result of the PTA since at least one of τ and τ^* falls from $\bar{\tau}$. However, it appears possible that Country 3's export price $p(\tau,\tau^*)-\tau^*$ increases, as both $p(\tau,\tau^*)$ and τ^* decrease except when $\bar{\tau}=1/(3+a)$. In the status-quo situation, the tariff-rate profile is $(\tau,\tau^*)=(\bar{\tau},\bar{\tau})$ and hence Country 3's export price for either good equals $p(\bar{\tau},\bar{\tau})-\bar{\tau}=(1-\bar{\tau})/2$. Under the PTA, on the other hand, the export price is $p(0,1/(3+a))-1/(3+a)=1/(3+a)$. Now, $(1-\bar{\tau})/2>1/(3+a)$ if and only if $\bar{\tau}<(1+a)/(3+a)$. Since $\bar{\tau}<1/3$ and $1/3<(1+a)/(3+a)$, however, this inequality always holds. Therefore, Country 3's export prices fall and its social welfare declines, as a result of the PTA between Countries 1 and 2.

If $\bar{\tau}<1/(3+a)$, on the other hand, the member countries select $(\tau,\tau^*)=(0,\bar{\tau})$. The member countries' social welfare rises, while the nonmember country's falls as (1) shows that Country 3's export prices decrease as a result.

Finally, consider the bloc formation under open regionalism, in which Countries 1 and 2 select τ so as to maximize $W(\tau,\tau,a)$. The first-order condition for this maximization is

$$D_1W(\tau,\tau,a)+D_2W(\tau,\tau,a)=\frac{1-a-(3-a)\tau}{4}.$$

Then, it follows from $D_1W(\tau,\tau,a)+D_2W(\tau,\tau,a)=0$ that $\tau=(1-a)/(3-a)$. If $\bar{\tau}>(1-a)/(3-a)$, the member countries reduce their internal and external tariff rates non-discriminatorily to $(1-a)/(3-a)$, which benefits the member countries. Then nonmember country also benefits from this economic integration, since Country 3's export price for the non-numeraire goods, $p(\tau,\tau)-\tau=(1-\tau)/2$, increases as a result. If $\bar{\tau}\leq(1-a)/(3-a)$, on the other hand, the constraint that the member countries are not allowed to raise the tariff rate against nonmember countries is binding, and hence Countries 1 and 2 will not form a trading bloc under open regionalism.

Notes

*I am grateful to Alan Deardorff, Gordon Hanson, Chong Xiang, and other participants at the CGP conferences at Keio University and University of Michigan for helpful comments.

[1] The failure of the World Trade Organization (WTO) meeting in Seattle in December 1999 reveals the difficulty of multilateral negotiations in recent years.

[2] See Baldwin and Venables (1995) and Panagariya (2000) for surveys of the literature on PTAs.

[3] See Bergsten (1997) for details on the definitions of open regionalism.

[4] See Chapter 2 above by Drusilla Brown, Alan Deardorff, and Robert Stern for a computational assessment of regional trading arrangements involving Japan and Chapter 12 below by Masahiro Endoh for a simulation analysis of various options involving APEC liberalization.

[5] Each indifference curve is an oval surrounding the most-favorable tariff vector $(0,1/(3+a))$.

[6] Indeed, I can show that at any point on the vertical axis, the slope of the indifference curve equals $a/(1+a)$.

[7] Caplin and Krishna (1988) point out the possibility that the MFN requirement raises cooperative tariff rates. See also Ludema (1991) for the impact of the MFN requirement on international trade negotiations.

References

Bagwell, Kyle and Robert W. Staiger. 1997a. "Multilateral Tariff Cooperation During the Formation of Free Trade Areas," *International Economic Review* 38:291-319.

Bagwell, Kyle and Robert W. Staiger. 1997b. "Multilateral Tariff Cooperation During the Formation of Customs Unions," *Journal of International Economics*, 42:91-123.

Baldwin, Richard E. and Anthony J. Venables. 1995. "Regional Economic Integration," in Gene M. Grossman and Kenneth Rogoff (eds.), *Handbook of International Economics*, Volume 3. Amsterdam: Elsevier Science.

Bergsten, C. Fred. 1997. "Open Regionalism," *The World Economy* 20:545-565.

Caplin, Andrew and Kala Krishna. 1988. "Tariffs and the Most-Favored-Nation Clause: A Game Theoretic Approach," *Seoul Journal of Economics* 1:267-289.

Grossman, Gene M. and Elhanan Helpman. 1995. "The Politics of Free Trade Agreements," *American Economic Review* 85:667-690.

Kemp, Murray C. and Henry Y. Wan Jr. 1976. "An Elementary Proposition Concerning the Formation of Customs Unions," *Journal of International Economics* 6:95-97.

Krugman, Paul R. 1991. "Is Bilateralism Bad?" in Elhanan Helpman and Assaf Razin (eds.), *International Trade and Trade Policy*. Cambridge: MIT Press.

Levy, Philip I. 1997. "Political-Economic Analysis of Free-Trade Agreements,"*American Economic Review* 87:506-519.

Ludema, Rodney D. 1991. "International Trade Bargaining and the Most-Favored-Nation Clause," *Economics and Politics* 3:1-20.

Ohyama, Michihiro (1972), "Trade and Welfare in General Equilibrium," *Keio Economic Studies*, 9, 37-73.

Panagariya, Arvind. 2000. "Preferential Trade Liberalization: The Traditional Theory and New Developments," *Journal of Economic Literature* 38:287-331.

Viner, Jacob. 1950. *The Customs Union Issue*, Carnegie Endowment for International Peace, New York.

Comment

Gordon H. Hanson

This paper develops a simple theoretical model of international trade between three countries and then compares national welfare in each country under three trade regimes: non-cooperative tariff setting, a preferential trade agreement (PTA), and open regionalism. Under a PTA, it is assumed that two of the countries eliminate tariffs on trade between them and then set external tariffs on the third country at a level which maximizes the two countries' joint welfare. Under open regionalism, in contrast, internal and external tariffs are assumed to be equal. The two countries set this common tariff to maximize their joint welfare. Open regionalism is intended to mimic the organization of APEC, in which countries agree to lower trade barriers with a large number of trading partners, without necessarily eliminating these trade barriers entirely. There is, then, a tradeoff between a PTA and open regionalism. PTAs completely eliminate trade barriers among a small number of countries, while open regionalism lowers, but does not eliminate, trade barriers among a larger number of countries.

The key results of the paper relate to how these different trade regimes affect the welfare of trading countries. As is standard in the literature, the author finds that welfare rises for countries joining a trade agreement when they move from non-cooperative tariff setting to a PTA. The PTA allows countries to avoid the welfare-reducing consequences of a trade war. Perhaps surprisingly, a PTA may also be superior to open regionalism. When tariffs set non-cooperatively are relatively small, PTAs yield member countries higher welfare than does open regionalism. The logic is that with small non-cooperative tariffs the trade diverting effects of a PTA, induced by driving internal tariffs to zero while possibly increasing external tariffs, are small. Thus, PTAs mainly create trade, and, since they eliminate tariffs between some countries, the trade creating effects dominate those of open regionalism. When non-cooperative tariffs are relatively large, however, the trade diverting effects of PTAs dominate the trade creation effects. In this case, open regionalism yields higher welfare, since its effects are purely trade creating.

This paper captures some key features of differing trade regimes with admirable simplicity and clarity. The author nicely summarizes the conditions under which the trade creating effects of PTAs dominate those of open regionalism, which serves as a caution to those who expect that APEC will dramatically raise welfare in Asia. Still, there are several issues the author does not address, which may help account for APEC countries' willingness to choose open regionalism over PTAs. First, if there are important asymmetries among

APEC countries, they may disagree on what the common external tariff should be. In this setting, open regionalism may raise welfare by producing lower variance in tariff rates across countries (though perhaps a higher mean). Second, if the dependence on non-APEC trade is large, the results on the superiority of PTAs could be reversed. One reason to be concerned about this issue is that many Asian countries effectively specialize in producing intermediate inputs for the United State and Europe, under, for instance, foreign outsourcing arrangements. In this setting, trade between APEC and non-APEC countries would be large, since APEC countries would export mainly inputs and import mainly final goods and thus have a large external trade dependence. Third, geopolitical concerns may also influence tariff setting. A higher external tariff under a PTA would perhaps anger the trading partners of APEC countries, including the politically powerful United States and European Union. To avoid trade disputes or diplomatic conflicts which could compromise national security in Asia, APEC countries might choose open regionalism as a means of reducing trade barriers within the region while not sacrificing international relations with powerful external countries.

Comment

Chong Xiang

This paper is motivated by the establishment of large preferential trade arrangements (PTAs) (e.g., EU and NAFTA) and "open regionalism" (e.g., APEC) in recent years, and proposes to examine the trade-off between these two forms of trade liberalization. I think this is an interesting question to ask. I also think that there are a few issues this paper could have addressed, and addressing them would make the paper richer and more interesting.

First, looking at a bigger picture, in real life situation countries could be members of both a PTA and Open Regionalism. For instance, the NAFTA members, United States, Mexico, and Canada, are also members of APEC. In other words, sometimes it could be a PTA *and* Open Regionalism instead of a PTA *versus* Open Regionalism. Thus, it could be interesting to consider ways to extend the analysis so that countries could choose to be in both a PTA and Open Regionalism.

Second, as the central question of this paper is Open Regionalism versus PTA, it could be really interesting if the results have cases in which Open Regionalism is preferred to PTA. Though seemingly counter-intuitive, this is a non-trivial theoretical possibility. As is well known, a PTA generates two effects, one beneficial and one detrimental. The beneficial effect is trade creation, that is, by lowering their internal tariff rates, the member countries harness the gains from trade. However, doing so reduces the demand for export from the rest of the world. If the rest of world happens to be the low-cost producer of the goods, the member countries suffer a welfare loss. This is the trade-diversion effect, and the member countries have an incentive to mitigate it by setting the internal tariff rate at a positive level, as Furusawa argues. Compared with a PTA, Open Regionalism allows the internal tariff rate to be set at any desired level, and so Open Regionalism might be preferred to PTA if trade diversion is strong enough.

However, Furusawa's finding suggests that a PTA always dominates Open Regionalism unless the government is politically motivated. This seems to suggest that trade diversion is weak in the model as presented. Is it then because of certain specific assumptions made, or does this result hold under more general setting? If so, what is the intuition? Addressing these issues seems to have a good prospect of making this paper even more interesting.

Finally, although a PTA maximizes the joint welfare of the member countries, an individual member country might have an incentive to deviate from its commitment. Given that the other member countries do not charge a tariff for its exports, this particular member country could probably do better by charging a positive tariff on the imports from the other member countries because doing so generates tax revenue. In other words, the commitment of zero internal tariff rates is not necessarily an individual member country's best response, and the PTA has an incentive problem. Therefore it might be interesting to consider the enforcement of PTA as well. Although it is hard to imagine countries openly denounce an international trade agreement by changing their tariff rates, they could still deviate covertly by creating non-tariff barriers.

CHAPTER 12

Is APEC a Building Block or Stumbling Block towards Trade Liberalization?*

Masahiro Endoh

I. Introduction

The current rise of "regionalism" in the world trading system, emerging in the late 1980s, was incarnated as various movements of regional economic organizations, such as the formation of the European Union (EU) and its enlargement to the north and east, the North American Free Trade Agreement (NAFTA), and the Mercosur customs union. In the 1990s, regionalism flourished to such an extent that it was considered a menace to "multilateralism" which promotes global free trade, based on the most-favored-nation (MFN) principle. This has been established through the General Agreement on Tariffs and Trade (GATT) and the World Trade Organization (WTO). The problems with regionalism insofar as it may impact negatively on the world trading system, has been phrased concisely by Bhagwati (1991, p. 77), in terms of whether or not regionalism may serve as a "building block" or "stumbling block" toward multilateral trade liberalization.

Regionalism generally signifies the formation of Preferential Trading Agreements (PTAs) such as Free Trade Areas (FTAs) or Customs Unions (CUs). Among the many existing regional economic institutions, however, the Asia-Pacific Economic Cooperation (APEC) is a unique forum in its process of trade liberalization. APEC does not aim at creating a PTA on a reciprocal basis. Rather, it is based on the idea of "open regionalism" to further trade liberalization among member countries. "Open regionalism" means the reduction or elimination of import tariffs levied by APEC members for imports from both member and non-APEC economies.[1] This means that tariff reductions will be extended to all countries on an MFN basis, with APEC providing coordination of the timing and perhaps the commodities and extent of the cuts. APEC's liberalization project was agreed upon in 1994 and aimed at freeing trade by the more advanced countries by 2010 and by all countries by 2020.

This chapter aims to analyze whether APEC, featured by its "open regionalism," will become a building block or a stumbling block, by using a political-economy approach and computer simulation.[2] The market structure is assumed to be imperfect competition, with oligopolistic firms producing goods that are perfect substitutes for each other. A large number of countries with asymmetric market size is taken into consideration to compare the effects of five methods of trade liberalizations on each country's welfare, world welfare, and the world trading system.

The next section presents the basic multi-country model used in analyzing the effects of trade liberalization. In Section III, the procedures of trade liberalization considered in the simulation are explained. Section IV reports the main results of the computer simulations. Conclusions and implications are presented in Section V. The Appendix provides a theoretical explanation of the market structure in the multi-country model employed in this chapter.

II. The Model

The model employed in this chapter is derived from works by Venables (1987), Yi (1996) and Krishna (1998). The support-for-government function, or the government policy objective, is a simplified version of Grossman and Helpman (1995a, 1995b).

Consider that countries trade one imperfect-competition good with each other. These countries can impose an import tariff t on its import. Countries that concluded PTAs eliminate their import tariffs with each other while levying tariffs on imports from non-PTAs countries.

Each country possesses one firm that produces this imperfect-competition good with marginal cost being one. Taking tariffs into account, each firm decides the quantity of export to each country for the purpose of maximizing profit from its market. It is prohibited, or impossible, to re-export. The price of this good in country j, P_j, is determined from the equation $P_j = A_j - \Sigma_i q_j^i$, where A_j is the market size of country j.

From these assumptions and some others described in the Appendix, the quantity supplied by a firm in country i, firm i, to country j's market, q_j^i, is derived as

$$q_j^i = \left[\frac{A_j - 1 + (l - m_j)\, t}{l + 1}\right],$$

if country i and country j form a PTA, and

$$q_j^i = \left[\frac{A_j - 1 - (m_j + 1)\, t}{l + 1}\right],$$

if they do not, where l is the number of countries composing this world and m_j is the number of countries that can supply the good to country j without tariffs, that is, country j plus the countries with which it forms PTAs. These equations mean that the larger the market size of country j and the fewer countries it forms PTAs with, the more firm i exports to this market, since these two factors increase the amount of rent that firm i receives from exporting to country j.

The profit of firm i gained by supplying the good in the amount of q^i_j to country j's market, π^i_j, can be calculated from this model setting as $\pi^i_j = \lfloor q^i_j \rfloor^2$ and the total profits of country i's firm from each country's market, Π^i, is $\Pi^i = \Sigma_j \pi^i_j$.

The objective of the government is assumed simply to gain political support from voters, which determines the potential number of votes for the existing government in the next election. The effect that trade policy has could be described as a change in the value of the support-for-government function. The potential number of votes comes from two domestic voting groups: a general voter group and a firm-owner group.

The support for country j's government, government j, from the domestic general voter group depends on labor income, Z_j, total tariff revenue, T_j, which is distributed to the general voter through the government, and total consumer surplus, $S_j = Q_j^2/2$. The potential number of votes from the general voter is assumed to have a linear linkage with the sum of these values mentioned above. The number of votes from the firm-owner group is also assumed to have a linear linkage with the profit of firms, that is, the total income of firm-owner group, Π^j. Thus, the support-for-government function, or the government policy objective of country j, W_j, takes the form:

$$W_j = \alpha\ \Pi^j + (1-\alpha)(Z_j + T_j + S_j), \quad 0 \le \alpha \le 1,$$

where α denotes the relative ability of the firm-owner group to gather votes, compared to the general-voter group. α has a large value when, for example, a pressure group made up of firm owners of the imperfect-competition-good industry heavily influences the political decision-making of the government. This is done through lobbying votes for the government. When α=0.5, the value of W_j is equal to the total surplus of this country.

III. Simulation Procedure

Five types of computer simulations are conducted and the results are compared with each other, in order to examine the effects of each method of trade liberalization on each country's welfare, world welfare, and the world trading system. The five methods of trade liberalization are: (1) voluntary tariff removal (VTR); (2) PTA; (3) PTA+APEC; (4) WTO; and (5) WTO+APEC.

In each case, 20 countries are considered and all are assumed to be members of the WTO. Their market sizes are determined by:

$$A_i = exp(c - d \cdot ln\, i), \quad i = 1, 2, \ldots, 19, 20$$

where c and d are parameters. This means that A is modeled to be distributed exponentially, according to the distribution of the population or GNP of actual countries fit along with the exponential distribution.

The value of parameter t is given as t = 20 throughout. This t can be interpreted as a tariff remaining after a series of trade negotiations held by GATT/WTO, and it is assumed that all 20 countries still impose tariff t = 20 on goods from all other countries. There are two combinations of values concerning c and d: (c, d) = (12, 2) and (15, 3). When (c, d) = (12, 2), the largest country's market size, $A_1 = 162{,}754.8$, is 400 (20^2) times that of the smallest country's market size, $A_{20} = 406.9$. $A_{20} = 406.9$ is the value that just satisfies the condition that all 20 countries trade with a positive quantity of trade under all circumstances. When (c, d) is (15, 3), this becomes 8,000 (20^3) times (A_1 = 3,269,017.4, $A_{20} = 408.6$).[3] As for α, it has five values: α = 0, 0.25, 0.5, 0.75, 1.

Throughout the simulations, it is assumed that international transfers do not exist, and that each country decides its trade policy only by considering the government-policy objective of its own country. Each country chooses the trade policy that increases domestic support for the government. It does not consider other countries' domestic support-for-government function or other countries' requests.

Case 1: Voluntary Tariff Removal (VTR)

VTR is defined as each country eliminating all tariffs voluntarily and unilaterally at once without the aid of WTO trade negotiations. In this case, unilateral elimination of import tariffs always reduces the firm profit gained from the home market because of the intensified competitiveness and reduced price, while the profit gained from the foreign market does not change. This can be seen from equation (4). Therefore the firm-owner group never supports voluntary tariff reduction. On the other hand, whether or not the general-voter group supports this type of tariff elimination is uncertain, because this affects tariff revenue and total consumer surplus in an opposite way.

Each country's decision to eliminate or impose import tariffs in order to increase domestic support depends only on the home country's condition. It does not need to consider other countries' reactions or the number of turns of decision-making when designing the simulation procedure. Therefore, the simulation procedure in this case can be stated as:

Step 1. *Select country 1 and give it an opportunity to (1) eliminate or (2) to impose tariffs in a non-preferential manner.*

Step 2. *This country selects its trade policy in order to increase its government-policy objective.*

Step 3. *Repeat Step 1 and Step 2 from country 2 to country 20.*

Case 2: Preferential Trading Arrangement (PTA)

The formation of PTA is to obtain complete liberalized trade among member countries. Firm-owner groups may approve the elimination of the home-country's tariffs if other countries simultaneously eliminate their import tariffs, which would then lead to an increase in exports and hence profits. Many PTAs in actuality are composed of three or more countries. However, in order to simplify the computer-simulation procedure and ease the grasp of the implications of the results, it is assumed that only bilateral trade agreements (BTAs) take place. Regional trade agreements composed of three or more countries can be considered as the accumulation of bilateral trade agreements.

Step 1. *Randomly select one country and give it an opportunity to decide whether (1) to conclude a new BTA, (2) to cancel an existing BTA, or (3) to do nothing.*

Step 2. *This country selects (1) or (2) depending on which one brings a larger increase in its government-policy objective. Note that to select (1), it is necessary that this conclusion raises the partner country's government policy-objective in order to acquire its support. If neither (1) nor (2) raises this country's government-policy objective, then this country chooses (3) and does not change its commercial policy.*

Step 3. *Repeat Step 1 and Step 2 until it reaches a stable state.*

The number of turns of decision-making may affect the results of the simulation. They then are programmed to be allotted randomly to countries (Step 2). One simulation trial consists of Step 1 to Step 3, and 100 trials are taken for each case from case 2 to case 5.

Case 3: Preferential Trading Arrangement (PTA) + APEC

Further trade liberalization by WTO countries involving PTAs and APEC is programmed here so that some member countries of APEC engage in open regionalism, which makes these countries lift all import tariffs unilaterally.[4] As will be seen in the next section, however, no incentive exists for any country to liberalize imports voluntarily and unilaterally. Therefore, APEC-type countries have to be chosen exogenously at the beginning of the simulation, disregarding their intentions about liberalizing trade. In other words, an assumption is made that APEC-type countries carry out an open-regionalism policy for exogenous reasons.

Step 1. *Out of 20 countries, select 4 countries and name them APEC. These APEC countries are ordered to eliminate their import tariffs unilaterally under all circumstances. The other 16 countries are classified as non-APEC.*

Step 2. *Randomly select one country from 20. If it is a non-APEC country, give it an opportunity to decide whether (1) to conclude a new BTA with non-APEC countries, (2) to cancel an existing BTA with non-APEC countries, (3) to eliminate an import tariff levied on an import from one APEC country,*

(4) to levy an import tariff on an import from one APEC country, or (5) to do nothing.

Step 3. *This country selects one option from (1) to (4), depending on which one brings the greatest increase in its government-policy objective. Note that to select (1), it is necessary that this raises the partner-country's government-policy objective in order to acquire its support. If these choices do not raise this country's government-policy objective, then this country chooses (5) and does not change its commercial policy.*

Step 4. *Repeat Step 2 and Step 3 until it reaches a stable state.*

This simulation is also conducted 100 times for each combination of parameters. At present, actual APEC member economies have not yet abolished import tariffs completely on the basis of open regionalism, and many PTAs concluded with/among APEC member(s) are in effect, different from the simulation procedure. My procedure therefore explains whether "an ideal APEC," which may actualize by 2020, is a "building block" or "stumbling block" towards trade liberalization.

Case 4: Multilateral Liberalization via the WTO

It is assumed that after a series of trade negotiations held by GATT/WTO, tariff t still remains among WTO member countries. Here, the process of further trade liberalization based on the WTO is modeled so that some member countries of WTO ("WTO-positive countries") intend to completely eliminate their tariffs with each other, while some other countries ("WTO-negative countries") are reluctant to do so.

Whether or not each WTO country should engage in further trade liberalization beyond its current situation depends on its home condition as well as other countries' attitudes towards trade liberalization. The relationship of cause and effect in each country about its decision to eliminate remaining tariffs connects infinitely with those of other countries. So a WTO trade round appears in order to facilitate negotiation and foster confidence among member countries about lifting tariffs, to conclude treaties with each other and actually eliminate tariffs, and to improve the procedure of settling disputes among member countries.

Considering the nature of this kind of decision-making, the simulation procedure to find "WTO-positive countries" is designed as follows:

Step 1. *Initially, all 20 countries are WTO-positive countries and do not impose any tariffs.*

Step 2. *Randomly select one country and give it an opportunity to decide whether (1) to be a WTO-positive country and provide other WTO-positive countries with free access into the domestic market, or (2) to be a WTO-negative country and return to the initial situation where the country imposes* tariffs t on import goods from all other countries, taking into account that other WTO-positive countries also impose tariffs on goods exported from this country.

Step 3. *This country selects (1) or (2) in order to increase its government policy objective.*

Step 4. *Repeat Step 2 and Step 3 until it reaches a stable state.*

Similar to the PTA, the turns of decision-making may also affect the simulation results. They then are programmed to be allotted randomly to countries (Step 2) and 100 trials are conducted per each combination of parameters.

With regard to this simulation, note first that while WTO-positive countries liberalize trade among WTO-positive countries, tariffs on import goods from WTO-negative countries remain. However, this is clearly against the MFN principle of the WTO. Second, since this program finds only WTO-positive countries from all WTO members, it cannot say that these WTO-positive countries actually abolish their tariffs on a reciprocal basis, because other WTO-negative countries may strongly oppose a proposal of this kind of trade liberalization. Consequently, this case shows some results of a supposed situation where WTO-positive countries can accomplish complete trade liberalization exclusively among themselves.[5]

Case 5: WTO + APEC

Lastly, consider the program of further trade liberalization using WTO and APEC's open regionalism. The characters of both have been depicted previously and here they form the program stated below. This simulation is conducted for 100 trials per each combination of parameters.

Step 1. *Out of 20 countries, select 4 countries and name them APEC. These APEC countries are ordered to eliminate their import tariffs unilaterally under all circumstances. The other 16 countries are classified as non-APEC. These non-APEC countries are all initially WTO-positive and do not impose any tariffs.*

Step 2. *Randomly select one country from 20. If this is a non-APEC country, give it an opportunity to decide whether (1) to be a WTO-positive country and provide for other WTO-positive countries plus APEC countries with free access into the domestic market, or (2) to be a WTO-negative country and return to the initial situation where the country imposes tariffs t on import goods from all other countries in exchange for other WTO-positive countries also imposing tariffs on goods exported from this country.*

Step 3. *This country selects (1) or (2) in order to increase its government policy objective.*

Step 4. *Repeat Step 2 and Step 3 until it reaches a stable state.*

IV. Results

In each simulation from case 2 to 5, all 100 trials end in the same results except for two combinations of parameters in Case 3, despite the randomness of decision-making turns allotted to countries. Even though these two cases are exceptions, the results of the 100 trials in these two cases are mostly the same and the differences that exist are fairly small (these two cases are shown below). Therefore, it can be concluded that the results of this simulation are robust and stable.

Case 1: VTR

As for the case of the VTR, the simulation results show no incentive for any country to lift tariffs voluntarily and unilaterally in a non-preferential manner, at both (c, d) = (12, 2) and (15, 3), and at any value of α. There are two reasons for this: for the firm-owner group, intensified competitiveness in the home market will only bring reduction in profit, while from the general-voter group's point of view, the decrease of tariff revenue exceeds the increase of total consumer surplus.[6] In this simulation, the phenomenon that the decrease of tariff revenue always surpasses the increase of total consumer surplus is verified from the fact that no countries adopt VTR even at $\alpha = 0$, where the government pays attention only to the general voter group. The initial situation does not change at all; hence the results of this case were excluded from the following tables.

Case 2 and 3: PTA with and without APEC

Table 1 summarizes the simulation results for the PTA case (case 2). It shows the number of countries that eliminate tariffs on import goods, i.e., the number of "freed channels," and the ratio of changing each country's government-policy objective compared to the initial situation, with the combination of parameter values and each country's market size (Ai). The maximum number of freed channels in each country is 19 (20 minus home country). In the case of a PTA, the number of freed channels is equal to the number of BTAs that each country arranges. The ratio of the changing government-policy objective is valued at $\alpha = 0.5$ and shown in table 1 as the percent of "change of surplus," although each government makes decisions through the simulation by changing α. This is because I wish to show the change of each country's total surplus (consumer plus producer) and world total surplus from an impartial and benevolent point of view, instead of its government-policy objective.

The results where $\alpha = 0$ are not shown in this table because no country wants to conclude a BTA with any other countries, being the same as VTR. The fact that the general-voter group in any country does not support tariff abolition to any other countries proves in this model that any tariff abolition must decrease this country's tariff revenue more than increase its total consumer surplus. On the other hand, the reason why the results at $\alpha = 0.75$ are not shown is that these results range evenly between those at $\alpha = 0.5$ and $\alpha = 1$.

Table 1 shows three features concerning each country's freed channels. First, in all cases, the largest country (country 1) liberalizes its imports from, i.e., concludes BTAs with, the least number of countries. The number of freed channels increases as market size decreases and after its number peaks between country 5 and country 10, it declines as market size decreases. The distribution of these numbers indicates that large countries form BTAs with only large countries and refuse to form BTAs with small countries. Table 2 shows with which countries they form BTAs in the case (c, d) = (12, 2) and $\alpha = 0.5$ as an example. Here, country 1 forms a BTA only with country 2 and 3, country 2 with countries 1, 3-7, country 6 and 7 with all other countries except country 1, and countries 14-19 could not form BTAs with countries 1-4.

Secondly, the larger the value of α, countries form more BTAs, at both (c, d) = (12, 2) and (15, 3), although there exist a few exceptions (country 5 and 20 at (c, d) = (12, 2) from $\alpha = 0.25$ to 0.5). This is because, as the value of α increases, governments put less weight on the intention of general-voter groups, which are opposed to lifting import tariffs. And thirdly, the larger the difference of each country's market size, the less the number of freed channels, indicated from the comparison of the case (c, d) = (12, 2) and (15, 3). This means that as some countries' market size increases compared with others, they lose their intention of liberalizing imports and concluding BTAs with other countries.

When the market size of one country increases, the optimal number of BTAs for this country diminishes. This phenomenon can be explained as follows. When other conditions are fixed and the market size of country i, A_i, increases, not only does the revenue of country i's firm gained from the domestic market increase, but the revenue of other countries' firms gained from country i's market also increases. Yet the revenue of country i's firm gained from other countries' markets does not change. Therefore, by canceling BTAs with some existing partner countries and imposing tariffs on imports from them, even though country i's firm will suffer the loss of profit caused by decreasing exports, this firm can gain profit from the home market in which market competition will ease by canceling BTAs with some countries. The firm-owner group in country i will then demand its government to cancel some of the BTAs in order to maximize its net gain, i.e., the gain from supplying more goods to the home market minus the loss caused by diminishing exports to the BTAs-canceled market.

From the point of view of a country's total surplus, table 1 shows two features. First, surpluses of all relatively small countries are decreased by forming BTAs, and the smaller the market size, the more decrease in its surplus. This is caused by discriminating methods of trade liberalization held by large coun-

Table 1. Results of Simulations in the Case (2) PTA

		(c, d) = (12, 2)					
Country		$\alpha = 0.25$		$\alpha = 0.5$		$\alpha = 1$	
No. (i)	Ai	No. of F. Ch.	Change of Surplus	No. of F. Ch.	Change of Surplus	No. of F. Ch.	Change of Surplus
1	162,754.8	1	-0.0001%	2	-0.0001%	3	-0.0003%
2	40,688.7	4	0.0350%	6	0.0322%	7	0.0295%
3	18,083.9	5	0.0166%	9	0.1503%	11	0.1397%
4	10,172.2	8	0.0550%	11	0.0299%	14	0.2859%
5	6,510.2	18	0.0956%	17	0.0561%	17	0.0262%
6	4,521.0	17	0.0109%	18	0.0717%	18	0.0378%
7	3,321.5	17	0.0161%	18	0.0808%	18	0.0448%
8	2,543.0	16	-0.0315%	17	-0.0283%	18	0.0492%
9	2,009.3	16	-0.0299%	17	-0.0266%	17	-0.0643%
10	1,627.5	16	-0.0287%	17	-0.0253%	17	-0.0633%
11	1,345.1	15	-0.0575%	16	-0.0770%	17	-0.0625%
12	1,130.2	15	-0.0569%	16	-0.0764%	17	-0.0619%
13	963.0	15	-0.0563%	16	-0.0759%	16	-0.1143%
14	830.4	15	-0.0559%	15	-0.1054%	16	-0.1139%
15	723.4	15	-0.0556%	15	-0.1051%	16	-0.1136%
16	635.8	15	-0.0553%	15	-0.1048%	15	-0.1432%
17	563.2	15	-0.0550%	15	-0.1046%	15	-0.1430%
18	502.3	15	-0.0548%	15	-0.1044%	15	-0.1428%
19	450.8	15	-0.0546%	15	-0.1042%	15	-0.1426%
20	406.9	15	-0.0544%	14	-0.1230%	14	-0.1614%
World	-----	268	0.0003%	284	0.0004%	296	0.0005%

Table 1 *(continued)*

		(c, d) = (15, 3)					
Country		α = 0.25		α = 0.5		α = 1	
No. (i)	Ai	No. of F. Ch.	Change of Surplus	No. of F. Ch.	Change of Surplus	No. of F. Ch.	Change of Surplus
1	3,269,017.4	0	0.0000%	1	0.0000%	1	0.0000%
2	408,627.2	1	0.0001%	3	0.0059%	4	0.0059%
3	121,074.7	3	0.0024%	5	0.0012%	6	0.0010%
4	51,078.4	4	0.0007%	7	0.0021%	8	0.0018%
5	26,152.1	6	0.0010%	8	-0.0007%	11	0.0022%
6	15,134.3	7	0.0002%	10	-0.0006%	12	-0.0008%
7	9,530.7	9	0.0002%	13	-0.0005%	14	-0.0008%
8	6,384.8	11	-0.0001%	16	-0.0014%	17	-0.0007%
9	4,484.2	15	-0.0001%	16	-0.0014%	16	-0.0017%
10	3,269.0	14	-0.0003%	15	-0.0018%	16	-0.0016%
11	2,456.1	14	-0.0002%	15	-0.0018%	15	-0.0020%
12	1,891.8	13	-0.0004%	14	-0.0020%	15	-0.0020%
13	1,487.9	13	-0.0004%	14	-0.0020%	15	-0.0020%
14	1,191.3	12	-0.0004%	13	-0.0021%	14	-0.0022%
15	968.6	12	-0.0004%	13	-0.0021%	14	-0.0022%
16	798.1	12	-0.0004%	13	-0.0021%	13	-0.0023%
17	665.4	11	-0.0005%	12	-0.0021%	13	-0.0023%
18	560.5	11	-0.0005%	12	-0.0021%	12	-0.0024%
19	476.6	11	-0.0005%	12	-0.0021%	12	-0.0024%
20	408.6	11	-0.0005%	12	-0.0021%	12	-0.0024%
World	-----	190	0.0000%	224	0.0000%	240	0.0000%

Table 2. Partner Countries of PTA at (c, d) = (12, 2) and α = 0.5

Ctry No.	1	2	3	4	5	6	7	8	9	10	11	12	13	14	15	16	17	18	19	20
1	-	o	o																	
2	o	-	o	o	o	o	o													
3	o	o	-	o	o	o	o	o	o	o										
4		o	o	-	o	o	o	o	o	o	o	o	o							
5		o	o	o	-	o	o	o	o	o	o	o	o	o	o	o	o	o	o	
6		o	o	o	o	-	o	o	o	o	o	o	o	o	o	o	o	o	o	o
7		o	o	o	o	o	-	o	o	o	o	o	o	o	o	o	o	o	o	o
8			o	o	o	o	o	-	o	o	o	o	o	o	o	o	o	o	o	o
9			o	o	o	o	o	o	-	o	o	o	o	o	o	o	o	o	o	o
10			o	o	o	o	o	o	o	-	o	o	o	o	o	o	o	o	o	o
11				o	o	o	o	o	o	o	-	o	o	o	o	o	o	o	o	o
12				o	o	o	o	o	o	o	o	-	o	o	o	o	o	o	o	o
13				o	o	o	o	o	o	o	o	o	-	o	o	o	o	o	o	o
14					o	o	o	o	o	o	o	o	o	-	o	o	o	o	o	o
15					o	o	o	o	o	o	o	o	o	o	-	o	o	o	o	o
16					o	o	o	o	o	o	o	o	o	o	o	-	o	o	o	o
17					o	o	o	o	o	o	o	o	o	o	o	o	-	o	o	o
18					o	o	o	o	o	o	o	o	o	o	o	o	o	-	o	o
19					o	o	o	o	o	o	o	o	o	o	o	o	o	o	-	o
20						o	o	o	o	o	o	o	o	o	o	o	o	o	o	-

o means these two countries form a bilateral trade agreement tries that do not eliminate tariffs against small countries. On the other hand, the medium- to large-sized countries show an increase in surplus. The largest country 1 suffers from a slight decrease in its surplus when (c, d) = (12, 2), but the decrease enlarges when country 1 concludes more BTAs with other countries and liberalizes access to its home market.

Secondly, the larger the value of α, the more, in general, the ratio of increase or decrease in regard to each country's total surplus, at both (c, d) = (12, 2) and (15, 3). This is brought by the increase of BTAs concluded by large countries. As α increases, large countries lift only their import tariffs against medium-sized, but not small-sized countries. This discriminating trade liberalization worsens the terms of trade for small countries and reduces the profit of the small countries' firm-owner gained from large countries. The changes of these ratios are fairly small at (c, d) = (15, 3), for two reasons: the number of BTAs becomes small and the market size of each country enlarges compared to the welfare effect of tariff policy produced with a given value of t = 20.

Table 3 similarly summarizes the simulation results in the case of PTA with APEC (case 3) at (c, d) = (12, 2). Here, two kinds of APEC groups are assumed and listed to compare the case where APEC is composed of 4 larger countries among 20 (countries 1, 6, 11, 16) with the case of smaller countries (countries 5, 10, 15, 20). Figures concerning the APEC-type countries in table 3 are written in italics. The number of freed channels in APEC-type countries is all set at 19 from their open regionalism. The results at (c, d) = (15, 3) are omitted from this table, as well as from the following tables, because they have the same characteristics as the results at (c, d) = (12, 2).

Among all combinations of parameters in this case, two combinations: (1) (c, d) = (12, 2), α = 0.25, with larger APEC countries, and (2) (c, d) = (15, 3), α = 0.5, with larger APEC countries, produce two or three kinds of different results by 100 trials, because of the path-dependency. In both of the simulations above, however, one dominant type of result exists which accounts for about 90 of the 100 trials. The remaining results show little difference from the dominant type.[7] Concerning these two combinations of parameters, table 3 shows the dominant type of results.

Comparing tables 1 and 3, two features are evident for the influence that open regionalism has on the number of freed channels. First, the total number of freed channels in the world increases more when APEC is composed of larger countries. This is because large countries conclude fewer BTAs in table 1, and therefore the increase in the number of freed channels by the adoption of open regionalism is large. Second, when α is small, the total number of freed channels in the world increases more with the case of APEC compared with the case of PTA alone. This is because, when open regionalism is adopted, a small α results in a small number of world BTAs, highlighting an increase in the number of freed channels in APEC-type countries, as well as a large α brings a large reduction in the number of freed channels in each non-

Table 3. Results of Simulations in the Case (3) PTA + APEC at (c, d) = (12, 2)

	APEC-type countries: 1, 6, 11, 16 (larger countries)					
	$\alpha = 0.25$		$\alpha = 0.5$		$\alpha = 1$	
Country No.(i)	No. of F. Ch.	Change of Surplus	No. of F. Ch.	Change of Surplus	No. of F. Ch.	Change of Surplus
1	*19*	*-0.0003%*	*19*	*-0.0004%*	*19*	*-0.0006%*
2	3	0.0017%	4	0.0007%	5	-0.0001%
3	4	0.0306%	7	0.0287%	8	0.0249%
4	7	0.0813%	9	0.0725%	11	0.0662%
5	8	0.1195%	11	0.1086%	15	0.1016%
6	*19*	*-0.0418%*	*19*	*-0.0667%*	*19*	*-0.0897%*
7	14	0.0521%	15	0.1455%	15	0.1340%
8	13	0.0055%	14	0.0384%	15	0.1410%
9	17	0.0085%	14	0.0411%	14	0.0290%
10	17	0.0102%	14	0.0429%	14	0.0308%
11	*19*	*-0.0472%*	*19*	*-0.0753%*	*19*	*-0.1012%*
12	16	-0.0177%	17	-0.0064%	14	0.0330%
13	15	-0.0364%	17	-0.0057%	13	-0.0192%
14	15	-0.0360%	16	-0.0352%	13	-0.0187%
15	15	-0.0356%	16	-0.0348%	13	-0.0183%
16	*19*	*-0.0477%*	*19*	*-0.0760%*	*19*	*-0.1022%*
17	15	-0.0350%	15	-0.0535%	12	-0.0475%
18	15	-0.0348%	15	-0.0533%	12	-0.0473%
19	15	-0.0346%	15	-0.0531%	12	-0.0471%
20	15	-0.0344%	15	-0.0529%	12	-0.0470%
World	280	0.0002%	290	0.0002%	274	0.0003%

Table 3 *(continued)*

APEC-type countries: 5, 10, 15, 20 (smaller countries)						
	$\alpha = 0.25$		$\alpha = 0.5$		$\alpha = 1$	
Country No. (i)	No. of F. Ch.	Change of Surplus	No. of F. Ch.	Change of Surplus	No. of F. Ch.	Change of Surplus
1	1	0.0001%	2	0.0001%	3	0.0000%
2	3	0.0368%	5	0.0343%	6	0.0316%
3	4	0.0231%	7	0.1568%	9	0.1466%
4	6	0.0653%	9	0.0418%	12	0.2985%
5	*19*	*-0.0567%*	*19*	*-0.0977%*	*19*	*-0.1334%*
6	13	0.0224%	14	0.0859%	14	0.0542%
7	13	0.0281%	14	0.0955%	14	0.0618%
8	12	-0.0192%	13	-0.0131%	14	0.0666%
9	12	-0.0176%	13	-0.0113%	13	-0.0465%
10	*19*	*-0.0721%*	*19*	*-0.1243%*	*19*	*-0.1697%*
11	15	-0.0444%	12	-0.0615%	13	-0.0447%
12	15	-0.0437%	12	-0.0610%	13	-0.0441%
13	15	-0.0432%	16	-0.0595%	12	-0.0964%
14	15	-0.0427%	15	-0.0891%	12	-0.0960%
15	*19*	*-0.0732%*	*19*	*-0.1261%*	*19*	*-0.1722%*
16	15	-0.0421%	15	-0.0885%	12	-0.0955%
17	15	-0.0418%	15	-0.0882%	11	-0.1249%
18	15	-0.0416%	15	-0.0880%	11	-0.1248%
19	15	-0.0414%	15	-0.0879%	11	-0.1246%
20	*19*	*-0.0733%*	*19*	*-0.1264%*	*19*	*-0.1726%*
World	260	0.0002%	268	0.0003%	256	0.0004%

APEC country. The latter effect can be said to be the non-APEC countries' "free-ride" on the APEC effort.

These two tables also show two features concerning the influence of open regionalism on the change of total surplus in each country. First, most APEC countries have a reduction in their rates of surplus change (the only exception is country 16 when APEC is composed of larger countries), while most non-APEC countries have an increase in their rates of surplus change (the exceptions are country 2-4 when, again, APEC is composed of larger countries), compared with rates in table 1. The complete elimination of import tariffs among APEC countries reduces APEC countries' tariff revenues and also reduces profits of APEC firms and the firms located in former BTA partners of some APEC countries, whereas it increases profits of firms located in countries that formerly did not conclude BTAs with some APEC countries. For most APEC countries, the former negative effect on surplus exceeds the latter positive effect, while for most non-APEC countries the positive effect of open regionalism on surplus exceeds its negative effect (some exceptions mentioned above are caused by inversion of the amounts of these effects). Second, the surplus in medium- to small-size countries has a larger increase or smaller decrease when APEC is composed of larger countries, because the larger APEC market, the more the revenues of firms located in the medium- to small-size countries, i.e., the more positive effect of APEC.

What can be said from this examination is that whether APEC will become "a building block" or "a stumbling block" depends on the circumstances. When APEC includes many large (small) countries or when each government takes into account relatively the intention of the general-voter group (the firm-owner group), APEC will have a positive (negative) effect on promoting world-wide trade liberalization. From the viewpoint of each country's surplus, an APEC that is composed of large countries is preferable to that composed of small countries, although both can increase most countries' domestic surpluses. Note that, however, APEC's positive effects on world-trade liberalization and on other non-APEC countries' surplus sacrifice APEC countries' domestic surplus.

Case 4 and 5: WTO with and without APEC

The simulation results in the case of the WTO (case 4) at (c, d) = (12, 2) are shown in table 4. The signs "p." or "n." indicate whether this country is WTO-positive or WTO-negative. This table shows that relatively smaller countries compose the WTO-positive group, and the greater the value of α, the more countries belonging to the WTO-positive group. The reasoning to explain this phenomenon is the same as that in the case of PTA. The most striking point in this table is that relatively small countries increase their surpluses, and, the smaller one country's market size is, the greater the ratio of increase in its surplus, while large countries decrease their surpluses. This result is quite the

Table 4. Results of Simulations in the Case (4) WTO at (c, d) = (12, 2)

Country	α = 0.25				α = 0.5			α = 1		
No. (i)	Ai	p./n.	No. of F. Ch.	Change of Surplus	p./n.	No. of F. Ch.	Change of Surplus	p./n.	No. of F. Ch.	Change of Surplus
1	162,754.8	n.	0	-0.0004%	n.	0	-0.0007%	n.	0	-0.0013%
2	40,688.7	n.	0	-0.0062%	n.	0	-0.0099%	p.	18	-0.0104%
3	18,083.9	n.	0	-0.0237%	p.	17	-0.0133%	p.	18	-0.0108%
4	10,172.2	p.	16	-0.0090%	p.	17	-0.0065%	p.	18	-0.0013%
5	6,510.2	p.	16	-0.0006%	p.	17	0.0030%	p.	18	0.0101%
6	4,521.0	p.	16	0.0064%	p.	17	0.0106%	p.	18	0.0187%
7	3,321.5	p.	16	0.0113%	p.	17	0.0158%	p.	18	0.0245%
8	2,543.0	p.	16	0.0146%	p.	17	0.0194%	p.	18	0.0284%
9	2,009.3	p.	16	0.0170%	p.	17	0.0218%	p.	18	0.0310%
10	1,627.5	p.	16	0.0187%	p.	17	0.0236%	p.	18	0.0329%
11	1,345.1	p.	16	0.0199%	p.	17	0.0249%	p.	18	0.0343%
12	1,130.2	p.	16	0.0208%	p.	17	0.0258%	p.	18	0.0353%
13	963.0	p.	16	0.0216%	p.	17	0.0266%	p.	18	0.0361%
14	830.4	p.	16	0.0221%	p.	17	0.0272%	p.	18	0.0367%
15	723.4	p.	16	0.0226%	p.	17	0.0276%	p.	18	0.0372%
16	635.8	p.	16	0.0230%	p.	17	0.0280%	p.	18	0.0376%
17	563.2	p.	16	0.0233%	p.	17	0.0283%	p.	18	0.0379%
18	502.3	p.	16	0.0235%	p.	17	0.0286%	p.	18	0.0382%
19	450.8	p.	16	0.0237%	p.	17	0.0288%	p.	18	0.0384%
20	406.9	p.	16	0.0239%	p.	17	0.0290%	p.	18	0.0386%
World	-----	--	272	0.0002%	--	306	0.0003%	--	342	0.0006%

opposite to the case of PTA. The reason for this contraposition is that, in the case of the WTO, large countries in the WTO-positive group (country 3 and 4 at $\alpha = 0.5$, for example) open their home market to small countries, while they keep levying tariffs against super-large WTO-negative countries (country 1 and 2 in this case), which promote exports from small countries to large countries in the WTO-positive group and increase firm profit located in small countries. Small countries can indeed export without tariff to medium- or large-size countries even in the case of a PTA. However, in this case, these importing countries also conclude free trade agreements with large countries and allow them to export goods without imposing tariffs. Consequently, the competition in medium- and large-size countries intensifies and the profit from these markets decreases. The larger the value of α, the larger increase of small countries' surpluses, which is brought by the increase of WTO-positive countries.

Table 5 shows the results of WTO with APEC (case 5) at (c, d) = (12, 2). The sign "A." indicates that this country belongs to APEC. Comparing table 4 and 5, it is found that open regionalism has two influences on the number of freed channels. First, the total number of freed channels in the world increases on a larger scale when APEC is composed of larger countries, which is the same result and involves the same reason as in the case of PTA with APEC. Second, the total number of freed channels in the world is larger when α is large. This contradictory result is because WTO can deter WTO-positive countries from "free-riding" on APEC effort.

Concerning the influence of "open regionalism" on the change in total surplus in each country, there are two notable features from the two tables. First, in almost all cases, the countries' surpluses increase when APEC is composed of larger countries, while they decrease when APEC is composed of smaller countries, when compared with the case of WTO alone. This is because the large APEC market produces the positive effect of open regionalism, more than its negative effect of APEC on each country's surplus. Second, most APEC countries increase their surplus in both cases when APEC is formed of larger countries and smaller countries, although the largest country (country 1 or 5) reduces its domestic surplus. This result is quite contrary to the case of PTA with APEC, where the surpluses of APEC countries decrease. The reason why surpluses of APEC countries increase in the case of WTO with APEC is that WTO can minimize the negative effect of open regionalism on APEC itself.

The judgment of whether APEC will become "a building block" or "a stumbling block" in the case of the WTO, again, depends on circumstances. When APEC includes many large (small) countries or when each government relatively takes into account the intention of the firm-owner group (the general-voter group), APEC will have a positive (negative) effect in promoting world-wide trade liberalization. From the viewpoint of each country's surplus, APEC composed of larger countries increases most countries' surplus, while APEC formed of smaller countries decreases them, compared with the case of the WTO. The advantage of the WTO system is that APEC countries sacrifice fairly little in order to liberalize world trade by open regionalism.

V. Concluding Remarks

This chapter has examined the conditions in which APEC will become a building block or a stumbling block to trade liberalization multilaterally. Three main criteria of being a building block that promotes trade liberalization emerge from the simulation results. First and foremost, the inclusion of many large countries in APEC is crucial. Second, open regionalism has beneficial and significant effects on world-trade liberalization and each country's surplus if it goes along with WTO-based liberalization. Third, when the method for furthering trade liberalization is by forming PTAs, it is important to deter non-APEC countries from "free-riding" on APEC efforts. In actuality, the form of open regionalism still remains in the proposal stage, and it is not clear whether any of the present economies or groups in APEC would follow it. However, the analysis shows that this policy has the potential ability to become a building block in the world-trading system.

This chapter's analyses demonstrate that the attitudes of the United States and Japan, the world's first and second largest GNP countries, toward APEC are crucial to APEC's role in contributing to world-trade liberalization and each country's welfare. Both countries may have the incentive to break away from APEC and retreat from multilateral-trade liberalization via the WTO in order to increase their domestic total surpluses. However, if they choose to form FTAs with other countries in disregard of APEC or WTO activities, most other countries, especially medium- and small-size countries, will suffer from the reduction of their economic welfare. U.S. and Japanese participation in APEC and WTO and their commitment to both APEC's open regionalism and WTO's multilateral trade liberalization will surely make APEC "a building block" towards world trade liberalization that will benefit the world economy.

The analysis developed in this chapter has much room for improvement. The interpretation of the structure of the basic model and the computer-simulation procedure alone raise many problems including: lack of the restriction of production and supply in each country; exogenous determination of APEC-type countries; disagreement of the MFN principle with the procedure of WTO-positive countries, and so on. The revision of these points may result in quite different outcomes and will be addressed in future research.

Appendix

This Appendix provides a theoretical explanation of the multi-country model employed in this chapter.

The world consists of l countries, and let L be the set of countries. Each country can impose an import tariff t, the rate of which is given,[8] on its import

Table 5. Results of Simulations in the Case (5) WTO + APEC at (c, d) = (12, 2)

APEC-type countries: 1, 6, 11, 16 (larger countries)									
Country	α = 0.25			α = 0.5			α = 1		
No. (i)	A./ p./n.	No. of F. Ch.	Change of Surplus	A./ p./n.	No. of F. Ch.	Change of Surplus	A./ p./n.	No. of F. Ch.	Change of Surplus
1	*A.*	*19*	*-0.0034%*	*A.*	*19*	*-0.0034%*	*A.*	*19*	*-0.0033%*
2	n.	0	0.0016%	n.	0	-0.0055%	p.	19	-0.0080%
3	n.	0	0.0062%	p.	18	-0.0024%	p.	19	-0.0013%
4	n.	0	0.0119%	p.	18	0.0146%	p.	19	0.0171%
5	n.	0	0.0158%	p.	18	0.0313%	p.	19	0.0348%
6	*A.*	*19*	*0.0360%*	*A.*	*19*	*0.0430%*	*A.*	*19*	*0.0469%*
7	p.	15	0.0420%	p.	18	0.0501%	p.	19	0.0545%
8	p.	15	0.0462%	p.	18	0.0547%	p.	19	0.0593%
9	p.	15	0.0491%	p.	18	0.0578%	p.	19	0.0625%
10	p.	15	0.0510%	p.	18	0.0599%	p.	19	0.0647%
11	*A.*	*19*	*0.0540%*	*A.*	*19*	*0.0619%*	*A.*	*19*	*0.0662%*
12	p.	15	0.0535%	p.	18	0.0625%	p.	19	0.0674%
13	p.	15	0.0543%	p.	18	0.0634%	p.	19	0.0683%
14	p.	15	0.0549%	p.	18	0.0640%	p.	19	0.0689%
15	p.	15	0.0554%	p.	18	0.0646%	p.	19	0.0695%
16	*A.*	*19*	*0.0576%*	*A.*	*19*	*0.0655%*	*A.*	*19*	*0.0699%*
17	p.	15	0.0561%	p.	18	0.0653%	p.	19	0.0702%
18	p.	15	0.0563%	p.	18	0.0656%	p.	19	0.0705%
19	p.	15	0.0566%	p.	18	0.0658%	p.	19	0.0708%
20	p.	15	0.0568%	p.	18	0.0661%	p.	19	0.0710%
World	--	256	0.0011%	--	346	0.0013%	--	380	0.0016%

Table 5 *(continued)*

Country	APEC-type countries: 5, 10, 15, 20 (smaller countries)								
	$\alpha = 0.25$			$\alpha = 0.5$			$\alpha = 1$		
No. (i)	A./ p./n.	No. of F. Ch.	Change of Surplus	A./ p./n.	No. of F. Ch.	Change of Surplus	A./ p./n.	No. of F. Ch.	Change of Surplus
1	n.	0	-0.0002%	n.	0	-0.0005%	n.	0	-0.0011%
2	n.	0	-0.0026%	n.	0	-0.0081%	p.	18	-0.0105%
3	n.	0	-0.0098%	p.	17	-0.0141%	p.	18	-0.0112%
4	n.	0	-0.0186%	p.	17	-0.0080%	p.	18	-0.0021%
5	*A.*	*19*	*-0.0068%*	*A.*	*19*	*0.0011%*	*A.*	*19*	*0.0092%*
6	p.	15	-0.0010%	p.	17	0.0083%	p.	18	0.0176%
7	p.	15	0.0034%	p.	17	0.0134%	p.	18	0.0233%
8	p.	15	0.0065%	p.	17	0.0169%	p.	18	0.0272%
9	p.	15	0.0087%	p.	17	0.0193%	p.	18	0.0298%
10	*A.*	*19*	*0.0117%*	*A.*	*19*	*0.0219%*	*A.*	*19*	*0.0321%*
11	p.	15	0.0114%	p.	17	0.0223%	p.	18	0.0330%
12	p.	15	0.0123%	p.	17	0.0232%	p.	18	0.0340%
13	p.	15	0.0130%	p.	17	0.0240%	p.	18	0.0348%
14	p.	15	0.0135%	p.	17	0.0246%	p.	18	0.0354%
15	*A.*	*19*	*0.0157%*	*A.*	*19*	*0.0260%*	*A.*	*19*	*0.0364%*
16	p.	15	0.0143%	p.	17	0.0254%	p.	18	0.0363%
17	p.	15	0.0146%	p.	17	0.0257%	p.	18	0.0366%
18	p.	15	0.0149%	p.	17	0.0260%	p.	18	0.0369%
19	p.	15	0.0151%	p.	17	0.0262%	p.	18	0.0371%
20	*A.*	*19*	*0.0171%*	*A.*	*19*	*0.0275%*	*A.*	*19*	*0.0378%*
World	--	256	0.0002%	--	314	0.0003%	--	346	0.0006%

goods from other countries. M_j is the set of countries that can supply goods to the market of country j without tariffs—in other words, country j plus countries on which country j lifts import tariffs. The number of M_j's elements is $m_j\ (0 \le m_j \le l)$. If country j ($j \in L$) lifts tariffs on five countries, for example, $m_j = 6$ including country j itself. $M_j \subseteq L$, of course. The tariff that country j imposes on goods from country i ($i \in L$), t_j^i, is therefore:

$$t_j^i = \begin{cases} t & if \quad i \notin M_j \\ 0 & if \quad i \in M_j \end{cases}$$

There are two kinds of goods produced in each country: a numeraire good and an imperfect-competition good. Both are produced under constant returns to scale with no fixed costs, and one unit of good requires one unit of labor as input. The numeraire good is produced and distributed competitively and priced at one per one unit on the world market. Therefore, the wage per one unit of labor is also one. These assumptions indicate that the marginal cost of two goods is one. If there exists Z_j units of labor in country j, the labor income of country j is Z_j. The numeraire good is transferred across countries to settle the balance of trade.

Regarding the imperfect-competition good, each country possesses one firm that produces this good.[9] The market structure is imperfect competition, with oligopolistic firms producing goods that are perfect substitutes for each other. Taking tariffs into account, each firm decides the quantity of export to each country with recognition that markets in different countries are segmented. The equilibrium concept is Cournot-Nash. The quantity supplied by a firm in country i, firm i, to country j's market is described as q_j^i. Hereafter the imperfect-competition good will mainly be referred to as "good".

Aggregate utility in country j, U_j, is assumed to take the form:

$$U_j(K_j, Q_j) = K_j + \left(A_j Q_j - Q_j^2/2\right), \tag{1}$$

where K_j denotes the consumption of the numeraire good in country j and $Q_j = \sum_i q_j^i$ denotes the total sales of the imperfect-competition good in country j. From equation (1), the price of the imperfect-competition good in country j, P_j:

$$P_j = A_j - Q_j. \tag{2}$$

Each firm regards each country as a separate market and therefore chooses its optimal quantity for each country separately. Under the Cournot assumption, firms are assumed to be maximizing profits by taking other firms' outputs as given, with all firms choosing their quantities simultaneously. Firm i decides the quantity of export to country j, q_j^i, by solving the following problem:

$$\max_{q_j^i} \pi_j^i = q_j^i\left[A_j - Q_j - \left(1 + t_j^i\right)\right]. \tag{3}$$

Solving and rearranging equation (3) yields:

$$\begin{aligned} q_j^i &= \left[\frac{A_j - 1 + \Sigma_k t_j^k}{l+1} - t_j^i\right] \\ &= \left[\frac{A_j - 1 + \left(l - m_j\right)\, t}{l+1} - t_j^i\right]. \end{aligned} \tag{4}$$

The meaning of each element in equation (4) is as follows. $\left(A_j - 1\right)/(l+1)$ denotes the amount of rent that firm i receives from exporting to country j. From equation (1), A_j indicates the degree of preference for the imperfect-competition good in country j. The higher the value of A_j, the higher its price, at a certain quantity of supply to country j. Or, from equation (2), A_j could be seen as the degree of market size, since at a certain price, the higher the value of A_j, the more demand for the good. And the greater (smaller) the value of A_j, the more (less) rent each firm will receive from the additional supply of the good to country j. This results in more (less) supply from country i to country j, q_j^i. $\left(l - m_j\right) t/(l+1) - t_j^i$ is the relative index of the tariff rate imposed by country j on the import good from country i. $\left(l - m_j\right) t/(l+1)$ is the index of the average tariff rate in country j (this is not the average tariff rate itself). When country j's tariff rate on firm i's export, t_j^i, is smaller (larger) than the index of the average tariff rate in country j, $\left(l - m_j\right) t/(l+1)$, this firm can export more (less) to country j.

The support-for-government function, or the government policy objective of country j, W_j, takes the form as mentioned in Section II:

$$W_j = \alpha\, \Pi^j + (1-\alpha)\left(Z_j + T_j + S_j\right), \quad 0 \le \alpha \le 1.$$

$\alpha\, \Pi^j$ shows the support from the firm-owner group, while $(1-\alpha)\left(Z_j + T_j + S_j\right)$ is the support from the general voter group. The tariff revenue $T_j = \Sigma_i t_j^i q_j^i$ is distributed to the general voter through the government,[10] and the total consumer surplus, S_j, is equal to aggregate utility minus total purchase cost, $S_j = U_j - \left(K_j + P_j Q_j\right) = Q_j^2/2$.

Download of Program

The program used in this paper is available from the following Website. http://www.fbc.keio.ac.jp/~endoh/download/dle.htm

Notes

* The author wishes to thank Jeffrey Bergstrand, Arvind Panagariya, Ken Suzuki, Gina Pei-Chun Liao, Akiko Tateishi, as well as conference participants at Keio University and the University of Michigan for their helpful comments. Nevertheless, the author alone is responsible for any errors.

[1] An alternative concept of "open regionalism" is that any group should allow any country to join that is already prepared to accept the agreements reached. Yi (1996) employs this definition and reaches the conclusion that this "open regionalism" could lead to world-wide free trade.

[2] See Chapter 2 above by Drusilla Brown, Alan Deardorff, and Robert Stern for a computational assessment of APEC liberalization and Chapter 11 by Taiji Furusawa for a theoretical analysis comparing preferential trading arrangements and APEC liberalization.

[3] When these differences are shown according to each country's GNP, compared with United States with the largest GNP of $7.8 trillion, we have for 1/400, Slovak Republic ($19.8 billion), Tunisia ($19.4 billion), Ecuador ($18.8 billion) and for 1/8000 Mongolia ($998 million), Burundi ($924 million), and Eritrea ($852 million). Using population, these differences are similar.

[4] This definition that APEC is a subset of WTO could be justified from the fact that among 18 economies belonging to APEC, only China and Taiwan are not WTO members presently but will be soon.

[5] In the case where WTO-positive countries abolish their tariffs on an MFN basis and do not impose tariffs on WTO-negative countries, the simulation procedure becomes the same as the case of VTR where no country wants to lift tariffs.

[6] In the case where the difference of each country's A is relatively small (small d) and the general-voter group heavily influences the government-policy objective (small α), the results of the simulations show that some small countries adopt VTR, when the increase of total consumer surplus exceeds the reduction in firm profit and tariff revenue. For example, at (c, d) = (9, 1) and $\alpha = 0$, the simulation shows that eight small countries adopt VTR. The combination of parameter values examined here, however, does not produce this phenomenon.

[7] For the case (c, d) = (12, 2), $\alpha = 0.25$, with larger APEC countries, 100 simulation trials produced two kinds of results concerning the number of freed channels at country 8: 88 trials resulted in 13, while 12 trials resulted in 17. On the other hand the case (c, d) = (15, 3), $\alpha = 0.5$, with larger APEC countries, 100 simulation trials produced three kinds of results concerning its numbers at country 17 and 18. In both countries, 93 trials produced a result of 10 as the number of freed channels. 6 trials produced a result of 14 in country 17 and 10 in country 18. The remaining 1 trial produced a result of 10 in country 17 and 14 in country 18. These results show that some countries sometimes eliminate tariffs on imports from four APEC countries by affecting the path-dependency of the turns of decision-making.

[8] Previous papers concerning the stability of PTAs, Riezman (1985), Kennan and Riezman (1990), Bond and Syropoulos (1996) and Yi (1996), among others, consider the import tariffs adjustable to optimal rates. Here, however, the rate of tariff t is treated as given. Therefore, for purposes of clarity, the choice for each country is to impose t or 0 on its imports.

[9] It makes little difference if more firms exist in one country, as in Krishna (1998). If the number of firms is determined endogenously in order to reduce excess revenue to zero, as in Venables (1987), the results may change significantly.

[10] If this model is modified to the situation that the firm-owner group can gain a part of the tariff revenue, some outcomes presented in the following are largely changed.

References

Bhagwati, Jagdish. 1991. *The World Trading System at Risk.* London: Harvester Wheatsheaf.

Bond, Eric W. and Constantinos Syropoulos. 1996. "The Size of Trading Blocs: Market Power and World Welfare Effects," *Journal of International Economics* 40:411-37.

Grossman, Gene M. and Elhanan Helpman. 1995a. "Trade Wars and Trade Talks," *Journal of Political Economy* 103:675-708.

________. 1995b. "The Politics of Free-Trade Agreements," *American Economic Review* 85:667-90.

Kennan, John and Raymond Riezman. 1990. "Optimal Tariff Equilibria with Customs Unions," *Canadian Journal of Economics* 23:70-83.

Krishna, Pravin. 1998. "Regionalism and Multilateralism: A Political Economy Approach," *Quarterly Journal of Economics* 113:227-51.

Riezman, Raymond. 1985. "Customs Unions and the Core" *Journal of International Economics* 19:355-65.

Venables, Anthony J. 1987. "Customs Union and Tariff Reform under Imperfect Competition," *European Economic Review* 31:103-10.

Yi, Sang-Seung. 1996. "Endogenous Formation of Customs Unions under Imperfect Competition: Open Regionalism is Good," *Journal of International Economics* 41:153-77.

Comment

Jeffrey H. Bergstrand

This is an interesting paper. It is subtle in terms of its scope and deals with an important topic. APEC will likely continue to be an important item on the world's trade policy agenda. Also, Endoh has nested the investigation of APEC theoretically in the context of—and alongside—further liberalization in the form of free trade agreements (FTAs) as well as in the form of further liberalization under the WTO. The three major questions of his paper are:

1. Is "open regionalism" defined in the context of APEC (i.e., unilateral liberalization) welfare enhancing?
2. Does open regionalism enhance or detract from the welfare changes associated with FTAs?
3. Does open regionalism enhance or detract from the welfare changes associated with continued multilateralism?

While Endoh cites earlier papers, he does not provide much motivation for his particular framework. Thus, I was left quite curious why he used it given numerous other approaches potentially available. Endoh's model is most closely related to Venables (1987) and Krishna (1998). On the producer and consumer side, it is virtually identical to Krishna's model, with firms treating markets as "segmented" and providing goods that are perfect substitutes. The other models cited all specify linear demand curves. Whereas Venables' model has free entry and exit allowing an endogenous number of firms, Endoh's model—with one firm producing the "imperfect competition" good in each country—is closest to Krishna's model, where there are an exogenous number of multiple producers in each country of "the good."

There are two notable differences from Krishna and Venables. First, the government's objective is potentially more realistic than in the Krishna or Venables models. In Krishna, the government only weighed producers' interests, i.e., producer rents. In essence, Krishna found that in the absence of trade diversion from an FTA with respect to ROW firms, an FTA is a zero-sum game. Firms gain from an FTA more the greater the trade diverted from the rest of the world. In Venables, only consumer welfare matters, since competition precludes producer surplus, and consumer welfare is a function of tariff revenue and consumer surplus.

In Endoh's model, in contrast, the government weighs both producer and consumer interests. Producer interests are represented the same as in Krishna. However, consumers potentially are affected here ambiguously by trade liberalization; consumers lose tariff revenue on the income side but gain in terms of lower prices for imported goods on the price side. The choice for the government objective between only firms' special interests vs. one representing both consumer and producer interests has been debated in the literature. I am more comfortable with the broader approach used here instead of that in Krishna, especially in light of the recent evidence in Goldberg and Maggi in the *American Economic Review* in December 1999 where they estimate a relatively strong weight for consumer welfare relative to producer interests in the government's objective function.

The second notable difference is that Endoh is interested in determining whether APEC's "open regionalism" is a welfare-enhancing approach to trade policy, either independent of free trade agreements or in conjunction with FTAs. Krishna focused on the impact of regionalism on multilateralism and did a comparative static analysis to show the conditions under which the entering into—in a first-stage—a bilateral free trade agreement might lead—in a second-stage—to *less* multilateralism. Endoh uses the same framework differently.

I will summarize what I consider the major findings in this paper and offer some criticisms. The first major finding is introducing in the model's context APEC in isolation (i.e., unilateral liberalization here). In the context of this model, unilateral liberalization is unambiguously welfare decreasing, and this is confirmed using computer simulation. Producers at home lose competitiveness and profits, while for consumers the loss of tariff revenue always exceeds the surplus gained, so that consumers also are always worse off with open regionalism.

Endoh notes that general voter support for open regionalism is uncertain, depending upon tariff revenue losses versus consumer surplus gains. While his model has numerous countries, I did some comparative statics of a simple 2-country version of his model. The conclusions of this comparative statics analysis for the simple case confirmed his simulation results. For specific tariff values on the imperfect-competition good that are no higher than marginal production costs (normalized in his paper to unity), unilateral liberalization is unambiguously welfare decreasing. Only if the specific tariff rate (in terms of the good) is higher than marginal production costs could consumer surplus gains ever potentially exceed the tariff revenue losses.

This result about open regionalism begs a couple of questions. First, and most obviously, why have so many countries—especially surrounding the Pacific Rim—pursued open regionalism if, as this theory suggests, it is always welfare decreasing? Such a contrast raises doubts about the limitations of the model. In reality, of course, every model is inherently falsifiable, so what is it in this model that might preclude welfare benefits from open regionalism?

One item that comes immediately to mind is the absence of variety effects. Goods here are perfect substitutes, à la Brander or Brander and Krugman. Second generation models of trade policy have incorporated this element over earlier perfect competition models, and allowing for variety may permit the possibility of consumer surplus to offset tariff revenue losses in this model.

Also, there is cursory evidence from policy discussions of reasons why countries have pursued open regionalism in the past two decades. One popular argument has been to spur competitiveness of domestic firms and export-related domestic firms and to augment growth and development. Yet such a channel cannot be recognized in the present parsimonious model. Thus, the model might somehow be modified to address this potentially important shortcoming to generate net welfare gains from unilateral liberalization.

The second major set of findings concerns the introduction of FTAs into this model with and without open regionalism. The results seem quite consistent with earlier ones in a similar framework. Large countries tend to form bilateral FTAs with other large countries. The intuition is the same as in Krishna: with a bilateral FTA the home producer gains better access to the partner's market. The larger the partner's market, the greater the gains.

While these results are consistent with Krishna, new findings arise due to the different government-objective function here, since the government's weight on producer vs. consumer interests can vary. Endoh finds that as producer interest weighs more heavily, countries do form more FTAs. The intuition is consistent with Krishna: there are potentially more markets to benefit from liberalization.

With APEC, Endoh finds additionally that the APEC countries incur a reduction in their rates of total surplus change, while the non-APEC countries incur an increase in their rates of total surplus change in the context of FTAs. This largely reflects, in the model's framework, the negative consumer-welfare and tariff-loss effects from the unilaterally liberalized economics.

Thus, the limitation from the earlier scenario surfaces again. Endoh points out that no country has an incentive to liberalize imports voluntarily and unilaterally. I find this outcome the most limiting aspect of the paper that is entitled "Is APEC a Building Block or Stumbling Block towards Trade Liberalization?"

Given this limitation, rather than moving on as he did to explore WTO liberalization with and without an accompanying APEC agreement, I would have preferred if he would have searched more thoroughly toward determining the limitations of this albeit parsimonious model to determine the *sensitivity* of the model at hand to assumptions that apparently preclude any potential net welfare gain from open regionalism.

The third and final major set of findings concerns further WTO-based multilateral liberalization with and without open regionalism. The modeling of further WTO-motivated liberalization by introducing WTO-positive countries (with intentions to completely eliminate mutual tariffs) and WTO-negative countries (countries who do not intend to liberalize) is a very interesting exercise. However, it seems beyond the scope of this paper, in light of the limitations noted above. However, I liked the construct of this simulation exercise, and if the constraints of the model are feasibly addressed, this is worth pursuing.

The limitation of this particular experiment, however, is that WTO-positive countries only liberalize *among themselves*. This introduces a bias in the computer-simulated results. APEC in the context here does not discriminate multilaterally. However, the WTO liberalization discriminates against WTO-negative countries. If such discrimination was absent (i.e., MFN treatment truly held), it is unclear what the outcomes theoretically would be. Endoh notes this shortcoming, and clearly the experiment needs to be redesigned before having more relevant economic content.

Overall, the scope of Endoh's chapter is perhaps too broad. It is difficult just trying to understand the relationships between unilateral liberalization, free trade agreements, and free trade agreements in the presence of APEC's open regionalization. It would have been preferable to focus on the foregoing issues and to leave the issues of the WTO and the WTO along with APEC's regionalism to a separate paper. A second major limitation is that unilateral liberalization is always welfare decreasing. This also influenced the results on APEC-enhanced FTAs as well as APEC-enhanced WTO liberalization. The model might well be broadened to introduce the positive gains from variety, especially since it is closely related to Venables' 1987 article. It is further important to explore the limitations of the linear demand curve for precluding potentially ambiguous results. Third, and the most ambitious challenge, if APEC's open regionalism has been pursued to advance growth, then dynamic factor-accumulation becomes an important feature that may induce positive welfare gains from open regionalism.

Comment

Arvind Panagariya

In this ambitious paper, Endoh simulates a theoretical model to address the question whether the pursuit of "open regionalism" by the Asia Pacific Economic Cooperation (APEC) forum will serve as a building block or stumbling block for multilateral trade liberalization. He also compares APEC's open regionalism to unilateral and multilateral liberalization. Endoh employs the one-good Cournot model along the lines of Krishna (1998) and Andriamananjara (1999), allowing for many countries that differ in market size.[1] He has done a commendable job of running a variety of simulations, offering a rich array of results.

My comments are divided into two parts. A narrower set of comments relates to the model while a broader set of comments addresses the issue of open regionalism itself, going beyond the model exercise in the paper. Beginning with the former, let me first note that the specification of the political-support function chosen by Endoh is somewhat problematic. The analysis is based on the following political-support function:

$$W = \alpha\Pi + (1-\alpha)(Z + T + S),$$

where Π stands for profit, Z for the wage income, T for tariff revenue, and S for *total* consumers' surplus. Symbol α is a constant such that $0 \leq \alpha \leq 1$. Two extreme cases are considered based on $\alpha = 1$ or $\alpha = 0$. The former case is straightforward in which only producers count in the political process and was indeed the basis of all of Krishna's original analysis. The case of $\alpha = 0$ is the problematic one.

In the standard Grossman-Helpman model, the political-support function turns out to be $\alpha\Pi + (1-\alpha)U$, where U stands for the economy-wide welfare and can be represented by $\Pi + (Z + T + S)$. This specification allows a straightforward interpretation of the two extreme cases. In particular, if $\alpha = 0$, the government maximizes welfare and if $\alpha = 1$, it maximizes the welfare of the owners of specific factors.

For the functions chosen by Endoh, the case $\alpha = 0$ has been interpreted to imply that the government cares only for the welfare of wage earners. This raises at least two problems. First, this interpretation requires the assumption that all tariff revenue is redistributed to wage earners. Typically, one would expect tariff revenue to be shared among all including profit earners. Second, even if one assumes that only wage earners get a share in the tariff revenue, S must include the consumers' surplus of wage earners only. But Endoh includes the consumers' surplus of profit earners in S as well.

My second point is that the Cournot model with just one non-numeraire good is much too limiting to address the questions at hand. In particular, the model does not give unilateral liberalization a fair play for two reasons. First, the terms of trade changes are central to the model, whereas the prescription of unilateral freeing of trade is given in the context of small countries; the Cournot model essentially rules out this important case. Second, in what is effectively a one-good model, with the numeraire good with constant marginal utility adjusting passively to ensure trade balance in the background, export interests do not get much play. In a more elaborate model, export interests could help push for unilateral liberalization, which turns out not to be possible in the present one-good model.

Finally, the agents in the model are assumed not to be forward looking. The decisions at the second stage follow from the decisions in the first stage rather than the other way round. Internal consistency would require solving the model by backward induction.

Next, let me briefly turn to the subject of "open regionalism" more broadly. Endoh has taken a particular definition of this concept: trade liberalization by a subset of countries on a nondiscriminatory basis. This is the definition I had employed in my early, detailed discussion of open regionalism in East Asia in Panagariya (1994) and concluded as follows: "Unilateral liberalization by the region as a whole must worsen the terms of trade. Moreover, given that the level of protection in the rest of the world is not much lower than that in East Asia, it is very likely that such a decline in the terms of trade will be welfare worsening." Based on the analysis in that paper, I concluded that this type of open regionalism is not feasible. Using a more formal model and numerical simulations, Endoh has reached much the same conclusion in his paper. In his analysis, open regionalism turns out to be neither a building block nor a stumbling block of multilateral liberalization for the simple reason that it fails to receive political support in the first place.

According to an alternative definition, open regionalism refers to open entry. Elsewhere (Panagariya, 1999), I have taken a critical view of this form of open regional approach as well. There are at least two reasons for this. First, open entry does not mean speedy entry. Until a country gains entry, it must still suffer discrimination vis-à-vis the union members. We know from experience that entry is rarely speedy. The Canada-U.S. Free Trade Agreement was signed in 1988. A dozen years later, it has only three members. Likewise, the European Union was conceived more than 40 years ago and has expanded from 6 to 15 members only. Second, open entry is not as innocuous as it sounds. As Bhagwati (1995, 1997) has noted, the admission price can include unpleasant "side payments" that are essentially unrelated to trade. These include acceptance of a stronger intellectual property rights regime, investment rules, and higher environmental and labor standards. In his future work, Endoh may wish to subject these ideas to a more formal examination.

Notes

[1] A comprehensive survey of the theoretical literature on preferential trading can be found in Panagariya (2000).

References

Andriamananjara, Soamiley. 1999. "On the Size and Number of Regional Integration Arrangements: A Political Economy Model," University of Maryland, mimeo.

Bhagwati, Jagdish. 1995. "U.S. Trade Policy: The Infatuation with Free Trade Areas," in Jagdish Bhagwati and Anne O. Krueger (eds.), *The Dangerous Drift to Preferential Trade Agreements*. Washington, D.C.: American Enterprise Institute for Public Policy Research.

Bhagwati, Jagdish. 1997. "Fast Track to Nowhere," *Economist*, October 18, pp. 21-23.

Krishna, Pravin. 1998. "Regionalism and Multilateralism: A Political Economy Approach," *Quarterly Journal of Economics* 113:227-251.

Panagariya, Arvind. 1994. "East Asia and the New Regionalism," *World Economy* 17:817-39.

Panagariya, Arvind. 1999. "The Regionalism Debate: An Overview," *World Economy* 22:477-511.

Panagariya, Arvind. 2000. "Preferential Trade Liberalization: The Traditional Theory and New Developments," *Journal of Economic Literature* 38:287-331.

Part Three: U.S.-Japan Bilateral Trade and Investment Issues

CHAPTER 13

U.S.-Japan Trade Policy and FDI Issues

Robert M. Stern

I. Introduction

The purpose of this chapter is to review the salient issues of U.S.-Japan trade policies and foreign direct investment (FDI). It covers these issues from a multilateral, bilateral, and regional perspective. To provide some background, I begin in Section II with a description of the recent patterns of trade and FDI of the United States and Japan. Section III considers U.S.-Japan multilateral trade relations and policy initiatives, with emphasis on the dispute settlement actions that each of the nations has taken vis-à-vis the other. Section IV discusses from a U.S. perspective its bilateral trade relations and policy initiatives with Japan, and Section V does the same from a Japanese perspective. Section VI covers the various regional trade policy initiatives in which the two nations are engaged or are actively considering. Section VII concludes.

II. Recent Patterns of Trade and Foreign Direct Investment of the United States and Japan

Before considering the policies of the United States and Japan, it is useful as background to provide an overview of the recent patterns of their trade and FDI.

Patterns of U.S. and Japanese External Trade

Information on the commodity composition of U.S. merchandise trade is given in nominal terms in Table 1 for 1998. It is evident that there are both sizable exports and imports in the merchandise trade categories listed. Most of the categories show net imports, with the exception of food, chemicals, power and other nonelectric machinery, and other transport equipment. The overall trade deficit in 1998 was $263.92 billion, with the largest net imports in fuels, nonferrous metals, office and telecommunications equipment, automotive products, clothing, and other consumer goods. Manufactures accounted in 1998 for more than 80 percent of U.S. exports and imports. Table 2 indicates U.S. merchandise trade by major trading partner and product in 1998. Scrutiny of the details shows some noteworthy variations by commodity group and regions in

Table 1. Commodity Composition of U.S. Merchandise Trade, 1998 (Billions of Dollars and Percent)

	Value (Billions of Dollars)			Percentage	
	Exp.	Imp.	Bal.	Exp.	Imp.
Agricultural products	69.85	62.40	7.45	10.3	6.6
Food	54.33	46.07	8.26	8.0	4.9
Raw materials	15.52	16.33	-0.81	2.3	1.7
Mining products	22.95	84.63	-61.68	3.4	9.0
Ores & other minerals	5.30	6.04	-0.74	0.8	0.6
Fuels	10.07	62.15	-52.08	1.5	6.6
Non-ferrous metals	7.57	76.44	-68.87	1.1	8.1
Manufactures	558.11	757.56	-199.45	82.0	80.2
Iron & steel	6.03	20.73	-14.70	0.9	2.2
Chemicals	69.30	56.44	12.86	10.2	6.0
Other semi-manufactures	39.00	66.85	-27.85	5.7	7.1
Machinery & transp. equip.	358.17	431.61	-73.44	52.6	45.7
Power gener. machinery	19.13	15.44	3.69	2.8	1.6
Other nonelec. machinery	65.40	61.37	4.03	9.6	6.5
Office & telecom. equip.	113.89	155.91	-42.02	16.7	16.5
Elec. mach. & apparatus	34.92	43.46	-8.54	5.1	4.6
Automotive products	61.01	129.83	-68.82	9.0	13.7
Other transp. Equipment	63.76	25.60	38.16	9.4	2.7
Textiles	9.22	13.46	-4.24	1.4	1.4
Clothing	8.79	55.72	-46.93	1.3	5.9
Other consumer goods	64.61	112.75	-48.14	9.5	11.9
Unspecified products	29.52	39.76	-10.24	4.3	4.2
Total	680.43	944.35	-263.92	100.0	100.0

Source: Adapted from WTO, *International Trade Statistics 1999*.

Table 2. U.S. Merchandise Trade by Major Trading Partner and Product, 1998 (Billions of Dollars)

	Canada			EU(15)			Japan			Mexico		
	Exp.	Imp.	Bal.	Exp.	Imp.	Bal.	Exp.	Imp.	Bal.	Exp.	Imp.	Bal.
Agricultural products	10.30	19.26	-8.96	12.07	9.95	2.12	13.80	0.63	13.17	7.04	5.94	1.10
Mining products	6.21	22.77	-16.56	4.95	6.26	-1.31	1.82	0.82	1.00	3.34	7.06	-3.72
Manufactures	132.92	123.29	9.63	125.21	156.24	-31.03	40.64	120.56	-79.92	64.98	79.05	-14.07
Semi-manufactures	29.09	31.90	-2.81	26.17	45.99	-19.82	7.81	14.92	-7.11	14.55	6.95	7.60
Machinery and transport equipment	85.34	77.92	7.42	79.34	82.94	-3.60	24.76	92.84	-68.08	38.84	54.96	-16.12
Textiles, clothing, and other consumer goods	18.49	13.46	5.03	19.69	27.31	-7.62	8.09	12.80	-4.71	11.59	17.14	-5.55
Total	154.15	177.92	-23.77	149.81	182.03	-32.22	57.88	125.09	-67.21	79	96.07	-17.07

	China			Taiwan			Rest of World			World		
	Exp.	Imp.	Bal.	Exp.	Imp.	Bal.	Exp.	Imp.	Bal.	Exp.	Imp.	Bal.
Agricultural products	1.68	1.18	0.50	2.11	0.50	1.61	22.85	24.94	-2.09	69.85	62.4	7.45
Mining products	0.46	0.98	-0.52	0.60	0.10	0.50	5.57	46.64	-41.07	22.95	84.63	-61.68
Manufactures	11.91	72.18	-60.27	14.79	32.98	-18.19	167.66	173.26	-5.60	558.11	757.56	-199.45
Semi-manufactures	2.63	7.25	-4.62	2.51	4.11	-1.60	31.57	32.90	-1.33	114.33	144.02	-29.69
Machinery and transport equipment	8.24	22.43	-14.19	10.75	21.14	-10.39	110.90	79.38	31.52	358.17	431.61	-73.44
Textiles, clothing, and other consumer goods	1.04	42.50	-41.46	1.53	7.73	-6.20	22.19	60.99	-38.80	82.62	181.93	-99.31
Total	14.26	75.09	-60.83	18.16	34.34	-16.18	207.17	253.81	-46.64	680.43	944.35	-263.92

Source: Adapted from WTO, *International Trade Statistics 1999.*

which the United States has net exports or net imports and the particular categories that contribute most to the U.S. trade deficit. Thus, for example, with respect to Japan, the United States has net exports of agricultural products and net imports of manufactures, especially machinery and transport equipment. The United States has sizable net imports of machinery and transport equipment and especially textiles, clothing, and other consumer goods from China and Taiwan. For the Rest of World, there are sizable U.S. net imports of mining products (particularly petroleum) and textiles, clothing, and other consumer goods and U.S. net exports of machinery and transport equipment.

Information on the commodity composition of Japan's merchandise trade in 1998 is shown in Table 3. Manufactures accounted for 94.2 percent of Japan's exports and 56.6 percent of imports. Japan's revealed comparative disadvantage in agricultural and mining products is thus evident from the sizable net imports indicated. Its revealed comparative advantage in the net exports of manufactures is also evident, especially for machinery and transport equipment. Clothing is the only category of manufactures in the table that shows net imports.[1] The geographic distribution of Japan's merchandise trade is shown in Table 4. Japan has net imports of agricultural and mining products from the United States and the other regions shown. Japan is a net exporter of semi-manufactures to the United States, East Asia, and Rest of World and a net importer from the EU-15. Japan's sizable net exports of machinery and transport equipment are evident to all of the countries/regions shown. Japan's trade in textiles, clothing, and other consumer goods is nearly balanced except for the sizable net imports from East Asia.

The nominal values of U.S. and Japanese exports and imports of commercial services for 1998 are indicated in Table 5. It is noteworthy that the United States had net services exports of $74.2 billion, with the largest amounts indicated for travel (i.e., tourism), financial services, royalties and license fees, and other business services. Transportation and travel accounted for 53.8 percent of total exports and 65.2 percent of total imports, with other commercial services accounting for the remainder. Japan had net services imports of $48.9 billion in 1998. The largest net services imports were recorded for travel (i.e., tourism) and other business services. Data on the geographic breakdown by type of service and major trading partner are not readily available for services.

Patterns of U.S. and Japanese Foreign Direct Investment (FDI)

Data on the sectoral distribution of the stock of U.S. inward and outward FDI are reported in Table 6 for 1987, 1992, 1997, and 1998. As indicated in the last row of the table, the U.S. stock of outward FDI was $980.6 billion in 1998 as compared to $314.3 billion in 1987. The U.S. stock of inward FDI was $811.8 billion in 1998 as compared to $263.4 billion in 1987. Manufacturing accounted for 41.7 percent of inward FDI and 31.1 percent of outward FDI in 1998. The share of services was more than half of inward and outward FDI in 1998 as compared to 47.4 percent and 37.4 percent, respectively, in 1987. This

Table 3. Commodity Composition of Japanese Merchandise Trade, 1998 (Billions of Dollars and Percent)

	Value (Billions of Dollars)			Percentage	
	Exp.	Imp.	Bal.	Exp.	Imp.
Agricultural products	4.09	56.59	-52.50	1.1	20.2
Food	2.05	44.47	-42.42	0.5	15.8
Raw materials	2.04	12.13	-10.09	0.5	4.3
Mining products	5.99	60.02	-54.03	1.5	21.4
Ores & other minerals	0.84	8.81	-7.97	0.2	3.1
Fuels	1.24	43.27	-42.03	0.3	15.4
Non-ferrous metals	3.91	7.94	-4.03	1.0	2.8
Manufactures	365.56	158.73	206.83	94.2	56.6
Iron & steel	14.87	3.20	11.67	3.8	1.1
Chemicals	27.24	20.57	6.67	7.0	7.3
Other semi-manufactures	17.08	12.14	4.94	4.4	4.3
Machinery & transp. equip.	268.47	74.88	193.59	69.2	26.7
Power gener. machinery	6.23	3.67	2.56	1.6	1.3
Other nonelec. machinery	47.76	10.30	37.46	12.3	3.7
Office & telecom. equip.	85.03	36.55	48.48	21.9	13.0
Elec. mach. & apparatus	28.25	9.82	18.43	7.3	3.5
Automotive products	77.61	7.81	69.80	20.0	2.8
Other transp. Equipment	23.59	6.73	16.86	6.1	2.4
Textiles	5.97	4.36	1.61	1.5	1.6
Clothing	0.41	14.72	-14.31	0.1	5.2
Other consumer goods	31.54	28.86	2.68	8.1	10.3
Unspecified products	12.50	5.29	7.21	3.2	1.9
Total	388.14	280.63	107.51	100.0	100.0

Source: Adapted from WTO, *International Trade Statistics 1999.*

Table 4. Japan's Merchandise Trade by Major Trading Partner and Product, 1998 (Billions of Dollars)

	United States			EU (15)			East Asia		
	Exp.	Imp.	Bal.	Exp.	Imp.	Bal.	Exp.	Imp.	Bal.
Agricultural products	0.55	17.00	-16.45	0.43	5.19	-4.76	1.89	8.46	-6.57
Mining products	0.87	2.33	-1.46	0.35	0.99	-0.64	3.34	4.00	-0.66
Manufactures	113.99	46.75	67.24	68.90	32.20	36.70	75.77	47.54	28.23
Semi-manufactures	13.91	9.00	4.91	8.14	10.13	-1.99	19.76	7.74	12.02
Machinery and transport equipment	89.58	28.76	60.82	52.59	13.54	39.05	44.72	16.98	27.74
Textiles, clothing, and other consumer goods	10.50	8.99	1.51	8.17	8.53	-0.36	11.29	22.82	-11.53
Total	119.85	67.48	52.37	71.69	39.09	32.60	83.65	61.13	22.52

	Rest of World			World		
	Exp.	Imp.	Bal.	Exp.	Imp.	Bal.
Agricultural products	1.22	25.94	-24.72	4.09	56.59	-52.50
Mining products	1.43	52.70	-51.27	5.99	60.02	-54.03
Manufactures	106.90	32.24	74.66	365.56	158.73	206.83
Semi-manufactures	17.36	9.04	8.32	59.17	35.91	23.26
Machinery and transport equipment	81.58	15.60	65.98	268.47	74.88	193.59
Textiles, clothing, and other consumer goods	7.96	7.60	0.36	37.92	47.94	-10.02
Total	112.95	112.93	0.02	388.14	280.63	107.51

Source: Adapted from WTO, *International Trade Statistics 1999*.

Table 5. U.S. and Japanese Trade in Commercial Services, 1998 (Billions of Dollars and Percent)

	United States				Japan			
	Exports		Imports		Exports		Imports	
	Value	Percent	Value	Percent	Value	Percent	Value	Percent
Total commercial services	240.0	100.0	165.8	100.0	61.8	100.0	110.7	100.0
Transportation	45.5	19.0	50.3	30.3	21.3	34.4	28.4	25.6
Sea transport	4.1	1.7	14.1	8.5	14.2	23.0	19.7	17.8
Air transport	24.5	10.2	23.0	13.9	7.0	11.4	8.6	7.8
Other transport	16.9	7.1	13.2	7.9	0.1	0.0	0.1	0.0
Travel	83.4	34.8	57.8	34.9	3.7	6.1	28.8	26.0
Other commercial services	111.1	46.3	57.8	34.8	36.8	59.1	53.5	48.3
Communication services	3.9	1.6	8.6	5.2	1.2	1.9	1.6	1.4
Construction services	4.1	1.7	0.7	0.4	7.7	12.5	5.5	5.0
Insurance services	2.8	1.2	6.9	4.2	0.0	0.1	2.4	2.1
Financial services	13.7	5.7	3.8	2.3	1.6	2.6	2.2	1.9
Computer and information services	4.0	1.7	0.5	0.3	1.3	2.2	3.5	3.2
Royalties and licence fee	36.8	15.3	11.3	6.8	7.4	12.0	8.9	9.1
Other business services	41.6	17.3	25.9	15.6	17.1	27.6	28.1	25.4
Personal, cultural, and recreational services	4.2	1.7	0.1	0.0	0.4	0.7	1.3	1.1

Source: Adapted from WTO, *International Trade Statistics 1999.*

Table 6. U.S. Stock of Foreign Direct Investment and Its Sectoral Distribution at Year-End, 1987, 1992, 1997, and 1998 (Billions of Dollars and Percent)

	Inward FDI				Outward FDI			
	1987	1992	1997	1998	1987	1992	1997	1998
Agriculture & fishing	0.5	0.3	0.3	0.3	0.2	0.1	0.1	0.1
Mining & quarrying	16.5	10.8	6.4	6.8	20.5	12.8	11.0	10.7
of which: Extraction of petroleum and gas	14.4	8.8	4.7	5.4	19.0	11.7	9.5	9.3
Manufacturing	35.6	37.2	40.8	41.7	41.9	37.1	32.4	31.1
of which:								
Food products	5.9	5.7	3.9	2.2	4.0	4.2	9.8	8.9
Textile and wood activities	3.0	3.6	5.2	5.2	2.5	2.8	2.3	2.4
Petroleum, chemical, rubber and plastic products	10.8	13.1	15.7	14.9	10.5	14.0	11.0	10.5
Metal and mechanical products	4.9	5.7	5.8	5.3	10.8	7.4	5.6	5.3
Office machinery, computers, radio, TV and communication equipment	4.0	4.1	4.3	4.7	3.2	3.2	3.7	3.5
Vehicles and other transport equipment	1.1	1.0	2.0	4.3	6.0	5.1	4.0	3.6
Electricity, gas & water	..	0.6	0.5	0.4	..	0.2	1.8	2.5
Construction	0.5	0.5	0.6	0.6	0.3	0.2	0.2	0.2
Trade & repairs	17.2	15.9	15.1	14.2	11.7	12.3	8.9	9.0
Hotels & restaurants	..	2.7	1.4	1.1	..	0.3	0.3	0.3
Transport & communication	..	0.9	3.1	2.8	0.5	1.6	0.7	0.8
of which:								
Land, sea and air transport	0.7	0.6	1.5	1.4	0.5	0.7	..	..
Telecommunications	0.1	0.3	1.6	1.4	0.0	0.9	1.2	1.2

	Inward FDI				Outward FDI			
	1987	1992	1997	1998	1987	1992	1997	1998
Financial activities	17.0	27.1	21.9	21.7	23.6	31.7	43.3	43.5
of which:								
Monetary institutions	..	6.6	5.5	5.5	..	4.9	4.6	4.3
Other financial institutions	..	3.0	6.3	6.3	..	23.0	33.9	34.4
of which: Financial holding companies	..	1.0	1.2	..	..	16.5	19.3	19.3
Insurance & activities auxiliary to insurance	..	8.4	10.2	9.9	..	3.9	4.8	4.8
Other financial institutions and insurance activities	..	9.7	16.4	16.2	..	26.8	14.4	14.9
Real estate & business activities	..	9.0	7.7	8.3	..	2.1	3.0	3.3
of which: Real estate	..	7.6	5.8	5.5	..	0.5	0.1	0.2
Other services	11.9	7.4	2.2	2.3	1.3	1.6	1.8	2.0
Unallocated	0.0	..	0.0	0.0	..	..	..	..
TOTAL (Percent)	100.0	100.0	100.0	100.0	100.0	1992.0	100.0	100.0
of which:								
PRIMARY	17.0	11.1	6.7	7.0	20.7	12.9	11.1	10.7
MANUFACTURING	35.6	37.2	40.8	41.7	41.9	37.1	32.4	31.1
SERVICES	47.4	51.8	52.5	51.3	37.4	50.0	56.5	58.2
TOTAL (Billions of Dollars)	263.4	427.6	693.2	811.8	314.3	502.1	865.5	980.6

Source: Adapted from OECD, *International Direct Investment Statistics Yearbook 1999*.

increased importance of services-related FDI is indicative of the fact that many services require a domestic presence in host countries. The geographic distribution of U.S. inward and outward FDI is reported in Table 7. More than 90 percent of inward FDI comes from OECD countries, whereas the OECD countries accounted for 71.3 percent of the outward stock in 1998. Outward FDI in Latin America/Caribbean and in the Asian countries accounted for the bulk of the remainder.

As noted in OECD (1999, p. 417), data on FDI for Japan come either from Japan's balance-of-payments statistics or are compiled on the basis of notifications collected by the Ministry of Finance (MOF). Stock data on Japan's FDI have been taken from balance-of-payments statistics since 1996. Before 1996, the stock data had been compiled by the MOF by accumulating flow data based on notifications. There is a break accordingly in the data reported by the OECD, so that inward and outward FDI stock data prior to 1996 are not comparable with the post-1996 stock data based on the balance-of-payments statistics.

The sectoral distribution of the stock of Japan's inward and outward FDI, based on notifications data, is reported in Table 8 for 1986, 1990, and 1994. As shown in the last row of the table, the absolute amount of Japan's inward FDI of $34.1 billion in 1994 is very small compared to its outward FDI of $463.6 billion. In 1994, 55.2 percent of inward FDI was in manufacturing, including 30.3 per cent in metal and mechanical products. The other 44.8 percent was in services, with 20.2 percent in trade & repairs and 7.1 percent in financial activities. The data on Japan's outward FDI indicate that about two-thirds of the stock was in services in 1994 as compared to 55.4 percent in 1988. The sectoral data based on balance-of-payments statistics are not yet available for 1996-97.

The large difference in Japan's inward and outward FDI has been remarked upon in the GATT/WTO trade policy review of Japan (1995, p. 35):

> "The authorities ascribe the relatively low levels of FDI into Japan largely to high production costs, land prices, and acquisition costs; these factors have been exacerbated by yen appreciation and domestic competition, which together have resulted in generally low profitability for foreign affiliates and thus tending to discourage possible new entrants....To these factors should be added, when considering the fairly low stock of FDI in Japan, past restrictions on FDI and the fact that, with domestic savings in excess of investment, the Government had not encouraged inward FDI, except in areas where specific technology was thought necessary, e.g., chemicals."

Notwithstanding the foregoing remark, there is reason to believe that the data reported in Table 8 are misleading. As noted in Fukao and Ito (2000), the MOF data cover only cross-border capital flows and therefore do not corre-

Table 7. Geographic Distribution of Stock of U.S. Foreign Direct Investment Position at Year-End, 1987, 1992, 1997, and 1998 (Billions of Dollars and Percent)

	Inward FDI				Outward FDI			
	1987	1992	1997	1998	1987	1992	1997	1998
OECD Countries	93.4	94.8	93.1	94.4	76.9	75.6	70.6	71.3
Africa	0.2	0.2	0.2	0.1	1.3	0.6	1.3	1.4
Latin America-Caribbean	3.7	3.8	4.4	3.5	13.6	15.5	17.8	17.4
Near & Middle East	1.9	1.1	1.0	1.0	1.3	1.1	1.0	1.1
Asian Countries	0.7	1.0	1.3	1.0	5.0	6.0	8.1	7.8
Other	0.1	-1.0	0.1	0.0	1.9	1.1	1.2	1.1
Total (Percentage)	100.0	100.0	100.0	100.0	100.0	100.0	100.0	100.0
Total (Billions of Dollars)	263.4	423.1	693.2	811.8	314.3	502.1	865.5	980.6

Source: Adapted from OECD, *International Direct Investment Statistics Yearbook 1999.*

Table 8. Japanese Stock of Foreign Direct Investment and Its Sectoral Distribution at Year-End, 1986, 1990, 1994 (Billions of Dollars and Percent)

	Inward FDI			Outward FDI		
	1986	1990	1994	1986	1990	1994
Agriculture & fishing	..	..	..	1.2	0.7	0.7
Mining & quarrying	..	..	..	12.7	6.1	4.4
of which: Extraction of petroleum and gas	..	..	..	..	..	..
Manufacturing	70.5	63.9	55.2	25.9	27.0	27.8
of which:						
Food products	2.4	1.7	1.7	1.2	1.4	1.6
Textile and wood activities	..	..	..	2.9	1.9	2.2
Petroleum, chemical, rubber and plastic products	34.3	21.9	3.3	..	..	..
Metal and mechanical products	29.1	37.0	30.3	7.5	5.9	5.8
Office machinery, computers, radio, TV and communication equipment	..	..	..	4.4	6.7	6.4
Vehicles and other transport equipment	..	..	..	..	..	..
Electricity, gas & water	..	..	..	..	..	..
Construction	0.8	0.5	0.3	1.0	0.8	0.9
Trade & repairs	12.6	16.0	20.2	13.4	10.5	10.7
Hotels & restaurants	..	..	..	..	..	..
Transport & communication	1.1	1.6	1.7	..	..	5.7
of which:						
Land, sea and air transport	0.6	0.8	0.7	7.3	5.8	5.7

	Inward FDI			Outward FDI		
	1986	1990	1994	1986	1990	1994
Agriculture & fishing	..	..	..	1.2	0.7	0.7
Telecommunications	0.5	0.8	1.0	..	..	..
Financial activities	2.4	3.7	7.1	16.1	21.3	18.9
of which:						
Monetary institutions	..	..	..	..	..	..
Other financial institutions	..	..	..	..	..	..
of which: Financial holding companies	..	..	..	..	..	..
Insurance & activities auxiliary to insurance	..	..	..	..	..	..
Other financial institutions and insurance activities	..	..	..	..	..	..
Real estate & business activities	..	..	..	..	..	..
of which: Real estate	..	..	..	..	..	..
Other services	12.6	14.4	15.5	17.6	28.9	29.3
Unallocated	..	..	..	2.6	1.8	1.6
TOTAL (Percent)	100.0	100.0	100.0	100.0	100.0	100.0
of which:						
PRIMARY	..	..	..	13.9	6.8	5.0
MANUFACTURING	70.5	63.9	55.2	25.9	27.0	27.8
SERVICES	29.5	36.1	44.8	55.4	67.2	65.5
TOTAL (Billions of Dollars)	7.3	18.4	34.1	117.4	310.8	463.6

Source: Adapted from OECD, *International Direct Investment Statistics Yearbook 1999*.

spond to the full extent of the actual activities of foreign affiliates in Japan and do not take into account the fact that branches of foreign firms have been set up in Japan to circumvent Japanese regulations. There is also evidence in more recent MOF data of a significant increase in inward FDI in recent years. Thus, in nominal terms on a notifications basis, there was more than a 5-fold increase in inward FDI between the 1994 and 1999 fiscal years in comparison to a 74 percent increase in outward FDI.[2] It appears therefore that the large differences in Japan's inward and outward FDI have been narrowing considerably.

The geographic distribution of Japan's stock of FDI is reported in Table 9. Most of the inward FDI comes from OECD countries, 80.5 percent in 1997. The OECD countries accounted for 48.9 percent of Japan's outward FDI in 1997 and the Asian countries, 25.2 percent.

III. U.S.-Japan Multilateral Trade Relations and Policy Initiatives

The World Trade Organization (WTO) came officially into existence in January 1995 and since then has become the center of focus for multilateral trade-policy activities for the member countries. There have been three WTO Ministerial Conference meetings in the intervening years, the most recent of these being the failed Seattle meeting held in early December 1999. In preparing for the Seattle meeting, there were some apparent differences between the United States and Japan concerning the establishment of the agenda for a new WTO negotiating round. The United States favored a somewhat narrow agenda that would be concentrated especially on issues of the built-in agenda that had been mandated in the Uruguay Round agreements concluded in 1993-94. This built-in agenda called for negotiations for the liberalization of agriculture and services to begin in the year 2000 together with actions needed to clarify and improve the implementation of a number of the Uruguay Round agreements. Japan, on the other hand, favored a broader agenda that would encompass such issues as competition policy and investment and the reopening of certain of the Uruguay Round agreements, antidumping in particular. It was also evident in the WTO discussions prior to the Seattle Meeting that the United States was pushing hard in collaboration with the Cairns Group to address issues of agricultural liberalization in a meaningful way. Japan and a number of other WTO members, especially the European Union (EU), were reluctant to make a commitment on agricultural liberalization at the time. Also, Japan had expressed concern about U.S. antidumping actions since it had been targeted so often, but for mainly domestic political reasons the United States was adamant in opposing reopening the antidumping agreement. In any event, despite the failure of the Seattle meeting, the year 2000 negotiations have begun on agricultural and services liberalization and review of the implementation of the Uruguay Round agreements. Progress on the agenda for a broader WTO negotiating round will evidently have to wait until after the November 2000 U.S. presidential election.

Table 9. Geographic Distribution of Stock of Japanese Foreign Direct Investment Position at Year-End, 1986, 1990, 1994, and 1997

	Inward FDI				Outward FDI			
	1986	1990	1994	1997[a]	1986	1990	1994	1997[a]
OECD Countries	89.3	86.7	86.9	80.5	56.5	70.1	70.2	48.9
Africa	..	..	..	..	3.5	1.9	1.7	0.1
Latin America-Caribbean	..	..	3.3	..	17.7	12.4	11.3	-0.4
Near & Middle East	..	..	..	0.3	2.8	1.1	1.0	0.5
Asian Countries	3.9	2.7	4.0	12.0	18.5	13.9	15.3	25.2
Other	6.8	10.6	5.8	7.2	1.1	0.6	0.5	25.8
Total (Percentage)	100.0	100.0	100.0	100.0	100.0	100.0	100.0	100.0
Total (Billions of Dollars)	7.3	18.4	34.1	29.1	106.5	311.3	463.6	292.0

[a]Pre-1997 stock data are based on compilations of FDI notifications and are not comparable with the post-1994 data based on balance-of-payments statistics.

Source: Adapted from OECD, *International Direct Investment Statistics Yearbook 1999*.

Notwithstanding the failure of the Seattle Ministerial Conference, it is important to note that there has been considerable activity in the past five years especially regarding consultation requests brought to the WTO Dispute Settlement Mechanism. It is useful accordingly to look at these actions more closely from the perspective of the United States and Japan.

Dispute Settlement Actions[3]

One of the most important features of the WTO was the redesign and strengthening of the Dispute Settlement Mechanism. Compared to the previous dispute settlement procedures in the GATT, it is now no longer possible to block establishment of a panel or for a party to block panel reports. Opportunities for arbitration have been increased, time limits applied for completion of panel investigations, standard terms of reference specified, and improvements made in surveillance of the implementation of the panel reports. Because WTO member countries have agreed, when possible, to use multilateral remedies in trade disputes, the scope for resort to unilateral trade measures may be reduced. Further, because the WTO has broader coverage than the GATT, more disputes may be referred to the WTO Dispute Settlement Body (DSB).

Hoekman and Kostecki (1995, pp. 49, 179-80) note that 132 complaints were lodged in the GATT dispute settlement procedure between 1948 and 1994. In contrast, according to WTO (2000), from 1 January 1995 to 22 June 2000, there have been 202 consultation requests made for dispute settlement on 159 "distinct matters." The consultation requests are broken down by complainant and respondents in Table 10.[4] It is evident that the United States has brought 65 complaints in total, including 5 against Japan, 25 against the European Communities (EC) and individual EC member countries, 6 against other industrialized countries, and 29 against developing/emerging economies. Japan has brought 7 complaints in total, including 4 against the United States.

As detailed in WTO (2000), the U.S. complaints brought against Japan involve:

- Taxes on Alcoholic Beverages (DS 11)—The United States—joined by the European Union and Canada—successfully challenged a discriminatory Japanese tax arrangement that placed high taxes on whisky, vodka, and other Western-style spirits, while applying low taxes to a traditional Japanese spirit (shochu). The Appellate Body Report and Panel Report were adopted on December 24, 1996. Under a December 1997 agreement, Japan agreed to eliminate tariffs on white spirits and to accelerate elimination of tariffs on brown spirits.

- Measures Concerning Sound Recordings (DS 28)—This complaint was brought under the TRIPS Agreement. The United States contended that Japan's copyright regime violated the TRIPS Agreement. A mutually sat-

Table 10. WTO Disputes: Consultation Requests January 1, 1995 to June 22, 2000

	Respondents					
Complaints by	United States	Japan	European Communities[a]	Other Ind. Countries	Develop-ing/Emerging Economies	Total[b]
United States	–	5	25	6	29	65
Japan	4	–	–	1	2	7
European Communities	18	6	–	3	24	51
Other Industrialized Countries	5	1	7	3	11	27
Developing/Emerging Economies	21	–	18	2	27	68
Total[b]	48	12	50	15	93	218

Notes:

[a]Includes complaints against the European Communities (EC) as well as individual EC member countries.

[b]Totals reflect individual cases involving more than one country requesting consultation with respondent.

Source: Adapted from World Trade Organization, "Overview of the State-of-play of WTO Disputes," http://www.wto.org./wto/ dispute/bulletin.htm, 22 June 2000.

isfactory solution to this dispute was reached on January 24, 1997, such that Japan will provide full copyright protection for sound recordings.

- Measures Affecting Consumer Photographic Film and Paper (DS 44)—This began as a Section 301 action on behalf of Eastman Kodak against the Fuji Photo Film company. A dispute panel was established on October 16, 1996. It was announced on December 5, 1997 that all 21 points in the U.S. filing had been dismissed on the grounds that the alleged Japanese Government barriers had no perceptible impact on the competition between imports and domestic products. No further action has been taken. The United States is monitoring the situation in the Japanese market.

- Measures Affecting Distribution Services (DS 45)—This action on June 13, 1996 was brought in parallel with Kodak-Fuji action and challenges Japan's Large-Scale Retail Stores Law. Further consultations were requested on September 20, 1996 to address additional legal claims and Japanese measures. Japan announced that it would abolish the Large Scale Retail Stores Law in December 1997.

- Measures Affecting Agricultural Products (DS 76)—Japan agreed to eliminate variety-by-variety testing for quarantine purposes and lifted various restrictions on the imports of certain varieties of fruit, including apples and cherries. The Appellate Body Report and the Panel Report were adopted on March 19, 1999.

Japan's complaints brought against the United States involve:[5]

- Imposition of Import Duties on Automobiles from Japan under Sections 301 and 302 of the Trade Act of 1974 (DS 6)—Japan alleged that these surcharges were in violation of the GATT. The dispute was settled on July 19, 1995.

- Measure Affecting Government Procurement (DS 95)—Japan contends that an Act enacted by the State of Massachusetts prohibiting the public procurement from persons doing business with Burma is in violation of the Government Procurement Agreement. A panel was requested (jointly with the European Union) on September 8, 1998, but its authority lapsed as of February 11, 2000. This case came before the U.S. Supreme Court on March 22, 2000. It was decided on June 19, 2000 that the Massachusetts Act was preempted by federal action on economic sanctions towards Burma taken by the U.S. Congress, and that it interfered with the President's authority granted by Congress to speak for the United States in developing a comprehensive and multilateral Burma strategy.

- Anti-Dumping Act of 1916 (DS 162)—Japan has challenged the U.S. 1916 Act and the decisions made under this Act as violating the GATT and the Antidumping Agreement. A panel was established on July 26, 1999.

- Anti-Dumping Measures on Certain Hot-Rolled Steel Products (DS 184)—Japan contends that the preliminary and final determinations of the U.S. Department of Commerce and International Trade Commission in their antidumping investigations were erroneous and based under deficient procedures and are in violation of the GATT and the Antidumping Agreement. Japan requested a panel on February 24, 2000.

It is evident from the foregoing that the United States is the single largest user of the Dispute Settlement Mechanism. While Japan has requested more consultations than under the GATT prior to 1995, its post-1995 requests appear small by comparison to the United States and European Union. Since there is no question about Japan's firm commitment to the principles and rules of the WTO, this difference may reflect a conscious decision by the Japanese authorities to pursue dispute settlement especially in cases in which its major export interests are in jeopardy (e.g., automobiles and steel) and to resist in cases in which its domestic firms are charged with ostensible restrictive behavior (e.g., photographic film and paper). This is in contrast to the more aggressive, unilateral actions that are typical of U.S. trade policies and that will be discussed in the next section.

IV. U.S. Bilateral Trade Relations and Policy Initiatives with Japan

The United States has for some time aggressively pursued bilateral trade objectives vis-à-vis Japan. As noted in U.S. President (2000, pp. 215-34), there have been extensive bilateral discussions and agreements negotiated with Japan designed to expand access for U.S. firms to Japan's domestic market. These have included:

- 38 market-opening trade agreements with Japan since 1993, coupled with monitoring and enforcement of these agreements, including the use of "objective" criteria to assess progress under each agreement. Some of the most significant developments are noted below.
    - **Insurance**: The 1994 U.S.-Japan Insurance Agreement was designed to achieve a substantial increase in market access and sales for foreign insurance providers and intermediaries in Japan. A second agreement (December 15, 1996) was designed to achieve substantial deregulation of the "primary" life and non-life sectors, which account for about 95 percent of Japan's insurance market, and to avoid radical change in the remaining sector that includes personal accident, cancer, and hospitalization insurance. There have been continuing official consultations under the two insurance agreements dealing with

specific matters to promote increased access and competition in the provision of insurance services in the Japanese market.

- **Flat Glass**: An agreement was concluded in January 1995 aimed at opening the Japanese market, which is dominated by three large producers, to increased imports of flat glass. There has not been any appreciable market penetration. The agreement expired at the end of 1999, and discussions of how to improve foreign market access are to be continued.
- **Auto and Auto Parts**: In August 1995, an Automotive Agreement was designed with the objective of eliminating market-access barriers and expanding sales opportunities for foreign firms in the Japanese market. The United States established an Interagency Enforcement Team to assess progress under the agreement. Due to the prolonged economic downturn in Japan, overall vehicle and parts sales have declined significantly, including sales by U.S. manufacturers. The United States has continued to discuss with Japan proposals for further deregulation, standards-related issues, measures to improve transparency, and actions to enhance competition in the automotive sector in Japan.[6] The Agreement expires in December 2000.
- **Government Procurement**: Bilateral government-procurement agreements have been concluded in the areas of: telecommunications (including an agreement covering NTT procurement); computers; supercomputers; satellites; medical technology; and construction/public works. The objective of these agreements is to expand Japanese public-sector procurement of foreign products and services. The agreements address such matters as: lack of consistent and equal access to information regarding upcoming procurements; insufficient opportunities to comment on, and participate in, the development of specifications; over-reliance on sole-sourced procurements; use of unique or Japan-specific technical standards as opposed to international standards; and lack of impartial bid protest systems.

- **Investment**: A U.S.-Japan Investment Agreement was concluded in July 1995. The Agreement focuses on both structural change and government facilitation designed to attract foreign direct investment to Japan. There are continuing consultations on measures needed to remove existing barriers in order to improve the FDI climate in Japan.

- **Sectoral Issues**
  - **Steel**: The United States has been concerned about the impact of increased steel imports from Japan on U.S. firms. These imports have been monitored since early 1999 and coupled with statements that safeguards and antidumping actions could be introduced unless imports are rolled back.[7] In 1999, dumping orders were issued against Japan on certain hot-rolled carbon steel flat products and stainless

steel sheet and strip in coils. A number of dumping investigations against Japan on other steel products have also been requested by U.S. steel producers.

- **Rice**: Japan established a minimum-access commitment for rice imports in the Uruguay Round negotiations. On April 1, 1999, Japan introduced a new rice regime that transformed the existing import-quota system into a tariff-quota system. Under "tarrification," a specific duty is applied to imports outside of Japanese minimum-access rice imports. The United States is now the single largest foreign supplier of rice to the Japanese market and is actively monitoring Japan's foreign rice purchases.
- **Consumer Photographic Film and Paper**: Following the unfavorable WTO Dispute Settlement panel ruling, the United States established an interagency and monitoring committee in February 1998 to conduct semi-annual reviews of the implementation of Japan's representations to the WTO regarding its efforts to ensure the openness of its markets and its distribution system to imports of photographic film and paper.[8]
- **Semiconductors**: On June 10, 1999, the United States, Japan, Korea, and the European Commission announced a new, multilateral Joint Statement on Semiconductors designed to ensure fair and open global trade in semiconductors. Chinese Taipei subsequently became a party to the Joint Statement. There were three previous semiconductor agreements designed to open the Japanese market to foreign semiconductors, improve cooperation between Japanese users and foreign suppliers, and eliminate tariffs. Since 1996, when the foreign share of the Japanese market averaged more than 30 percent, the climate has changed from confrontation to cooperation. Following the December 1996 WTO Singapore Ministerial Meeting, a multilateral Information Technology Agreement was negotiated that will substantially eliminate all semiconductor tariffs worldwide. The World Semiconductor Council was created so that member countries could regularly discuss and engage in cooperation concerning global semiconductor issues.
- **Deregulation**: Agreement on concrete deregulatory actions that Japan will take to improve U.S. sectoral access in telecommunications, housing, financial services, insurance, medical devices and pharmaceuticals, energy, and legal services, and to further structural improvements in distribution, competition policy, and transparency.[9]

    - Telecommunications: Japan agreed to bring interconnection rates to competitive, market-based levels and to develop guidelines to reduce restrictions faced by telephone carriers. Japan also committed to ensure that NTT's retail pricing of services, relative to interconnection rates, does not impair competition.

- Housing: Japan has adopted Public Comment Procedures to make it easier for building-material suppliers to participate in the formulation and implementation of revisions to the Building Standard Law, the cornerstone of Japan's housing policy, and to implement performance-based standards for certain types of wood housing. Discussions have been held, in the context of a new WTO negotiating round, for the purpose of eliminating tariffs on value-added wood products.
- Financial Services: Measures have been implemented under Japan's "Big Bang" initiative to liberalize transactions involving new financial products, increase competition and lower costs to facilitate financial trading, and enhance accounting and disclosure standards.
- Insurance: Measures are being taken to streamline the current product approval system and to clarify Japanese Government rules and regulations covering insurance so that Japanese consumers will have available a wider array of new, innovative, and cost-competitive insurance products.
- Medical Device/Pharmaceutical/Nutritional Supplement Products: More attention is to be given to pharmaceutical pricing reform and encouragement of innovations to improve the availability of pharmaceuticals, medical devices, and nutritional supplements.
- Energy: Japan is engaged in efforts to deregulate its electricity and natural gas sectors and to reduce energy costs.[10]
- Legal Services: Efforts are being made to remove barriers that restrict Japanese and foreign persons and firms from obtaining fully integrated transnational legal services for domestic and cross-border transactions.
- Distribution: Japan has taken steps to abolish the Large-Scale Retail Store Law and has agreed to decentralize the monitoring of establishment of large stores and to promote more competition.
- Competition Law and Policy: The Japan Fair Trade Commission (JFTC) has taken measures to enhance greater competition among trade associations, identify and rectify private restraints of trade, reduce administrative guidance that supports anticompetitive behavior, and provide for more consultation to enhance competition. Measures have also been taken to enhance greater transparency in public procurement procedures, and discussions are being held to design a private remedy system to deal with antimonopoly violations.
- Transparency and Other Government Practices: A foundation is being developed for a more transparent and accountable regula-

tory system to allow for public review and comment on draft regulations and enactment of an information disclosure law.

- **Administration of U.S. Trade Laws and Regulations**: The United States has a number of legal statutes and provisions that authorize the use of trade-remedy measures to deal with allegedly harmful effects that the policies of trading partners may have on U.S. interests. These measures include: safeguard actions; anti-dumping (AD) and countervailing duties (CVDs); Section 301 actions; and special arrangements for agricultural products and for textiles and clothing. Some of these measures of particular concern to Japan are noted below.
    - **Safeguard Actions**: Section 201 of the U.S. Trade Act of 1974 provides for safeguard relief to redress injury from increased imports for up to four years and possibly to a maximum of eight years. To obtain relief, the U.S. International Trade Commission (USITC) must make an affirmative determination that an industry has been seriously injured by increased imports. As of March 1, 2000, the United States had safeguard measures in place for: wheat gluten; lamb meat; certain wire (wire rod), and circular welded carbon quality line pipe. On February 1, 2000, the President imposed a tariff-rate quota on imports of wire rod for a period of 3 years on imports from all countries except Canada and Mexico. Import relief in the form of a tariff-rate quota was imposed for a period of 3 years on imports of line pipe on February 11, 2000.
    - **Anti-dumping (AD) and Countervailing Duties (CVDs)**: These measures have a long history as U.S. trade-law remedies, and the procedures and criteria used for investigations have been changed and elaborated over time in accordance with changes in U.S. legislation and agreements reached in periodic GATT negotiations. AD actions are aimed against presumptively "unfair" pricing practices of firms while CVD actions are aimed against practices (e.g., subsidies) of foreign governments. AD and CVD investigations are initiated at the request of firms, labor unions, or coalitions of parties and are addressed simultaneously to the USITC and International Trade Administration (ITA) of the U.S. Department of Commerce. Once the USITC makes a determination of material injury, the ITA then establishes the dumping-margin rate of duty to be applied. An analogous procedure is followed for CVD petitions.

      Information on U.S. anti-dumping investigations from 1980-1998 is provided in Table 11.[11] Initiations peaked in 1992 with 84 cases and declined to 15 in 1997. However, initiations (particularly involving steel) increased to 36 cases in 1998. The geographic distribution of AD orders in effect on January 1, 1999 is indicated in Figure 1. Japan, with 16.2 percent of the 297 cases was the single largest country affected. The importance of iron and steel and products thereof is evident, accounting for 41.1 percent of all products.

U.S. CVD investigations from 1980-1998 are noted in Table 12. They also peaked in 1992, with 22 cases, and have since fallen to 6 in 1997 and 11 in 1998. There were no CVD orders in effect involving Japan as of January 1, 1999, as is evident in Figure 2. The importance of iron and steel and products (58.8 percent) is further evident in the commodity breakdown in Figure 2.

- **Section 301 and Related Actions:** There is a panoply of U.S. trade tools that is applied in conjunction with bilateral and WTO mechanisms to promote foreign compliance with U.S. laws and, to an extent, address issues that are outside the scope of the WTO.
  - **Section 301** of the Trade Act of 1974 is the principal U.S. statute for addressing allegedly unfair foreign practices that may affect U.S. exports of goods or services. A procedure is provided whereby interested parties may petition the USTR to investigate a foreign government policy or practice and take action. The USTR may also self-initiate an investigation. The USTR is required to seek consultation with the foreign government involved, and, if no settlement is reached and the investigation involves a trade agreement, a WTO dispute settlement procedure must be invoked. Once the investigation is concluded and if no settlement is reached, the USTR will decide if any actions are to be taken to rectify damage being done to U.S. interests.

    An indication of Section 301 cases initiated in 1996-1998 is provided in WTO (1999b, pp. 87-89. One of the 18 cases was self-initiated by the USTR against Japan and involved Japan's prohibition on certain agricultural products. The United States requested consultation with Japan in the WTO dispute settlement mechanism (DS 76). A panel was appointed and found that Japan had acted inconsistently with the WTO Sanitary and Phyto-Sanitary (SPS) agreement, and the panel report was upheld by the Appellate Body in 1999.

    Earlier in October 1994, the USTR self initiated a Section 301 investigation of Japan's autos and auto parts policies. An agreement was reached in June 1995, but, as noted above, there has not been a significant improvement in the market positions of U.S. and foreign auto firms. The current Automotive Agreement will expire in December 2000.[12]

    In response to a petition filed by the Eastman Kodak Company regarding market access barriers in Japan's photographic film and paper market, USTR initiated a section 301 investigation in

Table 11. U.S. Anti-dumping Investigations, 1980-98

Year	1980 to 1985	86	87	88	89	90	91	92	93	94	95	96	97	98	1980 to 1998
Initiations	218	83	16	42	24	35	66	84	37	51	14	21	15	36	742
Prelim. Det.	156	52	45	35	23	25	43	47	67	46	23	16	16	28	629
Final Det.	107	43	58	17	40	18	28	28	80	31	38	12	15	17	533
Duty Orders	59	26	53	12	24	14	19	16	42	16	24	9	7	9	310
Revocations	37	8	9	0	5	10	7	1	3	28	12	6	4	25	145

Source: Adapted from WTO (1999b, p. 68).

Table 12. U.S. Countervailing Duty Investigations, 1980-98

Year	1980 to 1985	86	87	88	89	90	91	92	93	94	95	96	97	98	1980 to 1998
Initiations	173	28	8	17	7	7	11	22	5	7	2	1	6	11	305
Prelim. Det.	144	28	10	18	6	4	9	26	1	7	3	0	3	7	266
Final Det.	104	22	20	14	12	4	5	7	20	2	6	2	0	2	220
Duty Orders	65	13	14	7	6	2	2	4	16	1	2	2	0	1	135
Revocations	68	4	2	1	5	4	6	0	1	5	35	1	1	4	137

Source: Adapted from WTO (1999b, p. 72).

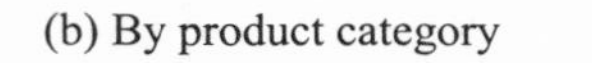

Figure 1. Anti-dumping Duty Orders in Effect on 1 January 1999

Per cent

(a) By country

(b) By product category

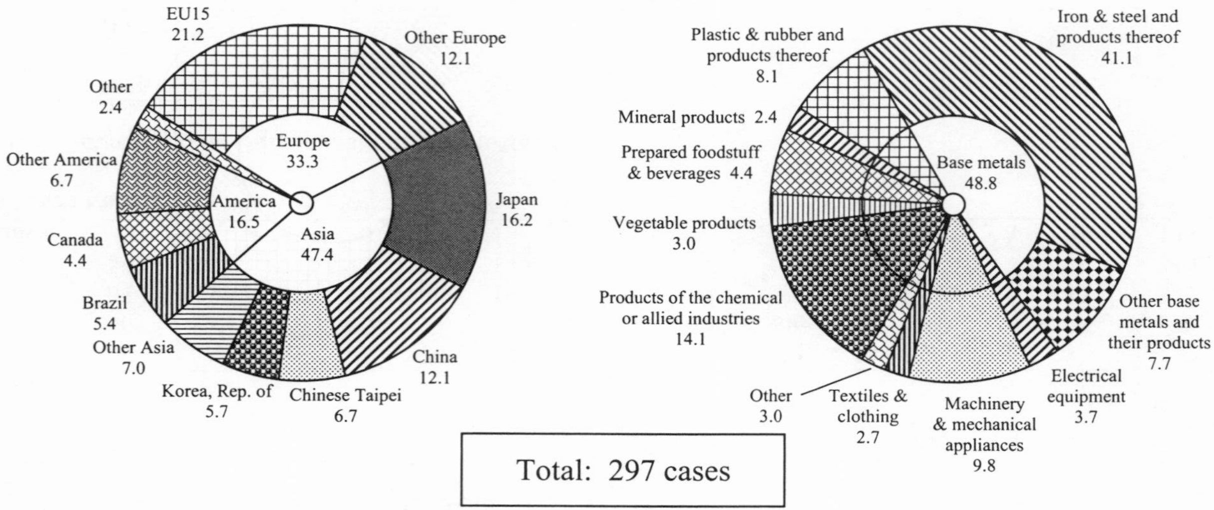

Source: Adapted from WTO Secretariat, based on information provided by the International Trade Administration.

Figure 2. Countervailing Duty Orders in Effect on 1 January 1999

Per cent

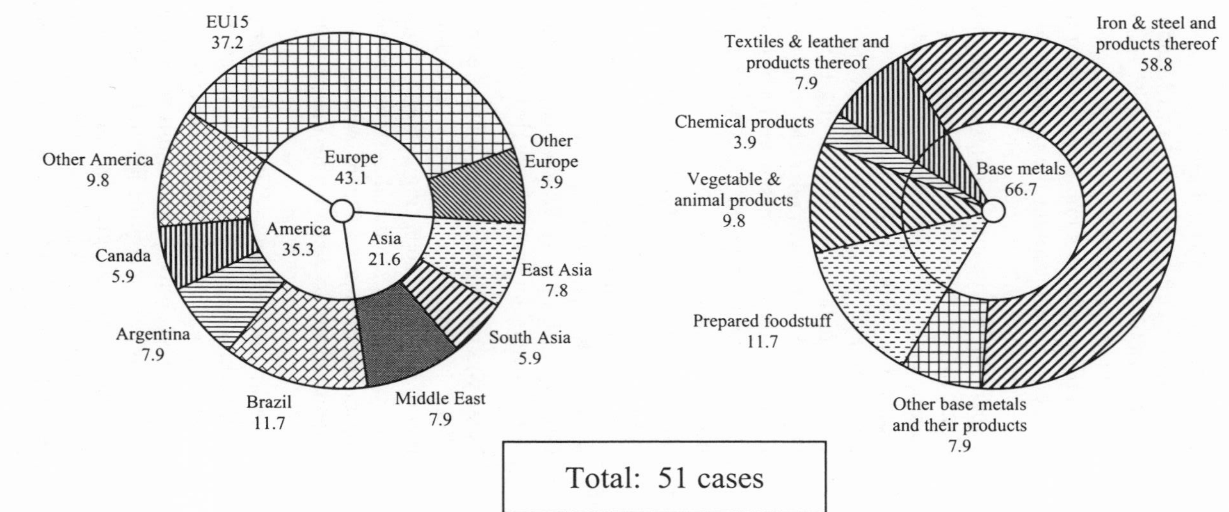

Source: Adapted from WTO Secretariat, based on information provided by the International Trade Administration.

July 1995 and WTO dispute settlement proceedings in June 1996. In January 1998, Japan was found not to be in violation of its WTO obligations. Subsequently, the USTR and Department of Commerce established a monitoring and enforcement committee to review Japan's implementation of its formal representation to the WTO concerning the openness of its market to imported photographic film and paper. Monitoring is continuing.[13]

- **Super 301** provisions were introduced in the Omnibus Trade and Competitiveness Act of 1988 and, after allowing them to lapse subsequently, they were reinstated in March 1994. The USTR is required to submit a report to Congress on U.S. trade expansion priorities and to identify "priority foreign country practices" whose elimination would benefit U.S. exports. This authority lapsed in 1998 but was reinstated on March 31, 1999. No priority foreign country practices were identified as of April 1999, but some dispute settlement cases were announced. None of these involved Japan.
- **Special 301** provides for investigation against "priority foreign countries" that may infringe on U.S. intellectual property rights (IPRs). In its annual *National Trade Estimates Report*, the USTR includes the following Special 301 categories: Priority Foreign Country List; Priority Watch List; Watch List; and Special Mention. Japan is not currently singled out under this authority.

  Japan was downgraded to a "monitored country" in 1997. But the USTR has expressed concern with end-user pirating and protection of digital broadcasting as well as with the protection of trade secrets in Japan's judicial system, protection of confidential information in Japan's Patent Agency, and with the burdens on patent holders to demonstrate that patents were used by infringers.
- **Telecommunications**—Section 1377 of the Omnibus Trade and Competitiveness Act of 1988 requires the USTR to review the operation and effectiveness of U.S. telecommunication trade agreements. Activity under this authority has been greatly expanded following completion and implementation on February 5, 1998 of the WTO Agreement on Basic Telecommunications. The USTR has conducted three reviews since the Agreement came into effect. In 1998, the United States sought new Japanese rules for international service so as to allow competition and to lower retail prices. In 1999, Japan eliminated restrictions on the use of leased lines by new entrants and eliminated a premium charged to competitors for calls to certain NTT customers. In 2000, Japan was called to task for its alleged failure to implement cost-

oriented interconnection rates, and discussions were held to address these issues. On July 18, 2000, it was announced that Japan had agreed to lower substantially its telecommunication interconnection rates.[14]

- **Government Procurement**—Title VII of the 1988 Omnibus Trade and Competitiveness Act has required the USTR to report annually on countries that are in violation of their obligations under the WTO Government Procurement Agreement (GPA) as well as non-signatory countries that are judged not to apply transparent and competitive procurement procedures and that may show evidence of corruption and bribery in procurement practices. This authority expired on April 30, 1996 but was reinstituted on March 31, 1999 and extended to the NAFTA and to other agreements on government procurement to which the United States was a party. Japan has not been singled out under the new authority.

  There is a 1994 U.S.-Japan Public Works Agreement that aims at reforming bidding and contracting procedures for public works in Japan as a means of enhancing transparency, objectivity, and competition as well as strengthening non-discrimination. The United States has continued to express concern about Japan's adherence to this Agreement. The annual consultation provision of the Agreement expired on March 31, 2000, and Japan has to date rejected the U.S. request to extend this provision. Depending on the outcome of discussions, Japan could be singled out under Title VII.

  Following a complaint in April 1996 that Japan's National Police Agency (NPA) was discriminating against a U.S. supplier in a wireless communication system, USTR determined that Japan was potentially in violation of both its WTO government procurement obligations and its obligations under the bilateral government-procurement agreement. The NPA subsequently agreed to reopen the procurement and issued a new Request for Proposals in August 1997.

It is evident from the preceding discussion that the United States pursues bilateral trade policies vis-à-vis Japan in an expressly deliberate manner. Many U.S. actions are designed to promote the interests of U.S. firms seeking greater access to Japan's domestic markets. This raises the question of how effective the U.S. bilateral policies have been in pursuing such greater market access. There have been a number of studies that have addressed the question of effectiveness. Greaney (2000) cites one type of study that relies on public documents and interviews with government and/or industry officials, and a second type that looks more directly at the trade impacts involved. She criticizes the first type of study as being subjective and possibly open to biased assessments, and the second type of study as being too aggregated or not well specified in terms of measuring the trade impacts. Greaney uses industry-level data for 1980-1995, and she finds only a few bilateral agreements and actions that suggest positive trade impacts, and a small number that may involve possible trade diversion rather than trade creation. In her conclusion, she asks why the U.S. Government is so keen to incur the costs involved in negotiating bilateral agreements with Japan when the benefits are so limited. She suggests the reason appears to be that the political gains from the actions taken may outweigh the economic gains.

V. Japan's Bilateral Trade Relations and Policy Initiatives with the United States

The preceding section was devoted to a discussion of U.S.-Japan trade relations and policy initiatives from a U.S. perspective. In this section, I address Japan's perspective on its bilateral relations with the United States. For this purpose, I will rely on the Ministry of International Trade and Industry (MITI) publication, *2000 Report on the WTO Consistency of Trade Policies by Major Countries*. Japan's major issues relating to the United States are listed on pp. iii-iv of the Executive Summary of the Report and discussed at length in the individual chapters. I summarize these issues below:

- **National Treatment Principle**

  Harbor Maintenance Tax (Harbor Services Fee): Since 1987, the United States has imposed ad valorem freight charges of 0.125 percent on imported products involving use of U.S. harbors. Ship owners or exporters voluntarily pay the tax quarterly. The Supreme Court ruled in 1998 that the tax on exports was unconstitutional and exports and exporters were therefore no longer required to pay the tax. In 1995, the U.S. Government introduced a bill to substitute a harbor services fee in lieu of the harbor maintenance tax. But no action has been taken to date on this bill, and there is concern that it may discriminate against foreign freight providers and therefore violate national treatment under the WTO.

- **Quantitative Restrictions**

  Import Restrictions on Yellow-fin Tuna—This is related to the tuna-dolphin case in which the U.S. import restrictions on yellow-fin tuna were found to be in violation of the GATT. The United States agreed that the import restrictions would be removed if an enforceable international agreement were reached in support of the Panama Declaration of 1992 that was designed to regulate the incidental intake of dolphins. The legally binding International Dolphin Preservation Agreement was agreed upon, but the United States has yet to remove the embargo on yellow-fin tuna that it had previously adopted.

Import Restrictions on Shrimp and Shrimp Products—This relates to the so-called shrimp-turtle case in which U.S. restrictions on imports of shrimp were imposed on those countries (including Japan) in which acceptable turtle-excluding devices were not being used. The U.S. measures were found in dispute settlement proceedings to be in violation of the WTO Agreement. But the United States has yet to change its measures to conform with its WTO obligations.

Export Restrictions on Logs—To conserve the habitat of spotted owls, the United States has banned the export of logs from federally owned forests and restricted exports from state-owned forests. However, the United States allows domestic sales of logs without any restriction and promotes exports of lumber. The ban and restrictions on exports of logs thus appear to be designed to protect U.S. domestic lumber mills and may therefore be in violation of the WTO Agreement.

- **Tariffs**

Method of Calculating Tariffs on Clocks and Wristwatches—The United States calculates tariffs on finished clocks and watches as the aggregate of the tariffs on their components. While this method of calculation is not a violation of WTO rules, it fails to take into account that mechanical clocks and watches have been almost completely replaced by new technology that does not lend itself to the breakdown of components. Japan has requested therefore that the United States assign a flat tariff rate to the finished product rather than on the individual components.

- **Antidumping Measures**

As we have already noted in our discussion of U.S. measures designed to deal with alleged, unfair trade practices, antidumping (AD) actions are of major concern to Japan. The most recent U.S. AD actions involve imports of Japanese steel products. But there is a longer history of Japan's complaints that can be cited.

Irregular Governmental Actions in the Super-Computer Case—In May 1996, a bid by the Japanese computer manufacturer, NEC, was selected for a computer system to be procured by the U.S. National Center for Atmospheric Research. However, before the negotiations were completed, AD charges were filed that led to decisions by the U.S. Department of Commerce and by the U.S. International Trade Commission that the U.S. computer manufacturer, Cray Research, had been threatened with material injury. Japan expressed concern that the preliminary analysis that dumping had occurred was announced prior to the beginning of the AD investigation. Japan has requested further explanation from the U.S. Government, and that such anomalous actions be avoided in the future.

Applying Anti-Circumvention Measures—The revised U.S. antidumping (AD) law departs from the WTO AD Agreement insofar as the U.S. law provides for measures to deal with anti-circumvention. Anti-circumvention may arise when companies subject to AD duties try to circumvent the duties by shifting production to the importing country or to third countries and selling from there, or selling products with only minor modifications from those covered by AD duties. The difficulty that arises is that there are no standards for judging whether circumvention exists and how much the AD duties should be. As a result, the investigating authorities have considerable discretion and may decide upon AD duties that obstruct trade. Anti-circumvention measures are to be addressed in the ongoing deliberations concerning the WTO AD Agreement.

Problems Involved in Determining Dumping—The United States has restructured the basis for price comparisons in assessing whether there is dumping. The new elements relate to calculation of the "constructed export price," comparisons at comparable levels of trade, and the offset for indirect selling expenses. As a consequence of the changes, the adjustments to be made when comparing the normal price with the constructed export price are problematic and subject to administrative discretion.

Problems Involved in Determining Injury—The conditions necessary to establish injury to firms in importing countries are not clearly defined in the AD Agreement. The U.S. International Trade Commission must make its preliminary determining regarding injury within 45 days, which may be too short a time for the exporting firms to prepare their arguments about whether there has been dumping and injury. Further, determination of the cause of injury needs to take into account other factors such as changes in trade policies, the presence of subsidies, and how market shares are calculated when domestic producers consume significant proportions of like products internally.

Like Products—The determination of like products poses many difficulties in AD investigations when it comes to calculating AD duties. This determination may therefore be subject to abuse by the investigating authorities, as has been alleged by Japan in the cases of television receivers and color picture tubes that involved differences in technology and were different products as compared to the products under investigation.

Sunset Review—Because past U.S. AD laws lacked a sunset provision, U.S. AD duties have tended to remain in force much longer than in other countries. The new AD Agreement provides for a sunset clause to the effect that AD duties expire automatically after five years unless a review concludes that dumping and injury are still present. In the new U.S. AD law, all AD measures imposed prior to January 1995 are to be reviewed. A total of 46 AD measures against Japan have come up for review. As of January 1, 2000, 21 measures had been terminated, 1 was revoked due to changed circumstances, and 6 were maintained. The remaining 19 are still in process of review and require monitoring to insure that the review is being administered properly.

AD Measures on Steel Products—Since the summer of 1997, AD complaints have been filed against steel products in 12 categories from 25 countries, including Japan. These investigations cover 80 percent of Japan's steel exports to the United States. The Japanese Government has expressed concern about the protectionist aspects of this abuse of the U.S. AD regime, and they have found evidence of violations of the provisions of the GATT and WTO AD Agreements. Japan requested establishment of a WTO dispute settlement panel to deal with the U.S. actions in February 2000.

Problems with the U.S. Antidumping Act of 1916—In November 1998, an AD suit was brought in the Federal District Court of Ohio alleging that nine importers, including three Japanese trading houses, had engaged in dumping with the intention of harming the U.S. steel industry. Japan sought consultations at the WTO on this matter since the 1916 Act provides for compensation for damages and criminal penalties as relief measures rather then tariffs, and the investigation did not follow WTO AD procedures. Japan requested a dispute settlement panel in June 1999, and a final report is expected sometime in the year 2000.

- **Subsidies and Countervailing Measures**
  Actions involving subsidies and countervailing measures are aimed against government practices and are the counterpart of AD measures just discussed. Japan has several concerns about countervailing duties (CVDs) that have been imposed by the United States.

Imposition of Countervailing Duties on Hot-rolled Lead and Bismuth Carbon Steel Products—The issue here involves the U.S. imposition of CVDs in 1995-1997 on certain types of steel products imported from the United Kingdom, even though the companies involved had sold their assets. The United States argued that the conditions responsible for the CVDs were transferred as part of the selling companies. The EU requested a WTO panel, which found that the United States was in violation of the WTO Subsidies Agreement. Japan was an interested third party, in agreement with the EU.

Tax Treatment for "Foreign Sales Corporations"—Since 1985, the United States has allowed foreign sales corporations (FSCs) to exempt a portion of their export income from taxes if their exports contain a specified level of U.S. products. Parent companies can also deduct from their income taxes dividends paid to them by these FSCs. The EU has claimed that this arrangement represented an export subsidy and was in violation of the WTO Subsidies Agreement. A WTO panel was established in September 1998, with Japan as an interested third party. The panel concluded that the arrangement constituted an export subsidy and recommended that the United States eliminate this arrangement by October 2000.

Debt Guarantees for the Steel Industry—Japan has expressed concern about a U.S. program initiated in 1999 to provide a total of $1 billion in debt guarantees for steel makers meeting certain lay-off and production-cut criteria. Since these guarantees may have a negative impact on Japan's steel industry according to the Subsidies Agreement, the arrangement is being monitored by Japan.

- **Safeguards**

  Safeguard Measures on Steel Products—On December 30, 1998, eight U.S. steel mills and the steelworkers' unions filed a petition with the USITC, claiming that an upsurge of imports of steel wire rods was causing serious injury and that safeguard measures be instituted. The USITC commissioners were equally divided in its determinations. On February 11, 2000, President Clinton announced safeguard measures in the form of a tariff-rate quota for a period of 3 years and a day, with an increase in the quota level of 2 percent annually and a threshold level of 1.58 net tons, additional import duties on the quota of 10 percent, 7.5 percent, and 5 percent, respectively, over the three years involved, and exemption for imports from NAFTA members (Canada and Mexico).

  On October 28, 1999, a similar petition was filed with the USITC regarding imports of welded carbon quality line pipe. The USITC commissioners were once again divided. The President announced on the same day, as in the case of steel wire rods, the introduction of safeguard measures that involved additional import duties of 19 percent, 15 percent, and 11 percent in each of the three years to be covered. In both of these cases, the Government of Japan has questioned the USITC findings of serious injury and the particular remedial measures introduced that were considered to be protectionist in intent.

  Lamb Meat—Following a petition on October 7, 1998 by seven American lamb producers and industry associations requesting safeguards action to deal with a claimed upsurge in imports of fresh, chilled, or frozen lamb meats, the president introduced a safeguards arrangement on July 7, 1999. Australia and New Zealand, the major exporters involved, asked for establishment of a WTO panel, which was constituted on November 19, 1999. Japan, Canada, the EU, and Iceland joined as a third party.

  WTO Consistency of Section 201 of the Trade Act of 1974—While Section 201 provides much of the basic structure of the WTO Agreement on Safeguards, Japan has expressed concern about using safeguards on the grounds that they may not be investigated adequately and may be invoked selectively against particular countries. Japan has also noted that voluntary quantitative restrictions on a country's exports are not permitted under the WTO Agreement.

Invocation of Transitional Safeguards—The United States invoked 28 transitional safeguards under the Agreement on Textiles and Clothing (ATC) in the first half of 1995. The ATC was created in the context of the eventual elimination of the Multi-Fibre Arrangement. Following WTO panel rulings in three cases against the United States that were filed by Costa Rica and India, the U.S. rescinded the measures. There remains some concern though about further actions that the United States might take that may be inconsistent with the ATC.

- **Rules of Origin**

Lack of Clarity and Consistency—It appears that U.S. rules of origin are rather complicated insofar as they cover a variety of circumstances in their application: (1) rules for origin marking; (2) rules for enforcement of quantitative restrictions of imports of textile products; (3) rules for enforcing other trade-related measures; (4) preferential rules applied to goods originating in developing countries; and (5) NAFTA rules of origin and origin marking. Rules of origin about marking may be confusing and unpredictable to exporters since they involve determining whether and to what extent a product has been "substantially transformed," and this is done on a case-by-case basis by the U.S. customs authorities. Efforts are underway to harmonize especially definitions of non-preferential rules of origin, but there is a continuing need to determine if the rules are administered in a consistent and impartial manner.

Amending the Rules of Origin for Textile Products—The issue here is to determine the country for which origin will be granted when textile products pass through individual phases of the production process that are performed in different countries. Examples include different countries in which the sewing and cutting of clothing are performed and where the activities of dip dyeing, printing, and other ancillary processes take place. The EU and United States had a WTO dispute about processing and exporting scarves using silk weaves from China and cotton weaves from Turkey and Egypt, and identifying the products as made in the EU. Japan has been an interested party in this dispute that is still ongoing, pending completion of the harmonization of non-preferential rules of origin.

- **Standards and Conformity Assessments**

American Automobile Labeling Act—Since 1992, all passenger cars and light trucks must carry labels indicating their domestic content percentage of value added in the United States and Canada. This system of labeling supposedly will help consumers make better purchasing decisions if they can determine the proportion of the automobile's price produced within the United States/Canada. Japan has countered that the system discriminates against foreign automobiles since: (1) it distinguishes between parts purchased from wholly-owned subsidiaries and independent suppliers; (2) calculations are based on model averages and tend to understate the content of cars produced by foreign automotive makers within the United States; (3) content is calculated at the point of final assembly, but the painting process has to be geographically separate from the location of final assembly, a requirement that discriminates against foreign companies using integrated production systems; (4) content is calculated only in terms of parts prices and excludes the labor and assembly costs for final assembly; and (5) U.S./Canadian content is handled jointly, which may disadvantage countries other than Canada and be in violation of Most-Favored-Treatment.

Regulation of Corporate Average Fuel Economy (CAFÉ)—CAFÉ regulations have required that domestic and imported vehicles be distinguished and their average fuel economy be calculated separately. Problems arise for foreign manufacturers of large cars with low fuel economy insofar as they are not permitted to include small cars with high fuel economy in meeting the CAFÉ regulations. The United States maintained in a case involving the EU that the CAFÉ regulations did not harm commercial interests.

Adoption of the Metric System—The fact that the United States has not adopted the metric system may constitute a significant barrier to international trade since the metric system is used by virtually all other countries in the world. Even though the United States made some commitments to adopt the metric system as part of the Structural Impediments Initiative agreements with Japan, it is estimated that only about 20 percent of private-sector businesses in the United States use the metric system. Japan and presumably other countries are therefore interested in encouraging greater adoption of the metric system in the United States.

- **Trade in Services**

State Regulations for Foreign Insurance Companies—Each U.S. state has its own insurance laws and insurance regulators, and there are no federal laws or regulatory agencies regulating insurance. As a consequence, many states have measures that may discriminate against foreign insurance companies. In the Japan-U.S. insurance pact of 1994 and the additional concessions in the WTO Agreement, the United States committed to: (1) relaxation of state regulations; (2) acceleration of licensing procedures; and (3) relaxation of nationality requirements for corporate executives. There has been some limited progress in improving regulations, but, on the whole, it appears that many regulations are still in place that make market entry difficult for foreign insurance companies.

Basic Telecommunications—While the United States has one of the most open telecommunications markets in the world, there are still some problems with the access of foreign companies to the U.S. markets. New Federal Communications Commission (FCC) regulations on the entry of foreign suppliers came into force in February 1998. The new rules: retain foreign ownership restrictions on wireless telecommunications services; provide the FCC with wide discretionary powers in specifying criteria for "public use" and "extremely high threat to competition" in the review standards for carrier certification and wireless station licensing; may allow licenses to be refused on grounds of "foreign policy and trade concerns"; and permit competing carriers to file petitions for licenses to be refused.

Maritime Services—The United States provides various forms of assistance to its domestic shipping industry. These include: a variety of cargo holding policies that require the use of U.S.-registered ships; retaliatory measures taken under the Jones Act against discriminatory actions by foreign governments that allegedly violate the interests of U.S. shipping; requiring that shippers operating in internal U.S. waters use ships built in or registered in the United States; requiring that U.S. ships with U.S. crews be used to transport Alaskan oil; providing operating cost subsidies for U.S.-registered ships; and giving the U.S. Federal Maritime Commission the authority in 1998 to regulate the shipping fees charged by foreign shipping companies.

- **Protection of Intellectual Property**

Hilmer Doctrine—The United States patent system includes the "first-to-invent" principle, which may negatively affect the stability of patent rights. The U.S. interpretation of the so-called Hilmer doctrine may be in breach of the Paris Convention for the Protection of Industrial Property. That is, the priority date in the Paris Convention has been interpreted judicially in the United States as not preventing the grant of a patent by another applicant.

Submarine Patents—It is possible in the United States for a patent applicant to keep the application secret and intentionally delay the process of patent examination. If, at a later time, a third party merchandises the same technology and there is an infringement of the patent, the original patent holder may collect royalties. In the U.S.-Japan Framework Talks in 1993, the United States agreed to establish an early publication system and to calculate a patent term not from the date on which the patent was granted but from the date the first application was filed. Subsequent legislation has addressed the issue of early publication. But there may still be delays in the U.S. patent-examining process and exemptions in the early publication system that are detrimental to Japanese interests and that need therefore to be monitored closely.

First-to-Invent Principle—The United States is the only country that uses the first-to-invent principle. This differs from the first-to-file principle under which a patent can be granted to the applicant who first filed an application for the same invention. While the first-to-invent principle is not in violation of the TRIPS Agreement, it may make the validity of a patent unpredictable and insecure if later challenged by a first inventor. This may be detrimental to Japanese interests, and it can be argued accordingly that the United States should switch to the first-to-file principle.

Re-examination System—The rights of third parties to request review of the validity of a U.S. granted patent are subject to problems arising from requirements about proving priority and participating in the re-examination process. Although U.S. legislation in 1999 made some improvements in the re-examination system, the difficulties faced by third parties apparently still remain and are in need of resolution.

Trademarks Systems—Section 211 of the Omnibus Act of 1998 states that the United States will not recognize renewal or exercise of rights for trademarks related to assets confiscated by Cuba. This provision appears to be in violation of the national treatment and most-favored-nation obligations of the TRIPS Agreement and is under discussion by interested nations.

Section 337 of the Tariff Act of 1930—This legislation targets unfair import practices by excluding imports that infringe upon valid U.S.-registered intellectual property. The Omnibus Trade and Competitiveness Act of 1988 removed the requirement of injury in actions taken. U.S. practice may be in violation of the national treatment provisions of the GATT, and it may also subject foreign suppliers to lengthy periods arising from the procedures for U.S. enforcement of intellectual property rights. While the United States has improved upon the Section 337 procedures, administrative problems still remain.

- **Government Procurement**

State of Massachusetts Act Regulating State Contracts Business with or in Burma—As mentioned in our earlier discussion of WTO dispute settlement actions, Japan has contended that the State of Massachusetts prohibition on public procurement involving in business with Burma is in violation of the Government Procurement Code. A panel was set up in 1998, but its authority lapsed in February 2000. The U.S. Supreme Court ruled in June 2000 that portions of the Massachusetts law were unconstitutional because they infringed on federal prerogatives.

"Buy American" Legislation—This legislation dates from 1933 and provides that U.S. federal purchasing grant preferential treatment for U.S. domestic products and thus expressly discriminates against foreign products. While some of the provisions of the legislation have been moderated over time, the basic Buy American Act has remained unchanged. There are also procurement laws at the state and local levels that contain provisions similar to the federal Act in giving preferential treatment to government procurement of goods produced domestically and locally. The United States has offered to include 37 states under the WTO Government Procurement Agreement, but adherence to the Agreement in many states has yet to be fully carried out.
National Security Exceptions—The 1994 Government Procurement Agreement permits signatories to use national security as a reason to refuse foreign tenders, but there are no clear standards as to when this would be applied. The issue then is that national security may be used as an excuse to limit competition and thereby improve the competitiveness of U.S. firms.

- **Unilateral Measures**
In Section IV above, I have described the numerous actions taken by the United States in the multilateral and bilateral contexts. The Japanese Government has taken exception especially to the U.S. unilateral measures under Section 301 and related provisions of U.S. Trade Acts. It is worth quoting Japan's official position as stated in MITI's *2000 Report on the WTO Consistency of Trade Policies by Major Trading Partner* (pp. 232-33):

> "The United States is making active use of WTO mechanisms to resolve trade disputes. Such action should be regarded as positive. Nonetheless, it is unfortunate that even after the strengthened WTO procedures took effect, the US stance to use the initiation of Section 301 investigations to pressure trading partners to concede to concessions remains unchanged. It should be noted that the United States has tended to divide issues of concern into 'areas covered by the WTO' and 'areas not covered by the WTO,' while simultaneously initiating WTO dispute settlement procedures and procedures that could be defined as unilateral measures. By using this combination in tandem, the United States maintains that it may use Section 301 to take unilateral measures in areas not covered by the WTO Agreement.
>
> Such activities are, at the very least, contrary to the spirit of the WTO dispute settlement mechanism, which is supposed to be a 'central element in providing security and predictability to the multilateral trading system.' Furthermore, we would like to stress that, even if a dispute is in an area not covered by the

> WTO Agreement, if the unilateral measures themselves violate the Agreement, it would be possible to refer those measures to a panel. Japan's stance to seek a solution according to WTO dispute settlement procedures when a unilateral measure is taken remains unchanged. Japan should also continue to challenge problems on every occasion."

Section 301 and Related Provisions of U.S. Law—In Section IV above, I described briefly the content of and procedures followed under Section 301 and related provisions. It is of interest to indicate Japan's official view of these essentially unilateral measures, as noted in MITI's *2000 Report:*

> **Section 301**—The USTR has broad authority under Section 301 as the result of its investigations to: (1) suspend, withdraw, or prevent the application of benefits of trade-agreement concessions; (2) impose duties and import restrictions on goods; and (3) levy or impose other restrictions on services such as restrictions on market entry for companies from the offending country. (p. 234)
>
> **Super 301**—"Super 301's automaticity introduced a new element of rigidity and unilateralism into US trade laws. Although USTR retained discretion in identifying priorities warranting immediate action, the annual process could prompt a USTR investigation without a petition ever being received from an interested party. In contrast, the decision to initiate an investigation under regular Section 301 procedures normally is prompted by a petition." (p. 241)
>
> **Special 301**—The investigation period under Special 301 is shorter than under the Uruguay Round TRIPS Agreement, which could create difficulties. Further, "The United States says that even if a country is in full compliance with the TRIPS Agreement, it will be designated a priority country if it is found to infringe on U.S. intellectual property rights in areas outside the scope of the Agreement. This stance reflects the U.S. position that unilateral measures without resort to WTO dispute settlement procedures are possible for items not covered by the WTO Agreement." (p. 243)
>
> **Telecommunications**—The two main features of the telecommunications provisions are a mandate for negotiations under threat of unilateral measures and review of trade agreement implementation. As noted above, the United States had taken issue with the high cost of interconnection rates. Following bilateral discussions, Japan has agreed to reduce its interconnection rates.
>
> **Government Procurement**—The United States has expressed concern about Japan's administration of government procurement ar-

rangements involving computers, super computers, construction, and telecommunications. The main issue is whether U.S action that might be taken is in conformance with the WTO Government Procurement Agreement.

Others—"The United States has certain internal laws that provide for the application of unilateral measures to natural and juridical persons outside the United States for trade or security reasons. Many of these laws that set penalties for enterprises that invest in the targeted country seriously constitute barriers to the activities of enterprises, such as direct investment. [These measures]...use domestic laws to determine whether foreign companies are 'violating' the rules according to [the U.S.]...own criteria." (p. 248)

Helms-Burton Act—The Cuban Liberty and Democratic Solidarity Act of 1996 (Helms-Burton Act) was passed in the aftermath of the shooting down of small, private American aircraft by the Cuban military. This Act prohibits trafficking of property that was confiscated by the Cuban Government after 1959 and provides authority to deny U.S. visas to any individuals involved with the confiscation of property. The European Communities (EC) challenged the Helms-Burton Act in the WTO, and a panel was created in October 1996. The EC requested in April 1997 that the panel suspend its work, following diplomatic discussions between the United States and EC and other interested parties concerning less forceful administration of the Act by the United States.

Iran-Libya Sanctions Act—This 1996 Act requires the U.S. president to impose sanctions on any U.S. or foreign person or company that makes investment in petroleum resources in excess of $40 million in these countries. The Act has met with great disapproval by several countries and companies, and, in response, the U.S. Government has not pursued enforcement.

"Excessive" Extraterritorial Application of Competition Law—This issue is not a matter of consistency with WTO rules, but concerns the extraterritorial application of domestic law that is not permissible under international law. "We particularly note that the current US notion to apply antitrust laws extraterritorially to the importing country's domestic market structure based on the "the exporter's benefit" goes beyond the international consensus on extraterritorial application of competition laws." (p. 255)

In Section III preceding, I had occasion to review the main features of U.S. trade policy directed at Japan from the U.S. perspective, and in this section to provide a Japanese perspective on its concerns regarding U.S. trade policy. My reading of the issues is that Japan's two main involve: (1) U.S. resort to anti-dumping (AD) and safeguards actions; and (2) U.S. unilateral measures directed at Japan under Section 301 and related authority. U.S. AD actions diminished during most of the 1990s, but have increased in the past few years. As indicated in Section III, imports of steel products especially from Japan and other supplying countries have become the object of complaints from U.S. producers under both the AD and safeguards provisions of U.S. trade law. While the U.S. responses to the alleged unfair trade practices of foreign exporters are generally consistent with WTO rules, the fact remains that there is a good deal of discretion involved in the way that the U.S. actions are administered. The U.S. steel industry has a long history of invoking AD actions when it feels under pressure from foreign competition, and it has been able to leverage considerable support from the U.S. Executive Branch. From Japan's perspective, it is necessary accordingly to resist AD protectionist pressures by seeking more transparent administration of the U.S. AD and safeguards authorities, in particular the ways in which dumping margins are calculated and whether or not and the extent to which U.S. steel firms have been seriously injured by imports.

Japan has been highly critical of the use of Section 301 and related provisions in U.S. law because they can be applied unilaterally and may not be WTO consistent. The United States is the only major trading nation that has such unilateral authority, and it is a continuing bone of contention for all of the countries at which the authority may be directed. It was believed with the creation of the WTO and the strengthening of the Dispute Settlement Mechanism that the United States might reduce its use of unilateral measures. Yet, as has been noted, the broad Section 301 authority is still widely used. This is the case even though it has been difficult to find clear evidence that the actions involved have had much effect in expanding U.S. exports to the countries being targeted. By the same token, it can be argued that U.S. pressures on Japan to change certain specified domestic policies and regulations may be in Japan's interest and can result in improved efficiency and gains in welfare. It seems clear that it would be preferable to use the WTO process to deal with these issues rather than relying on bilateral negotiations. Yet, we have to take as given the structure of U.S. unfair trade laws and the ways in which firms and workers can bring their self-interested pressures to bear on the Executive Branch and the Congress. Therefore, Japan and other countries must decide which U.S. unilateral initiatives and actions are acceptable to them on efficiency and welfare grounds and which initiatives and actions should be contended by resorting to the WTO process.

VI. Regional Trade Policy Initiatives

Both the United States and Japan are engaged in a number of regional arrangements. For the United States, this includes the North American Free Trade Agreement (NAFTA), which became effective in January 1994, and ongoing discussions and negotiations for a Free Trade Area for the Americas (FTAA). Both the United States and Japan are members of the Asia Pacific Economic Cooperation (APEC) forum. In an especially noteworthy change in its trade policy, according to the *Financial Times*, May 12, 2000, p. 1, Japan has recently been involved in discussing possible free trade agreements with Singapore and South Korea, and there has been some mention of similar arrangements with other Asian countries and possibly Mexico and Chile. There has also been some discussion of a so-called ASEAN Plus-3 free trade agreement in which Japan, China, and South Korea would join together with the ASEAN nations.[15]

Each of these regional arrangements raises the possibility of trade diversion. This has been of concern in the case of NAFTA, given the tariff differentials involved and the somewhat restrictive rules of origin that apply in such key sectors as textiles and clothing and automobiles. Thus far, however, there does not appear any clear evidence suggesting that trade diversion has occurred, especially since, as Krueger (2000) has noted, Mexico has increased its exports considerably not only to the United States but to non-NAFTA countries as well since the inception of NAFTA in 1994. The other regional initiatives noted are still in the discussion stages, and some time will elapse before any final negotiations are completed.

V. Conclusion

An effort has been made in this chapter first to provide background on some of the main features and patterns of the exports and imports of goods and services of the United States and Japan as well as the inward and outward foreign direct investment of the two nations. I then reviewed the multilateral dimensions of each nation's trade policies, focusing especially on the dispute settlement actions implemented since the creation of the World Trade Organization in 1995. This was followed by a lengthy discussion of U.S.-Japan bilateral trade relations and policies in recent years from the perspective of each nation. Regional trade relations and policies were also discussed briefly.

I had occasion to review the trade policies of Japan and the United States not too along ago in Stern (1996, 1998). What I find interesting in looking back is that the trade-policy relations of these two nations seem to have entered a relatively quiescent period in comparison to the often heated policy disputes that had arisen in previous years. This change in atmosphere may be attributed in part to the increasingly important role that the dispute settlement mechanism has played since the creation of the WTO. It may also reflect the differences in the economic performance of the two economies during the 1990s, with rapid and sustained economic growth in the United States and continuing stagnation in Japan. It is fairly well established that protectionist pressures are sensitive to macroeconomic conditions. This is borne out by the data showing a significant decline in the use of anti-dumping (AD) and countervailing actions in recent years by the United States. An important exception is evidence that U.S. AD actions have increased noticeably in the past two years, especially with regard to imports of steel, which is a sector of still great importance to Japan. The question then is whether U.S.-Japan trade relations will become more conflictual if there is a significant decline in the U.S. rate of economic growth.

Another factor of importance is Japan's apparent progress in recent years in promoting domestic deregulation in a number of key sectors. As a result, access to Japan's domestic market has been eased with respect both to imports of goods and services and inward FDI.[16] These changes may portend more favorable conditions for Japanese firms domestically as well as in external trade, as efforts are continued to encourage more rapid economic growth to overcome the long period of stagnation.

A final point concerns the recent decisions by Japan to seek bilateral free trade agreements with important trading partners in Asia and in the Western Hemisphere. It is not clear whether this is a reaction to the problems being encountered in initiating a new round of multilateral negotiations. But whatever the explanation, it marks a potentially important departure in Japan's support of the multilateral trading system and the concern of the possibility of trade diversion that could be detrimental to global welfare.

Notes

[1] More disaggregated data would also show net imports of such manufactured goods as pharmaceuticals, aircraft, and precision instruments.

[2] The Ministry of Finance data on foreign direct investment can be accessed at: http://www.mof.go.jp.english/e1008.htm.

[3] For other discussion of dispute settlement, see Chapter 5 by William Davey, Chapter 14 by Gary Saxonhouse, and Chapter 16 by Robert Howse.

[4] It should be noted that the total number of complaints (218) in Table 10 reflects individual cases involving more than one country requesting consultation with the respondent.

[5] As noted in Davey (2000), Japan has been frequently involved as a party and third party in WTO dispute settlement proceedings. These cases have involved in particular the automotive sector, antidumping measures, intellectual property, and U.S. Section 301 actions.

[6] For details, consult U.S. Department of Commerce and The Office of the U.S. Trade Representative (1999).

[7] See "White House Report to the Congress" (1999) for a statement on conditions in the steel industry and an action plan that encompasses: bilateral efforts to counter unfair trade practices and strong enforcement of U.S. laws; consideration of escape-clause (Section 201) safeguards actions; an early warning system to monitor import trends; restoration of global economic growth and ensuring market-based reform; tax relief for the steel industry; and adjustment assistance for steelworkers and their communities.

[8] See Office of the United States Trade Representative and United States Department of Commerce (1999) for the second report on access to Japan's photographic film and paper market.

[9] See Office of the United States Trade Representative (2000) for the third report under the U.S.-Japan Enhanced Initiative on Deregulation and Competition Policy.

[10] See "Comments of the United States Government on the Draft Report on Electricity Transmission by the Electric Utility Industry Council, Joint Subcommittee on Basic Policy Instruments and Electricity Charges," June 18, 1999.

[11] See Chapter 6 above by J. Michael Finger, Francis Ng, and Sonam Wangchuk for an empirical analysis of anti-dumping actions initiated by WTO member countries.

[12] See U.S. Department of Commerce and The Office of the U.S. Trade Representative (1999) for a report on autos and auto parts.

[13] See footnote 6 above.

[14] See Office of the United States Trade Representative, Press Release 00-55.

[15] See Chapter 2 above by Drusilla Brown, Alan Deardorff, and Robert Stern for a computational assessment of these bilateral free trade agreements.

[16] For some journalistic commentary on the changes that have been taking place, see the news articles in the *Wall Street Journal*, "Converging Forces: Distress, Deregulation and Diplomacy Breach Walls of Fortress Japan—Tokyo's Pragmatic Embrace of Western Investment Leads to a Trade Détente," December 28, 2000, p. A1; and "A Kinder, Gentler Way to Pry Open Japan: 'Post-Revisionists' Believe Collaboration Will Work Better Than Threats," January 11, 2001, p. A14.

References

"Comments of the United States Government on the Draft Report on Electricity Transmission by the Electric Utility Industry Council, Joint Subcommittee on Basic Policy Directions," June 18, 1999, http://ustr.gov/reports/usjpelec.pdf.

Davey, William J. 2000. "Japan, WTO Dispute Settlement and the Millennium Round," in Robert M. Stern (ed.), *Issues and Options for U.S.-Japan Trade Policies*, University of Michigan Press, forthcoming.

Executive Office of the President of the United States. 2000. *2000 Trade Policy Agenda and 1999 Annual Report of the President of the United States on the Trade Agreements Program.* USTR, Washington, D.C., March.

Fukao, Kyoji and Keiko Ito. 2000. "Foreign Direct Investment and Services Trade: The Case of Japan," prepared for the NBER Eleventh Annual East Asia Seminar on Economics, *Trade in Services*, June 22-24, Seoul, Korea.

General Agreement on Tariffs and Trade (GATT). 1995. *Trade Policy Review: Japan 1994.* Geneva: GATT Secretariat.

Greaney, Theresa. 2000. "Do U.S.-Japan Bilateral Trade Agreements Affect International Trade," in Robert M. Stern (ed.), *Issues and Options for U.S.-Japan Trade Policies*, University of Michigan Press, forthcoming.

Hoekman, Bernard and Michael M. Kostecki. 1995. *The Political Economy of the World Trading System: From GATT to WTO.* Oxford: Oxford University Press.

Krueger, Anne O. 2000. "NAFTA's Effects: A Preliminary Assessment," *The Americas Edition 2000, The World Economy* 23:761-775.

Office of the United States Trade Representative and United States Department of Commerce. 1999. "Access to Japan's Photographic Film and Paper Market: Report on Japan's Implementation of Its WTO Representations," June 9, http://www.ustr.gov/reports/index.html.

Office of the United States Trade Representative. 2000a. "Third Joint Status Report under the U.S.- Japan Enhanced Initiative on Deregulation and Competition Policy," July 19, http://www.ustsr.gov/reports/index.html.

Office of the United States Trade Representative. 2000b. "USTR Releases Super 301, Special 301 and Title VII Reports," Press Release 00-30, Washington: D.C., May 1.

Office of the United States Trade Representative. 2000c. "United States and Japan Agree on Interconnection Rates," USTR Press Release 00-55, http://ustr.gov/releases/index.html.

Organization for Economic Cooperation and Development (OECD). 1999. *International Direct Investment Statistics Yearbook 1999.* Paris: OECD.

Stern, Robert M. 1996. "The Trade Policy Review of Japan," *The World Economy, Global Trade Policy 1996* 19:133-155.

Stern, Robert M. 1998. "The WTO Trade Policy Review of the United States, 1996," *The World Economy* 21:483-514.

U.S. Department of Commerce and The Office of the U.S. Trade Representative. 1999. "Report to President William Jefferson Clinton of the Interagency Enforcement Team Regarding the U.S.-Japan Agreement on Autos and Auto Parts," June 3, http://ustr.gov/reports/index.html.

"White House Report to the Congress on Steel." January 7, 1999, http://www.ustr.gov/reports/index.html.

World Trade Organization. 1999a. *International Trade Statistics 1999.* Geneva: WTO.

World Trade Organization. 1999b. *Trade Policy Review: United States 1999.* Geneva: WTO, September.

World Trade Organization. 2000. "Overview of the State-of-play of WTO Disputes." http://www.wto.org/wto/dispute/ bulletin.htm, 23 March.

Comment

Yoko Sazanami

Robert Stern provides an excellent and comprehensive overview of U.S-Japan trade and FDI issues from the late 1980s to present. This is a period when the U.S. government has aggressively tried to open up the Japanese market. The response of the Japanese government has been well documented in the Ministry of International Trade and Industry's publication entitled *Report on the WTO Consistency of Trade Policies by Major Countries,* originally entitled *Whitepaper on Unfair Trade*. The major portion of the *Whitepaper on Unfair Trade* was devoted to pointing out the harmful effects of taking unilateral action to back up U.S. domestic interests of specific industries.

I share Stern's view in his Conclusion, in which he mentions that the two nations seem to have entered a relatively quiescent period compared to previous years. I agree that the dispute settlement mechanism in the WTO has played a very important role in alleviating frustrations on the Japanese side, both among government officials and the public at large, as reflected in the Japanese press.

I may stress one more reason for this recent quiescence. The bilateral policy initiatives policy to improve U.S. access in certain services—telecommunications, financial services, insurance and distribution in particular—by pressuring Japanese government for deregulation, have been effective in helping not only American but also other foreign firms to penetrate the Japanese market in the late 1990s.

According to notification data compiled by the Ministry of Finance in Table 1, Japanese outward FDI was on the average 9.5 times larger than inward FDI for the period between 1991 and 1997. In 1998 and 1999, this ratio was reduced to 3.9 times and 3.1 times, respectively. The industrial breakdown of Japanese inward FDI is in Table 2. The share of inward FDI in non-manufacturing,—telecommunication, trade & commerce, finance & insurance, service and others—in the total increased from 61% in 1997 to 77% in 1998. The data from the same source reports that inward FDI from North America (mostly representing FDI from the United States) in 1998 reached 352 billion yen in finance & insurance and 225 billion yen in services. In 1999, the share of non-manufacturing in total inward FDI was 59%, reflecting the large investment by Renault in manufacturing to help the restructuring of Nissan Motors. This investment pushed France to top of the list of Japanese inward FDI in the same year.

Deregulation policies carried out by the Hashimoto government's initiative were necessary in order to restructure the Japanese economy. However, when the weak recovery in 1995/1996 was aborted by fiscal tightening—specifically the increase in the consumption tax (VAT) rate from 3% to 5%—pessimistic sentiment among the public began to spread and the slowdown in household spending pushed Japan into recession. In the fall of 1997, bankruptcies of larger financial institutions such as Yamaichi Securities, Sanyo Securities, and Hokkaido Takushoku Bank triggered fears of weakening financial strength of the Japanese financial sector. In particular, the banks' huge bad loans and consequent credit crunch trying to recover their ailing balance sheet further aggravated the slump.

The political struggle between the ruling Liberal Democratic Party (LDP) and the opposition Democratic Party (DP) continued even after Prime Minister Hashimoto's resignation. The DP laid the responsibility for Japan's ailing financial sector to the bad policy response on the part of the LDP. In the meantime, the stock prices of banks listed on the Tokyo Stock Exchange started to decline towards the spring of 1997. The downfall of the Long-term Credit Bank and its subsequent nationalization had to wait until a new rescue law was enacted in 1998.

The financial turmoil of 1997/1998 evidently changed the public sentiments toward mergers and acquisitions (M&A) and toward foreign acquisition of Japanese financial institutions in particular. In 1999, GE Capital took over Nihon Leasing, for which the Long-term Credit Bank had formerly acted as main bank. Ripplewood Holdings and other U.S. firms bought out the Long-term Credit Bank in the same year. By 1999, some of the barriers to entering the Japanese market that foreign business had most frequently complained about, such as high housing costs and difficulty in recruiting talented Japanese staff were less heard owing to the post-bubble fall in land prices and increased mobility in labor market. Although it is still difficult to predict when these changes will pull the Japanese economy out of its decade-long current recession, it is clear that some changes are starting.

"Restructuring" implies that some people who used to enjoy vested interests will be hurt by the change. Japan faced multiple troubles in 1997. This was especially true for Japanese banks, with 70% of cross-border lending directed to Asia. The fall in the Thai baht in July 1997 and the subsequent downturn of the Asian economies put serious strain on Japanese business, including firms in the manufacturing field that had built networks with local firms in the region starting in the 1980s.

A number of reasons can be pointed out for Japan's recent interest in regional agreements, including the reported bilateral Free Trade Agreements (FTA) with Singapore and Korea. Since the success of Asian high growth in the 1980s and 1990s depended on liberalization of trade and investment, disappointment over U.S. leadership in launching a new trade round in Seattle was greater in Asia than in other regions. Also, in Japan, there were overt complaints expressed about the IMF policy response at the time of the Asian crisis.

There is strong business interest in FTAs as voiced as in the recent Keidanren Report, *Jiyuboeki Kyotei no Sekkyoku-teki na Suishin o Nozomu* (Toward an Aggressive Initiative for a Free Trade Agreement) published on July 18, 2000. The report points out four advantages of FTAs: (1) FTAs can expand business opportunities among member countries; (2) European and American countries are intensifying FTA relationships. Japanese firms must try to overcome the disadvantage of not being a member country. For example, as a result of the Mexico-EU FTA, European firms can export automobiles and electric machinery at a 10-20% tariff rate; (3) by joining, Japan can accelerate structural reform; and (4) FTA rules can complement liberalization in trade and foreign direct investment by supplementing the rules not covered by the WTO.

At the end let me present my own views on why Japan is joining FTAs and concluding bilateral trade agreements in Asia. From the experience with deregulation in Japan, depriving vested interests of advantages they have enjoyed in the past requires strong political will. An FTA can bring additional political and economic pressure for the change by removing entry barriers to foreign as well as domestic firms, including public enterprises. For the same reasons, a Japan-Korea Free Trade Agreement should include liberalization in services that require commercial presence of service providers as the first priority. The Asian financial crisis revealed the lack of a regional framework that can function as a safety net. To this end, a swap agreement between ASEAN plus three (Japan, China, and Korea) concluded in May 2000, can be one step forward. It was reported (the Nihon Keizai Shimbun, May 7, 2000) that the agreement includes an information-sharing mechanism regarding economic as well as financial conditions of member countries.

Table 1. Japanese Inward and Outward FDI, 1991-1999*

	1991	1992	1993	1994	1995	1996	1997	1998	1999
(1) Inward FDI	590	531	359	433	370	771	678	1,340	2,399
(2) Outward FDI	5,686	4,431	4,151	4,281	4,957	5,409	6,623	5,217	7,439
(2)/(1)	9.6	8.4	11.6	9.9	13.4	7.0	9.8	3.9	3.1

* Fiscal year April/March, figures are based on ex post facto report or prior notice.

Source: Adapted from http://www.mof.go.jp/1c008.htm (accessed date 10/23/2000).

Table 2. Japanese Inward FDI by Industry, 1991-1999*

	(billion yen)								
	1991	1992	1993	1994	1995	1996	1997	1998	1999
Manufacturing Total	258	208	184	206	141	311	267	313	979
Machinery	60	83	78	134	18	156	145	213	865
Other manufacturing	198	125	106	72	123	155	122	100	114
Non-Manufacturing Total	332	322	174	228	228	459	412	1,028	1,420
Telecomunication	14	6	3	3	5	2	3	17	330
Trade & commerce	107	155	100	114	68	166	100	176	348
Finance & Insurance	120	19	4	69	100	27	162	457	512
Services	74	107	24	37	49	236	89	318	206
Others	17	35	43	5	6	28	58	60	24
TOTAL	590	530	358	434	369	770	679	1,341	2,399

* Fiscal year April/March, figures are based on ex post facto report or prior notice.

Source: Adapted from http://www.mof.go.jp/1c008.htm (accessed date 10/23/2000).

Comment

John Ries

Overview

This paper is nicely written and provides a wealth of information about U.S.-Japan economic relations. Stern has done an impressive job of culling information from a variety of sources on trade, FDI, and international economic policies. He not only provides detailed FDI and trade data but also comprehensive lists and descriptions of trade cases and policy initiatives. It will serve as an excellent reference for those interested in Japanese and U.S. economic relations.

Stern concludes that the current state of economic relations is relatively amicable. The data support this view. The review of WTO cases between the two countries reveals only nine cases initiated in the period 1995-2000, with the majority of these already resolved. Currently, there are no countervailing duties on Japanese products. Moreover, bilateral negotiations have resulted in 38 agreements aimed at opening Japanese markets. These include insurance, flat glass, and automobile parts.

The only areas where there appears to be contention is U.S. antidumping duties and trade in steel products. These areas, of course, are not mutually exclusive as many of the 48 existing antidumping orders targeted towards Japan are for steel products. The United States continues to be concerned about Japanese steel imports and seems willing to use the tools at its disposal to reduce Japanese import penetration.

Comments

1. The current relatively positive relationship between Japan and the United States is a consequence of a number of factors.
   (a) As documented by Stern, there seems to have been general progress made at the negotiating table. The 38 market-opening trade agreements have relieved frictions in important sectors. Moreover, negotiations furthering the deregulation of service industries serve the interests of both nations—the United States gains market access whereas Japan benefits from improved market orientation and the infusion of competition and efficient practices.
   (b) The continued robustness of the U.S. economy: With joblessness at extreme lows, there is little need to point fingers at imports and perceived unfair trade practices.

(c) A more contentious view is that there has been a narrowing of ideological differences. It has been argued that Japanese business has traditionally been governed by market forces, government direction, and inter-firm cooperation. Consequently, government has been reluctant to surrender its control by allowing unfettered foreign competition and, when it has, foreign firms have been thwarted by cooperative arrangements between Japanese firms. The severe economic problems experienced by Japan and the success of the U.S. economy arguably have led to a fuller embrace of the market in Japan. This, in turn, has created a more open environment for deregulation and increased market access.

2. It seems remarkable that Japan continues to run large merchandise trade surpluses. Stern's figures show a $107.5 billion surplus for 1998. I am curious how this persistent surplus squares in the balance of payments. Some of it is offset by a $48.9 billion deficit in commercial services shown in Stern's paper. However, as a large creditor to the world, I would imagine Japan enjoys a large surplus in capital services. Thus, I presume that there is a large current account surplus that has to be offset by a capital account deficit. But how does Japan continue to be in a position to lend capital? With its financial-market turmoil, aging society, and government fiscal deficits, I have difficulty understanding Japan as a lending nation. I think this issue has implications for the future. When the U.S. economy turns down, people will see again see a trade surplus with Japan as a "problem" that the U.S. government must deal with. It would comfort me to know that future macroeconomic conditions will dictate a reduction or elimination of Japanese trade surpluses. However, I see little sign of that in the data presented by Stern.
3. Trade and the environment: A future problem area? An extremely problematic area for trade regulation concerns issues related to trade and the environment. Nations adopt measures ostensibly aimed at protecting public health or conserving natural resources. However, these measures may result in bans on imports of particular goods. Cases in point are the EU's ban on hormone-treated beef and the U.S. restrictions on the imports of shrimp. A developing trade dispute concerns EU restrictions on genetically modified (GM) foods. The problem is that the WTO has not exhibited consistency in dealing with this issue. To begin with, it is not clear whether these regulations even violate the GATT agreement. The GATT allows "internal regulatory measures" that do not discriminate between foreign and domestic goods. Thus, even import bans are not considered as violations when viewed as part of a non-discriminatory internal regulatory measure. There has been some inconsistency in GATT/WTO dispute resolution as to when such measures are GATT violations and hence require justification as an Article XX exemption. Another area of ambiguity is determining whether a measure is a "least-restrictive measure." A measure must be least restrictive in order to qualify for the exemption. Finally, en-

vironmentalists are applying extreme pressure for the WTO to accept the so-called "precautionary principle" as a basis for trade-restricting legislation.

The point is that there is much latitude for trade-restricting measures ostensibly aimed at protecting health or resources. The United States is under pressure from environmental groups to use trade policy as a tool for furthering environmental goals. For Japan, agricultural liberalization threatens powerful vested interests that might lobby for restrictions disguised as environmental protection measures.

Conclusion

Like Stern, I see a fairly positive picture. My only worry is that a downturn in the U.S. economy may give rise to renewed antagonism towards Japanese bilateral trade surpluses. I am also concerned that inconsistent treatment of trade restricting measures purportedly aimed at protecting health and the environment will provide an avenue that may be exploited by protectionist interests.

CHAPTER 14

Dispute Settlement at the WTO and the Dole Commission: USTR Resources and Success*

Gary R. Saxonhouse

I. The Passage of the Uruguay Round Agreements and the Dole Commission

After more than seven years of negotiation the Uruguay Round concluded with an historic agreement on December 15, 1993. Exactly four months later documents implementing this agreement were signed by representatives of the 117 Uruguay Round participants at a ministerial meeting at Marrakesh, Morocco. Even so, this signed agreement required ratification at home by the relevant legislative bodies of the agreement signatories.

Ratification of the Uruguay Round Agreements was viewed as virtually certain in all countries except the United States. While the new World Trade Organization was set to begin operations on January 1, 1995, as late as October, 1994, Senate Finance Committee Chair, Daniel Patrick Moynihan, could claim only 26 committed yes votes.[1] Many senators, including the Republican Minority Leader, Robert Dole, were said to be concerned about the WTO's newly enhanced Dispute Settlement Mechanism (DSM). The critical element of the revised DSM is the absence of the right of any country acting alone to block the formation of a Dispute Settlement panel or the adoption of panel findings. As the DSM had operated under the GATT, veto power was held, effectively, even by the accused party. In fact, this power was used in significant instances by losing parties to block adverse panel findings against them.[2] Under the WTO, however, panels get set up and proceed with their investigations and panel findings are adopted unless the WTO Council decides otherwise by consensus.[3] This is the polar opposite of the older *modus operandi*, and it was the loss of national sovereignty implicit in this new arrangement to which many senators objected.

That there should have been Congressional objections to the new DSM is ironic. In the 1988 Omnibus Trade Act that gave the Reagan Administration fast-track authority for the Uruguay Round, Congress mandated U.S. trade officials "to negotiate for more effective and expeditious dispute settlement mechanism and procedures" that would "enable better enforcement of U.S.

rights."[4] Actually, the inclusion of such language in the Trade Act of 1988 should be no surprise. U.S. interest in a revised DSM is of very long standing. Already during the Tokyo Round, the United States pressed both for an end to the single country veto and for expedited procedures.[5]

In Fall 1994, populist fears about the loss of sovereignty to the WTO were such that Senator Dole reported that his office was receiving 2,000 phone calls a day from opponents of the Uruguay Round Agreement.[6] Notwithstanding, on November 23, 1994, he agreed to support the enabling legislation and to encourage all Republican senators to support it in exchange for White House support for a Dole-conceived WTO "escape hatch." The escape hatch would be embodied in legislation to be introduced the following year that would establish a WTO Dispute Settlement Review Commission.[7] Dole intended that

- The Commission would consist of five Federal appellate judges appointed by the President in consultation with the leadership of both Houses and Chairmen and Ranking Members of the Senate Finance Committee and the House Ways and Means Committee.
- It would review all final WTO dispute settlement reports adverse to the United States to determine whether the panel exceeded its authority or acted outside the scope of the agreement. Following issuance of any affirmative determination by the Commission any member of either House would be able to introduce a joint resolution calling on the President to negotiate new dispute settlement rules that would address and correct the problem.
- If there were three affirmative determinations in any five-year period, any member of either House could introduce a joint resolution to disapprove U.S. participation in the WTO – and if the resolution were enacted by Congress and signed by the President, the United States would commence withdrawal from the WTO.

II. The History of the Dole Commission

Despite the wide-spread publicity given the Clinton-Dole WTO agreement and despite the Senate having passed the WTO implementing legislation on December 1, 1994, in the six years that have ensued, the so-called "Dole Commission" has not been set up. As early as January 4, 1995, on the very first day of the new Congress, with Republicans in control of both Houses for the first time in forty years, Senator Dole introduced legislation creating the Commission.[8] The bill was identical with the terms of the late November agreement with the exception of one significant provision. Section 7 of the proposed legislation would have guaranteed participation by private parties in the proceedings before the dispute-settlement panels.

Guaranteeing participation of private parties in dispute-settlement-panel proceedings, while it did not deter many of the Senate's leading figures on trade policy from co-sponsoring the bill, including Senators Moynihan, Baucus, D'Amato, Grassley, Murkowski, Lott, Pressler, Santorum and Simon, it was as controversial in 1995 as it is today.[9] The hearings held by the Senate Finance Committee on the Dole legislation found wide disagreement on this issue between two former Deputy United State Trade Representatives. Alan Wolff argued such private participation was necessary because

> "... even the best lawyer cannot do a first-rate job if he or she does not have the time or resources to devote to a case. The reality is that these very capable people at USTR are already overworked and if the WTO system spawns even more international trade litigation before panels, they will be stretched even thinner .... The result is that the United States will lose cases it should win."[10]

Alan Holmer countered that

> "... in dispute settlement, the U.S. Government needs to be able to act efficiently and speak with one voice. This is not a mere theoretical issue. Some WTO cases will involve issues that have a direct economic impact on dozens of U.S. industries, trade associations, or companies. Will each of them have the right to represent the interests of the United States before the panel? What if, while supporting the overall U.S. Government position (USG), their view of the law or the facts is different from that of the USG? Moreover, inevitably there will be differences in strategic approaches to cases, particularly where the best U.S. legal argument in one case may have a detrimental interest in another case. The role of the Administration in dispute settlement proceedings is not to represent one company or interest group. Rather, its role is to represent the national interest."[11]

The Clinton Administration took Ambassador Holmer's side in this dispute and refused to support the legislation as Senator Dole had submitted it.[12] It was only in the following November that the original Dole legislation was re-introduced, this time with offending Section 7 removed.[13] In his eagerness to have this legislation passed prior to the beginning of the 1996 presidential primaries in which he would be a candidate and in which he would face protectionist opposition, Senator Dole agreed to allow Robert Byrd, a very senior Democratic member of the Senate, to submit an amendment that would set up two new WTO review commissions in addition to the one comprised of members of the Federal judiciary. One commission would consist of senators whose mandate would be to review all aspects of the WTO's workings and to recommend legislation wherever appropriate. This commission of senators would be advised by a second commission comprised of trade lawyers, former government officials, scholars and labor leaders.[14]

The Byrd Amendment doomed the Dole legislation. Key members of the Senate Finance Committee, led by its Chair, William Roth, changed their views and now opposed the Dole proposal fearing first, that the new commission of senators would be a threat to the Finance Committee's jurisdiction over trade issues, and, second, that the private-sector commission would be prone to domination by special interests.[15] This latter concern was also shared by the Clinton Administration. One last attempt was made to pass this legislation during the last few days before Senator Dole's resignation from the Senate. A compromise was reached to drop the new commission of senators and to refashion the private sector commission so that 1) half the nominees would be appointed by the White House and 2) the new commission would report directly to the Senate Finance Committee and the House Ways & Means Committee.[16] Notwithstanding this compromise, opposition from protectionist textile interests, who were hostile to anything that might legitimize the WTO in any way, was sufficient to prevent the legislation from coming to a vote at that time.[17] In fact, while periodically re-introduced, the legislation was not voted on in that Congress at all, nor in any subsequent Congress.[18]

III. Congressional Review of WTO Treatment of U.S. Interests

While the WTO Dispute Settlement Review Act has never been passed by Congress and does not have any immediate prospect of passage, the sovereignty issues raised at the time that it was under active consideration remain politically salient. There may be no federal judiciary review of WTO decisions adverse to U.S. interests, but the Uruguay Round Agreements Act does require a five year review for the Congress by the USTR of U.S. participation in the WTO.[19] This report appeared in late February 2000. At that time, by USTR's count, 32 WTO cases in which the United States had been involved in a significant way had been completed. Of these cases, the United States prevailed in 24, either as a result of a Dispute Settlement panel finding or because of a settlement highly favorable to U.S. interests prior to a formal panel report being issued. The USTR, emphasizing both the large number of cases in which the United States prevailed, particularly as a plaintiff, and the overall high win-rate, concluded that the DSM is operating in a way highly beneficial to U.S. interests.[20] By implication, by these indices, the USTR suggests that the fears that spawned the original interest in the Dole Commission were unwarranted. Indeed, the U.S. rate of success with the DSM since the WTO commenced is slightly better than it was during the 1980s when the DSM first came to be used intensively as means of resolving trade disputes.[21]

Whatever the views of the USTR, and irregardless of the non-existence of the Dole Commission, the same section of the Uruguay Round Agreements Act that provides for a five-year review of U.S. participation in the WTO, also provides that within 90 days of Congress receiving this report, just as with the Dole Commission bill, any member may introduce a joint resolution of both Houses calling for U.S. withdrawal from the WTO.[22] Such a resolution must be placed on the calendar for action no later than 45 days after being introduced. If passed by the Congress and signed by the President, it would trigger U.S. withdrawal subject to the six months advance notification required by the

WTO's Article XV. In response to the USTR's five-year report and citing the eight decisions that have gone against the United States, a joint resolution calling for U.S. withdrawal from the WTO was introduced within a matter of days of the report's release.[23] Because of the expedited schedule required by the Uruguay Round Agreements Act, hearings were held on the resolution within a month of its filing. A little more than two months after hearings were held, the resolution was voted down on the House floor by a margin of 363 to 56, a margin of victory much wider than the 288-146 vote on whether to join the WTO in November, 1994.[24] Notwithstanding the December 1999 turmoil at the failed WTO Summit in Seattle, Congressional support for the WTO was stronger than it had been five years earlier. Significantly, during the floor debate on the joint resolution, the USTR's high rate of success at the WTO was raised repeatedly by opponents of the resolution.[25]

IV. Resources and U.S. Performance at the WTO

It is possible that the absence of a review commission composed of respected jurists may actually increase the political sensitivity of each adverse WTO outcome for the United States and lead to undue focus on quantitative indicators of success at the DSM. In this connection, the resources that the USTR has at its disposal to pursue litigation at the WTO does become an issue. It may be as Alan Wolff forecast in his testimony before the Senate Finance Committee that the USTR is losing cases it should win at the WTO because its lawyers are "overworked."[26] While it may seem obvious that more resources should strengthen the position of the United States in international economic disputes, senior U.S. trade officials have often taken the opposite view. Ambassador Mickey Kantor, when he was USTR, argued that his agency's great virtue was its small size, and that this small size was the key to its success.[27] Whether because of Ambassador Kantor's views, or because of the constraints imposed by the large Federal budget deficits that Congress faced during much of the 1990s, despite the creation of the WTO, NAFTA, and APEC, to mention just a few new responsibilities, until the very last months of the Clinton Administration, USTR was no larger than it was in 1993 when the Clinton Administration took office.[28] USTR had 203 full-time equivalent authorized positions in both fiscal year 1993 and in fiscal year 2000. In recent years, USTR Charlene Barshefsky regularly asked for, but was denied large increases in her staff.[29] Finally, only a few months before her departure from public life, Congress did approve Ambassador Barshefsky's request for 25 new full-time, career positions within USTR.[30]

V. Resources, Success and Success Rates

Now that the USTR's size is changing, what can be expected to happen to U.S. performance at the WTO? To analyze this issue, and leaving aside until Section VII of this paper all questions of strategic behavior including reactions of trading partners,[31] assume that the USTR has the utility function:[32]

$$U\left(a(X,\delta), b(X,\delta) \right) \ ,$$

where

a(X, δ) is the proportion of cases won at the WTO

b(X, δ) is the number of cases won at the WTO

X is the number of cases brought before the WTO

δ is the resources the USTR will use above the minimum K required per case

The utility function posited here reflects USTR interest, as evident in its recent report on U.S. performance at the WTO, and in the Congressional debate on continued U.S. participation in the WTO, in its success-rate as well as in its total number of wins. Note further that f(y) is the 'base' probability that case number 'y' is won by the US, with f '(y)<0, that is, potential WTO cases can be ordered according to their probability of success on the assumption that only K resources are used per case. The probability of success can be affected by δ g(δ) is the increased likelihood that any particular case is won due to 'extra' resources (independent of which case):

$g'(\delta)>0,\ g''(\delta)<0$ with $\quad lim_{\delta \to \infty}\ g(\delta) < 1 - lim_{X \to 0}\ f(X)$

(Impossible to guarantee any win).

The problem for the USTR is:

$$Max_{X,\delta} U\left(\underset{+}{a(X,\delta)}, \underset{+}{b(X,\delta)} \right) subject\ to\ (K+\delta)X \le m,$$

where m is the total resources available to the USTR.

VI. The Comparative Statics of the USTR's Problem

The total number of U.S. wins at the WTO is clearly increasing in USTR resources[33]

$$\frac{db}{dm} = \overset{+}{\frac{db}{dX}}\overset{+}{\frac{dX}{dm}} + \overset{+}{\frac{db}{d\delta}}\overset{+}{\frac{d\delta}{dm}} \ .$$

This presumably is the relationship that Ambassador Wolff had in mind. Once again, as in the USTR report on the WTO, Congressional debate on continued U.S. participation in the WTO, and Ambassador Barshefsky's own Congressional testimony makes clear, however, there is also interest in a, the rate of success. Here the results are ambiguous:

$$\frac{da}{dm} = \overset{-}{\frac{da}{dX}}\overset{+}{\frac{dX}{dm}} + \overset{+}{\frac{da}{d\delta}}\overset{+}{\frac{d\delta}{dm}},$$ which can be positive or negative.

This can be restated as the effect that marginal resources have on the marginal success rate depends on the effect of marginal resources on the impact of each of the USTR's two possible uses of these resources:

Resources per U.S. case at the WTO
Number of U.S. cases at the WTO

Using the results from Appendices 1 and 2, decreasing (increasing) $g''(\delta^*)$, that is a lessening (increasing) of the effect of above-minimum resources K per case, decreases (increases) the denominator of $\frac{d\delta}{dm}$, and therefore $\frac{d\delta}{dm}$ is increased (decreased) while $\frac{dX}{dm}$ is decreased (increased), thereby increasing (decreasing) $\frac{da}{dm}$. In other words, the less (more) rapidly the effectiveness of marginal resources used per case ($g''(\delta^*)$) is falling (from the equilibrium amount of resources per case, $K+\delta^*$), the greater (smaller) the share of any increase in marginal resources will be used to increase resources per case. Because resources per case is what is assumed to increase WTO success rates, less (more) rapid marginal decline in the effect of resources used per case correspond with greater resources increasing (lowering) success rates.

Decreasing (increasing) $f''(X^*)$, that is, increasing (decreasing) the rate at which the 'base' success rate is falling at X^*, decreases (increases) $\frac{d^2a}{dX^2}$ (guaranteeing the Hessian given in Appendix 1 is negative semi-definite) and decreases (increases) the denominator of $\frac{d\delta}{dm}$. Once again $\frac{d\delta}{dm}$ is increased (decreased), $\frac{dX}{dm}$ is decreased (increased) and $\frac{da}{dm}$ is increased. This means the more rapidly (slowly) the probability of success with a new case at the WTO ($f'(X)$) is falling (from the marginal U.S. WTO case, X^*, in equilibrium), the lower (higher) the share of any marginal increases in resources that will go towards bringing additional U.S. cases at the WTO. Instead, more of these marginal increases in resources will go towards increasing resources per case (starting new cases) and therefore to higher (lower) success rates.

The impact that USTR preferences have on the allocation of its resources can be seen with the use of the first-order conditions:

$$(K+\delta)X = m\text{, and therefore } X = \frac{m}{K+\delta}$$

Substituting this into $U_a g'(\delta) + XU_b g'(\delta) = X\lambda$ gives:

$$((K+\delta)U_a + mU_b)g'(\delta) = m\lambda .$$

Suppose there is an increase (decrease) in importance to the USTR of the success rate. Because utility is homogeneous in degree zero the comparative statics for such a change are the same sign as if U_a is increased (decreased) and U_b decreased (increased) in the ratio necessary to leave λ unchanged. Since $g''(\delta)<0$ and the above condition must hold for all utility functions, δ must increase (decrease). Given $X = \frac{m}{K+\delta}$, this means that X must decrease (increase). Because the USTR success rate at the WTO is increasing in δ and decreasing in X, the success rate increases (decreases).

The results in this section are also presented in figure 1.[34] m^o is the original resource constraint, m' is the new resource constraint, and w_{USTR} is the USTR iso-welfare curve through the original equilibrium. a^o is the locus of points with a^o proportion of wins, and b^o is the locus of points with b^o wins. Points to the left (right) and below (above) a^o represent a higher (lower) proportion of wins than a^o . Points to the right (left) and above (below) b^o represent a higher (lower) number of wins. With the new resource constraint m', if the new equilibrium is to the left (right) and above (below) a^o, this will be the outcome most consistent with Ambassador Wolff's (Kantor's) 1995 Congressional testimony. Where this new equilibrium will be depends critically (though not exclusively) on the shape of a^o, which, in turn, depends on $g''(\delta)$ and $f''(y)$.

It does appear that the view implicit in Congressional appropriations for USTR until last year, and explicit in Ambassador Kantor's remarks, under some conditions, can be correct. Less resources for the USTR can mean a higher success rate. In thinking about this issue, it is important to keep in mind that it is the USTR itself that ultimately controls the number of U.S. cases that go before the WTO. The more cases the USTR allows to go before a dispute settlement panel, the more cases it will win. But assuming the cases with the highest chance of success at the WTO are taken there first, the more cases it will also lose.[35] To the extent that both the number of successes and the rate of success are politically salient, there is a trade-off here. The trade-off will depend on how quickly the probability of success in an additional case taken to the WTO declines by comparison with how much investing additional resources on cases already at the WTO raises the probability of success with them. Depending on how much the USTR values the number of successes versus success rates will determine together with these two factors how its resources are allocated. If additional cases bring with them very low probability of success by comparison with investing additional resources in existing cases, new resources for the USTR will raise both the success rate and the number of wins. Paradoxically, if there remain promising cases that are not being

Figure 1. Equilibrium

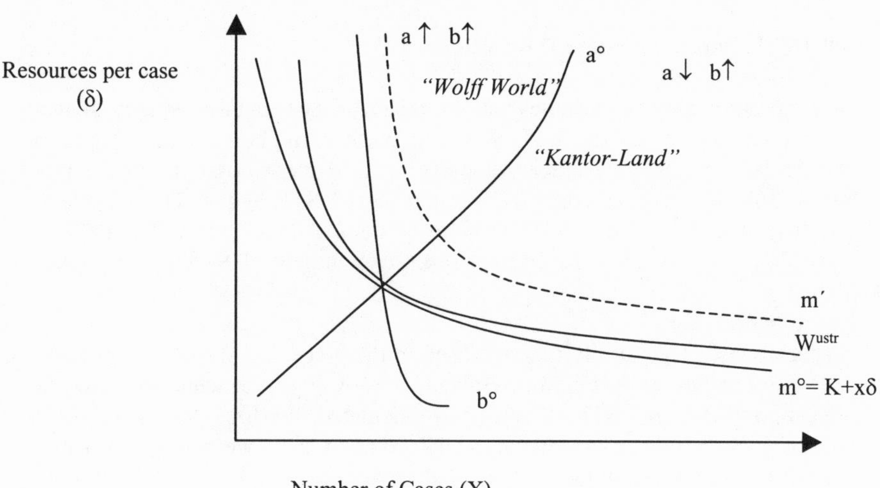

brought to the WTO because of a lack of resources, new resources for the USTR can lower its rate of success at the WTO even while it increases the number of wins.

VII. USTR Behavior and MITI Reactions

The preceding analysis assumes that the USTR values all cases equally. It also does not discuss reactions that U.S. trading partners might make in response to an increase in USTR resources. Suppose instead these possibilities are now allowed for in a simple example.[36] Assume that USTR and MITI are contesting two cases before the WTO Dispute Settlement Mechanism. The issue is how USTR and MITI will split their resources. Suppose USTR's utility function is

$$U = \alpha a + \beta b^*,$$

a special case of the utility function used in the preceding sections. While a is still the win rate with wins unweighted, b* now weights wins according to their importance to USTR. When b* is calculated, the first case is weighted more significantly than the second. USTR gives Case 1 a weighting of 1, while Case 2 is given a weighting of w.

$$1 > w > 0$$

is the amount USTR weights a win in Case 2. As before, the more resources USTR uses per case, the greater the chance of winning that case. Once again, K resources are the 'base' resources used per case (here set exogenously to 0). τ are the additional resources the USTR will use for the first case. n represents total USTR resources (set exogenously to 1).

MITI is assumed to have a utility function of the same form as USTR.

$$U' = \rho c + \theta d^*$$

c is MITI's win rate and d* is its weighted number of wins. For MITI, Case 1 also has a weight of 1, while Case 2 is weighted h with

$$1 > h > 0$$

As is likely, both USTR and MITI will find Case 1 more important. For MITI, as for USTR, the more resources, the more likely a case will be won before the USTR. K are the base resources that MITI uses per case (here also set exogenously to zero). γ are the extra MITI's resources used for Case 1. m are MITI's total resources (also set exogenously to 1)

As before, there is an exogenous 'base' probability that USTR will win each of the two cases. This probability is denoted f(1) and f(2) for Cases 1 and 2, respectively. Resources affect USTR chances according to the following relationship, also a special case of the function used in the preceding sections.

$$g(case) = -e^{-\nu\tau} + e^{-\nu\gamma} - \mu\tau\gamma$$

where

v > 0 is a measure of the effect of extra resources (set exogenously to 2)

$\mu > 0$ is a measure of the degree of strategic interaction (set exogenously to 1).

For the purposes of illustration here, it is assumed that USTR acts as a strategic substitute. The more resources that MITI puts on one case, the less valuable USTR's resources on that case become, and the less resources USTR wants to put on that case. The opposite is true for MITI. It acts as a strategic complement.[37] The more resources that USTR puts on a case, the more valuable MITI's resources on that case become and the more resources that MITI wants to put on that case.

From the above, USTR maximizes

$$(.5\alpha+\beta)(f(1)-e^{-v\tau}+e^{-v\gamma}-\mu\tau\gamma+(.5\alpha+x\beta)[f(2)-e^{-v(1-\tau)}$$
$$+e^{-v(1-\gamma)}-\mu(1-\tau)(1-\gamma)],$$

with the first-order condition:

$$(1-w)(\beta(ve^{-v\delta}-\mu\gamma)-\mu(\frac{1}{2}\alpha+\beta)(n-2k)=0.$$

The second-order condition is satisfied for the assumed parameters:

$$-(1-x)\beta(v^2e^{-v\tau})<0$$

In the same way, MITI maximizes

$$(.5\rho+\theta)(1-f(1)+e^{-v\tau}-e^{-v\gamma}-\mu\tau\gamma)+$$
$$(.5\rho+w\theta)[1-f(2)+e^{-v(1-\tau)}-e^{-v(1-\gamma)}+\mu(1-\tau)(1-\gamma)] \quad ,$$

with the first-order condition:

$$(1-h)\theta(ve^{-v\gamma}+\mu\tau)-\mu(\frac{1}{2}\rho+h\theta)(m-2k)=0.$$

Once again, the second-order condition is satisfied for the assumed parameters:

$$-(1-h)\theta(v^2e^{-v\gamma})<0.$$

Table 1 summarizes the equilibria for the setup just presented. The base case assumes $\alpha = \beta = \rho = \theta = 1$ and h = w = 0.5. Values of .05 for h and w mean that Case 1 is much more important to both USTR and MITI than is Case 2.

The baseline in Table 1 indicates how USTR and MITI divide the extra increment of resources that each gets. Despite USTR and MITI both valuing the first case twenty times more than the second, USTR, unlike MITI, will devote a disproportionate amount of its resources to Case 2. This result follows from the assumption that the USTR acts as a strategic substitute and MITI as a strategic complement.

Δ1 explores what happens when USTR puts less of a weight on Case 2 than does MITI. Unsurprisingly relative to the baseline, USTR becomes more likely to win Case 1 and less likely to win Case 2. More surprisingly in Δ2, when USTR puts more weight on Case 2 than does MITI, giving USTR more

Table 1. USTR and MITI: Likelihood of Success with Incremental Resources and Differential Weights on Outcomes

		Baseline	Δ 1a	Δ 1b	Δ 2a	Δ 2b	Δ 3	Δ 4a	Δ 4b	Δ 5a	Δ 5b
	α	1	1	1	1	1	1	1.25	1.5	1	1
	β	1	1	1	1	1	1	1	1	1	1
	ρ	1	1	1	1	1	1	1	1	1.25	1.5
	θ	1	1	1	1	1	1	1	1	1	1
action	δ	0.1825	0.21	0.24	0.16	0.14	.1845	0.15	0.12	.225	.265
action	γ	0.8093	0.75	0.67	0.78	0.75	.7612	.771	.732	.705	.601
	h	.05	0.1	0.15	0.05	0.05	.075	0.05	0.05	0.05	0.05
	x	0.05	0.5	0.5	0.1	0.15	.075	0.05	0.05	0.05	0.05
result g (case 1)		-.6437	-.59	-.52	-.6408	-.637	-.6137	-.6415	-.6431	-.552	-.4473
result g (case 2)		.332	.203	0.05	0.27	0.21	.2298	.25402	.1772	.1134	-.073

resources, when MITI will get matching resources, will make it less likely that USTR will win Case 2 while it is more likely to win Case 1 relative to the outcome in the baseline. With Δ3 the more important USTR and MITI find Case 2 relative to Case 1, the more likely relative to the baseline, USTR is to win Case 1, but the less likely it is to win Case 2.

Δ4 and Δ5 explore how the allocation of incremental resources for USTR and MITI changes when, unlike the baseline and the preceding simulation, USTR and MITI place different weights on the success rates and the winning of cases weighted by their importance. Surprisingly for Δ4 the more importance that USTR places on the success rate relative to MITI, the less likely it is to win Case 2, while becoming no more likely to win Case 1. For Δ5, and in contrast with the results for USTR, if MITI places relatively more importance on success rates than does USTR, MITI becomes more likely to win Case 2, but somewhat less likely to win Case 1.

From the perspective of the issues discussed in the preceding section, in each instance (though least for the base case), extra resources actually lower the success rate for USTR. Even for Δ4, the more important the success rate for USTR, with extra resources for both USTR and MITI, the lower the success rate is likely to be for them. Unlike the preceding section, this finding does not follow from extra resources encouraging USTR to take on additional cases with a low probability of success. Rather as a strategic substitute, it is poorly suited to improve its welfare in an environment where both sides have more resources. For example, were USTR to attempt to bring only the first case and not the second to the WTO, both USTR and MITI would put all their resources on this case and g(1) = - 1. For the setup here, it makes sense for USTR to try both cases. The results for MITI, which are the exact opposite of those for USTR, show that for a strategic complement, more resources can lead to both a higher success rate and a greater likelihood of winning the most important cases notwithstanding USTR getting the same increment in new resources.

VIII. Consistency and the Use of the WTO Dispute Settlement Mechanism

Since the enhancement of the DSM with the creation of the WTO, there has been an upsurge in its use. During the 1980s, 127 complaints were taken to the DSM.[38] During its first five years of operation alone, the WTO's DSM has received 185 complaints.[39] U.S. use of the DSM reflects these general trends. Between 1980 and the beginning of 1990, the United States brought 39 complaints to the DSM.[40] Between 1995 and the beginning of 2001, the United States has brought 60 complaints.[41] This implies an increase in the annual incidence of complaining to the WTO by the United States of over 200%.

The greatly increased U.S. use of the DSM cannot be the result of increased resources. In the late 1990s, the USTR budget has been no greater than it was in the 1980s. Nor does it seem likely, given all the emphasis on USTR's success rate a, that in recent years more emphasis is being put on total successes b.[42] Rather, it has been suggested that the WTO's DSM might be used more often now because the Uruguay Round Agreements texts, being new, are inherently ambiguous.[43] A more predictable environment allows parties to a conflict to save themselves the trouble of using up scarce resources by resolving their dispute outside the WTO, anticipating what would happen if they went through the DSM process. While this is a plausible view of the relationship between uncertainty and the use of the DSM, in theory, the inverse relationship is also plausible. Consider the following.

Suppose USTR has a case that it believes has merit φ. It is assumed USTR's information about the merit of the case that it can take to the WTO is private information.[44] If USTR takes the case to the DSM, it will get:

$$(1 - \rho)\,\varphi + \rho\,\varepsilon\,,$$

where ρ is a noise parameter and ε is a population mean of a random drawing of possible remedies for USTR's complaints. Both USTR and MITI know ρ and ε. If $\rho = 1$, the DSM result is pure noise, if $\rho = 0$, there will be an outcome with merit φ. Suppose that MITI offers p settlement to USTR. MITI gets $-p$, if USTR accepts but $-[r+(1-\rho)\varphi+(\rho\varepsilon)]$ if USTR rejects where n is the resource cost of pursuing the case at WTO.

USTR will accept p if $p \geq (1-\rho)\varphi + \rho\varepsilon$ or $(p-\rho\varepsilon)/(1-\rho) \geq \varphi$. MITI's expected payoff (not knowing φ) is:

$$pF[\frac{p-\rho\varepsilon}{1-\rho}] + \int_{\frac{p-\rho\varepsilon}{1-\rho}}^{\infty} \{(1-\rho)\varphi + \rho\varepsilon + r\}dF(\varphi),$$

where F is prior on φ.

Solving for offer p in equilibrium, the first-order condition is:

$$F[\frac{p-\rho\varepsilon}{1-\rho}] + \frac{p}{1-\rho}F'[\frac{p-\rho\varepsilon}{1-\rho}] - \frac{p+r}{1-\rho}F'[\frac{p-\rho\varepsilon}{1-\rho}] = 0\ ,$$

or $(1-\rho)\frac{F}{F'} = r$,

when F is uniform $p = \varepsilon\rho + n$ ($\varepsilon = ½$).

In this case USTR will accept if:

$$r \geq (1-\rho)\varphi \text{ or } \frac{r}{1-\rho} \geq \varphi\,.$$

Thus, with a uniform distribution, more noise ρ:

1) increases offer p;

2) increases the probability that the conflict will not be taken to the WTO.

This suggests that it may not be a new, untested and unpredictable WTO that is generating more cases. In fact, the set-up allows the inference that perhaps the new WTO's DSM is more rather than less predictable than the GATT's forty-year old DSM.[45] The speed and automaticity (panel findings accepted except if opposed by a consensus of WTO Council Members) of the new DSM may make the whole WTO more predictable than before, notwithstanding the inevitable vagueness of a new trade treaty.[46] And, because it is more predictable than before, it is being used.[47]

IX. Conclusions

At the time the Uruguay Round Agreements were passed by Congress, particular concern was expressed about their implications for U.S. national sovereignty. Concern was sufficiently great that the Clinton Administration committed its support to the creation of a commission that would review each adverse decision against the United States by the WTO. The commission was designed such that the outcome of its review process might trigger a serious Congressional consideration of U.S. withdrawal from the WTO.

While the so-called Dole Commission was never created, the Congressional controversy surrounding the ratification of the Uruguay Round Agreement has led to particular concern with USTR performance at the WTO. Curiously, enhanced Congressional concern has not gone hand in hand with more resources for USTR. Over the 1990s, USTR has rarely asked for, and, until 2000 has not received additional resources for its work.

The analysis here shows that if the USTR is concerned not only about the number of cases it wins but also about its rate of success, having more resources may have an ambiguous impact on the USTR's rate of success. Depending on how relatively promising are the additional cases that may yet be brought by USTR to the WTO, and how usefully additional resources may be applied to existing cases, it is possible that more resources can lower USTR's success rate. This is true, though for different reasons, when explicit allowance is made for the response by the other party to the dispute to a USTR commitment of additional resources.

More resources cannot explain the increased use that the USTR has made since the WTO was established, because until recently USTR has received no additional resources. Rather, a more predictable DSM may have encouraged more rather than fewer cases to be brought to the WTO in preference to further efforts at extra-WTO bilateral settlements.

Appendix 1

The problem for the USTR is:

$$Max_{X,\delta}U\left(a(\underset{+}{X},\delta),b(\underset{+}{X},\delta)\right) \textit{ subject to } (K+\delta)X \le m.$$

Note the success rate, $a(X, \delta) = \frac{1}{X}\int_0^X f(y)dy + g(\delta)$ with:

$$\frac{da}{dX} = \frac{1}{X}f(X) -- \frac{1}{X^2}\int_0^X f(y)dy < 0$$

$$\frac{d^2a}{dX^2}=\frac{1}{X}f'(X)-\frac{2}{X^2}f(X)+\frac{2}{X^3}\int_0^X f(y)dy \gtrless 0$$

$$\frac{d^2a}{dXd\delta}=0$$

$$\frac{da}{d\delta}=g'(\delta)>0$$

$$\frac{d^2a}{d\delta^2}=g''(\delta)<0$$

and the number of wins, b(X, δ)= $Xa(X,\delta)=\int_0^X f(y)dy+Xg(\delta)$

$$\frac{db}{dX}=f(X)+g(\delta)>0$$

$$\frac{d^2b}{dX^2}=f'(X)<0$$

$$\frac{d^2b}{dXd\delta}=g'(\delta)>0$$

$$\frac{db}{d\delta}=Xg'(\delta)>0$$

$$\frac{d^2b}{d\delta^2}=Xg''(\delta)<0\,.$$

The USTR's problem written as a LaGrangean is:

$$L(X,\delta,\lambda)=U(a(X,\delta),b(X,\delta))-\lambda((K+\delta)X-m),$$

which leads to the first order conditions

$$\frac{\partial U}{\partial a}\frac{da}{dX}+\frac{\partial U}{\partial b}\frac{db}{dX}=(K+\delta)\lambda$$

$$\frac{\partial U}{\partial a}\frac{da}{d\delta}+\frac{\partial U}{\partial b}\frac{db}{d\delta}=X\lambda$$

(K+δ)X=m.

The Hessian here is:

$$\begin{bmatrix} \frac{\partial U}{\partial a}\overset{><0}{\frac{d^2a}{dX^2}}+\frac{\partial U}{\partial b}\overset{<0}{f'(X)} & \frac{\partial U}{\partial b}g'(\delta)>0 \\ \frac{\partial U}{\partial b}g'(\delta)>0 & \frac{\partial U}{\partial a}g''(\delta)+\frac{\partial U}{\partial b}Xg''(\delta)<0 \end{bmatrix}.$$

The Hessian is negative semi-definite as long as g'(δ) is not too big, and $\frac{d^2U}{dX^2}$, (the top left corner) is negative.

Appendix 2

Totally differentiating the first-order conditions given in Appendix 1 with respect to (X, δ,λ, m) leads to:

$$\frac{\partial U}{\partial a}\left(\frac{d^2 a}{dX^2}\frac{dX}{dm}\right)+\frac{\partial U}{\partial b}\left(f'(X)\frac{dX}{dm}+g'(\delta)\frac{d\delta}{dm}\right)=\lambda\frac{d\delta}{dm}+(k+\delta)\frac{d\lambda}{dm}$$

$$\frac{\partial U}{\partial a}\left(g''(m)\frac{d\delta}{dm}\right)+\frac{\partial U}{\partial b}\left(g'(\delta)\frac{dX}{dm}+Xg''\frac{d\delta}{dm}\right)=\lambda\frac{dX}{dm}+X\frac{d\lambda}{dm}$$

$$(K+\delta)\frac{dX}{dm}+X\frac{d\delta}{dm}=1$$

These three equations can be solved as a system to find $\frac{dX}{dM}$ *and* $\frac{d\delta}{dm}$.

$$\frac{d\delta}{dm}=\left[X+\frac{1}{K+\delta}\left(\frac{-U_b(K+\delta)Xg''(\delta)-U_a(K+\delta)g''(\delta)-X\lambda}{U_b(K+\delta)g'(\delta)-U_aX\frac{d^2a}{dX^2}-(K+\delta)\lambda}\right)\right]^{-1}$$

and

$$\frac{dX}{dm}=\frac{1}{(K+\delta)}\left(1-X\frac{d\delta}{dm}\right)$$, or δ and X are substitutes.

Notes

* The first four sections of this paper rely on the research assistance of Chan Ho Song. Rodney Wallace played a major role in formulating Sections V and VI as did Joel Sobel with Section VII. Their help is much appreciated and none of them are to blame for the context within which their insights and analyses have been used. The comments of CGP Conference participants are also much appreciated, particularly those of Theresa Greaney, Jude Hays, Rob Howse, T. N. Srinivasan and David Weinstein.

[1] See the discussion on this point in Ernest H. Preeg, *Traders in a Brave New World* (Chicago: University of Chicago Press, 1995) p. 182.

[2] Alan Wm. Wolff, "Hearing on the WTO Dispute Settlement Review Commission Act," Senate Finance Commission, Washington, D.C., May 10, 1995.

[3] John H. Jackson, "Testimony Prepared for the U.S. Senate Finance Committee Hearing, March 23rd, 1994 on Uruguay Round," University of Michigan Research Forum on International Economics Discussion Paper No. 353. Panel findings can be brought to the Appellate Body by the losing party. The decisions of the Appellate Body are adopted by the WTO except where a consensus of the WTO Council decides otherwise.

[4] Alan Wm. Wolff, "Hearing on the WTO Dispute Settlement Review Commission Act."

[5] John H. Jackson, "Strengthening of the Dispute Settlement Function and Future GATT Activities," in *The Uruguay Round: Appraisal and Implications for Investment Trade and Investment*, Tokyo: Fair Trade Center, p. 182. Already during the years prior to the WTO's establishment, no country (or even the EC as a whole) made more use of the DSM than did the United States. Almost one-third of all cases brought to the DSM stemmed from complaints by the United States. See Robert E. Hudec, *Enforcing International Trade Law: The Evolution of the Modern GATT Legal System* (Salem, New Hampshire: Butterworth Legal Publishers, 1993) p. 316.

[6] Peter Behr, "Dole Joins President on GATT," *Washington Post*, November 24, 1994. The strength of populist sentiment fanned by import-competing industries has led some political scientists to argue that the new DSM by removing the single country veto may allow national political leaders too little flexibility in dealing with aggrieved domestic interests. This lack of flexibility may stifle further liberalization. See, for example, Judith Goldstein and Lisa L. Martin, "Legalization, Trade Liberalization and Domestic Politics: A Cautionary Note," *International Organization* Vol. 54 No. 3 Summer, 2000, pp. 603-632, and George W. Downs and David Rock, *Optimal Imperfection?: Domestic Uncertainty and Institutions in International Relations*, Chapter 4 (Princeton, NJ: Princeton University Press, 1995). Not all observers agree that the WTO's DSM allows political leaders little flexibility. Monika Butler and Heinz Hauser, "The WTO Dispute Settlement System: A First Assessment from an Economic Perspective," *The Journal of Law, Economics and Organization*, Vol. 16, No. 2, October, 2000, pp. 503-534, appear to conclude just the opposite.

[7] The establishment of such a review commission as a by-product of the passage of controversial legislation is not unprecedented. The Spring 2000 discussion of a joint White House Congressional commission with powers to review human rights, labor policies and development of the rule of law in China in connection with legislation to grant China permanent Most-Favored Nation status is just the latest instance of the use of this device. For example, see Joseph Kahn, "To Aid Trade Bill, Democrat Creates Plan for Rights Panel," *New York Times*, May 4, 2000.

[8] Congressional Record Senate Volume 141 No. 1, January 4, 1995.

[9] Keith M. Rockwell, "Dole Prepared to Compromise on WTO Review Panel Plan," *Journal of Commerce*, May 11, 1995, p. 3A.

[10] Alan Wm. Wolff, "Hearing on the WTO Settlement Review Commission Act."

[11] Alan E. Holmer, "Hearing on the WTO Dispute Settlement Review Commission Act," Senate Finance Commission, Washington, D.C., May 10, 1995.

[12] Alan Wm. Wolff and John A. Ragosta, "How the Uruguay Round Will Change the Practice of International Trade Law in the United States" (July, 1996).

[13] United States Senate Bill No. 1438, 104th Congress (November 30th, 1995).

[14] John Maggs, "Dole Makes Another Push for WTO Oversight Bill," *Journal of Commerce*, December 6, 195. p. 3A.

[15] John Maggs, "Dole Unlikely to Pass WTO Bill in '95," *Journal of Commerce*.

[16] John Maggs, "Dole Paves Way for Commission to Review WTO," *Journal of Commerce*, June 10, 1996, p. 3A.

[17] John Maggs, "Dole Gives Bill Final Push," *Journal of Commerce*, June 12, 1996, p. 3A.

[18] See, for example, House of Representatives Bill No. 4706, 106th Congress, 2nd Session, June 21, 2000. This bill, introduced at the time of the floor debate of a resolution that would lead to U.S. withdrawal from the WTO, includes only those provisions to which the Clinton Administration had originally agreed 5-1/2 years earlier. While this bill had bi-partisan sponsorship, it had no chance of passage.

[19] Office of the United States Trade Representative, *2000 Trade Policy Agenda and 1999 Annual Report of the President of the United States on the Trade Agreements Program* (Washington, D.C., 2000), Chapter 2.

[20] Both export industries and import-competing industries appear to agree that a higher USTR success rate at the WTO is an indication that the revised DSM is working in accord with U.S. interests. See James McCall Smith, "Domestic Politics and WTO Dispute Settlement Reform," paper prepared for delivery at the 2000 Meeting of the American Political Science Association. See also Chapter 5 by William Davey and Chapter 13 above by Robert Stern and Chapter 16 below by Robert Howse for other discussion of dispute settlement.

[21] In 77 cases in the 1980s, as either plaintiff or defendant, the United States prevailed in 57. Overall, for the period between 1948 and 1998 in 125 cases, the United States prevailed in 84. See Robert E. Hudec, *Enforcing International Trade Law*, pp. 302-325.

[22] 103rd Congress, 2nd Session, *Uruguay Round Agreements Acts*, Section 125.

[23] Bruce Stokes, "Preparing to Bypass the WTO," *Financial Times* March 29, 2000, p.13. Actually, the joint resolution was initially introduced even before the USTR report was sent to Congress, because the USTR report was sent late. The resolution was then withdrawn and re-introduced ("House Members Move to Sponsor Resolution for U.S. WTO Withdrawal"), *Inside U.S. Trade*, Vol. 18, No. 2 March 3, 2000.

[24] James McCall Smith, "Domestic Politics and WTO Dispute Settlement Reform."

[25] See the remarks of Members of Congress Benjamin Cardin (Democrat, Maryland), Doug Bereuter (Republican, Nebraska), Nancy Johnson (Republican, Conecticut), Kenneth Bentsen (Democrat, Texas), and Phillip Crane (Republican, Illinois) opposing House Joint Resolution 90 in the 106th Congress, 2nd Session, *Congressional Record*, Vol. 146, No. 6 H4787-H4807.

[26] Alan Wm. Wolff, "Hearing on the WTO Dispute Settlement Review Commission Act."

[27] Michael Kantor, "Hearings," House International Affairs Committee, August 4, 1995, *JEI Report* No. 31B, p. 9.

[28] In 1993, this consisted of 173 positions with USTR and 30 authorized detailees from other agencies. In 2000, USTR had 178 positions with 25 authorized detailees (Michael Kantor, "Hearings," House Appropriations Committee, Subcommittee on Commerce, Justice, State, the Judiciary and Related Agencies, April 5, 1995; Charlene Barshefsky, "Hearings on USTR Agenda and Budget Request," House Appropriations Committee, Subcommittee on Commerce, Justice State and the Judiciary, April, 2000). While global and regional agreements have created new responsibilities for USTR, it is also true that it is not yet engaged in a round of world-wide multilateral negotiations as it was in the early 1990s.

[29] Charlene Barshefsky, "USTR Agenda and Budget Request," House Appropriations Committee, Sub-Committee on Commerce, Justice, State, the Judiciary and Related Agencies, March 17, 1999.

[30] Office of the United States Trade Representative, "Budget Proposal for Fiscal Year 2002," April 9, 2001.

[31] For the purposes of this section, it can be assumed that the trading partner on the opposing side of the case refuses to engage in bilateral negotiations under any circumstances. Clearly, this is only one of many assumptions that might be made.

[32] The justification for a USTR utility function of this form is outlined in Sections I, II and III of this paper.

[33] See Appendix 1.

[34] Figure 1 is taken from David Weinstein's October, 2000 comment on this paper.

[35] On the last three points, see Robert E. Hudec, *Enforcing International Trade Law*, p. 326.

[36] I would like to thank participants in the May Pre-Conference, particularly Theresa Greaney and Rob Howse, for their suggestion that this section be written. Needless to say, they are not to blame for the form it has taken.

[37] The assignment of these roles to USTR and MITI is arbitrary. The roles could equally well be reversed. The analysis here is merely meant to be illustrative.

[38] Robert E. Hudec, *Enforcing International Trade Law*, p. 319.

[39] Young Duk Park and Barbara Eggers, "WTO Dispute Settlement 1995-99: A Statistical Analysis," *Journal of International Economic Law*, Vol. 3 No. 1 (March 2000) pp. 183-204.

[40] Robert E. Hudec, *Enforcing International Trade Law*, p. 316.

[41] Young Duk Park and Barbara Eggers, "WTO Dispute Settlement 1995-99: A Statistical Analysis," p. 195.

[42] As noted in the analyses in Section V, were this to happen, it would lead to the USTR taking more cases to the WTO.

[43] John H. Jackson, *The Jurisprudence of GATT and the WTO* (Cambridge: Cambridge University Press, 2000) pp. 179-80.

[44] It is assumed in this analysis that the plaintiff in a WTO case knows more about the merits of the case it brings then does the defendant. For example, a plaintiff government knows better whether its constituent firms have been injured by the failure of a defendant government to meet its WTO obligations than the defendant government itself. While this may not always be the case, it is not inconsistent with assuming that both parties to the dispute know ρ, the quality of the DSM, and ε, the random drawing of all possible remedies.

[45] In the conventional legal setting, there is a substantial literature that finds that the more information there is about judicial outcomes, the more probable it is that litigants will risk a trial. See, for example, John B. Gould, "The Economics of Legal Conflicts," *Journal of Legal Studies*, June, 1973 2(2) pp. 225-251; Robert H. Mnookin and Lewis Kornhauser, "Bargaining in the Shadow of the Law: The Case of Divorce," *Yale Law Journal*, April, 1979, 88 (5) pp. 951-997; Henry S. Farber and Harry C. Katz, "Interest Arbitration, Outcomes, and the Incentive to Bargain," *Industrial and Labor Relations*

Review, October, 1979. Unlike the analysis presented here, this literature assumes that the litigants are risk-adverse.

[46] William J. Davey, "The WTO Dispute Settlement System," *Journal of International Economic Law* Vol. 3 No. 1 (March, 2000) pp. 15-18.

[47] There is already a substantial analytical literature on the resolution of trade disputes whether inside or outside the GATT or WTO. See, for example, Kathryn E. Speir and David E. Weinstein, "Retaliatory Mechanisms for Eliminating Trade Barriers: Aggressive Unilateralism vs. GATT Co-operation" in Winston W. Chang and Seiichi Katayama (eds.) *Imperfect Competition in International Trade* (Boston: Kluwer Academic Publishers, 1995). None of this work, however, allows for USTR concern with success rates.

Comment

Jude C. Hays

Given that the political salience of U.S. success in WTO mediated disputes is high (or may be high at some point in the future), what steps can be taken to improve the USTR's performance at the WTO? The answer that immediately comes to mind is to provide the USTR with more resources. In this paper, Saxonhouse forces us to reevaluate this strategy by showing how increased funding could actually undermine the USTR's performance at the WTO. Thus, Saxonhouse makes an important theoretical contribution to what is, at least potentially, an important policy debate. In the first three sections of the paper, Saxonhouse considers the domestic politics of the WTO's Dispute Settlement Mechanism (DSM). He then presents three separate models examining the relationship between the USTR's resources and its success rate at the WTO as well as the relationship between uncertainty and the use of the WTO's DSM. I discuss these topics in order below starting with domestic politics and ending with the formal models.

I. Motivation: Domestic Politics and the WTO Dispute Settlement Mechanism

One of the most interesting aspects of this paper is its focus on domestic trade politics in the United States. In fact, Saxonhouse uses domestic politics, specifically the political salience of the WTO's DSM, to motivate the theory he develops. Before turning to the models, he writes: "It is possible that the absence of a review commission composed of respected jurists may actually increase the political sensitivity of each adverse WTO outcome for the United States and lead to undue focus on quantitative indicators of success at the DSM. In this connection, the resources the USTR has at its disposal to pursue litigation at the WTO does become an issue." If the USTR's success rate with the WTO's DSM is politically salient, then we need to think rigorously about the factors that affect this win rate. Dissatisfaction with the WTO's dispute-resolution procedures could reduce overall support for the international organization and potentially lead to a U.S. withdrawal. Of course, the degree to which domestic politics serves to motivate the theory depends on how serious the political risks are. My only concern with Saxonhouse's treatment of domestic politics and the WTO's DSM is that there is no attempt to assess the seriousness of these political risks, be they current or future.

Perhaps this is because the risks are so small. It is clear that there is currently substantial U.S. political support for the WTO. The strongest evidence of widespread support is the fact that the Congressional vote in the House of Representatives extending participation in the WTO in June of 2000 was 363 to 56, a much larger victory than the original 288-146 vote on the WTO in November of 1994. For institutional reasons we would expect the House to be more responsive to organized interests than the Senate (e.g., the length of its terms and the size of its districts). Yet, after five plus years of operation, support for the WTO did not decline in the House. If anything, support for the WTO has increased over the years. The fact that the Dole Commission was never passed provides similar evidence. In some ways, this support undermines the motivating role domestic politics plays for the paper. However, there is no guarantee that the high levels of political support will continue into the future, especially if the number of WTO dispute-settlement outcomes perceived as adverse to U.S. interests begins to increase.

Saxonhouse could strengthen his treatment of the politics of the WTO's DSM by drawing on the theoretical research that links domestic politics and international trade. Much of this literature, which begins with Olson (1965, 1982), is directly relevant to Saxenhouse's topic. For example, Downs and Rocke (1995, Ch. 4) have developed an argument about the "optimal imperfection" of the GATT enforcement system that stems from politicians uncertainty about future interest group pressures. According to them, the GATT system provided sanctions for noncompliance that were high enough to get states to obey most agreements most of the time, yet low enough to allow politicians to break them if the domestic costs were too high. Sometimes politicians are compelled to break free trade agreements. This likely explains why so many politicians are concerned about the inflexibility of the WTO's DSM and leads to the conclusion that domestic political support for the WTO might drop once politicians begin to feel its constraints.

In sum, domestic politics provides an important motivation for Saxonhouse's analysis. There are good reasons why we might expect the WTO's DSM to generate significant domestic political opposition (See also, Goldstein and Martin 2000). This opposition has not been influential yet but could change in the future, especially if the USTR's win rate begins to drop (for reasons unrelated to its resource base). Therefore, it is important that we begin to theorize about USTR success rates. Saxonhouse begins this task.

II. The Models

Saxonhouse presents three separate models. The first two focus on the effect of USTR resources on its success rate in WTO disputes. The first model is simply an optimization problem for the USTR. The USTR's utility is a function of the number of cases won at the WTO and its win rate. The USTR chooses the number of cases to take to the WTO and the amount of resources (above the minimum required) to be devoted to the cases. Interestingly, Saxonhouse finds that more resources might actually lower the USTR's success rate at the WTO. If investing additional resources in existing cases only brings small increases in the probability of success, the USTR will bring new cases and its overall success rate will drop. The problem with this model is that complaints always involve two actors (at least). There needs to be some strategic interaction.

This shortcoming is addressed in the second model. Here the number of cases is fixed at two, but the marginal effect of additional resources spent on each case depends on the spending of two actors: the USTR and MITI. The functional form is

$$g(case) = -e^{-\nu\tau} + e^{-\nu\tau} - \mu\tau\gamma \tag{1}$$

where g is the increase in the probability (over the baseline) that the USTR will win a particular case, τ is the additional resources the USTR uses for the first case, γ is the extra resources the USTR uses for the first case, ν determines the effect of extra resources, and μ determines the degree of strategic interaction. The last term implies that the USTR acts as a strategic substitute. It gets very little additional benefit from expending resources on a case where MITI is spending a lot. MITI, on the other hand, is a strategic complement. Again, more resources reduce the success rate for the USTR, although this time the result stems from the fact that the USTR is assumed to be a strategic substitute. Given the importance of this assumption, more time should spent justifying the functional form for g in equation (1). Why should we expect the USTR to act as a strategic substitute?

The third model has a different purpose: to show how a more predictable environment can make it more likely that the WTO's DSM will be used. The conventional wisdom suggests the opposite. If actors can anticipate the outcome, then they should settle their dispute privately and save the cost of taking the case to the WTO. In the model, if the USTR takes the case to the DSM, it expects to get

$$(1-\rho)\varphi + \rho\varepsilon \tag{2}$$

where φ is the USTR's belief about the complaint's merit, ρ is a noise parameter, and ε is the mean of the population of possible remedies for the complaint. If the complaint goes to the DSM, MITI expects

$$-[n + (1-\rho)\varphi + \rho\varepsilon] \tag{3}$$

where n is the cost of taking the case to the WTO. MITI, however, does not know φ. Therefore, the only uncertainty for MITI drops out of (3) when $\rho = 1$. With this specification, maximum noise (in the outcome) is associated with lower levels of uncertainty (for MITI) about what will be a successful proposal.

Again, some of model three's assumptions are not adequately justified. Why should ε be known to both actors while φ is not? Furthermore, the logic behind the result should be discussed in more detail. And finally, because it addresses a different topic than the other two, it would be helpful if more time were spent tying model three to the rest of the paper.

III. Conclusions

I applaud Saxonhouse's attention to domestic trade politics. However, his treatment leaves a key question unanswered: How serious are the risks posed by the political opponents of the WTO's DSM? His models generate very interesting results that challenge conventional beliefs. In this way, Saxonhouse makes an important theoretical contribution. But do the models provide correct predictions/explanations? Will additional resources actually reduce the success rate of the USTR? Is the DSM being used because the texts of the Uruguay Round are unambiguous? In order to convince the reader of the importance of these results, more effort should be devoted to justifying the assumptions that drive them.

References

Downs, George W. and David M. Rocke. 1995. *Optimal Imperfection? Domestic Uncertainty and Institutions in International Relations.* Princeton: Princeton University Press.

Goldstein, Judith and Lisa L. Martin. 2000. "Legalization, Trade Liberalization, and Domestic Politics: A Cautionary Note," *International Organization* 54(3): 603-632.

Olson, Mancur. 1965. *The Logic of Collective Actions: Public Goods and the Theory of Groups.* Cambridge: Harvard University Press.

Olson, Mancur. 1982. *The Rise and Decline of Nations: Economic Growth, Stagflation, and Social Rigidities.* New Haven: Yale University Press.

Comment

David E. Weinstein

David Weinstein notes in his comment that Gary Saxonhouse has made an important contribution to the political economy of trade literature. To understand where it fits in, one needs to keep track of how this literature has progressed. Initially work focused, quite rightly, on understanding what the effects of commercial police were. The literature then moved to understand under what conditions particular policies were optimal. This, however, was unsatisfactory because it left out institutions and the political process. Recent work by Bagwell and Staiger has greatly furthered the debate by helping us to understand how the rules of the GATT and WTO function. Although their contributions are important, work by Helpman and Grossman has also served to help us gain an understanding of the political economy behind protection.

In all of this work, the question of how these policies are implemented has been left unanswered. Previous work has postulated that governments are influenced by special interests, but governments always are able to implement whatever policy they want. However, as Saxonhouse suggests, this is a major simplification that misses a lot about how trade policy is actually implemented. The area that he examines is Dispute Settlement—an area that almost by definition involves a disagreement over whether a treaty has been abrogated. GATT or WTO disputes typically involve serious questions about whether a particular policy constitutes a violation of a trade agreement. Importantly, neither the governments involved nor the agents making the decisions have perfect information about the veracity of the claims since these often involve injured parties or beneficiaries.

Saxonhouse's question, then, is how should governments proceed when they know that they will have only imperfect information about the world? Saxonhouse models this by considering a principal-agent problem. In particular, he reasons that it is going to be impossible for individual senators or members of Congress to understand the complexities of every case. Instead they are forced to rely on agents, in this case the USTR, to enforce the treaties. The problem is how does the funding of the USTR affect its performance?

Here Saxonhouse proposes a very sensible utility function for the USTR, which depends both on the quantity of cases it wins and its win rate. The U.S. government can only control the USTR through its budget. Depending on the structure of the utility function, increasing the USTR budget will increase the win rate at the expense of the number of cases, increase the number of cases at the expense of the win rate, or increase both. The fact that the win rate may fall as the USTR budget increases is a particularly interesting result.

This result raises a number of questions, however. The first concerns the utility function. Although the utility function that Saxonhouse proposes is sensible, it is a reduced-form equation. Where does this function come from? Presumably it is derivable from either the agents or the laws drafted by Congress. If it is the former, it would be nice to see what underlying preferences generate it. If it is the latter, it may be worth asking why the USTR is structured to care about these two variables using the weights that it has. In future work, it would be interesting to push the principal-agent problem back one step further and ask how the utility functions arise from the underlying utilities of the actors.

It is important also to consider some questions not asked by Saxonhouse. In particular, one might want to ask what is the optimal structure of the USTR. To paraphrase the old saw, an under-funded USTR will presumably lose some cases that it should have won, but an over-funded USTR will win some cases it should have lost! It would have been useful to see some more discussion of optimal funding levels of the USTR. There is also the potential for welfare losses arising from what Bhagwati has called "Directly Unproductive Profit-Seeking" or DUPS. These losses arise as lawyers (and other lobbyists) burn up vast quantities of money writing briefs and conducting lobbying in order to achieve a favorable decision. This is particularly apropos of the second main model in which both MITI and USTR are agents. Saxonhouse focuses on the outcomes, but I would also like to know more about the welfare implications. In particular it would be desirable to do some additional work on what the optimal policy is, or how dispute settlement can be structured so that small countries with inadequate funds to pursue cases can be protected. Perhaps the system needs something akin to court-appointed attorneys!

The foregoing comments notwithstanding, Saxonhouse's work is a fascinating and provocative account of the political economy underlying trade protection.

CHAPTER 15

Do U.S.-Japan Bilateral Trade Agreements Affect International Trade?

Theresa M. Greaney[*]

I. Introduction

Economists have good reason to maintain a certain level of skepticism regarding bilateral trade agreements. Viner (1950) showed that a preferential trading arrangement, a customs union, may cause welfare losses if the effects of trade diversion overwhelm those of trade creation. For completely different reasons, some U.S. trade negotiators have developed a strong sense of skepticism regarding bilateral trade agreements with Japan, in particular. The "new emphasis on explicitly mandated results has arisen from the perception that previous market-opening initiatives with Japan have failed because the standard process- or rule-based approach is too easily undermined or subverted by Japanese countermeasures" (Irwin, 1994, p. 12). These sentiments contrast sharply with the often positive reports issued by the U.S. Trade Representative, boasting of positive progress in expanding market access for "U.S. exporters and others with competitive products and services to offer" (USTR, 1999, p. 205). Which of these conflicting views on the potential impacts of U.S.-Japan bilateral trade agreements holds true? Do these agreements divert trade to favor U.S. exporters, have little impact on trade, or have significant positive impacts on trade that benefit all exporters to Japan?

This study finds some evidence to support each of the three viewpoints by using trade data for 1980-1995 to assess the impacts of 15 U.S.-Japan trade agreements. In most cases, the data suggest limited impacts on Japan's imports of targeted manufactured products, particularly from the United States. In fact, in many sectors, growth in Japan's imports of targeted products from the United States slowed after an agreement was signed. However, in two high-profile cases involving autos and semiconductors, I do find some evidence that suggests positive impacts of the agreements on bilateral trade flows. In the auto case, I find evidence consistent with trade diversion, favoring imports from the United States over those from the European Union (EU), rather than pure trade creation. In a few more cases, the trade data suggest positive effects of an agreement on Japan's imports from producers located outside the United States. However, the details of the trade agreements in most of these cases make it difficult to draw a firm causal link between the agreements and the trade movements.

These results address an ongoing need for better assessment of the impacts of U.S.-Japan trade agreements. U.S. trade negotiators have emphasized implicit, rather than explicit, trade barriers in recent talks with Japanese officials.[1] Since implicit trade barriers often are difficult to define, much less to measure in any traditional way, trade agreements related to these types of barriers may not produce the effects that one would expect based on traditional trade theory. In particular, trade-liberalizing agreements may have very limited impacts on trade flows if negotiators misidentify the source of market barriers or overestimate their significance. Given the economic and political costs involved in these bilateral negotiations, it is imperative that policymakers, trade negotiators, and industry representatives have some means of assessing the outcomes of past bilateral trade agreements. Since there is no formal mechanism requiring a U.S. government agency to conduct such an assessment, the initiative to pursue one must come from the outside.[2]

Several recent studies have attempted to address this assessment need. The distinguishing features of these studies are their different sources of assessment information, which can be used to place the studies into one of two groups. One group mainly has relied upon information culled from public documents and interviews with informed insiders (i.e., government and/or industry officials) to evaluate U.S. bilateral agreements. Bayard and Elliott (1994) and Elliott and Richardson (1997) used reports from the USTR's office, along with interview data, to rate the outcomes of cases pursued under Section 301 of U.S. trade law. The American Chamber of Commerce in Japan (ACCJ) also used information provided by interested parties to assess the outcomes of 45 major bilateral-trade agreements signed by the United States and Japan between 1980 and 1996 (ACCJ, 1997). For each agreement, evaluations were "sought from representatives of American companies and business associations in both the United States and Japan, all of whom had firsthand knowledge of how the trade situation changed after the relevant agreement was concluded" (ACCJ, p. 19).

Evaluations of trade agreements provided by knowledgeable insiders in the trade representative's office and in industry provide valuable information for an assessment effort. However, these subjective evaluations introduce the possibility of biased assessments. Those involved in lengthy and costly trade negotiations may be reluctant to criticize the final outcome of their efforts. On the other hand, those planning for subsequent rounds of negotiations and agreements are unlikely to express complete satisfaction with past efforts. The relative strengths of these two opposing sources of bias in an assessment likely differ across industries, across time, and across individual assessors. Therefore, the subjective assessments should be compared to more objective means of evaluation.

The more objective approach taken by two previous studies and by this study is to use trade data to assess the impacts of bilateral trade agreements.

Noland (1997) used the residuals from gravity-model regressions of U.S. bilateral exports and foreign direct investment as measures of implicit trade and investment barriers. He found no significant impacts of the bilateral-trade actions on the levels of or changes in implicit barriers. However, his analysis at the targeted country level may have been too aggregated to detect effects at the targeted country and industry level. In a Congressional Research Service report to Congress, Gold and Nanto (1991) use trade data to assess the cross-industry impacts specifically of U.S.-Japan bilateral trade agreements. They compared nominal growth in U.S. exports to Japan in sectors targeted by bilateral agreements with growth in total U.S. exports to Japan and to the entire world for the 1985-1990 period. They concluded that the bilateral agreements had positive effects on bilateral trade flows since trade growth in the targeted sectors exceeded total trade growth.

Noland (1997) and Gold and Nanto (1991) draw very different conclusions regarding the effectiveness of U.S. trade policies in part due to their different assumptions regarding the ultimate goals of the policies. Noland assumes that the U.S. objective is to lower implicit trade (and investment) barriers while Gold and Nanto assume a more direct, mercantilistic goal of raising U.S. exports. This chapter considers both objectives and arrives at conclusions that lie somewhere in between the previous studies. I find evidence that suggests positive trade impacts of a few bilateral agreements, but these cases are in the minority and some involve the possibility of trade diversion rather than trade creation.

I arrive at these conclusions by using industry-level trade data to examine the impacts of past U.S.-Japan trade agreements on Japan's manufactured imports from the United States. and from the rest of the world.[3] I improve upon Gold and Nanto's (1991) approach by using: (1) a fuller set of industry-level, trade-growth data rather than just aggregate data for comparative purposes; (2) real rather than nominal trade-growth data; and (3) a longer time period (1980-1995) that is divided into pre-agreement and post-agreement periods for each targeted industry. I also conduct formal tests for instability in trade-growth paths that might correspond with the signing of a bilateral-trade agreement. Finally, I develop an objective set of ratings based on the trade data and then compare these ratings to those provided by the ACCJ's industry insiders and by the sector-specific research based on USTR reports. Overall, I find very limited correspondence across the different ratings. This may indicate a broader or different set of criteria used by the industry and government officials in evaluating the outcomes of these trade agreements. For example, lowering the costs of doing business in Japan may be the primary goal rather than increasing sales revenues in that market.

I present the methodology used in evaluating the bilateral-trade agreements in the next section, followed by a description of the trade data employed. The results of my trade-based assessment are presented in section four, along with a comparison of my assessment ratings with those from the ACCJ (1997) and Bayard and Elliott (1994) reports. In the final section, I summarize and interpret the overall results and discuss a few industry-specific results for the high-profile agreements in automobiles and semiconductors.

II. Methodology

I use industry-level data on Japanese and U.S. trade patterns from 1980-1995 to analyze the impact of bilateral trade agreements on manufacturing industries. All of the agreements analyzed focus on increasing access to Japan's market. Before trying to assess the impacts of the agreements, trade growth in each targeted sector is compared with trade growth in non-targeted sectors on average to see whether targeted sectors appear "different." Of course, any differences in average annual growth rates between targeted and non-targeted sectors may be due to a variety of influences that affect industries disparately, such as trade agreements, or to selection bias in choosing sectors to target in bilateral negotiations. To avoid the problem of selection bias, most of my analysis is based on variations in trade growth within industries rather than direct comparisons of trade growth across industries.

As a first step towards assessing the impact of an agreement, I examine whether trade in the targeted sector(s) grew at a faster pace after an agreement was signed between the two countries. Growth in Japan's imports from the United States is compared with growth in Japan's imports from the European Union (EU) and from all non-U.S. sources to detect the possible bilateral and multilateral effects of an agreement. The EU is chosen for comparison purposes since trade patterns between developed countries tend to be more similar to those between other developed countries than to those between a developed and a developing country. In addition to examining Japan's imports from various sources, U.S. exports to Japan are compared with U.S. exports to both EU and all non-Japanese destinations in an attempt to distinguish between demand-side and supply-side effects on trade growth. A sharp increase in Japan's imports of a particular good from the United States may be a singular event driven by demand-side forces or it may reflect a sharp increase in U.S. exports of that good to all foreign destinations (i.e., a supply-side influence).

To examine the potential effects of the bilateral trade agreements, I use the differences between trade growth in the pre-agreement and post-agreement periods to create various ratings for each agreement relative to the other agreements. These ratings are based on the premise that the goal of a U.S.-Japan bilateral trade agreement is to increase Japan's targeted-sector imports from the United States and possibly from other sources as well. Some of the ratings focus only on the potential impact on U.S.-based producers while others include potential impacts on producers located elsewhere. These trade-based ratings then are compared with those devised by the ACCJ (1997) and by Bayard and Elliott (1994).

In addition to using differences between pre- and post-agreement trade growth as suggestive evidence of the potential impact of the bilateral trade agreements, I conduct formal tests of instability in the trade growth paths. I use Chow tests to test for instability in each industry's trade growth in the year of an agreement or the following year, which allows for some lag in detecting the effects of an agreement. The Chow tests use the following regression:

$$(1) \quad y_{it} = \alpha_i + \beta_{1i} t + \beta_{2i} postyr + \beta_{3i} postyr \cdot t + \varepsilon_{it} ,$$

where y_{it} = the annual import (or export) growth rate for industry i at time t and postyr is a dummy variable for the breakpoint year being tested. For $t \geq yr$, postyr = 1; otherwise postyr = 0. Confidence levels of 95% and 90% are used to define valid breakpoints.[4] If a valid breakpoint closely follows a bilateral trade agreement, and Japan's imports (U.S. exports) of the targeted good increased at a faster pace in the post-agreement period, then this provides some evidence to support a positive assessment of the agreement. If breakpoints coincide with faster growth for Japan's import from the United States but slower growth for imports from elsewhere, this suggests a trade diversion, rather than pure trade creation, effect.

In an attempt to control for macroeconomic influences, such as exchange rate and income changes, that affect all industries, I also test for instability in the trade growth paths of the targeted industries after differencing out the annual trade growth in non-targeted industries. This test should identify breakpoints that are truly industry-specific and eliminate breakpoints caused in large part by events, such as the yen's appreciation in late 1985 or the bursting of Japan's bubble economy in 1991, that affect all industries.

After identifying breakpoints that correspond with faster post-agreement trade growth, I examine the contents of these agreements as a final check to see if a credible argument can be made for a causal link. In a few cases, the trade agreements involved discussions, agreements on data collection, agreements on topics for future negotiations and/or concessions in other sectors but very little that could reasonably be expected to cause a sharp increase in Japan's imports of the targeted good(s).

III. Data

The ACCJ (1997) report identified and assessed 45 major bilateral trade agreements between 1980 and 1996. Agreements were selected from among this group if they satisfied the following criteria: (1) the agreement targeted specific manufactured products (i.e., SITC 5-8 industries), rather than broad structural issues, services, or agricultural products; and (2) the agreement was concluded after 1982 and before 1994. The first criterion is based on this study's focus on the issue of Japan's manufactured imports, which have been the target of many complaints involving implicit trade barriers. The second criterion is based on the availability of the trade database for years 1980-1995 and the need to have at least two years of trade growth data in the pre- and post-agreement periods. Table 1 lists all of the agreements that satisfy the first criteria, and of these, 15 also satisfy the second criteria. These 15 agreements

Table 1. Manufacturing Industries Targeted in Major Bilateral Trade Agreements, 1980-96

	SITC #	ACCJ Rating	B&E Rating
Telecommunications			
NTT Procurement (1980)	764	2	
Telecomm. Equip. & Services—MOSS (1986)	764	5	
Telecomm.--Cellular & Third-Party Radio (1989)	764	3	
Telecomm.--Cellular & Third-Party Radio (1994)	764	10	
Computers & High Technology			
Electronics—MOSS (1986)	752, 759, 776	7	
Medical/Pharmaceutical Products—MOSS (1986)	541, 872	8~9	
Medical Technology Procurement (1994)	541, 872	8~9[1]	
Non-R&D Satellite Procurement (1990)	792	9	10
Supercomputer Procurement (1990)	752	6	6.7
Computer Products Procurement (1992)	752, 759	7	
Semiconductors (1986)	776	8	3.3
Semiconductors (1991)	776	8	
Semiconductors (1996)	776	--[2]	
Transportation			
Autos & Auto Parts—MOSS (1987)	781,784	--[3]	
Autos & Auto Parts (1992)	781,784	--[4]	
Autos & Auto Parts (1995)	781,784	8	3.3[5]

	SITC #	ACCJ Rating	B&E Rating
Materials Manufactures			
Wood Products—MOSS (1986)	634, 635, 641	3	
Wood Products (1990)	634, 635	6[6]	6.7
Paper Products (1992)	641, 642	4	
Building and Construction			
Flat Glass (1995)	664	3~6	

Source: ACCJ (1997) provided the list of major agreements, the information used by the author to assign SITC codes to agreements, and the ACCJ agreement ratings (on a 1 to 10 scale). Bayard and Elliott (1994) provided ratings of agreements that involved Section 301 cases on a four-point scale, which the author transformed onto a ten-point scale (B&E ratings) to match the ACCJ ratings scale. Bold type indicates inclusion in this study.

[1] The respondents gave one rating for both the 1986 and 1994 agreements, but noted that the high rating was more reflective of the former.

[2] The respondents gave one rating for both the 1986 and 1991 agreements but no rating for the most recent (1996) agreement.

[3] No rating was reported but the respondents notes that the agreement's objectives were limited so few results were expected.

[4] No rating was reported but the respondents noted significant results.

[5] Elliott and Richardson (1995) provided this rating for the auto part portion of the agreement in their update and extension on Bayard and Elliott (1994).

[6] The respondents boosted the rating to an "8" when the agreement was considered in conjunction with subsequent Section 301 watch list action initiated in 1994.

(shown in bold type in table 1) covered products in 16 different three-digit SITC code industries. With some of the agreements covering multiple industries and some industries targeted by several agreements, the 16 industries and 15 agreements create 27 industry-agreement pairs.

Bilateral trade data are obtained from Statistics Canada's (SC's) World Trade Database (WTDB). The four-digit SITC trade data are aggregated to the three-digit level to cover the range of products included in each agreement. To convert the nominal dollar-denominated trade data into real dollar and yen trade values, I use the U.S. export-price index and the average annual exchange rate from the IMF's *International Financial Statistics* (IFS), and Japanese price indices from the Bank of Japan's Price Indexes Annual. Specifically, U.S. export figures are converted into real 1990 dollars using the IFS export-price index. Japanese import figures are converted into nominal yen using the IFS exchange rate. Since the aggregate import-price index for Japan is heavily influenced by oil price changes, I instead use industry-level import-price indices to deflate the nominal yen figures for the targeted industries. For example, Japan's import-price index for electrical machinery is used to deflate imports in SITC 764, 752 and 759.[5] For imports in all of the nontargeted sectors, Japan's wholesale price index (WPI) is used as a deflator.[6]

IV. Results

As a preliminary step in evaluating the various trade agreements, I present summary statistics for the average annual growth rates of each of the targeted industries in table 2. In this table and subsequent tables, I present U.S.-Japan bilateral trade growth figures alongside the same statistics for Japanese or U.S. trade with the rest of the world and with just the EU.[7] These statistics allow for comparisons of the potential effects of the bilateral trade agreements on trade with all other countries in aggregate, and with other major industrialized countries in particular. In table 2 and subsequent tables, growth data for Japan's imports from the United States and that for U.S. exports to Japan differ somewhat due to the respective conversions into real yen and real dollar figures.

Four industries stand out as having significantly faster growth in U.S.-Japan bilateral trade relative to the growth in Japan's imports from non-U.S. sources and relative to U.S. exports to non-Japanese destinations: SITC 759 (computer and office machine parts and accessories), 781 (passenger cars), 611 (leather) and 635 (wood manufactures). Industries in which Japan's imports from the United States appear rather slow relative to imports from non-U.S. or EU sources are: SITC 764 (telecommunications equipment), 752 (computers), 792 (satellites and other small aircraft), 634 (wood and plywood), and 642 (paper and paperboard cut to size or shape). However, only SITC 642 shows significantly slower growth in U.S. exports to Japan than to the other destinations. Some of these differences in trade-growth rates can be explained by cross-sectional differences in initial trade levels. In particular, U.S.-Japan

Table 2. Average Annual Trade Growth in Targeted vs. Non-Targeted Sectors, 1980-95

SITC	Japan's Import Growth from...			America's Export Growth to...		
	US	Non-US	EU	Japan	Non-Japan	EU
764	18.58	26.02	31.03	16.11	10.10	7.68
752	14.50	32.17	22.72	11.95	8.67	5.11
759	30.64	21.92	15.89	26.76	4.97	4.92
776	33.83	31.41	20.45	24.56	19.08	10.74
541	5.59	9.84	12.32	5.39	6.08	6.45
872	12.83	14.80	14.09	12.85	9.07	9.94
792	2.88	14.25	24.76	6.57	3.37	4.07
781	32.24	18.69	18.58	39.50	6.86	30.72
784	12.03	15.70	14.58	14.90	6.11	9.10
611	16.51	6.95	15.14	17.38	4.83	4.81
612	12.52	14.22	12.74	14.50	9.53	3.09
851	9.95	13.62	14.30	12.03	9.59	11.19
634	8.28	26.75	12.99	14.23	7.34	6.53
635	17.92	8.07	16.15	22.04	5.96	9.00
641	5.78	11.28	11.74	6.93	6.46	3.65
642	-0.46	16.87	7.61	0.45	8.67	3.00
All targeted industries*	12.37	18.75	15.23	11.54	7.18	5.71
All non-targeted industries*	4.69	8.50	6.74	6.87	4.76	3.29

*Trade-weighted average

trade flows in SITC 781 and 611 in 1980 are low relative to both of their comparison trade flows, which helps to explain their relatively rapid growth rates. Similarly, the relatively slow bilateral trade growth in SITC 752, 792 and 642 can be explained by large initial bilateral trade flows relative to the comparison trade flows.

The trade-growth rates for the targeted sectors also can be compared to the average annual trade-growth rates for all non-targeted manufacturing industries (SITC 5-8), shown at the bottom of table 2. Bilateral trade in almost all of the targeted sectors outpaced that in the average non-targeted industry, with SITC 642 being the only noteworthy exception.

Although table 2 provides basic information on identifying fast- versus slow-growing sectors between 1980 and 1995, it provides little information on the role of the bilateral trade agreements. Table 3 provides more suggestive evidence by comparing the trade growth during the pre-agreement and post-agreement periods for each industry-agreement pair. A successful agreement presumably will increase the flow of the targeted products into Japan. For agreements that occurred during the month of January, the breakpoint between the pre- and post-agreement periods readily can be defined as the year the agreement was signed.[8] Similarly, for agreements signed in December, the breakpoint is well-approximated by using the following year. For all agreements concluded in mid-year (i.e., any month except for Dec. or Jan.), two breakpoints are considered: the year of the agreement and the following year. In table 3, the second entry in each box corresponds with using the year after the agreement was signed as the breakpoint.

Table 3 shows a number of unexpected outcomes. Note that 13-18 (depending upon the breakpoint) of the 27 targeted industry cases show Japan's imports from the United States growing more slowly after a bilateral trade agreement was signed. This can be compared with only 8-9 (7-10) cases in which Japan's import growth in these same sectors from non-U.S. sources (from the EU) slowed in the post-agreement periods. Of the 13-18 cases of slower post-agreement import growth from the United States, 9-12 (depending upon the breakpoint) have faster post-agreement slowdowns than that for the average non-targeted industry.[9] On the U.S. exports side, 13-16 cases stand out as having slower post-agreement growth rates for exports to Japan. These 13-16 cases slightly exceed the 11 (7-10) cases where growth in U.S. exports to non-Japan (EU) destinations slowed in the post-agreement periods.

On an individual industry basis, the results in table 3 can be used as suggestive evidence of the success or failure of an agreement. For example, the results for SITC 759 (computer and office machine parts and accessories), 1986, and 781 (passenger cars), 1987 and 1992, show evidence consistent with successful bilateral agreements. The flow of these goods from the United States to Japan increased at a faster rate in the post-agreement periods even though growth in U.S. exports to the rest of the world and to the EU alone declined. Japan's imports of computer parts from the EU grew faster as well, while imports of autos increased at a faster pace only for U.S.-made autos (using 1988 as the breakpoint for the Aug., 1987 agreement). This suggests that the main, and possibly the only, beneficiaries of the auto agreement were U.S.-based producers, whereas the agreement affecting computer parts may have assisted all producers outside Japan. In contrast, cases in which the U.S.-Japan entries are negative while all other entries are positive suggest poor agreements in terms of U.S.-based interests, although these agreements may have benefited producers located elsewhere. These cases of apparent failure for U.S.-based interests are: 541 (1986), 611 (1985) and 851 (1985). Note that the participation of multinational enterprises in these trade flows to some extent weakens the assumed link between production location and national producer interests. This issue is discussed in greater detail in the conclusion below.

To go beyond merely identifying outlying cases of pre- and post-agreement trade growth differences shown in table 3, these differences are used to create a series of ratings for each agreement. The ratings attempt to address two basic questions: (1) did U.S.-based producers competing in the Japanese market benefit as a result of the agreement? and (2) did U.S.-based and other foreign-based producers competing in the Japanese market benefit as a result of the agreement? A significant increase in the post-agreement average annual trade growth rate in a targeted sector is taken as evidence that foreign producers benefit from an agreement.[10] The "significance" of any change is judged relative to changes in non-targeted sectors and to changes in targeted sector trade with other countries.

I address the first question by assigning ratings on a scale from 1 to 10 using the following statistics:[11]

U_{non}^{us}: pre-post difference for Japan's targeted industry imports from the United States—pre-post difference for Japan's average non-targeted industry imports from the United States;

U_{tar}^{row}: pre-post difference for Japan's (U.S.) targeted industry imports from the United States (exports to Japan)—pre-post difference for Japan's (U.S.) targeted industry imports from (exports to) the rest of the world; and

U_{tar}^{eu}: pre-post difference for Japan's (U.S.) targeted industry imports from the United States (exports to Japan)—pre-post difference for Japan's (U.S.) targeted industry imports from (exports to) the EU,

where "pre-post difference" refers to the difference between the pre-agreement and post-agreement average annual trade growth, as shown in table 3. For each rating, the subscript represents the industry and the superscript indicates the market that is being used for comparison purposes. The U_{non}^{us} rating answers the question, "To what extent does U.S. targeting of this industry seem to have given it an advantage over the average U.S. non-targeted industry in expanding sales in Japan?" This rating is the same whether the calcu-

Table 3. Quantitative Differences between Pre- and Post-Agreement Trade Growth in Targeted Sectors, 1980-95

SITC	Agreement Date	Japan's Post-Agreement Import Growth - Pre-Agreement Import Growth from ...			America's Post-Agreement Export Growth - Pre-Agreement Export Growth to ...		
		US	NON-US	EU	Japan	Non-Jpn	EU
764	Jan. 9, 1986	13.53	36.81	54.12	8.99	9.07	13.73
764	June 30, 1989	7.90	15.15	54.41	2.43	8.56	9.88
		-2.77	9.32	51.33	-4.64	6.62	3.81
752	Jan. 10, 1986	8.88	43.28	35.75	4.87	1.32	3.78
759	Jan. 10, 1986	33.39	-12.85	35.50	28.09	-2.08	-7.49
776	Jan. 10, 1986	-3.79	33.78	24.30	-12.47	-2.08	11.09
541	Jan. 9, 1986	-12.32	12.88	14.25	-7.39	3.88	2.87
872	Jan. 9, 1986	1.80	6.41	3.38	10.78	5.52	7.84
792	June 15, 1990	-3.14	-5.79	-15.04	-0.72	-4.74	-11.72
		-21.14	-2.08	-9.68	-20.50	-10.60	-19.63
752	June 15, 1990	-7.87	44.68	30.31	-9.32	-3.27	-6.43
		-6.52	50.10	35.35	-8.00	-3.28	-6.79
752	Jan. 22, 1992	-3.00	53.87	39.52	-3.39	-2.34	-5.32
759	Jan. 22, 1992	-9.38	15.37	42.65	-8.03	-5.76	-13.77
776	Sept. 2, 1986	-3.79	33.78	24.30	-12.47	-2.08	11.09
		2.72	31.44	12.46	-8.22	-1.98	13.31
776	June 11, 1991	-3.87	13.50	-5.04	-10.05	0.68	6.42
		3.81	26.33	2.25	-1.29	4.21	9.06
781	Aug. 18, 1987	56.64	3.48	4.00	53.32	-1.61	11.52
		43.41	-8.60	-8.46	33.54	-1.25	-14.23
784	Aug. 18, 1987	-3.23	-3.81	-0.71	-0.88	4.41	11.46
		5.06	-6.30	-5.98	4.06	3.49	11.12

SITC	Agreement Date	Japan's Post-Agreement Import Growth - Pre-Agreement Import Growth from ...			America's Post-Agreement Export Growth - Pre-Agreement Export Growth to ...		
		US	NON-US	EU	Japan	Non-Jpn	EU
781	Jan. 11, 1992	12.69	-10.25	-10.71	4.43	-4.52	-46.60
784	Jan. 11, 1992	-0.60	-21.60	-13.46	-2.07	6.36	19.70
611	Dec. 20, 1985	-15.25	19.05	28.23	-22.45	9.44	15.68
612	Dec. 20, 1985	-9.08	42.71	39.92	-14.02	-5.93	23.24
851	Dec. 20, 1985	-7.48	19.39	20.90	-11.71	25.24	15.35
634	Jan. 9, 1986	6.27	-5.55	14.81	25.54	19.97	24.41
635	Jan. 9, 1986	11.80	1.62	-2.80	32.31	22.57	17.11
641	Jan. 9, 1986	-2.47	1.16	-6.27	7.21	20.23	27.61
634	June 15, 1990	-7.39	-34.37	6.29	-4.95	-3.60	-3.66
		-9.48	-29.86	1.90	-2.55	-7.09	-8.05
635	June 15, 1990	-2.40	-3.90	-14.11	0.99	6.55	0.70
		-7.12	-0.67	-12.50	0.70	5.82	-3.99
641	Apr. 5, 1992	-1.01	1.97	1.68	5.80	6.63	4.55
		0.14	8.24	15.31	8.07	8.02	5.71
642	Apr. 5, 1992	10.09	1.68	-2.54	17.14	38.20	-4.59
		12.01	4.30	1.77	20.14	3.42	9.08

Note: In cases where two entries appear in a cell, the first entry corresponds with using the year of the agreement as the breakpoint and the second corresponds with using the following year as the breakpoint.

lation is based on Japan's imports from the United States or U.S. exports to Japan, so the statistic is reported only once in table 4. For Japan's imports from the United States, the U^{row}_{tar} and U^{eu}_{tar} ratings answer the questions, "To what extent did U.S. targeting of this industry appear to give U.S.-based producers an advantage over non-U.S.-based producers or over EU-based producers in expanding sales in Japan?" When the same statistic is applied to U.S. exports, the U^{row}_{tar} and U^{eu}_{tar} ratings address the questions, "To what extent did U.S. targeting of this industry appear to give U.S.-based producers an advantage in the Japanese market that they did not realize in making sales elsewhere or in the EU in particular?" Table 4 shows both U^{row}_{tar} and U^{eu}_{tar} ratings and an average for all five U^{i}_{j} ratings, along with the ACCJ and Bayard and Elliott (B&E) ratings for comparison.

In addition, table 4 presents two ratings that address the second question posed above regarding the potential benefits for U.S.-based and other foreign-based producers from U.S.-Japan bilateral agreements. These ratings are based on the following statistics:

UR_{non} : $(U^{us}_{non} + R^{row}_{non})/2$, and

UE_{non} : $(U^{us}_{non} + E^{eu}_{non})/2$, where

R^{row}_{non} = pre-post difference for Japan's targeted industry imports from the rest of the world (i.e., excluding the United States)—pre-post difference for Japan's average non-targeted industry imports from the rest of the world, and E^{eu}_{non} is the equivalent statistic for imports from the EU.

These two statistics give equal weight to gains made by U.S.-based producers and by producers based elsewhere. The ratings that correspond with these statistics use the ratings scale established by the U^{us}_{non} statistic so that these three ratings can be compared directly. For example, the 1987 auto agreement (SITC 781) appears to have had a much more positive impact on Japan's imports from the United States than on imports from the rest of the world or from the EU since adding either drops the agreement's rating from an average of 9.6 or 9.8 down to a 6 or 7, depending upon the breakpoint used. On average, however, the ratings that include the rest-of-world or EU impacts are more likely to exceed than fall short of the ratings that use only the U.S. impact.

The trade-based ratings in table 4 that focus on U.S.-based producers' interests exclusively (i.e., U^{i}_{j}) give the highest marks to agreements affecting SITC 759 (1986) and 781 (1987) and (1992). The lowest U^{i}_{j} ratings are received by SITC 776 (1986)[12] and 611, 612 and 851 (1985). The low trade-based rating received by the semiconductor agreement contrasts sharply with the high rating it received in the ACCJ (1997) report.

The various ratings in table 4 suggest that the criteria used for each assessment of the trade agreements differ significantly. The lack of consistent, positive correlations across the ratings systems is confirmed by pair-wise correlation coefficients.[13] At the 5% significance level, the ACCJ and Bayard and Elliott (B&E) ratings had no significant correlation coefficients with my trade-based ratings or with each other. This comparison demonstrates why supporters and critics of bilateral trade agreements sometimes use the same agreements to defend their views. The criteria for measuring success of an agreement appear to differ widely between U.S. business people, the USTR, and the trade data used in this paper.

The lack of strong correlations between my ratings, the ACCJ ratings, and the B&E ratings is reflected in many individual cases shown in table 4. Using an arbitrarily chosen three-point spread (i.e., 1.5 on each side) around each mean U^i_j rating as a criterion for finding approximately equal ratings, cases where the ACCJ ratings fall outside and above this range are the most numerous, with 13 cases covering 9 different industries and 8 agreements. These high-ratings cases are: SITC 752 and 776 (Jan. 1986), 541 and 872 (1986), 792 (1990), 752 (1990), 752 and 759 (1992), 776 (Sept. 1986) and (1991), 611, 612 and 851 (1985). The B&E ratings also were high for 5 of these cases (i.e., SITC 792 (1990), 752 (1990), 611, 612 and 851 (1985)), and for SITC 634 and 635 (1990). The ACCJ ratings appear too low for 3 industries involved in 2 of the agreements: SITC 634 and 635 (1986) and 642 (1992), while none of the B&E ratings appears too low. This leaves only 7 cases for which the ACCJ ratings match up relatively closely with my ratings based on trade growth (i.e., SITC 764 (1986) and (1989), 759 (1986), 641 (1986), 634 and 635 (1990) and 641 (1992)), and one case for the B&E ratings (i.e., SITC 776 (Sept. 1986)).

The cases where the industry insiders appear to provide overly optimistic ratings relative to the trade data are concentrated mainly in the computer and high technology sectors, with the only exception being the overly high rating given to the leather and leather footwear 1985 agreement (affecting SITC 611, 612 and 851). A possible explanation for this mismatch between the views of the ACCJ industry insiders and the trade results is the multinational aspect of production in the computer and high technology sectors. The industry officials in these sectors likely represent companies with substantial production capacity outside the United States, so their ratings may be more reflective of the market opening results of an agreement on a multilateral basis rather than on a bilateral basis.[14] In almost all of the high ratings cases, the ACCJ ratings more closely match the trade ratings that include sales gains made by non-U.S.-based producers rather than those that focus exclusively on U.S.-based producers.

In comparing the various ratings, the overly pessimistic ratings are concentrated solely in the materials manufactures sector. It is unfortunate that no ratings are available for the auto sector agreements because the high U^i_j rat-

Table 4. Ratings of Bilateral Trade Agreements, 1980-1995

		Rating Using Japan's Import Growth Rates					Rating using America's export growth rates		Mean		
SITC	Date	UR_{non}	UE_{non}	U^{us}_{non}	U^{row}_{tar}	U^{eu}_{tar}	U^{row}_{tar}	U^{eu}_{tar}	U^{i}_{j} rating*	ACCJ rating	B&E rating
764	1/86	6	8	5	4	2	5	4	4.0	5	--
764	6/89	5	7	4	5	1	4	4	3.6	3	--
		5	8	5	5	1	3	4	3.6		
752	1/86	6	6	4	3	3	5	5	4.0	7	--
759	1/86	4	8	8	10	5	8	9	8.0	7	--
776	1/86	5	4	2	1	3	3	2	2.2	7	--
541	1/86	3	3	1	3	3	3	4	2.8	8~9	--
872	1/86	3	3	3	5	5	5	5	4.6	8~9	--
792	6/90	3	2	3	6	7	5	6	5.4	9	10
		2	2	1	4	4	3	5	3.4		
752	6/90	6	5	2	1	2	4	4	2.6	6	6.7
		7	6	3	1	2	4	5	3.0		
752	1/92	7	6	3	1	2	4	5	3.0	7	--
759	1/92	4	6	2	3	1	4	5	3.0	7	--
776	9/86	5	4	2	1	3	3	2	2.2	8	3.3
		4	4	1	3	5	4	2	3.0		
776	6/91	5	4	3	4	6	3	3	3.8	8	--
		4	3	3	4	6	4	4	4.2		
781	8/87	6	7	10	10	10	10	9	9.8	--	--
		7	7	10	10	10	8	10	9.6		

		Rating Using Japan's Import Growth Rates					Rating using America's export growth rates		Mean		
SITC	Date	UR_{non}	UE_{non}	U^{us}_{non}	U^{row}_{tar}	U^{eu}_{tar}	U^{row}_{tar}	U^{eu}_{tar}	U^{i}_{j} rating*	ACCJ rating	B&E rating
784	8/87	1	2	1	6	5	4	3	3.8	--	--
		2	2	2	7	7	5	4	5.0		
781	1/92	4	4	6	8	8	5	10	7.4	--	--
784	1/92	2	3	4	8	7	4	2	5.0	--	--
611	12/85	3	3	1	3	1	1	1	1.4	4	6.7
612	12/85	5	5	1	1	1	4	1	1.6	4	6.7
851	12/85	3	3	2	3	3	1	2	2.2	4	6.7
634	1/86	3	4	4	7	5	5	5	5.2	3	--
635	1/86	3	3	5	7	7	6	6	6.2	3	--
641	1/86	2	2	2	5	6	3	2	3.6	3	--
634	6/90	1	3	2	8	4	4	5	4.6	6	6.7
		1	4	3	8	5	5	5	5.2		
635	6/90	3	2	3	6	7	4	5	5.0	6	6.7
		3	3	3	5	6	4	5	4.6		
641	4/92	4	4	4	5	5	4	5	4.6	4	--
		3	4	3	5	4	5	5	4.4		
642	4/92	4	4	5	6	7	6	7	6.2	4	--
		4	4	5	6	7	6	6	6.0		

*Not including UR_{non} and UE_{non} ratings.

-ings corresponding with both the 1987 and 1992 agreements for the passenger car industry (SITC 781) seem likely to clash with the negative perception developed by industry insiders, as reflected in the continuing lobbying efforts of the American Automobile Manufacturers Association (AAMA).[15]

All of my analysis thus far compares pre-agreement and post-agreement trade-growth rates in search of evidence suggestive of an agreement's impact. Another means of testing for the impact of an agreement is to run a formal test for instability in an industry's trade growth path at the time of an agreement. The valid breakpoint years identified by Chow tests are shown in table 5. Asterisks indicate the breakpoint years that coincide with increases in post-agreement average annual trade growth.

The Chow test results do not provide much evidence that is supportive of positive effects of the agreements on U.S.-based producers. The agreement year or subsequent year tested as a valid breakpoint in only six cases for U.S.-Japan trade flows. Three of these cases are characterized by declines in post-agreement average annual trade growth, SITC 764 (1990), 752 (1990) and 541 (1986). In another case, SITC 635 (1990), the increase in post-agreement trade growth is so marginal (i.e., less than 1%) for U.S. exports to Japan that it disappears when the data are converted into real yen rather than real dollars. In addition, in this case and in the case of SITC 634 (1986), trade-growth instability and increases in the post-agreement growth rates are found for U.S. exports not only to Japan but to non-Japanese and EU destinations as well. This makes it more difficult to credit the bilateral agreement for the export surge to Japan.

The only case that provides good evidence that is consistent with a bilateral agreement having a significant positive impact on U.S.-Japan trade flows is SITC 781 (1987), passengers cars. Japan's import growth from the United States in this sector peaked at 155% in 1988 while import growth from the rest-of-the-world and the EU fell somewhat. These declines in 1988 caused the instability found in Japan's imports from these other sources. The data suggest the possibility that some of the extra sales made by U.S. auto producers immediately following the agreement may have come at the expense of European auto producers. In fact, the breakpoint identified for imports from the EU (which account for almost all of Japan's imports from non-U.S. sources) meets the more stringent (5%) level of significance as compared to the breakpoint found for imports from the United States. Of the 27 industry-agreement cases, only one (marginally) satisfies the criteria for having had a positive impact on U.S.-based producers, and in this case the agreement may have caused trade diversion rather than trade creation.

In comparison, there are ten cases where an identified breakpoint matches an agreement year (or subsequent year) and a post-agreement increase in Japan's imports from non-U.S. and/or EU sources. By eliminating four cases in which the breakpoint corresponds with a sharp decline in the industry's annual trade growth even though post-agreement growth increases on average, six cases remain as possible examples of successful agreements from a multilateral perspective: SITC 764 (1986), 776 (1986), 541 (1986), and 611, 612 and 851 (1985). The cases involving SITC 541, 611 and 851 were mentioned previously as cases that appeared to be failures for U.S.-based interests, but possible successes for producers located elsewhere. The Chow test results strengthen the suspicion that these cases may have been successes for non-U.S.-based interests. The three other cases exhibit characteristics similar to this group in that all show significant increases in Japan's imports from the relevant non-U.S. sources in the post-agreement period but more limited increases or declines in imports from the United States.

Admittedly, many influences aside from trade agreements could be causing the cases of trade-growth instability presented in Table 5. To control for macroeconomic influences that affect all industries, I repeat the Chow tests after differencing the annual trade growth in the non-targeted industries from that in each targeted industry. In the first tests on differenced data, I used industry-level, import-price indices to deflate the targeted industries' data and Japan's WPI to deflate the non-targeted industries' data for Japan's import growth. To make sure that differences in the movements of these price indices do not unduly influence the results for Japan's imports, I also did the Chow tests after differencing out trade growth in the non-targeted industries when both the non-targeted and targeted industries' data are deflated using Japan's WPI. These results are reported in detail in Greaney (2001).

Of the seven agreements initially identified in the discussion of table 5 as possible evidence of positive impacts of trade agreements, one failed to be confirmed by differencing out trade growth in non-targeted sectors, 541 (1986). This means that in six of the 27 industry-agreement cases the trade data provide evidence that could be used to support a conclusion of positive effects from a bilateral agreement. Only in one of these six cases do the data support a conclusion of positive effects for producers located within the United States. This case involved the auto agreement in 1987. In this case, all three Chow tests identified a breakpoint for Japan's imports from non-U.S. and EU sources in 1988 that corresponds with a decline in post-agreement trade growth. The confirmation of the results using three variations on the trade data strengthen the suspicion that this agreement may have caused a substitution of U.S. autos for European autos in Japan's imports rather than an increase in market access for all foreign producers. However, this interpretation of the trade evidence becomes more difficult to defend when the details of the actual agreement are examined. According to ACCJ (1997, p. 96), the

> "Market-Oriented, Sector-Selective (MOSS) talks on transportation machinery is primarily a record of discussions on trade in autos and auto parts. Not a trade agreement in a formal sense, it nevertheless includes a few helpful announcements by the Japanese side regarding the compilation of statistics and the enforcement of auto inspection regulations."

Table 5. Agreement Years Identified as Valid Breakpoints by Chow Tests

SITC	Date	Japan's Import Growth from ...			America's Export Growth to ...		
		US	Non-US	EU	Japan	Non-Jpn	EU
764	1/86	90	86*, 87*;		90		87*;
	6/89		**89*, 90***				**89*, 90***
752	1/86	**90, 91**	92*	87*	**90, 91**		**86*, 87*;**
	6/90						**90**, 91
	1/92						
759	1/86						
	1/92						
776	1/86		**91***	86*, 87*;			
	9/86			**91**			
	6/91						
541	1/86	**86, 87**	**86***, 87*	**86***			87*
872	1/86					**86***	**86***
792	6/90					**90, 91**	**90, 91**
781	8/87	87*, 88*	**88**	88	87*, 88*		**87*, 88**
	1/92						
784	8/87		**92**				
	1/92						
611	12/85		86*, **87***	**86*, 87***			**86*, 87***

SITC	Date	Japan's Import Growth from ...			America's Export Growth to ...		
		US	Non-US	EU	Japan	Non-Jpn	EU
612	12/85		**86*, 87***	**86*, 87***		87*	86*, 87*
851	12/85		**86*, 87***	**86*, 87***		**86***	
634	1/86				**87***	**86***	**86***
	6/90						
635	1/86	**91**		90, **91**	**90*, 91***	86*;	87*;
	6/90					**90*, 91***	**90*, 91**
641	1/86					86*;	92*, **93***
	4/92					**92*, 93***	
642	4/92						**92**

Bold numbers represent rejection of the null hypothesis of parameter stability at the 5% level of significance. Non-bold numbers represent rejection only at the 10% level.

*The agreement year (or subsequent year) breakpoint identified by the Chow test coincides with an increase in post-agreement trade.

This description makes it seem unlikely that the 1987 "agreement" on autos would have produced the effects found by the Chow tests, unless one takes a broader view of the agreement. If the agreement is viewed as a lengthy process involving negotiations and media attention for a prolonged period of time rather than just a final written document of mutually agreeable points, it seems possible to argue that the agreement had a significant impact on trade. For example, the media attention given to U.S. auto producers during the negotiations may have served as free advertising.[16]

The auto case is not the only one where the Chow test results seem to suggest more significant impacts than one would expect given the details of the actual agreements identified. Of the five confirmed cases where valid breakpoints corresponded with post-agreement increases in Japan's import growth from non-U.S. or EU sources, the three involving leather trade present the strongest evidence of positive trade effects. However, the agreement for these cases is the least likely of any of the agreements to have caused significant positive effects on targeted industry imports, especially from non-U.S. sources. The 1985 leather agreement contained more concessions related to imports of aluminum and other goods than to imports of leather goods.

This leaves only two cases where it seems reasonable to interpret the Chow test results as evidence of a significant positive effect of a trade agreement on Japan's imports from non-U.S. or EU sources. The 1986 agreements in telecommunications equipment, SITC 764, and semiconductors, SITC 776, contained some market-opening aspects that may be linked to the increased import growth from non-U.S. and EU sources, respectively.

A final case that deserves further consideration is the 1991 semiconductor (SITC 776) agreement. The initial stability tests indicated instability in Japan's imports from non-U.S. and EU sources in the year of the agreement, but this instability corresponds with a sharp decline in import growth. Although import growth from the United States also fell in 1991, the decline was not sharp enough to be identified as a source of instability in the trade growth path. The differences in the trade-growth slowdowns in 1991 suggest the possibility that the agreement served to shield U.S. semiconductors exporters from the full brunt of the downturn in demand that coincided with Japan's economic slowdown in that year. The 1991 agreement made explicit the 20% market-share target for foreign semiconductor producers that had been mentioned in a side-letter to the 1986 agreement. Although the agreement set the market-share target for all foreign producers selling in Japan, some feared that it would be interpreted as a need to buy more specifically from U.S. producers.[17] In this case, distinguishing between trade creation and trade diversion effects is not possible without more detailed, industry-level analysis.

V. Conclusions

The 27 industry-agreement cases reviewed in this study provide evidence for both skeptics and advocates of U.S.-Japan bilateral trade agreements. The skeptics, however, can embrace the bulk of the cases for which the trade data from 1980-95 do not support a conclusion of significant positive impacts of the trade agreements on Japan's imports of targeted manufactured products. At the bilateral level, most cases showed a decline in Japan's real import growth of targeted products from the United States after an agreement was signed. Of the cases where import growth from the United States increased in the post-agreement period, only one case displayed instability in the trade growth path at the time of a bilateral trade agreement. In this particular case, involving the automobile agreement in 1987, the trade data suggests trade diversion benefiting U.S.-based producers at the expense of European producers. The semiconductor agreement in 1991 is a less-definitive second case where the trade data can be used to support a claim of positive impacts on U.S.-based producers from a bilateral trade agreement. In this case, the agreement may have served to soften the negative impact of Japan's economic downturn in 1991. At the multilateral level, only two cases were found where the trade evidence and details of the agreements support a claim that non-U.S.-based producers benefited from the increased market access sought by a U.S.-Japan trade agreement. These cases involved bilateral agreements covering telecommunications equipment and semiconductors signed in 1986.

The latter finding provides some support for the USTR's claims of negotiating bilateral agreements to increase access to Japan's markets on a multilateral basis. It does not, however, explain the tendency for U.S. industry insiders to rate agreements highly despite their apparently limited benefits on U.S.-based producers in terms of increasing sales in Japan. This may indicate that these business people have a more multinational perspective since they may work for multinational enterprises with production facilities in non-U.S. locations. Alternatively, it may indicate that the results of the agreements are too subtle or too slow in their realization to be detected by the stability tests or be reflected in the trade flow statistics at the three-digit SITC level. The true effects of the agreements may be masked by simultaneous changes in other sector-specific economic conditions or they may be realized through cost savings that do not necessarily prompt increased sales activity. Another possible reason for some of the discrepancy is that trade agreements with less ambitious agendas may have received more favorable ratings than more ambitious agreements. Ratings from industry representatives may be more reflective of the differing levels of implementation of the agreements than of their impacts on trade.

The results from two high-profile trade disputes help to illustrate some of reasons for the discrepancies noted between the trade-based assessments of the agreements and the assessments made by industry or government insiders. Japan's imports of passenger cars (SITC 781) from the United States showed much more rapid growth following the 1987 agreement, giving this case the highest trade-based ratings. However, lobbying by the AAMA has continued to emphasize the failure of Japan to comply with past agreements. This mismatch between trade flows and perceived success of past agreements is likely due, at least in part, to the activities of Japanese auto transplant facilities in the United States. Japanese imports from these facilities have increased at a much faster pace than have imports of Chrysler, Ford and General Motors autos in the years following the 1987 trade agreement.[18] In this case, although Japan's imports of U.S.-made Japanese cars are helping to support jobs in the United States, the lingering complaint from AAMA representatives is that the jobs are not in "American" auto (and auto parts) companies, though this distinction is becoming increasingly unclear.

Another high-profile trade dispute that shows a wide discrepancy between the different ratings is the semiconductor case, which involved trade agreements in 1986 and 1991. These agreements received a very favorable combined rating of 8 out of 10 from U.S. industry representatives but much lower average ratings of 2.2 to 4.2 based on U.S.-Japan bilateral trade flows. In fact, Japan's import growth rate from the United States of products within SITC 776, which includes semiconductors, slowed following each agreement. The gap between the ratings may be due to the expanding multinational production base of U.S. semiconductor producers. This means that greater market access in Japan could produce expanded Japanese imports not from the United States but from U.S. production facilities in South-East Asia, for example. In fact, Japan's imports from non-U.S. sources grew more rapidly following both trade agreements. Another possible explanation for the low trade-based ratings is that the three-digit SITC category may be too aggregated to detect the effects of the agreement on the semiconductor market alone.[19] Alternatively, this case may provide an example of an upward bias in the ratings on the part of industry insiders who are eager to stress the positive value of such agreements.

These two cases illustrate the potential pitfalls involved in trying to draw a direct link between bilateral, sectoral trade flows and national producer interests. However, as long as such linkages continue to be made in the context of bilateral trade disputes, it seems appropriate to apply these criteria as one means of assessing the effects of bilateral trade agreements. If expanding exports of U.S.-based manufactures is the true goal of U.S. negotiators in pursuing bilateral agreements with Japan, my results support a rather negative assessment of these efforts. This presents an obvious question for future research: why has the U.S. government been so willing to undertake the costs involved in negotiating so many bilateral agreements with Japan when the benefits appear to be so limited? One possibility is that political gains may be more important outcomes of these agreements than economic gains. Saxonhouse (1998) found that the 1995 U.S.-Japan auto agreement produced no measurable effects on the profitability of U.S. or Japanese auto producers, but it produced measurable positive effects on President Clinton's reelection chances.

Notes

[*] The author thanks Chihwa Kao, Gary Kikuchi, James Levinsohn, J. David Richardson, Shujiro Urata and seminar participants at the American Chamber of Commerce in Japan, Japan Economic Seminar meeting, Empirical Investigations in International Trade, Syracuse University, Union College, University of Hawaii and University of Michigan for helpful comments, and Donald Bruce and Seth Giertz for excellent research assistance. This research was assisted by a grant from the Abe Fellowship Program of the Social Science Research Council and the American Council of Learned Societies with funds provided by the Japan Foundation Center for Global Partnership.

[1] Implicit trade barriers that Japan has been accused of maintaining tend to involve non-transparent or discriminatory practices by the government or private sector.

[2] A report by the American Chamber of Commerce in Japan (ACCJ, 1997) states that ACCJ members were "astonished to learn that no US Government agency has a readily accessible list of all US-Japan trade agreements or their complete texts" (p. 14), much less any formal means of assessing the outcomes of past agreements.

[3] I focus on manufactured imports because Japan has been singularly criticized for its low level of such imports, particularly in sectors where Japan exports similar products. For example, see Lawrence (1987) and (1991).

[4] Results that satisfy the lower confidence level are included due to the high level of volatility in some of the industry-level trade growth paths.

[5] The industry-level, import-price indices used for the other SITC cases are available from the author upon request.

[6] Japan's WPI also is used to deflate the targeted industries' data for some of the stability tests on differenced data (i.e., non-targeted industry trade growth differenced from targeted industry trade growth) as a check for robustness.

[7] The industries are listed in table 2 and subsequent tables in the same order that they appear in the sector groupings shown in table 1.

[8] The breakpoint indicates the first year's growth rate included in the post-agreement period. For a breakpoint of 1986, the trade growth from 1985 to 1986 would be the first post-agreement annual growth rate.

[9] The changes in trade growth for the average non-targeted industry for each different breakpoint are not shown due to space constraints.

[10] These ratings are based on the generous assumption that significant increases in post-agreement average annual trade growth are caused mainly by the agreement, rather than by other economic events. Stability tests on the trade-growth paths at the time of the agreement will serve to test the assumed correlation between the agreement and the trade movements, though they cannot test for direct causation.

[11] The boundaries for each of the ratings are defined by the minimum and maximum statistic, which correspond with ratings of 1 and 10, respectively. Ratings intervals divide the full statistics' range into 10 equal partitions.

[12] Using annual trade data, I cannot distinguish between the potential effects of the Jan. 1986 and Sept. 1986 agreements involving semiconductors.

[13] See Greaney (2001) for detailed results.

[14] Data from the 1989 *Benchmark Survey of U.S. Direct Investment Abroad* supports the contention that these industries are heavily involved in overseas production. Sales by overseas affiliates relative to sales by U.S. parents for all manufacturing enterprises were 42%, using sales data by industry of affiliate and by industry of U.S. parent, and 44%, using sales data by industry of sales. The corresponding percentages for computers and office equipment were 85% and 89%, and for electronic components and accessories 97% and 68%.

[15] A possible explanation for this discrepancy between the trade-based ratings and the AAMA's lobbying efforts is presented in the conclusion below.

[16] AAMA representative Andrew Card complained during a panel discussion in 1995 that Japanese consumers do not know where to go to buy U.S. cars, even though many would consider buying one. He blamed the exclusive dealership arrangement in Japan for this problem rather than insufficient effort or advertising by AAMA members. (C-SPAN video, 1995)

[17] The European Community challenged the 1986 agreement for this very reason (i.e., violation of the most-favored nation principle), but it lost in a GATT panel decision in 1988. (Irwin 1994, p. 65-66.)

[18] This trend is reflected in statistics from the Japan Automobile Importers Association for new import car registrations. In 1986, new import car registrations in Japan include zero attributed to Japanese transplants in the United States and 2,341 attributed to the Big Three's U.S. production plants. These numbers rapidly changed in the ensuing years; Japanese transplants outnumbered the Big Three for the first time in 1991, with 16,328 versus 13,711 registrations. The difference is even larger by 1995, with 84,722 versus 38,111 cars registered.

[19] Unfortunately, this hypothesis cannot be tested with the World Trade Database used in this study because it provides only aggregated data for SITC 776 so that analysis at a more detailed, four-digit level is not possible.

References

American Chamber of Commerce in Japan. 1997. *Making Trade Talks Work: Lessons from Recent History*. Tokyo: American Chamber of Commerce in Japan.

Bayard, T. O. and K. A. Elliott. 1994. *Reciprocity and Retaliation in U.S. Trade Policy*. Washington, D.C.: Institute for International Economics,

C-SPAN video. 1995. "Closed Markets or Lazy Businessmen?," Economic Strategy Institute, June 26.

Elliott, K. A. and J. D. Richardson. 1997. "Determinants and Effectiveness of 'Aggressively Unilateral' U.S. Trade Actions," in R. C. Feenstra (ed.), *The Effects of U.S. Trade Protection and Promotion Policies*. Chicago: University of Chicago Press.

Gold, P. L. and D. K. Nanto. 1991. "Japan-U.S. Trade: U.S. Exports of Negotiated Products, 1985-1990," CRS Report for Congress. Washington, D.C.: Congressional Research Service, The Library of Congress.

Greaney, T. 2001. "Assessing the Impacts of US-Japan Bilateral Trade Agreements, 1980-1995," *The World Economy* 24:127-57.

Irwin, D. A. 1994. *Managed Trade: The Case Against Import Targets*. Washington, D.C.: AEI Press,

Lawrence, R. Z. 1987. "Imports in Japan: Closed Markets or Minds?" Brookings Papers on Economic Activity 2: 517-48.

Lawrence, R. Z. 1991. "How Open is Japan?" in P. Krugman (ed.), *Trade with Japan: Has the Door Opened Wider?* Chicago: University of Chicago Press.

Noland, M. 1997. "Chasing Phantoms: The Political Economy of USTR," *International Organization* 51:365-87.

Saxonhouse, G. R. 1998. "Trade Policy, Constituent Interests and Politics in US-Japan Economic Relations," Research Seminar in International Economics Discussion Paper No. 417, University of Michigan.

USTR. 1999. *National Trade Estimate*, www.ustr.gov/reports/nte/1999/contents.html.

Viner, J. 1950. *The Customs Union Issue*, New York: Carnegie Endowment for International Peace.

Comment

Shujiro Urata

I would like to make my comments in the following order. First, I discuss Greaney's paper and then describe the methodologies used in the analysis. After summarizing the major findings briefly, I present my evaluation and comments.

Greaney's purpose is to study the impacts of U.S.-Japan bilateral trade arrangements on Japan's imports of targeted manufactured products from the United States and non-U.S. sources. She also attempts to compare the objective assessment of the effectiveness of the agreements based on trade data and subjective assessments by industry and government insiders.

To address these questions, Greaney analyzes the changes in the growth rates of Japan's import volume between pre- and post-arrangements periods. If the growth rate of Japan's import volume in the post-arrangement period is found to be higher than the corresponding growth rate for the pre-arrangement period, the arrangement is evaluated to be effective, and if not, it is evaluated as ineffective. In addition to straightforward comparisons of these average growth rates between pre- and post-arrangement periods, a more sophisticated statistical analysis of identifying the presence or absence of a structural shift in the growth rates in Japan's imports is conducted by applying the Chow tests. If a structural shift is detected in the year or the following year of trade arrangement, the arrangement is evaluated effective. Furthermore, Greaney devises an index of trade impact by aggregating various measures, which are used to evaluate Japan' s imports, in order to compare her evaluation of the trade arrangements with those of others.

Greaney found that the impacts of trade arrangements are limited. The Chow test results indicate that, out of 27 trade arrangements, only one case had a positive impact on U.S.-Japan trade flows, while only two cases had a positive impact on Japan's imports from non-U.S. sources. Her objective assessment of trade arrangement is found to be very different from the subjective assessments made by industry or government insiders, which tend to give higher evaluations.

As for my comments, it is very important to evaluate the effectiveness and the impacts of policies. However, relatively few attempts have been made. Moreover, most of these attempts have been less than satisfactory as the analyses have not been rigorous enough to draw reliable conclusions. Greaney examines the issues carefully from various aspects by applying several methodologies, and it thus contributes significantly to the area of policy-oriented research.

I would like to make two major points and one minor point. The first point regards the possible mismatch between the objective of trade arrangements and the measure that Greaney employed for the evaluation of the arrangements. This mismatch, which I will describe below, may result in the unexpectedly limited impacts of trade arrangements as well as a very different evaluation of the arrangements between Greaney and industry or government insiders. Although she assumes that the expansion of U.S. exports to Japan is the purpose of the trade arrangements, it is not clear if that is the case for all the arrangements under study. Indeed, she notes that the 1985 leather agreement contained more concessions related to imports of aluminum and other goods than to imports of leather goods. She also notes that the 1991 semiconductor agreement made explicit the 20% market-share target. These observations cast doubt on the purpose of these trade arrangements being to expand U.S. exports of these products to Japan. If the objective of the agreements is not to increase the quantity of imports, then one should not evaluate the impact of trade arrangements on the basis of trade expansion in volume terms. Similarly, one should not expect the evaluation by industry and government insiders to be similar to that based on trade volume. To deal with this possible mismatch problem, one has to examine the contents and objectives of the agreements in detail before conducting the analysis or the evaluation of the arrangements. As to the criterion for the evaluation, I wonder if export value or market share rather than export volume may be better indicators, considering that industry and government representatives may be more interested in export value or market share, which may be more easily measured, rather than export volume.

The previous comment does not lessen the importance of examining the impacts of trade agreements on the quantity of Japan's imports, as it provides important information on the impacts of trade arrangements. The author conducted the analysis using only trade statistics. Although such analysis may provide useful information given limited data availability, it ignores some important factors. Ideally, one should estimate import-demand functions and export supply functions by explicitly incorporating variables other than trade variables such as domestic prices and income and then examine the presence or absence of structural changes by applying the Chow test. Let me state clearly here that Greaney realizes the importance of these factors, but, in my view, these factors are not fully taken into account. Indeed, one could evaluate the effectiveness of the arrangements by conducting simulation exercises based on a model consisting of demand and supply functions. To analyze the impacts of trade arrangements, I would like to emphasize the importance of a detailed industry study that takes into account industrial organization and other important industry characteristics. This is because the impacts of trade agreements crucially depend on the behavior of import-competing firms in Japan and exporting firms in the United States and other countries.

I would like to add a somewhat minor point. It is the definition of the rest of the world in the analysis. Does the rest of the world include the EU? If it does, the figure for the rest of the world is influenced strongly by the EU, and thus it should exclude the EU. Following on this point, it may be interesting to isolate East Asia from the rest of the world. Multinational firms have invested heavily in East Asia to set up an export base, and thus they may benefit from market opening measures applied to Japan as they are enabled to expand their exports to Japan.

CHAPTER 16

Multilateralism, Unilateralism, and Bilateralism in U.S.-Japan Trade Relations: A WTO Law Perspective

Robert Howse

I. Introduction

Although Japan and the United States have frequently resorted to dispute settlement under multilateral (GATT/WTO) rules to settle their trade disputes (see Chapter 13 above), unilateral trade-policy instruments such as the U.S. Section 301 legislation, as well as bilateral market-access agreements (auto parts, for example) have played an important role in the management by the United States of its trading relations with Japan. Among most advocates of multilateral trade liberalization, unilateral and bilateral "managed trade" approaches to trade conflict are viewed either as illegal under multilateral rules or system-threatening (see, for example, Bhagwati, 1988). Some, however, while not indifferent to the real risks identified by Bhagwati and others, see a complex interrelationship between unilateralism, bilateralism, and multilateralism. Sykes (1992) has argued that Section 301 has often been effective in addressing market-access complaints through the threat alone of unilateral trade-restricting action, thereby enhancing market access without the need for actual defection on multilateral trade-liberalization commitments. Yarbrough and Yarbrough (1986) maintain that bilateral arrangements can have mutual hostage-taking characteristics that increase the cost of defection from, and thereby improve compliance with, trade-liberalization commitments. Chang (1994) and Howse (1998, 1999) have argued, with respect to trade and environment, that unilateral action, or the threat of it, may help to overcome hold out or other collective-action problems and facilitate new, bargained multilateral norms or, in the labor context, may create needed pressure to make multilateral approaches work more effectively (Howse, 1999).

This chapter examines recent WTO jurisprudence that has clarified the legality, or legal preconditions, for certain kinds of unilateral and bilateral trade-policy instruments, and then goes on to consider the implications of the jurisprudence for the future management of Japan-U.S. trading relations. The cases are *Turtles*, *Section 301*, and *Canadian Autos*.[1]

II. Turtles

In *Turtles*, the WTO Appellate Body (AB) considered an appeal from a panel that found a U.S. embargo of shrimp fished with turtle-unfriendly technology a violation of Art. XI of the GATT, and not justifiable under Art. XX. Much along the lines of the earlier *Tuna/Dolphin* panels, the panel in *Turtles* basically excluded from the possibility of Art. XX justification unilateral-trade measures targeting environmental practices or policies in other countries as per se inconsistent with the spirit or character of the multilateral trading system.[2]

Upon appeal, the AB took a very different approach. It viewed unilateral-trade measures targeting other countries' policies as in principle capable of justification under the particular heads of Art. XX (in this case, exhaustible natural resources) and made the strong statement that: "It is not necessary to assume that requiring from exporting countries compliance with, or adopting certain policies (although covered in principle by one or other of the exceptions) prescribed by the importing country, renders a measure *a priori* incapable of justification under Article XX" (para. 121). However, in examining whether the U.S. embargo was in relation to the conservation of exhaustible natural resources, the AB body raised, but did not answer, the question of whether some kind of territorial nexus between the country taking the measures and the resources being conserved was necessary to satisfy the requirement that the measures be "in relation to exhaustible natural resources." The AB considered that it was not necessary to answer this question, because even *if* such a nexus were required, it would be satisfied in this case, apparently by virtue of the fact that some of the endangered species of sea turtles migrated through U.S. territorial waters. But what if none of the turtles swam through U.S. territorial waters? Would the AB have viewed the "commons" nature of the endangered species, as reflected in relevant international agreements, as a sufficient nexus with U.S. interests, again assuming one is actually required? It is possible that the AB body was divided on whether a nexus was required, and what kind of nexus it might be. Perhaps the AB, or some of them, were groping towards something equivalent to the "effects" doctrine in international anti-trust.

Having found the U.S. embargo to be justified under Art. XX(g), the AB went on to consider whether the United States had met the requirement under the "chapeau" of Art. XX that the measure not be *applied* "in a manner that would constitute arbitrary or unjustified discrimination between countries where the same conditions prevail, or a disguised restriction on international trade." Here, the AB found several elements of arbitrary or unjustified discrimination in the application of the scheme. The United States had engaged in serious negotiations with some countries to deal with its conservation concerns but had not made comparable efforts with the complainants in this case. Although the statute provided flexibility as to what equivalent technologies employed by other countries' shrimpers could satisfy the requirement of turtle-friendliness, when the scheme was *applied*, all shrimp not caught with the U.S.-prescribed TED technology were embargoed. And customs decisions on which shrimp could be imported, and which not, under the scheme were apparently arbitrary and non-transparent. The AB strongly implied that the straightforward extraterritorial application of domestic environmental regulation, indifferent to divergent conditions that prevail in different countries, would be unlikely to satisfy the requirements of the "chapeau." It suggested that the detailed application of embargoes of this nature would be judged against the expectation (found within certain international environmental agreements themselves, e.g., the Rio Declaration) that a state would not normally resort to unilateral action of this kind without having first seriously attempted to enter into negotiations with the other state(s) concerned, in order to find a way of achieving the environmental objectives in question in a manner consistent with the different conditions prevailing in the other state(s).

While being faithful to the entire text of Art. XX, which does not *per se* exclude such unilateralism, (see excellent commentary on the decision in Mavroidis, 2000, and DeBurca and Scott, 2001), the AB arguably struck a balance that is beneficial to the enhancement of multilateral or plurilateral cooperation to solve environmental commons problems. On the one hand, a state that contemplates unilateralism cannot go forward with it—as an automatic reflex, as it were—without being prepared to make a significant investment in the attempt to achieve a cooperative solution, which includes addressing different conditions in the other countries that may make them justifiably reluctant to adopt U.S. environmental standards . On the other hand, a state or states that refuse to enter into serious negotiations and frustrate cooperative solutions to environmental commons problems will not be protected against unilateralism by WTO law. In sum, the effect of the balance struck in *Turtles* is to create significant incentives for all sides caught in a trade and environment dispute to negotiate.

These implications of the *Turtles* ruling are very much at issue in the wake of Malaysia's recent claim, under Art. 21.5 of the WTO dispute settlement Understanding (DSU), that the United States has failed to implement the ruling, and must withdraw its scheme. In addition to making changes that address the due process concerns identified by the Appellate Body, the United States has also participated with Malaysia in negotiations on a regional accord regarding turtle conservation, beginning with the Perth Conference in October 1999, and continuing with a meeting hosted by Malaysia itself in July 2000.[3]

In light of these on-going negotiations, and the emphasis by the Appellate Body on the importance of cooperative solutions to such commons problems, Malaysia's challenge to U.S. implementation seems untimely. It was clear to Malaysia, as well as to other countries, that the negotiations constituted an important element in U.S. actions to implement the Appellate Body ruling—based upon notions of good faith, and the requirement in the DSU that Members exercise self-restraint in dispute settlement proceedings, and not engage in dispute settlement as a "contentious act" (Art. 3.7, 3.10), it would have been more appropriate to let the negotiations run their course, before challenging U.S. implementation. However, Malaysia's 21.5 claim may well be struck down on procedural grounds, since its request for a panel does not state any particulars concerning provisions of the WTO Agreement that it claims are violated by the U.S. measures as altered in light of the AB ruling.

The *Turtles* ruling has significant implications for the current dispute between the United States and Japan with respect to whaling. Whales are an endangered species, protected under a multilateral environmental agreement to which both the United States and Japan are signatories, *The International Convention for the Regulation of Whaling.* Under the *Convention*, the International Whaling Commission (IWC) may impose restrictions on whaling to safeguard whales as an exhaustible natural resource (Art. V).[4] Such decisions are to be taken by supermajority vote (Art. III). Pursuant to these procedures, the Commission has enacted a moratorium on whaling. However, Art. V:3 of the *Convention* allows individual signatories to lodge objections to decisions of this kind by the IWC, within a specified time frame, with the result that the decision in question is not binding on that signatory. Thus, Norway has engaged in commercial whaling subsequent to the moratorium, pursuant to an objection that it filed within the required time period.

While Japan did not file such an objection, it has for some time vigorously opposed the moratorium, arguing that there is scientific evidence that a complete ban on commercial whaling is no longer necessary to protect the viability of the species. Japan's manner of protesting the moratorium has been to engage in killings of whales for purposes of scientific research, which is permitted as an exception under the *Whaling Convention* (Art. VIII:1). Under the practice of the Commission this exception is interpreted narrowly; its guidelines in effect create a least restrictive means test, asking whether the research result could be achieved by non-lethal means, and also whether the sought research results are actually required for legitimate scientific purposes. When Japan's proposal for much expanded scientific research-based killings of whales was examined in the Scientific Committee of the IWC, the opinion of scientists was deeply divided as to whether the proposed activity would meet the guidelines for application of the exception, and the Committee was unable to endorse the Japanese proposal as consistent with the exception in Art. VIII of the Convention (Scientific Committee Report, IWS/52/4, 2000). Accordingly, the IWC promulgated a resolution stating that "gathering information on interactions between whales and prey species is not a critically important issue which justifies the killing of whales for research purposes" and that "information on stock structure, which may be relevant to management, be obtained using non lethal means." Therefore, the Japanese Government was urged to refrain from issuing the permits proposed under its program.[5]

Japan, however, refused to comply with the resolution and proceeded to issue permits for the whaling in question. After expressing U.S. concern through subtler measures of diplomatic pressure, President Clinton, announced in fall 2000 one sanction against Japan—a prohibition on Japanese fishing in certain U.S. waters—and there is possible consideration of trade sanctions pursuant to the Pelly Amendment. The Japanese government has made suggestions that it could commence a WTO action in the event that trade sanctions are imposed.

How would such a dispute be resolved under WTO law as interpreted in the *Turtles* case? There would be obviously no difficulty in characterizing the whales as exhaustible natural resources within the meaning of Art. XX(g). What, however, of the requirement that there be a rational relationship or connection between such sanctions and the protection of whales as an exhaustible natural resource? In the *Turtles* case, the Appellate Body found that such a rational relationship could exist where the trade measures were designed to "influence countries to adopt national regulatory programs" that would serve the protection of the endangered species (para. 138). However, it also seemed important to the Appellate Body that the U.S. measure was designed (although not applied) in such a manner as to permit entry into the United States of shrimp that were caught in a turtle-friendly manner, rather than being a prohibition on *all* shrimp from *jurisdictions* that catch shrimp in a turtle unfriendly manner (para. 141).

From an observation along these lines, the AB concluded that "it appears to us that Section 609, *cum* implementing guidelines, is not disproportionately wide in its scope and reach in relation to the policy objective of protection and conservation of sea turtles" (para. 141). Now here the AB does not actually say what *would* have been disproportionately wide in scope and reach. Given that the AB actually accepts that measures that operate through suasion of other governments in their policies have a rational relationship to the objective in question, it could not come to the conclusion that a ban on all shrimp would necessarily be "disproportionately wide" in scope and reach, if such a ban could reasonably be viewed as appropriate to the kind of suasion at issue. Trade in whale meat and by-products is already banned by virtue of the Convention on International Trade in Endangered Species (CITES). Thus, the statement of the AB in para. 141 of *Turtles* leaves us wondering what additional measures *would* be disproportionately wide in scope and reach. What about import restrictions on Japanese automobiles? Or television sets? In the *Reformulated Gasoline* case, the AB severely criticized the panel below for interpreting the language "relating to" in Art. XX(g) in such a way as to assimilate the kind of fit required between a measure and objective in the case where the treaty language used the word "necessary" to the kind of fit required in the case of Art. XX(g). So we know from *Reformulated Gasoline* that the AB cannot have in mind here a test as strict as that of least-restrictive-means.

My sense is that what the AB is saying here is that the trade-restricting scheme must be rationally coherent in light of the objective it purports to serve. Such rational coherence might be undermined, for example, if the scheme sanctioned Japan not only for killing whales but also other species not endangered or not protected as such under international law. Such coherence could also be undermined if the choice of imports to which the sanctions apply were chosen in such a way, not to maximize appropriate commercial pressure on Japan, but to maximize protective rents to domestic American producers for whom the products in question represent fierce import competition. Another example might be a case where the scheme provides for the sanctions to continue, say, for six months after the offending conduct has been discontinued. Such an extension could be regarded as punitive or protectionist or both, but not as well-tailored to the goal of inducing the other state to engage in the desired conservationist behavior.

Thus, the recommendations of the Commerce Secretary to the President should take into account the AB concerns that measures under XX(g) not be disproportionately wide in scope and reach, by designing a scheme that avoids features not well-tailored or closely connected to the goal of stopping the offending whaling, or which would seem to allow other purposes or goals (protection of domestic industries) to intrude into and disrupt the means-ends coherence of the overall scheme. Discussion so far appears to revolve around restricting imports of Japanese fish products into the United States. To the extent that the dispute revolves around Japan's fisheries practices, and more importantly to the extent that these are not products that are in competition with domestic U.S. production, this seems a sensible approach. To the extent that products that are in competition with domestic U.S. production cannot be avoided for the sanctions to have the needed impact, the import restrictions could be balanced by export restrictions, say of pollock and salmon. Thus, any protective benefit to U.S. producers in the fisheries sector could be balanced by an at least equivalent burden to those producers (and the export restrictions would put further pressure on Japan, because these are products favored by Japanese consumers).

A different challenge posed by this dispute for WTO law is that Japan may possibly argue that the U.S. measures are not rationally related to conservation of exhaustible natural resources, because the Japanese practice at which they are targeted does not impair the conservation of those resources. Here, Japan would present the scientific evidence that it claims to be able to muster that certain whale populations have increased to the point where takings are not endangering. Could one really say that the "scientific" killings, even on the scale now engaged in by Japan, make a real difference as to whether the species are endangered or not?

But it only takes a moment's reflection on the "tragedy of the commons" to appreciate the speciousness of such a potential line of argument. The tragedy of the commons does not occur because an individual user, unconstrained, depletes the commons to the point of exhaustion—indeed an individual user might well have enough incentives in terms of future availability of the commons resource to itself, not to deplete to that extent. The tragedy occurs because the unconstrained, or uncoordinated exploitation, of the commons by multiple users has the combined effect of exhausting the commons resource.

The real issue therefore is the relation of the conduct being sanctioned to the collective management of the commons resource in question with a view to avoidance of a tragedy of the commons. Refusing to abide by a resolution of the IWC that suggests its conduct falls outside of what is permitted under the multilateral regime for the management of whales as a global commons resource, Japan has effectively defected from a cooperative approach to the management of this commons resource. Where defections go unsanctioned, such regimes of multilateral cooperation may well unravel (Keohane, 1985; Axelrod and Keohane, 1985). In sanctioning such defection, the U.S. measures would be rationally related to preserving a multilateral regime for the conservation of whales.

The application of the U.S. measures would also have to be consistent with the chapeau of Art. XX. Here, it should be recalled that in the *Turtles* case, the AB found "unjustified discrimination" within the meaning of the chapeau because the U.S. scheme was applied differently to the complainants than to some other countries. Thus, in the case of certain countries in the Western hemisphere, the United States had proceeded to engage in negotiations that resulted in a cooperative approach to the problem of turtles as an endangered species, whereas with respect to the complainants, it had ended up imposing import restrictions without giving negotiations a serious try.

One source of consternation in Japan about the possibility of U.S. trade sanctions, is that the United States has not sanctioned Norway, which actually has an active commercial whaling industry, having reserved against the obligation to implement the IWC moratorium, as noted above. Despite its reservation, the IWC has also promulgated a resolution urging Norway to stop whaling. Is, then, the application of trade sanctions pursuant to the Pelly Amendment against Japan but not Norway "unjustified discrimination" within the meaning of the chapeau? I do not believe so. The meaning of "unjustified" must be read in light of the Rio Convention objective of advancing multilateral, cooperative solutions to environmental commons problems, noted by the AB in *Turtles*. However objectionable Norway's behavior may be from the perspective of conservationist values and policies, Norway is not "cheating" or defecting from the relevant multilateral regime. Japan is using a "loophole" in the *Convention* which the IWC has determined that it is not entitled to use under the circumstances, and is thus threatening the coherence and integrity of that regime. Norway is operating under an objection or reservation to the IWC decision on a moratorium, which it is legally entitled to, under the terms of the treaty itself. I believe that the United States is justified in taking into account this difference in the character of the two countries' behavior from the perspective of sustaining the legal and institutional framework for cooperative management of the exhaustible resource n question.

It is true that Japan questions the premise of the current approach of the multilateral regime, i.e., whether a ban is any longer necessary for preservation of the species in question. The IWC itself, since 1994, has been developing an alternative approach, based upon catch limits set in light of best available information on the situation with regard to individual species. However, there are considerable uncertainties in estimates of whale populations. Therefore, in the absence of solving issues with respect to the reliability of data, it is understandable that the IWC has yet to implement this alternative approach. This could be said to reflect the precautionary principle, which the AB in *Hormones* viewed as an established principle of international environmental law, albeit not of international law more generally. In any case, the bargaining costs entailed in reaching agreement among a range of state actors with divergent interests on specific catch limits, could be sufficiently high that a moratorium might remain the most efficient rule, even if, in a world where bargaining costs were, zero the optimal conservation rule would rather consist of more specific limits on takings.

III. Section 301

In this case, the European Union challenged provisions of U.S. S. 301 legislation that permitted unilateral U.S. determinations that a Member had violated WTO rules, determinations that would, at least potentially or in part, occur outside the framework and timetable for dispute settlement of the WTO itself. These provisions were connected to the threat (which was realized or close to being realized in the *Bananas* case) that the United States might take retaliatory trade action before, or without the authorization to do so by WTO dispute settlement organs, pursuant to the DSU. Relying on Art. 23 of the DSU, the EU made the following claim: "By imposing specific strict time limits within which unilateral determinations must be made that other WTO members have failed to comply with their WTO obligations and trade sanctions must be taken against such WTO members, this legislation does not allow the United States to comply with the rules of the DSU and the obligations of GATT 1994 in situations where the (DSB) has, by the end of those time limits, not made a prior determination that the WTO Member concerns has failed to comply with its WTO obligations and has not authorized the suspension of concessions or other obligations on that basis." Art. 23.2(a) of the DSU provides that: "Members shall: (a) not make a determination to the effect that a violation has occurred, that benefits have been nullified or impaired, or that the attainment of any objective of the covered agreements has been impeded, except through recourse to dispute settlement in accordance with the rules and procedures of this Understanding, and shall make any such determination consistent with the findings contained in the panel or Appellate Body report adopted by the DSB or an arbitration award rendered under this understanding." In understanding the decision in the *S.301* case, it is crucial to appreciate that the EU was not challenging as violations of Art. 23.2(a) the actual conduct of the United States authorities pursuant to S. 301 in the *Bananas* case (this was the subject of parallel proceedings in dispute settlement), but rather the very existence of the statutory provisions themselves. It is also important to appreciate that this case could not easily be resolved by characterizing the U.S. provisions as falling clearly on one side or the other of the divide between "mandatory" and "discretionary."

On the one hand, the provisions did mandate a *determination* of *whether* a violation had occurred, and thus required the USTR to put itself in a position where there was a significant possibility that it would make a finding of violation outside the WTO dispute settlement framework, thereby running afoul of DSU 23.2(a) On the other hand, the legislation could be argued to fall on the "discretionary" side of the divide in the sense that there was a hypothetical possibility that in every case where the statute mandated a *determination*, the USTR would make a finding that no violation had occurred. Thus, the frequently suggested notion that legislation which mandates conduct in violation of WTO obligations is itself WTO-inconsistent, whereas that while merely allows such violations on a discretionary basis does not, was unworkable as a principled approach to the problem in this case.The panel's ruling in this case is a masterful and subtle reconciliation of the GATT *acquis*—which suggested that in important respects a threat of violation can itself be a violation—with the basic approach to state responsibility in public international law. The panel accepted the notion that, since many provisions of the WTO treaties, and indeed the system as a whole, were aimed at protecting the expectations of individual traders, not simply states parties, the chilling effect on the conduct of traders of the insecurity created by a threat to violate could itself, depending on the treaty provision in question, constitute a violation of WTO law. At the same time, the panel rejected the idea that the WTO system had a quasi-constitutional or constitutional *telos* of direct legal effect: " . . . the GATT/WTO did *not* create a new legal order the subjects of which comprise both contracting parties or Members and their nationals"(emphasis in original).

It would thus be incorrect to *substitute* for the public-international-law framework of state responsibility, a constitutional understanding of the legal security provided to individual traders under the WTO treaties. However, in considering the way that the international-law framework of state responsibility *applies* to the WTO system, one must take into account the significance of the systemic goal of securing the trading opportunities of individual traders. Under the international-law framework for state responsibility, "legislation under which an eventual violation could, or even would, subsequently take place does not normally in and of itself engage State responsibility" (para. 7.80). What the panel appreciated was this: where the *benefit* from the *specific* treaty provision at issue is fundamentally undermined or impaired by the *threat* of a violation, not to consider the threat of violation as itself a violation would undermine the effectiveness of the treaty. On the other hand, if every *possibility* arising from a domestic statute that a violation might occur were interpreted as a "threat" and thus a violation in itself, this would be tantamount to replacing the public-international-law rules of state responsibility with a conception of direct effect—an absolute obligation on member states to translate WTO obligations into domestic legal guarantees to individual traders, i.e., providing individual legal rights against the *possibility* of WTO violations by domestic authorities.

It is this subtle appreciation of the need to read the *telos* of the WTO system and the framework for state responsibility in public-international law as complementary and consistent with one another, that informed the panel's overall approach to the U.S. measures at issue: "Construing a WTO obligation as prohibiting a domestic law that "merely" exposes Members and individual operators to risk of WTO inconsistent action should not be done lightly. It depends on the specific WTO obligation at issue, the measures under consideration and the specific circumstances of the each case." In examining the statutory provisions at issue, the panel found that these gave rise to a "real risk or threat" of WTO violation. There was thus a *prima facie* violation of Art. 23 of the WTO. However, this *prima facie* violation need not result in a definitive violation; the "threat" created by the statute itself could be curtailed or removed through lawful action, including action of a non-statutory character. In this case, the panel pointed to the Statement of Administrative Action (SAA) submitted by the President to Congress, and approved by Congress, which stated *inter alia* that it was the expectation of Congress that the executive branch would "base any section 301 determination that there has been a violation or denial of U.S. rights . . . on the panel or Appellate Body findings adopted by the DSB." It also pointed to underlying U.S. constitutional doctrine that requires the interpretation of U.S. law in a manner consistent with international treaty obligations, where possible. Finally, the panel noted assurances provided by the United States in the course of the panel proceedings that the USTR was to be bound by the Statement of Administrative Action to base a determination of a violation of U.S. WTO rights on a prior decision of a WTO panel or the Appellate Body. Taken together, the panel viewed these various aspects of the overall legal and administrative framework of U.S. trade law as removing the *prima facie* "real risk or threat" of violation created by the statute itself.

In backing off from a definitive finding of violation, the panel has been widely understood to have engaged in a pragmatic political compromise, allowing both the EU and the United States to accept the panel ruling, facilitating its adoption without appeal, and with each side claiming it has won. However, I believe that this disposition of the case follows logically from the jurisprudential foundations elaborated by the panel prior to its analysis of the U.S. measures. To have demanded of the United States that it explicitly change its statute, in effect that it guarantee directly and as of right to individual traders that WTO obligations would not be violated by U.S. executive action, would be tantamount to reading into the WTO system the requirement of "direct effect" of WTO obligations in domestic law. "Constitutionalizing" the WTO system in this way would have been an overly-ambitious and probably illegitimate act of judicial activism. Consistent with the basic approach to state responsibility in public-international law, and adapting that approach to the WTO context while not undermining it, the test the panel created for state responsibility in this context was whether, overall, legal acts (whether administrative, legislative or judicial) of a member state gave rise to a serious risk of violation, *not* whether the member state had provided statutory guarantees, enforceable by private parties, that WTO obligations would *not* be violated. Of course there is the discrete issue of whether the panel correctly applied its real or serious risk standard to the facts.

Given that the WTO system does not require that rights be *directly* conferred on private traders (even the TRIPS Agreement stays within the parameters of international-law state responsibility, allowing Members choices as to how it implements the requirement to provide legal security to IP rights holders), do the various acts relied on by the panel meet the more flexible standard for state responsibility discerned by the panel in its integration of WTO law with the public international law framework for state responsibility? In other words do these acts amount to a sufficient curtailment of the real risk or threat created by the statute, such as to fulfill state responsibility in this context?

An answer to this question might easily have been thought to depend on the panel's appraisal of complex and ambiguous facts, and even on its speculations about the political economy of U.S. trade law. Yet the panel was able to avoid such indeterminacy in the end, through the application of an international-law benchmark. It viewed the U.S. statements before the panel in the light of international-law jurisprudence on the legal status of unilateral declarations by states, specially the International Court of Justice (ICJ) *Eastern Greenland* and *Nuclear Test Ban* cases. In these cases, the ICJ held that a unilateral declaration made deliberately and with an apparent binding intent could have the legal effect of requiring the declaring state to conduct itself in accordance with the declaration. While acknowledging that in this instance "the U.S. statements do not go as far as creating a new legal obligation" (they could not, since the United States was already under an obligation to observe WTO law), it concluded that "[a]s a matter of international law, the effect of the U.S. undertakings is to anticipate, or discharge, any would be State responsibility that could have arisen had the national law under consideration in this case consisted of nothing more than statutory language" (para. 7.126).

In my view, this is a very elegant solution to the challenge of applying of the "real risk" standard to the facts of this case, because it is so thoroughly grounded in the general propositions of jurisprudence announced by the panel at the outset. In effect, the panel was saying: the United States has provided as much legal security against the real risk or threat of WTO violation posed by the statutory text itself as can be provided through *international* legal obligation—it has made a declaration that is sufficiently solemn and deliberate that the declaration could, if necessary, be itself viewed as a binding international law commitment. To ask for more, would amount to requiring "direct effect" and would obliterate the flexibility that the international law framework of state responsibility gives to states in deciding how effectively to implement international obligations within their own domestic legal system.

Some critics of the panel decision have questioned whether statements by a state made in a litigation context should be interpreted as intended to be binding, as opposed to being part and parcel of advocacy (see for example, Chang, 2000, p. 1188). The answer to this criticism lies in the recognition that the United States would have seen in the Interim Report of the panel the particular effect that the panel purported to give to its words. The failure of the United States to object to the panel making such use of the statements as it did certainly amounts to an intent to be bound, even if there is uncertainty as to whether any such intent might have existed at the time when the statements themselves were made. Similarly, if the United States objected to the interpretation of international law on the basis of which the panel read its statements to be the equivalent of binding unilateral declarations, this could have been appealed by the United States to the Appellate Body.

Another criticism sometimes made of the panel ruling, is that the panel failed to apply Art. XVI:3 of the WTO Agreement, which states: "Each Member shall ensure the conformity of its laws, regulations and administrative procedures with its obligations as provided in the annexed Agreement" (Chang, 2000, pp. 1189-1190). However, as the panel itself implied (para. 7.24), XVI:3 merely sets out question to be asked in a case like *S. 301*: *what* must a Member do, in the circumstances, to "ensure conformity" with Art. 23 of the DSU? Art. XVI:3 does not set out the demands of State responsibility, it merely articulates the *concept* of State responsibility as it applies to the WTO treaties. Some argue that the wording "ensure" in Art. XVI:3 denotes something equivalent to direct effect, or at least a significantly higher standard than that provided for in the general international law rules of State responsibility. Yet, singled out in this way, there is nothing in the ordinary meaning of the word "ensure" that goes beyond the standard articulations of the general international law principles of *pacta sunt servanda*/good faith. (see *Advisory Opinion on Treatment of Polish Nationals and Other Persons of Polish Origin in Danzig Territory*, 1932, P.C.I.J., Ser. A/B, No. 44).

Other critics see great danger in the notion that non-statutory action might cure statutory violations of WTO rules; it should be understood, however, that from the perspective of *international* law statutory acts do not have a status distinct from other internal acts of that have consequences for its international law obligations. As the International Court of Justice states in the *Polish Upper Silesia Case*, 1926, P.C.I.J., "municipal laws are merely facts which express the will and constitute the activities of states in the same manner as do legal decisions or administrative measures" (p. 19). It is thus a question of determining whether, on the basis of *all* the relevant "facts," a state has discharged its obligations of state responsibility in the circumstances.

In the *Indian Patents* case, the panel made a factual determination that India *could* not assure its conformity with the TRIPS Agreement by the administrative action it had taken, because of the specific relationship between statutes and administrative action in the Indian legal system, and the existence of apparently conflicting statutory obligations. At the same time, the panel made a number of statements of law that suggested an understanding of state responsibility that verged on "direct effect"—particularly the manner in which it developed the idea of "legal security." The Appellate Body modified some of these legal pronouncements, but of course could not alter the factual determination the panel made as to the effects of India's administrative action within the Indian legal system as a whole (a factual determination which, by the way, I find questionable in a number of respects). Because based on that factual determination, India had not met *any* plausible standard of state responsibility, the AB in *Indian Patents* did not need to articulate fully an alternative to the extremely intrusive legal standard for state responsibility of the panel in that case, in order to uphold the result, and could leave matters at expressing reservations about the panel's articulation of the legal standard. In *S. 301*, the panel has developed the law further, very much in the spirit of these reservations, articulating a context- and treaty text-sensitive standard for state responsibility that integrates the WTO system with the general international law framework for state responsibility.

In a subsequent case, *United States-Anti-Dumping Act of 1916*, Japan and the European Communities challenged certain provisions of this U.S. anti-dumping statute, which included possible criminal penalties and prosecutions for anti-dumping. The complainants claimed that various provisions of the statute violated the WTO Anti-Dumping Agreement and the GATT. As a defence, the United States in this case returned to the old mandatory/discretionary distinction that was the basis for determining state responsibility for legislation prior to the *S. 301* panel. The United States appealed from the panel ruling in *United States-Anti-Dumping* that United States had not shown the law to be "discretionary legislation" within the meaning of the older GATT doctrine. While upholding this narrow finding of the panel, the Appellate Body explicitly declined to consider the broader issue of the extent to which the mandatory/discretionary distinction is still relevant to state responsibility in the WTO—it did, however, in *dicta*, suggest that whether legislation is "discretionary" is not necessarily dispositive of whether it amounts to a violation of WTO law. The Appellate Body noted in this regard, with apparent approval, the *S. 301* panel (para. 99 and accompanying fn. 59). To me, this suggests that, in a future case where it was required to decide the broader issue, the AB might well be inclined to endorse the general approach in *S. 301*.

IV. Canada-U.S. Auto Pact Case

Japan and the United States have not infrequently resorted to bilateral agreements, often arguably of a "managed trade" character, in order to resolve their trade differences. These range from explicit Voluntary Export Restraints and import targets, to agreements concerning various domestic policy measures, for example the Japan-United States Automotive Agreement. Under the GATT system that preceded the creation of the WTO, these kinds of bilateral responses to trade conflict were not, in general subject to great discipline or scrutiny, one exception being the EC complaint against Japan in the *Semiconductor* case. In another GATT case, Canada successfully challenged EC beef import regulations that favored beef inspected by U.S. meat inspection authorities, the context of which was a bilateral understanding between the United States and EC concerning relaxation of certain measures of agricultural protection at least as applied to U.S. exports to the EC. However, bilateral deals of various kinds proliferated in the 1970s and 1980s, as responses to the limits of the current multilateral system in solving trade tensions, and most were not subject to challenge, for instance by other GATT Contracting Parties, as violations of MFN.

In the Uruguay Round, most forms of "voluntary" managed trade arrangements were outlawed in Art. 11. Indeed, the scope of this ban is pretty broad, as indicated in the footnote to this Article, which indicates that among the prohibited measures include "export moderation, export-price or import-price monitoring systems, export or import surveillance, compulsory import cartels and discretionary export or import schemes, any of which afford protection." Although many of the provisions of the Japan-U.S. Automotive Agreement for instance are worded in an MFN friendly way, even it might fall afoul of Art. 11, since there are provisions that related to export and import surveillance. Of course, in the case of "voluntary" arrangements a third country must be found that has a legal interest in challenging the measures under the Safeguards Agreement. However, with regard to formal standing rules, the concept of legal interest in WTO dispute settlement law is rather broad (see *Bananas*). This of course, does not mean that third countries would frequently, but for evidence of trade diversion or "fortress" effects, see themselves as having a concrete commercial interest in mounting such challenges.

Interestingly, the most significant challenge to bilateral managed trade so far brought to WTO dispute settlement is by Japan itself, claiming, inter alia, violations of MFN treatment in the Canada-U.S. auto pact arrangement, a long standing managed trade agreement, that—as anyone living in the Detroit/Windsor area is profoundly aware—has been used to divvy up plants and jobs between localities on the two sides of the border. Here, at issue was an import-duty exception that applied to certain listed manufacturers of automobiles with facilities in North America. However, on its face the exception was non-discriminatory with respect to the origin of the imports. Nevertheless, holding that Art. I of the GATT includes *de facto* discrimination, the AB upheld the panel's finding that, since the manufacturers in question imported almost exclusively from their own subsidiaries in particular countries, the import-duty exemption violated Art. I. I believe that this ruling will make it fairly difficult to devise bilateral-trade/managed-trade deals that pass Art. I, even if they do not get impugned under the *Safeguards Agreement*. Certainly, it will not be enough, as in the Japan-U.S. Automotive Agreement to phrase the market access commitments in MFN-friendly terms. The panels will look more deeply into the design or structure of the commitments, to see if they are devised so as to meet the needs of exporters from particular member countries.

Which is of course almost always the real-world negotiating context of such arrangements!

V. Conclusion

The recent case law of the World Trade Organization discussed above clearly suggests that the interpretation of multilateral rules at the WTO will have a significant influence on unilateral or bilateral approaches to Japan-U.S. trade relations. While multilateralism is often discussed as an *alternative* to unilateralism and bilateralism in trade relations, not only trade lawyers but all those concerned with trade policy, should pay attention to how evolving multilateral jurisprudence may alter the costs and benefits of unilateral and bilateral approaches in the years to come.

Notes

[1] For other discussion of WTO-related cases, see above Chapter 5 by William Davey, Chapter 13 by Robert Stern, and Chapter 14 by Gary Saxonhouse.

[2] In this case, unlike the *Tuna/Dolphin* cases, the panel had relied in a very loose and imprecise way on the language in the preambular paragraph of Art. XX, or "chapeau" about "unjustified and arbitrary discrimination." For a detailed analysis and critique of the panel decision, see Howse (1998).

[3] United States Department of State, "WTO Shrimp/Turtle Case Talking Points For Use in Consultations with the Government of Malaysia," unclassified document, October 19, 2000.

[4] An aside—in the *Turtles* case, the Appellate Body of the WTO, as noted above, considered the meaning of the expression "exhaustible natural resources" in Art. XX(g) in light of evolving norms of international environmental law and policy. This is entirely appropriate in light of the evolutionary nature of treaty interpretation reflected in the Vienna Convention on the Law of Treaties. However, some have argued that the meaning of natural resources in international law at the time the GATT Agreement was negotiated was the relevant meaning for interpretation, and that this meaning encompassed only non-living resources. However, the preamble to the *Whaling Convention*, done in 1946, refers to whales as "great natural resources."

[5] IWC Resolution 2000-5: Resolution on Whaling under Special Permit in the North Pacific Ocean.

References

Axelrod, R. and R. Keohane. 1985. "Achieving Cooperation Under Anarchy," in K. Oye (ed.), *Cooperation Under Anarchy*. Princeton, NJ: Princeton University Press.

Bhagwati, J. 1988. *Protectionism*. Cambridge, MA: MIT Press.

Chang, H. F. 1995. "An Economic Analysis of Trade Measures to Protect the Global Environment," *Georgetown Law Journal* 83:2131-2209.

Chang, S. W. 2000. "Taming Unilateralism Under the Trading System: Unfinished Job in the WTO Panel Ruling on United States Sections 301-310 of the Trade Act of 1974," *Law and Policy in International Business* 31:1151-1226.

DeBurca, G. and J. Scott. 2001 (forthcoming). "The Impact of the WTO on EU Decision-making," in G. DeBurca and J. Scott (eds.), *The WTO and the EU Constitution*. Oxford: Hart Publishing.

Howse, R. 1998. "The Turtles Panel—Another Environmental Disaster in Geneva," *Journal of World Trade* 32:73-100.

Howse, R. 1999. "The World Trade Organization and the Protection of Workers' Rights," *The Journal of Small and Emerging Business Law* 3:131-72.

Keohane, R. 1985. *After Hegemony: Cooperation and Discord in the World Political Economy*. Princeton, NJ: Princeton University Press.

Mavroidis, P. 2000. "Trade and Environment After the Shrimps-Turtles Litigation," *Journal of World Trade* 34 (February):73-88.

Sykes, A. 1992. "Constructive Unilateral Threats in International Commercial Relations: The Limited Case for Section 301," *Law and Policy in International Business* 23:263-330.

Yarbrough, B. and R. Yarbrough. 1986. "Reciprocity, Bilateralism, and Economic 'Hostages': Self-enforcing Agreements in International Trade," *International Studies Quarterly* 30:7-21.

Contributors

Kenzo Abe

Kenzo Abe is a Professor in the Graduate School of Economics, Osaka University in Japan. He has a B.A. from Keio University, and a M.A. and a Ph.D. from the Kobe University of Commerce. He specializes in international trade theory. He works on pure theories of international trade, trade policy, international transfer, and trade and environment. He has published a number of academic papers in professional journals.

Jeffrey H. Bergstrand

Jeffrey H. Bergstrand is Associate Professor of Finance and Business Economics at the University of Notre Dame. He received his B.A. in Economics and Political Science from Northwestern University in 1974, and his Ph.D. in Economics from the University of Wisconsin at Madison in 1981. From 1981-86, he was an economist at the Federal Reserve Bank of Boston. In 1986, he joined the faculty of the College of Business Administration at Notre Dame. His research on exchange rates, international trade flows, international finance, and open-economy macroeconomics has been published in leading journals and conference volumes. Since 1996, he has been a coeditor of the *Review of International Economics.*

Drusilla K. Brown

Drusilla K. Brown is an Associate Professor of Economics at Tufts University. She received her Ph.D. from the University of Michigan in 1984. Her research focuses primarily on the use of Applied General Equilibrium Models to evaluate trade negotiations and preferential trade agreements. In addition, she has worked on the theoretical issues concerning international labor standards and child labor.

William J. Davey

William J. Davey is the Edwin M. Adams Professor of Law at the University of Illinois College of Law, where he has taught courses in international trade law, European Community law, and corporate/securities law since 1984. From 1995 to 1999, he was the Director of the Legal Affairs Division of the World

Trade Organization. He is the author of *Pine & Swine: Canada-United States Trade Dispute Settlement* (1996), *Legal Problems of International Economic Relations* (1995, with Jackson & Sykes; 1986, with Jackson), *European Community Law* (1993, with Bermann, Goebel & Fox) and *Handbook of WTO/GATT Dispute Settlement* (1991-2000, with Pescatore & Lowenfeld), as well as various articles on international trade law issues. After his graduation from the University of Michigan Law School in 1974, he served as a law clerk to Judge J. Edward Lumbard (US Court of Appeals-New York) and Justice Potter Stewart (US Supreme Court) and worked in Brussels and New York for the law firm of Cleary, Gottlieb, Steen & Hamilton. He is a member of the American Law Institute.

Alan V. Deardorff

Alan V. Deardorff is John W. Sweetland Professor of International Economics and Professor of Public Policy at the University of Michigan. He received his Ph.D. in economics from Cornell University in 1971 and has been on the faculty at the University of Michigan since 1970. He served as Chair of the Department of Economics from 1991 to 1995. He has also served as a consultant to many government agencies and is currently on the editorial boards of the *World Economy*, *International Trade Journal*, and *Journal of International Economic Law*. He is co-author, with Robert M. Stern, of *The Michigan Model of World Production and Trade and Computational Analysis of Global Trading Arrangements*. He has published numerous articles on various aspects of international trade theory and policy. His current research interests include: the interactions between trade patterns and economic growth, the causes and effects of fragmentation, the importance of trade barriers for trade patterns, and the appropriate use of trade policies for issues of economic inequality, including labor standards and child labor.

Masahiro Endoh

Masahiro Endoh is Associate Professor, Faculty of Business and Commerce, Keio University. He held a previous academic appointment as Associate Professor in the Faculty of Commerce, Otaru University of Commerce (1996-99). He received a Bachelor's, Master's, and Ph.D. degree from the Keio University Faculty of Business and Commerce in 1991, 1993, and 2000, respectively. He has published papers on trade-related topics in *Applied Economics*, *The Journal of Asian Economics*, *Economia Internazionale*, and *Keio Business Review*, and has several manuscripts in process.

J. Michael Finger

Michael Finger is a Lead Economist in the International Trade Team at the World Bank. His general area of responsibility is trade reform, with a current focus on the implementation of the developing countries of their Uruguay Round obligations. He manages the Bank's partnership with the World Trade Organization and supports Bank programs that relate to client countries' WTO obligations. He has published 3 books and over 100 scholarly articles on international trade theory and policy.

Kyoji Fukao

Kyoji Fukao is Professor of Economics at the Institute of Economic Research, Hitotsubashi University. He has been at Hitotsubashi since 1986. He holds an M.A. in economics from the University of Tokyo. He has been a visiting researcher of the Research Institute of International Trade and Industries, MITI, and the Economic Research Institute, Economic Planning Agency. He is the author of numerous journal articles, chapters, and research papers dealing with foreign direct investment and open-economy macroeconomics.

Taiji Furusawa

Taiji Furusawa received his B.A. in Economics from Hitotsubashi University in 1987, M.A. in Economics from Hitotsubashi University in 1989, and Ph. D. in Economics from the University of Wisconsin-Madison in 1994. He taught at Brandeis University in 1994-95 and at Fukushima University in 1995-97. Since 1997, he has been an associate professor at Yokohama National University. His major research interest is in international trade negotiations and cooperation. He has published papers in the *Journal of International Economics*, *Review of International Economics*, and *Journal of Labor Economics*.

Yoshihisa Godo

Yoshihisa Godo is associate professor of economics at Mejii Gakuin University. He received Ph. D. from the Department of Agronomy, University of Kyoto, in 1994. He has published numerous papers/articles in professional journals and newspapers regarding Japan's agricultural policy. He is also the organizer of Theoretical Economics and Agriculture, one of the leading academic societies among Japanese agricultural economists, which was founded in 1952.

Theresa M. Greaney

Theresa Greaney specializes in the study of the Japanese economy and U.S.-Japan trade relations. She has recently published several analyses of Japan's voluntary import expansion (VIE) policies, examining the implications of "results-oriented" trade policy for the behavior of imperfectly-competitive firms. Her ongoing research examines Japan's changing import behavior and the impact of keiretsu relationships and outsourcing on international trade and trade policy. She completed her undergraduate studies at Stanford and received a Ph.D. in economics from the University of Michigan. She joined the faculty of the University of Hawaii at Manoa in August, 2000, after teaching for several years at Syracuse University.

Gordon H. Hanson

Gordon H. Hanson is Professor of International Economics in the Graduate School of International Relations and Pacific Studies at the University of California, San Diego. He received his Ph.D. in economics from the Massachusetts Institute of Technology in 1992. Prior to joining UCSD, he was a faculty member at the University of Michigan and the University of Texas. Professor Hanson is also a Research Associate in the National Bureau of Economic Research. His current research addresses multinational enterprises, U.S.-Mexico trade and migration, and the globalization of production in Asia and Latin America.

Jude C. Hays

Jude C. Hays is Assistant Professor of Political Science and Public Policy at the University of Michigan. His research focuses on the interconnections between the international economy and domestic politics. He has studied the effects of electoral politics on foreign exchange and bond markets and the role that democratic institutions play in mediating the impact of economic globalization on public finance. He received his Ph.D. from the University of Minnesota.

Keith Head

Keith Head is an Associate Professor of Strategy and Business Economics in the Faculty of Commerce and Business Administration at the University of British Columbia. He holds the HSBC Professorship in Asian Commerce. He teaches courses on international business management and managerial economics. He obtained his B.A. at Swarthmore College in 1986 and his Ph.D. in economics from the Massachusetts Institute of Technology in 1991. His research interests include foreign direct investment, international trade policy, and economic geography. His current research focuses on (1) the relationship between direct investment abroad and skill intensity at the parent firm and (2) how market size affects firm location decisions. His recent publications include: "Increasing Returns Versus National Product Differentiation as an Explanation for the Pattern of US-Canada Trade," with John Ries, in *The American Economic Review*; and "Non-Europe: The Magnitude and Causes of Market Fragmentation in the EU," with Thierry Mayer, in *Weltwirtschaftliches Archiv*. He is currently writing a book entitled *Elements of Multinational Strategy*.

Keisaku Higashida

Keisaku Higashida is an Associate Professor in the Faculty of Economics, Fukushima University in Japan. He has a B.A and a M.A. from Hitotsubashi University in Japan. His specialization is international trade theory, and he has been working on trade and environment.

Robert Howse

Robert Howse was educated at the University of Toronto (B.A. 1980, LL.B., 1989, co-editor in chief of the Law Review, 1998-1999) and Harvard Law School (LL.M., 1990). In 1999, he joined the University of Michigan Law School as Professor of Law. He taught previously at the University of Toronto Faculty of Law and as a Visiting Professor at Harvard Law School. He has also been a Lecturer in the Academy of European Law, European University Institute, Florence. Howse is an international fellow of the C. D. Howe Institute, a member of the faculty of the World Trade Institute, Bern, Switzerland, and serves on the editorial advisory boards of *Legal Issues in Economic Integration* and the *European Journal of International Law*. Between 1982 and 1986, he served in various positions in the Canadian foreign ministry, including on the Policy Planning Secretariat and at the Canadian Embassy in Belgrade, Yugoslavia. He is the author of *Economic Union, Social Justice and Constitutional Reform* (1992) and co-author, editor or co-editor of 6 other books, including the *Regulation of International Trade*, 2nd edition, 1999, with Michael J. Trebilcock. He has also published numerous contributions to edited volumes and articles in journals. With Kalypso Nicolaidis of Oxford University he is currently editing a volume of essays on the federal vision in the United States and European Union, to be published by Oxford University Press.

In 1994, Howse served on a panel advising the South African Justice Minister on the legal framework for the Truth and Reconciliation Commission. He has been a frequent adviser and consultant to the Canadian government, including the Law Commission of Canada. He has also consulted with international institutions and has worked on law reform issues in transitional countries.

Jota Ishikawa

Jota Ishikawa is an Associate Professor in the Graduate School of Economics, Hitotsubashi University in Japan. He has a B.A. and an M.A. from Hitotsubashi University and a Ph.D. from the University of Western Ontario in Canada. His specialization is in international trade theory. He has been working on economic growth, trade policy under imperfect competition, and trade and environment, and has published a number of academic papers in professional journals. He is currently the managing editor of *Hitotsubashi Journal of Economics*.

Fukunari Kimura

Fukunari Kimura obtained a Bachelor of Laws from the Faculty of Law, University of Tokyo in 1982 and worked as a researcher at the International Development Center of Japan for four years in the field of economic cooperation with developing countries. He received a Ph.D. in economics from the University of Wisconsin-Madison in 1991. He taught at the State University of New York from 1991-94, and then he moved to the Faculty of Economics, Keio University, where he is currently a professor of economics. His specialties are international trade and development economics. He has extensively written academic/semi-academic papers and articles particularly on foreign direct investment, regionalism and WTO, and industrial promotion of developing countries.

Will Martin

Will Martin is lead economist in the Development Research Group of the World Bank. He has been at the World Bank since 1991, where he has worked on trade policy-related issues with emphasis on the WTO and developing countries, and on trade policy reform in East Asian developing countries, particularly China. With Bernard Hoekman, he leads the Bank's major research and capacity-building project on the WTO and the developing countries. He has coordinated a number of major research projects, organized conferences on a range of issues, including "Trade and Poverty," and "The Uruguay Round and the Developing Economies," and played an active role in the formulation of World Bank policy positions. He is the editor or author of a number of books, chapters in books, and articles in international journals. Prior to joining the World Bank, Martin was a Senior Research Fellow at the Australian National University and a senior staff member at the Australian Bureau of Agricultural and Resource Economics. He holds a Ph.D. from Iowa State University, a B.Econ from the Australian National University, and a B.Agr Sc from the University of Queensland.

Keith E. Maskus

Keith E. Maskus is Professor of Economics at the University of Colorado. He is also a visiting research fellow at the Institute for International Economics, and associate editor of the *Review of International Economics*. Maskus has had visiting appointments as Senior Economist at the Federal Reserve Bank of Kansas City, Senior International Economist at the Department of State, and Professor of Economics at the University of Adelaide. He is a consultant for the USAID, World Bank, United Nations Conference on Trade and Development, World Intellectual Property Organization, and the Asia Foundation. His research focuses on empirical determination of the international pattern of trade and foreign direct investment, the economic impacts of trade-policy reform in developing countries, and aspects of international technology transfer, with reference especially to the effects of protecting intellectual property rights. His work has appeared in the *Journal of International Economics*, *American Economic Review*, *Review of Economics and Statistics*, *Journal of Development Economics*, *The World Economy*, and numerous other journals. His recent book entitled *Intellectual Property Rights in the Global Economy* was published in August 2000 by the Institute for International Economics. He received his Ph.D. from the University of Michigan in Ann Arbor in 1981.

Sadao Nagaoka

Sadao Nagaoka is Professor of Management and Economics at the Institute of Innovation Research in Hitotsubashi University. He holds a Ph.D. from MIT. His research interests are in the intersections between industrial organization and international trade. His recent publications include: "Competitive Impact of International Trade-A Case of Import Liberalization of Oil Product Market in Japan," *Journal of the Japanese and International Economies*, 1999; "International Trade Aspects of Competition Policy," in *Deregulation and Interdependence in the Asia-Pacific Region* edited by Ito and Krueger, University of Chicago Press, 2000; and a book on *The Economics of International Price Differentials—Productivity Approach* in Japanese, published by the NTT Press, 1999. Before joining Hitotsubashi University, he was employed in Seikei University, the Ministry of International Trade and Industry of Japan, and the World Bank. He has also served as an advisor and consultant to the OECD, WIPO, and Japanese government agencies.

Francis Ng

Francis Ng is a member of the research staff of the International Trade Team in the Development Research Group at The World Bank. He holds an MBA from the Catholic University of America and an M.A. and Ph.D. in economics from Washington International University. He is currently doing research on various international trade issues, including trade-policy reform in Sub-Saharan Africa, market access for developing countries, trade and production fragmentation in East Asia and Central European economies, and competition policy in the Middle East.

Arvind Panagariya

Arvind Panagariya is a Professor of Economics and Co-director, Center for International Economics, University of Maryland at College Park. He holds a Ph.D. degree in Economics from Princeton University. Prior to joining Princeton, he studied at Rajasthan University in India. He spent 1989-93 as a research economist at the World Bank and has been a consultant to various international institutions including the World Bank, Asian Development Bank, IMF, WTO, and UNCTAD. He has written or edited several books including *The Economics of Preferential Trade Agreements*, 1996, AEI Press (with Jagdish Bhagwati), *The Global Trading System and Developing Asia*, 1997, Oxford University Press (with M.G. Quibria and N. Rao), and *Lectures on International Trade*, 1998, MIT Press (with J. Bhagwati and T. N. Srinivasan). A collection of his essays on regionalism was published in 1999 by the World Scientific Press. Panagariya has written extensively on trade reforms in developing countries and is an editor of the *Journal of Policy Reform* and an Associate Editor of *Economics and Politics*. His technical papers and policy papers have appeared in leading journals. He writes a monthly column in the *Economic Times*, India's top financial daily.

John Ries

John Ries is an Associate Professor in the Faculty of Commerce and Business Administration of the University of British Columbia where he holds the HSBC Professorship in Asian Business. He teaches courses on international business, international trade policy, government and business, and the Asian business environment. He has a B.A. from UC-Berkeley and received a Ph.D. in Economics from the University of Michigan in 1990. His primary research interests are international trade and business and the Japanese economy. He has published articles in numerous academic journals, including the *American Economic Review*, *Journal of International Economics*, *Journal of Industrial Economics*, and the *Canadian Journal of Economics*. His current research includes an assessment of the effects of the Canada-U.S. FTA on North American manufacturing and an analysis of the role of vertical networks on the pattern of U.S. auto-parts trade.

Stephen W. Salant

Stephen W. Salant received his Ph.D. in economics from the University of Pennsylvania in 1973. He was an economist with the Federal Reserve Board in Washington, D.C. from 1972-78 and a Senior Economist with the Federal Trade Commission from 1979-81. During 1981-85, he was a Senior Economist with the RAND Corporation and served as the first co-editor of the *RAND Journal of Economics*. He joined the Michigan faculty in 1986 and has taught microeconomic theory, industrial organization and natural resource economics at the undergraduate and graduate levels. His recent research deals with cost asymmetries in the Cournot oligopoly model, the dynamics of common property extraction, spatial aspects of landfill depletion, and inefficiencies in gold extraction. His articles have appeared in leading journals.

Gary R. Saxonhouse

Gary Saxonhouse is Professor of Economics at The University of Michigan and Director of its Committee on Comparative and Historical Research on Market Economies (CCHROME). Besides holding his present position, Professor Saxonhouse has been on the faculty at Harvard, Yale and Brown. His publications include numerous articles on topics ranging from the structure and operation of the Japanese economy, U.S.-Japanese economic relations, technology transfer and econometrics, to English, Japanese and Indian economic history. His research has appeared in leading journals in the United States and Japan. In addition to his research papers, Saxonhouse has co-authored or co-edited six books, most recently *Finance, Governance and Competitiveness in Japan* (co-edited with Masahiko Aoki), published by the Oxford University Press. In recognition of his research achievements, the Association for Asian Studies awarded him its Distinguished Lectureship for 1979-80. During the academic years 1984-85, 1995-96, and again in 1999-2000, he was a Fellow at the Center for Advanced Study in the Behavioral Sciences at Stanford. He has been a frequent consultant to government and business, has testified on numerous occasions before Congressional committees, and served on Congressional and Japanese Government advisory panels and committees.

Yoko Sazanami

Yoko Sazanami has been a Professor of Economics at Meikai University since 1998, and prior to her retirement a long-time faculty member in economics at

Keio University. She has been a member of several Japanese Government committees and councils. Her recent publications cover topics in both international trade and international finance.

T. N. Srinivasan

T. N. Srinivasan is Samuel C. Park Jr. Professor of Economics at Yale University. He holds a Ph.D. in economics from Yale. His fields of research are International Trade and Economic Development. His recent book publications include *Developing Countries and the Multilateral Trading System: GATT 1947 to the Uruguay Round and Beyond* (Boulder, Colorado: Westview Press, 1998); and *Eight Lectures on India's Economic Reforms* (New Delhi: Oxford University Press, 1999). He has taught at numerous universities and has worked extensively with the World Bank. He is co-editor of several journals and a Fellow of the American Philosophical Society, the Econometric Society, the American Academy of Arts and Sciences, and a Foreign Associate of the National Academy of Science.

Robert M. Stern

Robert M. Stern is Professor of Economics and Public Policy (Emeritus) at the University of Michigan. He received his Ph.D. in economics from Columbia University in 1958. He was a Fulbright scholar in the Netherlands in 1958-59, taught at Columbia University for two years, and joined the faculty at the University of Michigan in 1961. He has been an active contributor to international economic research and policy for more than four decades. He has published numerous papers and books on a wide variety of topics, including international commodity problems, export-led growth, quantitative international economics, the determinants of comparative advantage, price behavior in international trade, balance-of-payments policies, the computer modeling of international trade and trade policies, trade and labor standards, and services liberalization. He has been a consultant to and done research under the auspices of several U.S. Government agencies and international and regional organizations. He is currently working with Drusilla Brown (Tufts University) and Alan Deardorff on the computational modeling and analysis of multilateral and regional trade liberalization, assessment of the post-1991 liberalization of economic policies in India, issues in U.S.-Japan international economic relations, and issues of child labor and international labor standards.

Jiro Tamura

Jiro Tamura is a Professor at the Law Faculty of Keio University, Tokyo. He received his L.L.B. from Keio University in 1981, his LL.M from Harvard in

1985 (Fulbright Scholarship), and completed his Ph.D. at Keio University in 1987. He was a guest scholar at the Brookings Institution and the American Enterprise Institute from 1991-93 and is an active consultant to various ministries in Japan. His publications have focused generally on comparative aspects of U.S. and Japanese Antitrust Laws, and he has also co-authored a book on the WTO.

Shujiro Urata

Shujiro Urata is Professor of Economics, School of Social Sciences, Waseda University and Research Fellow at the Japan Center for Economic Research in Tokyo. He is a graduate of Keio University, and holds an MA and Ph.D in economics from Stanford University. He was formerly a Research Associate at the Brookings Institution and an Economist at the World Bank. He specializes in international economics and economics of development. He is an author or coauthor of numerous articles in professional journals including the *Review of Economics and Statistics*, *Journal of Development Economics*, *Journal of Comparative Economics*, and *Mathematical Programming Study*. He has also published a number of books on international economic issues in English and Japanese, including *Measuring the Costs of Protection in Japan* (1995, Institute of International Economics) and *Asia & Europe: Beyond Competing Regionalism* (1998, Sussex Academic Press).

Sonam Wangchuk

Sonam Wangchuk works for the Ministry of Trade and Industry of the Royal Government of Bhutan. He is the Regional Director at the Regional Trade and Industry Office, Gelephu, Bhutan. Currently on study leave as a Joint Japan/World Bank scholar, he is completing the Program in Economic Policy Management (PEPM) course at Columbia University and is doing an internship at the World Bank.

David E. Weinstein

David Weinstein is the Carl S. Shoup Professor of the Japanese Economy at Columbia University and the Research Director of Columbia's Center for Japanese Economy and Business. In addition, he is a Research Associate at the National Bureau of Economic Research and also serves as an editor of the *Journal of International Economics* and the *Journal of the Japanese and International Economies*.

John Whalley

John Whalley is Professor of Economics at the Universities of Western Ontario (Canada) and Warwick (UK). He is also a Research Associate with the National Bureau of Economic Research (NBER). He is best known for his contributions to numerical simulation analysis (general equilibrium) of policy issues, work he started in the Tokyo Round and continued through the Uruguay Round. He has also written extensive policy commentary on trade policy, emphasizing issues confronting developing countries in the trading system. He recently co-authored a book with Peter Uimonen on *Environmental Issues in the New World Trading System* (MacMillan, 1997). He was a panelist at the Spring 1999 WTO High Level Symposium, and in June 2000 presented work in Geneva on "Special and Differential Treatment in the Millennium Round."

Chong Xiang

Chong Xiang is a Ph.D. student at the University of Michigan, and his main area of interest is international trade.

STUDIES IN INTERNATIONAL TRADE POLICY

Studies in International Trade Policy includes works dealing with the theory, empirical analysis, political, economic, legal relations, and evaluations of international trade policies and institutions.

General Editor: Robert M. Stern

John H. Jackson and Edwin Vermulst, Editors. *Antidumping Law and Practice: A Comparative Study*

John S. Odell and Thomas D. Willett, Editors. *International Trade Policies: Gains from Exchange between Economics and Political Science*

Stephen V. Marks and Keith E. Maskus, Editors. *The Economics and Politics of World Sugar Policies*

J. Michael Finger, Editor. *Antidumping: How It Works and Who Gets Hurt*

Horst Herberg and Ngo Van Long, Editors. *Trade, Welfare, and Economic Policies: Essays in Honor of Murray C. Kemp*

David Schwartzman. *The Japanese Television Cartel: A Study Based on* Matsushita v. Zenith

Alan V. Deardorff and Robert M. Stern, Editors. *Analytical Perspectives and Negotiating Issues in the Global Trading System*

Edwin Vermulst, Paul Waer, and Jacques Bourgeois, Editors. *Rules of Origin in International Trade: A Comparative Study*

Alan V. Deardorff and Robert M. Stern, Editors. *The Stolper-Samuelson Theorem: A Golden Jubilee*

Kent Albert Jones. *Export Restraint and the New Protectionism: The Political Economy of Discriminatory Trade Restrictions*

Alan V. Deardorff, James A. Levinsohn, and Robert M. Stern, Editors. *New Directions in Trade Theory*

Robert Baldwin, Tain-Jy Chen, and Douglas Nelson. *Political Economy of U.S.–Taiwan Trade*

Bernard M. Hoekman and Petros C. Mavroidis, Editors. *Law and Policy in Public Purchasing: The WTO Agreement on Government Procurement*

Danny M. Leipziger, Editor. *Lessons from East Asia*

Tamin Bayoumi. *Financial Integration and Real Activity*

Harry P. Bowen, Abraham Hollander, and Jean-Marie Viaene. *Applied International Trade Analysis*